D0953967

THE THREE PILLARS OF ZEN

 The

TEACHING,

compiled & edited, with

Three Pillars of Zen

PRACTICE, AND ENLIGHTENMENT

translations, introductions, & notes by PHILIP KAPLEAU

foreword by HUSTON SMITH

REVISED AND EXPANDED EDITION

ANCHOR BOOKS

Anchor Press / Doubleday   Garden City, New York   1980

A NOTE ON THE DECORATIONS   The section-heading devices, dating from about one to five centuries ago, are *kao,* the fanciful brush-drawn "signatures" or personal ciphers that were often adopted by Zen priests and other cultured Japanese in their literary and artistic avocations. Kao were only vaguely related to orthography and are used here, not for meaning, but abstractly, for their decorative quality. On the title page is the kao of Butcho-kokushi, a seventeenth-century Zen master.

Library of Congress Cataloging in Publication Data

Kapleau, Philip, 1912–   ed.
   The three pillars of Zen.

   Includes bibliographical references and index.
   1.   Zen Buddhism.   I.   Title.
BQ9265.4.K36   1980   294.3'927

The Anchor Books edition of *The Three Pillars of Zen* is a revised and expanded edition of the original published by John Weatherhill, Inc. in 1965. The book has had four hardcover printings by Weatherhill and Harper & Row, and fourteen printings in paperback by Beacon Press.
Anchor Books edition: 1980

ISBN: 0-385-14786-4
Library of Congress Catalog Card Number 78-22794
Copyright © 1980 by The Zen Center, Inc.
Copyright © 1965 by Philip Kapleau.
All Rights Reserved
Printed in the United States of America

Dedicated with respect and gratitude to my teachers: Harada-roshi, late abbot of Hosshin Monastery; Yasutani-roshi, late master of Taihei Temple; and Nakagawa-roshi, retired abbot of Ryutaku Monastery, all of whom have selflessly taught the truth of the Dharma for the welfare of men in the East and the West.

CONTENTS

FOREWORD / by HUSTON SMITH /

Tradition has it that it was in the sixth century A.D., with the journey of Bodhidharma from India to China, that Zen Buddhism first moved east. Six hundred years later, in the twelfth century, it traveled east again, to Japan. Now that more than another six hundred years have elapsed, is it to take a third giant stride eastward, this time to the West?

No one knows. Current Western interest in Zen wears the guise of the fad it in part is, but the interest also runs deeper. Let me cite the impression Zen has made on three Western minds of some note, those of a psychologist, a philosopher, and a historian. The book C. G. Jung was reading on his deathbed was Charles Luk's *Ch'an and Zen Teachings: First Series,* and he expressly asked his secretary to write to tell the author that "he was enthusiastic . . . When he read what Hsu Yun said, he sometimes felt as if he himself could have said exactly this! It was just 'it'!"[1] In philosophy, Martin Heidegger is quoted as saying: "If I understand [Dr. Suzuki] correctly, this is what I have been trying to say in all my writings."[2] Lynn White is not the molder of modern thought that Jung and Heidegger have been, but he is a fine historian, and he predicts: "It may well be that the publication of D. T. Suzuki's first *Essays in Zen Buddhism* in 1927 will seem in future generations as great an intellectual event as William of Moerbeke's Latin translations of Aristotle in the

[1] From an unpublished letter from Dr. Marie-Louise von Franz to Charles Luk dated September 12, 1961.

[2] In William Barrett (ed.), *Zen Buddhism: Selected Writings of D. T. Suzuki* (Garden City, N.Y.: Doubleday Anchor Books, 1956), p. xi.

thirteenth century or Marsiglio Ficino's of Plato in the fifteenth."[3]

Why should the West, dominated to the extent it currently is by scientific modes of thought, go to school to a perspective forged before the rise of modern science? Some think the answer lies in the extent to which the Buddhist cosmology anticipated what contemporary science has empirically discovered. The parallels are impressive. Astronomical time and space, which irrevocably smashed the West's previous world view, slip into the folds of Buddhist cosmology without a ripple. If we turn from macrocosm to microcosm, from the infinite to the infinitesmal, we find the same uncanny prescience. While the Greeks were positing atoms that were eternal because not composite (*a-tomas*—indivisible, that which cannot be cut), Buddhists were teaching that everything corporeal is impermanent (*anicca*) because constituted of dharmas as miniscule in duration as they are in space—remarkably like the fleeting blips that particles register on the scientists' oscilloscopes.

To return for a moment to the macrocosm, it is not just the dimensions of the scientific cosmology that Buddhism previsioned, but its form as well. We have become familiar with the debate between George Gamow's "big bang" and Fred Hoyle's "steady state" cosmogonies, the first arguing that the universe is the continuing consequence of the explosion of a single primeval atom; the second, that the universe has always been in the state in which we know it, fresh hydrogen being continuously created to replace that which is being emptied out through the stars' recession once they exceed the speed of light. The latest word from Mount Palomar is that both these theories appear to be wrong. The red shifts on the spectrographic reports from distant galaxies suggest they are slowing down. The hypothesis this evokes is that after expanding for a while the universe contracts, only to repeat the cycle indefinitely. As the Harvard astronomer Harlow Shapley puts the matter, instead of the "big bang" or the "steady state" theories, we have the "bang . . . bang . . . bang" theory. "Very interesting," says the Buddhist, this being what his cosmology has taught him all along.

[3] *Frontiers of Knowledge in the Study of Man* (New York: Harper and Brothers, 1956), pp. 304–5.

The West may find such instances of Buddhism's scientific pre-science striking, but this cannot account for Buddhism's appeal. For one thing, the West cannot feel that in science it has anything to *learn* from Buddhism; the most it can do in this sphere is give the Buddhists good marks for some precocious hunches. But there is the further fact that it is not Buddhism in general that is intriguing the West so much as the specific school of Buddhism that is Zen. We understand the specific attraction of *Zen* Buddhism when we realize the extent to which the contemporary West is animated by "prophetic faith," the sense of the holiness of the *ought*, the pull of the way things could be and should be but as yet are not. Such faith has obvious virtues, but unless it is balanced by a companion sense of the holiness of the *is*, it becomes top-heavy. If one's eyes are always on tomorrows, todays slip by unperceived. To a West which in its concern to refashion heaven and earth is in danger of letting the presentness of life—the only life we really have—slip through its fingers, Zen comes as a reminder that if we do not learn to perceive the mystery and beauty of our *present* life, our *present* hour, we shall not perceive the worth of *any* life, of *any* hour.

There is the further fact that with the collapse of metaphysics, natural theology, and objective revelation, the West is facing for the first time as a civilization the problem of living without objectively convincing absolutes—in a word, without dogmas. As Christ walked on the waters, so is the contemporary Westerner having to walk on the sea of nothingness, buoyant in the absence of demonstrably certain supports. Facing this precarious assignment, the Westerner hears of men across the sea who have for centuries taken up their abode in the Void, come to feel at home in it, and to find joy within it. How can this be? The West does not understand, but the Nothingness of which it hears from across the sea sounds like something it may have to come to terms with.

Zen tells us that the *is* is holy and the Void is home, but such affirmations are not Zen. Rather, Zen is a method for attaining to the direct experience of the truth of these affirmations. This brings us to the present book, for I know of no other that gives the reader so full an understanding of what this method is. For one thing, it presents for the first time in English Yasutani-roshi's "Introductory Lectures on Zen Training," lectures which have deservedly won the highest of praise in Japan as being, in the words of Ruth Fuller Sasaki, the director of the First Zen Institute of America in Japan, "the best introduction to Zen Buddhism yet written."

But the book contains another prize that is even more striking. Up to now it has been all but impossible for those who have not themselves undergone Zen training to get much of an inkling of what transpires in one crucial phase of the process, namely *dokusan*—the series of solemn, private interviews in which the roshi guides the student's meditation toward its goal of enlightenment—for the substance of these interviews has been considered personal and not to be divulged. Now a roshi, convinced that our new age occasions new procedures, has permitted a series of these interviews to be reproduced. Such material has never appeared even in Japanese; for it to appear in English, in this book, is a major breakthrough.

No one but Philip Kapleau could have written this book. He knows Zen from thirteen years of ardent training in Japan, three of these years in both Soto and Rinzai monasteries. He knows the Japanese who have colaborated to render his translations of little-known material impeccable. He knows the Japanese language well enough himself to have served as interpreter for his roshi's interviews with Western students. He has the skill of years of training as a court reporter to have recorded these interviews rapidly in shorthand as soon as they were over. And he has a literary style that is lucid and graceful. This assemblage of talents is unique. It has produced a remarkable book that is certain to assume a permanent place in the library of Zen literature in Western languages.

HUSTON SMITH
Professor of Philosophy
Massachusetts Institute of Technology

EDITOR'S PREFACE /

Briefly stated, Zen is a religious practice with a unique method of body-mind training whose aim is awakening, that is, Self-realization. In this volume I have tried to convey the religious character and spirit of Zen—yes, its rituals and devotions, its appeal to the heart no less than to the mind—for as a Buddhist Way of liberation Zen is most assuredly a religion. Grounded in the highest teachings of the Buddha, it was brought from India to China, where the methods and practices which are characteristically Zen's were evolved, and then through the centuries further elaborated in Japan, Korea, and Vietnam. Zen Buddhism is thus the consummation of the spiritual experiences of a number of Asian civilizations. In Japan today this tradition is still very much alive; in Zen temples, monasteries, and private homes men and women from every walk of life can be found actively engaged in zazen, the principal discipline of Zen.

At its profoundest level Zen, like every other great religion, transcends its own teachings and practices, yet at the same time there is no Zen apart from these practices. Attempts in the West to isolate Zen in a vacuum of the intellect, cut off from the very disciplines which are its *raison d'être*, have nourished in places a pseudo-Zen that is little more than a mind-tickling diversion.

The best way to correct this distortion, it seemed to me, was to compile a book setting forth the authentic doctrines and practices of Zen from the mouths of the masters themselves—for who knows these methods better than they?—as well as to show them come alive in the minds and bodies of men and women of today. This I have done chiefly through a contemporary Soto master, Yasutani-roshi; a fourteenth-century Rinzai master, Bassui-zenji; and the enlightenment stories of Japanese and American followers of Zen. Yasutani-roshi's introductory lectures on Zen practice, his lecture *(teisho)* on the koan Mu, and his private instructions *(dokusan)* to ten of his Western students form a unity which embraces the whole structure of Zen training in its traditional sequence. One lacking access to a bona fide roshi yet wishing to discipline himself in Zen will find this material to be nothing less than a manual for self-instruction.

Both the Soto and Rinzai disciplines are presented here—for the first time in a European language, we believe—as one integral body of Zen teaching, and this not academically but as living experience. The aims and methods of shikan-taza, the heart of Soto meditative discipline, as well as those of koan zazen, the mainstay of the Rinzai sect, are authoritatively expounded by Yasutani-roshi, who utilizes both in his own system of teaching.

In the introductions I have presented background and supplementary material which I felt would aid the reader to grasp the substance of each section, but I have resisted the temptation to analyze or interpret the masters' teachings. This would only have encouraged the reader to reinterpret my interpretations, and willy-nilly he would find himself sucked into the quicksands of speculation and ego-aggrandizement, from which one day, if he would seriously practice Zen, he would painfully have to extricate himself. For precisely this reason "idea-mongering" has always been discouraged by the Zen masters.

This book owes much to many people. First and foremost it owes an enormous debt to Zen Master Yasutani, whose teachings encompass more than half of it and who has graciously allowed them to be made available here to a wider public. My collaborators and I, all his disciples, are deeply grateful for his sagacious counsel and magnanimity of spirit which inspired us throughout.

My debt of gratitude to Kyozo Yamada-roshi, the Dharma heir of Yasutani-roshi, cannot be put into words. Friend and teacher, he was a tower of strength to lean on. Were it not for his wise advice and generous assistance, my overall task would have been immeasurably more difficult, if not impossible. We collaborated on the translations of Bassui's Dharma talk on One-mind and his letters, portions of the Iwasaki letters, the Ten Oxherding Verses, the quotations from Dogen and other ancient masters, and the extract from Dogen's *Shobogenzo*.

Akira Kubota, my second collaborator, was one of Yasutani-roshi's foremost disciples, having trained under him for some fifteen years. Together we translated the lecture on the koan Mu, parts of the Iwasaki letters, and the fourth and sixth accounts in the section on enlightenment experiences. I acknowledge my huge debt to him for his conscientious labors.

My special thanks are due Dr. Carmen Blacker, of Cambridge University. Her on-the-spot translations of many of Yasutani-roshi's lectures on Zen practice were incorporated by me into the translations which appear in this book. Further, I have taken the liberty of adopting without alteration several paragraphs from her own translation of sections of this same material which was published in the British Buddhist magazine *The Middle Way*, since her expression was so felicitous that I could hardly hope to have improved upon it.

I am exceedingly grateful to Dr. Huston Smith, Professor of Philosophy at the Massachusetts Institute of Technology and author of *The Religions of Man*, for his invaluable advice and encouragement at an early stage of the manuscript, and for his Foreword.

Brigitte D'Ortschy, a Dharma friend, was exceedingly helpful. Her thoughtful reading of the entire manuscript produced many valuable suggestions which have improved the book.

The Ten Oxherding Pictures of section VIII are used by kind permission of the artist, Gyokusei Jikihara. He is a highly esteemed contemporary painter in Kyoto and a lay disciple of Shibayama-roshi, the former abbot of Nanzen Monastery, under whom he trained in Zen for many years.

My debt to my wife, deLancey, is no small one. At all stages of the writing she has encouraged and worked with me. Indeed, for several years these labors constituted her major practice of zazen.

In our translations we have striven to avoid the evils of either a free, imaginative rendering on the one hand or an exactly literal reading on the other. Had we yielded to the first temptation, we might have achieved a stylistic elegance now lacking, but only at the expense of that forthright vigor and calculated repetition which is a characteristic feature of Zen teaching. On the other hand, had we slavishly adhered to the letter of the texts, we inevitably would have done violence to their spirit and thus obscured their deep inner meaning.

Our translations are interpretive in the sense that all translation involves the constant choice of one of several alternative expressions which the translator believes may convey the meaning of the original. Whether a translator's choices are apposite depends, in the ordinary translation, on his linguistic skill and his familiarity with his subject. Zen texts, however, fall into a special category. Since they are invariably terse and pithy and the ideograms in which they are written susceptible of a variety of interpretations, one key character often conveying a whole spectrum of ideas, to select the shade of meaning appropriate to a particular context demands from a translator more than philological acuity or an extensive academic knowledge of Zen. In our view, it requires nothing less than Zen training and the experience of enlightenment, lacking which the translator is almost certain to distort the clarity and emasculate the vigor of the original.

It may not be out of place, therefore, to point out that every one of the translators has trained in Zen for a considerable time under one or more recognized masters and opened his Mind's eye in some measure.

Since this book is addressed to the general reader rather than to scholars or specialists in Zen Buddhism, I have dispensed with all diacritical marks, which are apt to prove annoying to those unfamiliar with Japanese, Chinese, or Sanskrit. However, they have been inserted in the Zen vocabulary section. Even at the risk of some inconsistency, I have also dispensed with as much disruptive italicizing as seemed reasonable. In the body of the book I have followed the Japanese custom of writing the names of the Chinese Zen masters and other Chinese terms according to their Japanese pronunciation, just as we speak of *Zen* rather than *Ch'an* Buddhism, but in the vocabulary notes of the final section I have indicated the usually accepted Chinese pronunciations in parentheses. Chinese scholars who find this practice irritating are asked to bear in mind that Zen Buddhism has been in Japan almost a thousand years and hence is a legitimate part of Japanese life and culture. It could scarcely have survived so long or made such a strong impact on the Japanese had they not abandoned the foreign and, for them, cumbersome Chinese pronunciation.

In writing the names of the ancient Japanese masters I have adhered to the traditional Japanese custom of listing the chief Buddhist name first. In the case of modern Japanese, however, whether masters or laymen, I have followed the Western style, which of course is just the reverse, since this is the way they themselves write their names in English. Where a title comes immediately after a name (such as Yasutani-roshi or Dogen-zenji), for the sake of euphony the name and the title have been written according to traditional Japanese style as here indicated.

Technical Zen names and special Buddhist terms not defined in the text are explained in section x, "Notes on Zen Vocabulary and Buddhist Doctrine."

While the organization of the book follows the natural pattern of teaching, practice, and enlightenment, each section is complete in itself and can be read at random according to the reader's taste.

All footnotes throughout the book are mine.

PHILIP KAPLEAU

Kamakura, December 8, 1964

PREFACE TO THE REVISED EDITION /

This new Doubleday edition has given me the welcome opportunity to eliminate a number of minor errors of fact that have been called to my attention since the book was first published; to retranslate a few passages in the light of my own growing understanding of the Buddha's Dharma and the research of scholars in Buddhism; and to revise and expand some definitions in the vocabulary section that now appear to have been inadequate. It has also enabled me to delete from my own introduction material made obsolete by the passage of time and to insert new information making it easier, I believe, to understand the translated matter of the masters. Essentially, however, the texts remain unchanged.

Two new sections and a set of drawings have been added to this edition. The first consists of responses, put in narrative form, by Yasutani-roshi to questions asked him at the Zen Center following a sesshin. This material has been inserted under "Yasutani-roshi's Introductory Lectures on Zen Training," with the title of "Oneness and Manyness." Also included, in the section on "Postures," is a series of questions and answers concerning the physical difficulties that beginners experience in zazen, and how they can be corrected. These were culled from workshops held in Rochester over the years. A few of the responses were made by me in the course of my talks, but most were given in demonstrations and instructions by Ruth Sandberg, a senior member of the Zen Center who has trained under several well-known Indian teachers and has herself taught hatha yoga professionally for fifteen years. The drawings of Zen postures, the sketches of stretching exercises, and the cover design were made expressly for this edition by Richard

Wehrman, a professional illustrator and designer and a senior member of the Center. I acknowledge my huge indebtedness to both of them.

My deepest thanks also to Polly Papageorge and Bodhin, who assisted me in all phases of the preparation of this new edition.

PHILIP KAPLEAU

Rochester, New York
April 8, 1979

THE THREE PILLARS OF ZEN

PART ONE / TEACHING AND PRACTICE

I / YASUTANI-ROSHI'S INTRODUCTORY LECTURES ON ZEN TRAINING /

EDITOR'S INTRODUCTION / Westerners eager to practice Zen yet lacking access to a qualified master have always faced an imposing handicap: the dearth of written information on what zazen is and how to begin and carry it on.[1] Nor is this lack confined to English and other European languages. In the writings of the ancient Chinese and Japanese Zen masters which have come down to us there is little on the theory of zazen or on the relation of the practice of zazen to enlightenment. Neither is there much detailed information on such elementary matters as sitting postures, the regulation of the breath, concentration of the mind, and the incidence of visions and sensations of an illusory nature.

There is nothing strange in this. Sitting in zazen or meditation has been so accepted as the approved path to spiritual emancipation throughout Asia that no Zen Buddhist had first to be convinced that through it he could develop his powers of concentration, achieve unification and tranquility of mind, and eventually, if his aspiration was pure and strong enough, come to Self-realization. An aspirant, therefore, was simply given a few oral instructions on how to fold his legs, how to regulate his breathing, and how to concentrate his mind. Through the painful process of trial and

---

[1] Zazen is not "meditation" and for this reason we have retained this Japanese word throughout. Its precise meaning will become clear as the book progresses. Pronounced "zah-zen," each syllable is accented equally. ·

error and periodic encounters (*dokusan*) with his teacher, he eventually learned in a thoroughly experiential way not only proper sitting and breathing but the inner meaning and purpose of zazen.

But since modern man, as Yasutani-roshi points out, lacks the faith and burning zeal of his predecessors in Zen, he needs a map which his mind can trust, charting his entire spiritual journey, before he can move ahead with confidence. For these reasons Harada-roshi, Yasutani-roshi's own master, devised a series of introductory lectures on Zen practice some forty years ago, and it is this material which forms the basis of these lectures by Yasutani-roshi.

This present translation is a compilation of a number of such lectures which Yasutani-roshi has given, without notes, to beginners over the past several years. No new student may receive dokusan until he has heard them all.

These talks are more than a compendium of instructions on the formal aspects of zazen, that is, sitting, breathing, and concentration. They are an authoritative exposition of the five levels of Zen, of the aims and essentials of zazen, and of the all-important relation of zazen to enlightenment (*satori*). With them as map and compass the earnest seeker need not grope along hazardous bypaths of the occult, the psychic, or the superstitious, which waste time and often prove harmful, but can proceed directly along a carefully charted course, secure in the knowledge of his ultimate goal.

No account of the history and development of Zen, no interpretations of Zen from the viewpoint of philosophy or psychology, and no evaluations of the influence of Zen on archery, judo, haiku poetry, or any other of the Japanese arts will be found here. Valuable as such studies can be, they have no legitimate place in Zen training and would only burden the aspirant's mind with ideas that would confuse him as to his aims and drain him of the incentive to practice. For this reason they are deliberately omitted by Yasutani-roshi.

Yasutani-roshi's emphasis on the religious aspect of Zen Buddhism—that is, on faith as a prerequisite to enlightenment—may come as a surprise to Western readers accustomed to "intellectual images" of Zen by scholars devoid of Zen insight. This derives for the most part from the teachings of Dogen-zenji, one of the imposing religious personalities of Japanese history, who brought the doctrines of the Soto sect of Zen Buddhism from China to Japan. Without even a sketchy knowledge of the circumstances of Dogen's life that led him to become a Zen monk and to journey to China, where he attained the Great Way, one would find it difficult to understand the Soto Zen doctrine which forms the core of Yasutani-roshi's own teachings.

Born of an aristocratic family, Dogen even as a child gave evidence of his brilliant mind. It is related that at four he was reading Chinese poetry and at nine a Chinese translation of a treatise on the Abhidharma. The sorrow he felt at his parents' deaths—his father when he was only three and his mother when he was eight—undoubtedly impressed upon his sensitive mind the impermanence of life and motivated him to become a monk. With his initiation into the Buddhist monkhood at an early age, he commenced his novitiate at Mount Hiei, the center of scholastic Buddhism in medieval Japan, and for the next several years studied the Tendai doctrines of Buddhism. By his fifteenth year one burning question became the core around which his spiritual strivings revolved: "If, as the sutras say, our Essential-nature is Bodhi (perfection), why did all Buddhas have to strive for enlightenment and perfection?" His dissatisfaction with the answers he received at Mount Hiei led him eventually to Eisai-zenji, who had brought the teachings of the Rinzai sect of Zen Buddhism from China to Japan. Eisai's reply to Dogen's question was: "No Buddha is conscious of its existence [that is, of this Essential-nature], while cats and oxen [that is, the grossly deluded] are aware of it." In other words, Buddhas, precisely because they are Buddhas, no longer think of having or not having a Perfect-nature; only the deluded think in such terms. At these words Dogen had an inner realization which dissolved his deep-seated doubt. In all likelihood this exchange took place in a formal encounter (dokusan) between Eisai and Dogen. It must be borne in mind that this problem had perplexed Dogen for some time, giving him no rest, and that all he needed was Eisai's words to trigger his mind into a state of enlightenment.

Dogen thereupon commenced what was to be a brief discipleship under Eisai, whose death took place within the year and who was succeeded by his eldest disciple, Myozen. During the eight years Dogen spent with Myozen he passed a considerable number of koans and finally received *inka*.

Despite this accomplishment Dogen still felt spiritually unfulfilled, and this disquiet moved him to undertake the then-hazardous journey to China in search of complete peace of mind. He stayed at all the well-known monasteries, practicing under many masters, but his longing for total liberation was unsatisfied. Eventually at the famous T'ien-t'ung Monastery, which had just acquired a new master, he achieved full awakening, that is, the liberation of body and mind, through these words uttered by his master, Ju-ching: "You must let fall body and mind."

These words are said to have been uttered by Ju-ching at the commencement of the formal zazen period, in the early morning, as he was making his round of inspection. Spying one of the monks dozing, the master reprimanded him for his half-hearted effort. Then addressing all the monks, he continued: "You must exert yourselves with all your might, even at the risk of your lives. To realize perfect enlightenment you must let fall [that is, become empty of all conceptions of] body and mind." As Dogen heard this last phrase his Mind's eye suddenly expanded in a flood of light and understanding.[2]

Later Dogen appeared at Ju-ching's room, lit a stick of incense (a ceremonial gesture usually reserved for noteworthy occasions), and prostrated himself before his master in the customary fashion.

"Why are you lighting a stick of incense?" asked Ju-ching. Needless to say, Ju-ching, who was a first-rate master, and who had received Dogen many times in dokusan and therefore knew the state of his mind, could perceive at once from Dogen's walk, his prostrations, and the comprehending look in his eyes that he had had a great enlightenment. But Ju-ching undoubtedly wanted to see what response this innocent-sounding question would provoke so as to fix the scope of Dogen's satori.

"I have experienced the dropping off of body and mind," replied Dogen.

Ju-ching exclaimed: "You have dropped body and mind, body and mind have indeed dropped!"

But Dogen remonstrated: "Don't give me your sanction so readily!"

"I am not sanctioning you so readily."

---

[2] For a discussion of the significance of a single word or phrase precipitating enlightenment, see p. 97.

Reversing their roles, Dogen demanded: "*Show* me that you are not readily sanctioning me."

And Ju-ching repeated: "*This* is body and mind dropped," demonstrating.

Whereupon Dogen prostrated himself again before his master as a gesture of respect and gratitude.

"That's 'dropping' dropped," added Ju-ching.

It is noteworthy that even with this profound experience Dogen continued his zazen training in China for another two years before returning to Japan.

At the time of his great awakening Dogen was practicing *Shikan-taza*,[3] a mode of zazen which involves neither a koan nor counting or following the breaths. The very foundation of shikan-taza is an unshakeable faith that sitting as the Buddha sat, with the mind void of all conceptions, of all beliefs and points of view, is the actualization or unfoldment of the inherently enlightened Bodhi-mind with which all are endowed. At the same time this sitting is entered into in the faith that it will one day culminate in the sudden and direct perception of the true nature of this Mind—in other words, enlightenment. Therefore to strive self-consciously for satori or any other gain from zazen is as unnecessary as it is undesirable.[4]

In authentic shikan-taza neither of these two elements of faith can be dispensed with. To exclude satori from shikan-taza would necessarily involve stigmatizing as meaningless and even masochistic the Buddha's strenuous efforts toward enlightenment, and impugning the patriarchs' and Dogen's own painful struggles to that end. This relation of satori to shikan-taza is of the utmost importance. Unfortunately it has often been misunderstood, especially by those to whom Dogen's complete writings are inaccessible. It thus not infrequently happens that Western students will come to a Soto temple or monastery utilizing koans in its teaching and remonstrate with the roshi over his assignment of a koan, on the ground that koans have as their aim enlightenment; since all are

---

[3] For Yasutani-roshi's comments on *shikan-taza,* see pp. 56–57.

[4] The conscious thought "I must get enlightened" can be as much of an impediment as any other which hangs in the mind.

intrinsically enlightened, they argue, there is no point in seeking satori. So what they ask to practice is shikan-taza, which they believe does not involve the experience of enlightenment.[5]

Such an attitude reveals not only a lack of faith in the judgment of one's teacher but a fundamental misconception of both the nature and the difficulty of shikan-taza, not to mention the teaching methods employed in Soto temples and monasteries. A careful reading of these introductory lectures and Yasutani-roshi's encounters with ten Westerners will make clear why genuine shikan-taza cannot be successfully undertaken by the rank novice, who has yet to learn how to sit with stability and equanimity, or whose ardor needs to be regularly boosted by communal sitting or by the encouragement of a teacher, or who, above all, lacks strong faith in his own Bodhi-mind coupled with a dedicated resolve to experience its reality in his daily life.

Because today, Zen masters claim, devotees are on the whole much less zealous for truth, and because the obstacles to practice posed by the complexities of modern life are more numerous, capable Soto masters seldom assign shikan-taza to a beginner. They prefer to have him first unify his mind through concentration on counting the breaths; or where a burning desire for enlightenment does exist, to exhaust the discursive intellect through the imposition of a special type of Zen problem (that is, a koan) and thus prepare the way for *kensho*.

By no means, then, is the koan system confined to the Rinzai sect as many believe. Yasutani-roshi is only one of a number of Soto masters who use koans in their teaching. Genshu Watanabe-roshi, the former abbot of Soji-ji, one of the two head temples of the Soto sect in Japan, regularly employed koans, and at the Soto monastery of Hosshinji, of which the illustrious Harada-roshi was abbot during his lifetime, koans are also widely used.

Even Dogen himself, as we have seen, disciplined himself in koan Zen for eight years before going to China and practicing shikan-taza. And though upon his return to Japan Dogen wrote at length about shikan-taza and recommended it for his inner band of disciples, it must not be forgotten that these disciples were dedicated truth-seekers for whom koans were an unnecessary encouragement

[5] For the attitude of one such novice, see p. 137.

to sustained practice. Notwithstanding this emphasis on shikan-taza, Dogen made a compilation of three hundred well-known koans,[6] to each of which he added his own commentary. From this and the fact that his foremost work, the *Shobogenzo* (A Treasury of the Eye of the True Dharma), contains a number of koans, we may fairly conclude that he did utilize koans in his teaching.

Satori-awakening as Dogen viewed it was not the be-all and end-all. Rather he conceived it as the foundation for a magnificent edifice whose many-storied superstructure would correspond to the perfected character and personality of the spiritually developed individual, the man of moral virtue and all-embracing compassion and wisdom. Such an imposing structure, Dogen taught, could be erected only by years of faithful zazen upon the solid base of the immutable inner knowledge which satori confers.

What then is zazen and how is it related to satori? Dogen taught that zazen is the "gateway to total liberation," and Keizan-zenji, one of the Japanese Soto patriarchs, had declared that only through Zen sitting is the "mind of man illumined." Elsewhere Dogen wrote[7] that "even the Buddha, who was a born sage, sat in zazen for six years until his supreme enlightenment, and so towering a spiritual figure as Bodhidharma sat for nine years facing the wall."[8] And so have Dogen and all the other patriarchs sat.

For with the ordering and immobilizing of feet, legs, hands, arms, trunk, and head in the traditional lotus posture,[9] with the regulation of the breath, the methodical stilling of the thoughts and unification of the mind through special modes of concentration, with the development of control over the emotions and strengthening of the will, and with the cultivation of a profound silence in the deepest recesses of the mind—in other words, through the practice of zazen—there are established the optimum preconditions for looking into the heart-mind and discovering there the true nature of existence.

[6] In *Nempyo Sambyaku Soku* (Three Hundred Koans with Commentaries).

[7] In his *Fukan Zazengi* (Universal Promotion of the Principles of Zazen).

[8] Following Bodhidharma's example, Soto devotees face a wall or curtain during zazen. In the Rinzai tradition sitters face each other across the room in two rows, their backs to the wall.

[9] See p. 33 and section IX.

Although sitting is the foundation of zazen, it is not just any kind of sitting. Not only must the back be straight, the breathing properly regulated, and the mind concentrated beyond thought, but, according to Dogen, one must sit with a sense of dignity and grandeur, like a mountain or a giant pine, and with a feeling of gratitude toward the Buddha and the patriarchs, who made manifest the Dharma. And we must be grateful for our human body, through which we have the opportunity to experience the reality of the Dharma in all its profundity. This sense of dignity and gratitude, moreover, is not confined to sitting but must inform every activity, for insofar as each act issues from the Bodhi-mind it has the inherent purity and dignity of Buddhahood. This innate dignity of man is physiologically manifested in his erect back, since he alone of all creatures has this capacity to hold his spinal column vertical. An erect back is related to proper sitting in other important ways, which will be discussed at a later point in this section.

In the broad sense zazen embraces more than just correct sitting. To enter fully into every action with total attention and clear awareness is no less zazen. The prescription for accomplishing this was given by the Buddha himself in an early sutra: "In what is seen there must be just the seen; in what is heard there must be just the heard; in what is sensed (as smell, taste or touch) there must be just what is sensed; in what is thought there must be just the thought."[10]

The importance of single-mindedness, of bare attention, is illustrated in the following anecdote:

One day a man of the people said to Zen Master Ikkyu: "Master, will you please write for me some maxims of the highest wisdom?"

Ikkyu immediately took his brush and wrote the word "Attention."

"Is that all?" asked the man. "Will you not add something more?"

Ikkyu then wrote twice running: "Attention. Attention."

"Well," remarked the man rather irritably, "I really don't see much depth or subtlety in what you have just written."

[10] Udana I, 10 (translation by Nyanaponika Thera).

Then Ikkyu wrote the same word three times running: "Attention. Attention. Attention."

Half-angered, the man demanded: "What does that word 'Attention' mean anyway?"

And Ikkyu answered gently: "Attention means attention."[11]

For the ordinary man, whose mind is a checkerboard of crisscrossing reflections, opinions, and prejudices, bare attention is virtually impossible; his life is thus centered not in reality itself but in his *ideas* of it. By focusing the mind wholly on each object and every action, zazen strips it of extraneous thoughts and allows us to enter into a full rapport with life.

Sitting zazen and mobile zazen are two functions equally dynamic and mutually reinforcing. One who sits devotedly in zazen every day, his mind free of discriminating thoughts, finds it easier to relate himself wholeheartedly to his daily tasks, and one who performs every act with total attention and clear awareness finds it less difficult to achieve emptiness of mind during sitting periods.

Zazen practice for the student begins with his counting the inhalations and exhalations of his breath while he is in the motionless zazen posture. This is the first step in the process of stilling the bodily functions, quieting discursive thought, and strengthening concentration. It is given as the first step because in counting the in and out breaths, in natural rhythm and without strain, the mind has a scaffolding to support it, as it were. When concentration on the breathing becomes such that awareness of the counting is clear and the count is not lost, the next step, a slightly more difficult type of zazen, is assigned, namely, following the inhalations and exhalations of the breath with the mind's eye only, again in natural rhythm. The blissful state which flows from concentration on the breath and the value of breathing in terms of spiritual development are lucidly set forth by Lama Govinda:[12] "From this state of perfect mental and physical equilibrium and its resulting inner harmony grows that serenity and happiness which fills the whole body with

[11] From the *Zenso Mondo* (Dialogues of the Zen Masters), translation by Kuni Matsuo and E. Steinilber-Oberlin.

[12] *Foundations of Tibetan Mysticism*, by Lama Govinda (New York: E. P. Dutton, 1960), pp. 151–52.

a feeling of supreme bliss like the refreshing coolness of a spring that penetrates the entire water of a mountain lake . . . Breathing is the vehicle of spiritual experience, the mediator between body and mind. It is the first step towards the transformation of the body from the state of a more or less passively and unconsciously functioning physical organ into a vehicle or tool of a perfectly developed and enlightened mind, as demonstrated by the radiance and perfection of the Buddha's body . . . The most important result of the practice of 'mindfulness with regard to breathing' is the realization that the process of breathing is the connecting link between conscious and subconscious, gross-material and fine-material, volitional and non-volitional functions, and therefore the most perfect expression of the nature of all life."

Until now we have been speaking of zazen with no koan. Koan zazen involves both motionless sitting, wherein the mind intensely seeks to penetrate the koan, and mobile zazen, in which absorption in the koan continues while one is at work, at play, or even asleep. Through intense self-inquiry—for example, questioning "What is Mu?"—the mind gradually becomes denuded of its delusive ideas, which in the beginning hamper its effort to become one with the koan. As these abstract notions fall away, concentration on the koan strengthens.

It may be asked: "How can one concentrate devotedly on a koan and simultaneously focus the mind on work of an exacting nature?" In practice what actually happens is that once the koan grips the heart and mind—and its power to take hold is in proportion to the strength of the urge toward liberation—the inquiry goes on ceaselessly in the subconscious. While the mind is occupied with a particular task, the question fades from consciousness, surfacing naturally as soon as the action is over, not unlike a moving stream which now and again disappears underground only to reappear and resume its open course without interrupting its onward flow.

Zazen must not be confused with meditation. Meditation involves putting something into the mind, either an image or a sacred word that is visualized or a concept that is thought about or reflected on, or both. In some types of meditation the meditator envisions or contemplates or analyzes certain elementary shapes, holding them in his mind to the exclusion of everything else. Or he may contemplate in a state of adoration a Buddha or a Bodhisattva image, hoping to evoke in himself parallel states of mind. He may ponder such abstract qualities as loving-kindness and compassion. In Tantric Buddhist systems of meditation, mandalas containing various seed syllables of the Sanskrit alphabet—such as *Om*, for example—are visualized and dwelt upon in a prescribed manner. Also employed for meditational purposes are mandalas consisting of special arrangements of Buddhas, Bodhisattvas, and other figures.

The uniqueness of zazen lies in this: that the mind is freed from bondage to *all* thought-forms, visions, objects, and imaginings, however sacred or elevating, and brought to a state of absolute emptiness, from which alone it may one day perceive its own true nature, or the nature of the universe.

Such initial exercises as counting or following the breath cannot, strictly speaking, be called meditation since they do not involve visualization of an object or reflection upon an idea. For the same reasons koan zazen cannot be called meditation. Whether one is striving to achieve unity with his koan or, for instance, intensely asking, "What is Mu?" he is not meditating in the technical sense of this word.

Zazen that leads to Self-realization is neither idle reverie nor vacant inaction but an intense inner struggle to gain control over the mind and then to use it, like a silent missile, to penetrate the barrier of the five senses and the discursive intellect (that is, the sixth sense). It demands energy, determination, and courage. Yasutani-roshi calls it "a battle between the opposing forces of delusion and bodhi."[13] This state of mind has been vividly described in these words, said to have been uttered by the Buddha as he sat beneath the Bo tree making his supreme effort, and often quoted in the *zendo* during *sesshin:* "Though only my skin, sinews, and bones remain and my blood and flesh dry up and wither away, yet never from this seat will I stir until I have attained full enlightenment."

The drive toward enlightenment is powered on the one hand

[13] This statement is made from the standpoint of practice or training. From the standpoint of the fundamental Buddha-mind there is no delusion and no bodhi.

by a painfully felt inner bondage—a frustration with life, a fear of death, or both—and on the other by the conviction that through awakening one can gain liberation. But it is in zazen that the body-mind's force and vigor are enlarged and mobilized for the break-through into this new world of freedom. Energies which formerly were squandered in compulsive drives and purposeless actions are preserved and channeled into a unity through correct Zen sitting; and to the degree that the mind attains one-pointedness through zazen it no longer disperses its force in the uncontrolled prolifera-tion of idle thoughts. The entire nervous system is relaxed and soothed, inner tensions eliminated, and the tone of all organs strengthened. Furthermore, research involving an electrocardio-graph and other devices on subjects who have been practicing zazen for one to two years has demonstrated that zazen brings about a release in psychophysical tension and greater body-mind stability through lowered heart rate, pulse, respiration, and metabolism.[14] In short, by realigning the physical, mental, and psychic energies through proper breathing, concentration, and sitting, zazen estab-lishes a new body-mind equilibrium with its center of gravity in the vital *hara.*

Hara literally denotes the stomach and abdomen and the func-tions of digestion, absorption, and elimination connected with them. But it has parallel psychic[15] and spiritual significance. Accord-ing to Hindu and Buddhist yogic systems, there are a number of psychic centers in the body through which vital cosmic force or energy flows. Of the two such centers embraced within the hara, one is associated with the solar plexus, whose system of nerves governs the digestive processes and organs of elimination. Hara is thus a wellspring of vital psychic energies. Harada-roshi, one of the most celebrated Zen masters of his day,[16] in urging his disci-ples to concentrate their mind's[17] eye (that is, the *attention,* the summation point of the total being) in their hara, would declare:

---

[14] *Psychological Studies on Zen,* edited by Yoshiharu Akishige.

[15] "Psychic" here does not relate to extrasensory phenomena or powers but to energies and body-mind states which cannot be classified either as physiological or psychological.

[16] For further information about him, see pp. 285–88.

[17] See "mind" in section x.

"You must realize"—that is, make real—"that the center of the universe is the pit of your belly!"

To facilitate his experience of this fundamental truth, the Zen novice is instructed to focus his mind constantly at the bottom of his hara (specifically, between the navel and the pelvis) and to radiate all mental and bodily activities from that region. With the body-mind's equilibrium centered in the hara, gradually a seat of consciousness, a focus of vital energy, is established there which influences the entire organism.

That consciousness is by no means confined to the brain is shown by Lama Govinda, who writes: "While, according to Western conceptions, the brain is the exclusive seat of consciousness, yogic experience shows that our brain-consciousness is only *one* among a number of possible forms of consciousness, and that these, according to their function and nature, can be localized or centered in various organs of the body. These 'organs,' which collect, transform, and distribute the forces flowing through them, are called *cakras,* or centers of force. From them radiate secondary streams of psychic force, comparable to the spokes of a wheel, the ribs of an umbrella, or the petals of a lotus. In other words, these *cakras* are the points in which psychic forces and bodily functions merge into each other or penetrate each other. They are the focal points in which cosmic and psychic energies crystallize into bodily qualities, and in which bodily qualities are dissolved or transmuted again into psychic forces."[18]

Settling the body's center of gravity below the navel, that is, establishing a center of consciousness in the hara, automatically relaxes tensions arising from the habitual hunching of the shoulders, straining of the neck, and squeezing in of the stomach. As this rigidity disappears, an enhanced vitality and new sense of freedom are experienced throughout the body and mind, which are felt more and more to be a unity.

Zazen has clearly demonstrated that with the mind's eye centered in the hara the proliferation of random ideas is diminished and the attainment of one-pointedness accelerated, since a plethora of blood from the head is drawn down to the abdomen, "cooling" the brain and soothing the autonomic nervous system. This in

[18] *Foundations of Tibetan Mysticism*, p. 135.

turn leads to a greater degree of mental and emotional stability. Thus, one who functions from his hara, is not easily disturbed. He is, moreover, able to act quickly and decisively in an emergency owing to the fact that his mind, anchored in his hara, does not waver.

With the mind in the hara, narrow and egocentric thinking is superseded by a broadness of outlook and a magnanimity of spirit. This is because thinking from the vital hara center, being free of mediation by the limited discursive intellect, is spontaneous and all-embracing. Perception from the hara tends toward integration and unity rather than division and fragmentation. In short, it is thinking which sees things steadily and whole.

The figure of the Buddha seated on his lotus throne—serene, stable, all-knowing and all-encompassing, radiating boundless light and compassion—is the foremost example of hara expressed through perfect enlightenment. Rodin's "Thinker," on the other hand, a solitary figure "lost" in thought and contorted in body, remote and isolated from his Self, typifies the opposite state.

The ability to think and act from the hara is, like joriki, only indirectly related to satori and not synonymous with it. Satori is a "turning about" of the mind, a psychological experience conferring inner knowledge, while hara is no more than what has been indicated. Masters of the traditional Japanese arts are all accomplished in thinking and acting from the hara—they would not merit the title "master" if they were not—but few if any achieve satori without Zen training. Why not? Because their cultivation of hara is essentially for the perfection of their art and not satori, the attainment of which presupposes, as Yasutani-roshi points out in his introductory lectures, faith in the reality of the Buddha's enlightenment and in their own immaculate Buddha-nature.

With body and mind consolidated, focused, and energized, the emotions respond with increased sensitivity and purity, and volition exerts itself with greater strength of purpose. No longer are we dominated by intellect at the expense of feeling, nor driven by the emotions unchecked by reason or will. Eventually zazen leads to a transformation of personality and character. Dryness, rigidity, and self-centeredness give way to flowing warmth, resiliency, and compassion, while self-indulgence and fear are transmuted into self-mastery and courage.

Because they know from centuries of experience this transforming power of zazen, the Japanese masters have always placed greater reliance on zazen to foster moral conduct in their disciples than upon the mere imposition of the precepts from the outside. Actually, the precepts and zazen, both grounded in the identical Buddha-nature, which is the source of all purity and goodness, are mutually reinforcing. The strongest resolution to keep the precepts will at best be only sporadically successful if it is not supported by zazen; and zazen divorced from the disciplined life which grows out of a sincere effort to observe the precepts cannot but be weak and uncertain. In any case, contrary to what is believed in some sects of Buddhism, the precepts are not just simple moral commandments which anyone can easily understand and keep if he has the will to. In reality their relative-absolute sense cannot be grasped as living truth except after long and dedicated zazen. This is why Zen students are normally not given the book of problems called *Jujukinkai,* which deals with the ten cardinal precepts from the standpoints of the Hinayana doctrines, the Mahayana, the Buddha-nature itself, Bodhidharma's view, and Dogen's view, until the very end of their training, when their enlightenment and zazen power have deepened and matured. Indeed, the Japanese and Chinese masters stress that only upon full enlightenment can one truly know good from evil and, through the power of zazen, translate this wisdom into one's everyday actions.

That a strong sense of social and personal responsibility is inherent in the spiritual freedom of the satori man was made clear by Yasutani-roshi in response to a question addressed to him in America by a group of university students. "If, as we have been led to believe, satori makes clear that past and future are unreal, is one not free to live as one likes in the present, unconcerned about the past and indifferent to the future?"

In reply Yasutani-roshi made a dot on the blackboard and explained that this isolated dot represented their conception of "here and now." To show the incompleteness of this view, he placed another dot on the board, through which he drew a horizontal line and a vertical one. He then explained that the horizontal line stood for time from the beginningless past to the endless future and the vertical for limitless space. The "present moment" of the enlightened man, who stands at this intersection, embraces all these dimensions of time and space, he emphasized.

Accordingly, the satori-realization that one is the focus of past and future time and space unavoidably carries with it a sense of fellowship and responsibility to one's family and society as a whole, alike to those who came before and those who will follow one. The freedom of the liberated Zen man is a far cry from the "freedom" of the Zen libertine, driven as the latter is by his uncontrolled selfish desires. The inseparable bond with all human beings that the truly enlightened feels precludes any such self-centered behavior.

As well as enriching personality and strengthening character, zazen illumines the three characteristics of existence which the Buddha proclaimed: first, that all things (in which are included our thoughts, feelings, and perceptions) are impermanent, arising when particular causes and conditions bring them into being and passing away with the emergence of new causal factors; second, that life is pain; and third, that ultimately nothing is self-subsistent, that all forms in their essential nature are empty, that is, mutually dependent patterns of energy in flux, yet at the same time are possessed of a provisional or limited reality in time and space, in much the same way that the actions in a movie film have a reality in terms of the film but are otherwise insubstantial and unreal.

Through zazen the first vital truth—that all component things are ephemeral, never the same from one moment to the next, fleeting manifestations in a stream of ceaseless transformation— becomes a matter of direct personal experience. We come to *see* the concatenation of our thoughts, emotions, and moods, how they arise, how they momentarily flourish, and how they pass away. We come to *know* that this "dying" is the life of every thing, just as the all-consuming flame constitutes the life of a candle.

That our sufferings are rooted in a selfish grasping and in fears and terrors which spring from our ignorance of the true nature of life and death becomes clear to anyone compelled by zazen to confront himself nakedly. But zazen makes equally plain that what we term "suffering" is our evaluation of pain from which we stand apart, that pain when courageously accepted is a means to liberation in that it frees our natural sympathies and compassion even as it enables us to experience pleasure and joy in a new depth and purity.

Finally, with enlightenment, zazen brings the realization that the substratum of existence is a Voidness out of which all things ceaselessly arise and into which they endlessly return, that this Emptiness is positive and alive and in fact not other than the vividness of a sunset or the harmonies of a great symphony.

This bursting into consciousness of the effulgent Buddha-nature is the "swallowing up" of the universe, the obliteration of every feeling of opposition and separateness. In this state of unconditioned subjectivity I, *selfless* I, am supreme. So Shakyamuni Buddha could exclaim: "Throughout heaven and earth, I alone am the honored One." Yet since awakening means also an end to being possessed by the idea of an ego-I, this is as much a world of pure objectivity. Therefore Dogen could write: "To learn the Way of the Buddha is to learn about oneself. To learn about oneself is to forget oneself. To forget oneself is to experience the world as pure object. To experience the world as pure object is to let fall one's own body and mind and the 'self-other' body and mind."[19]

To help awaken us to this world of Buddha-nature, Zen masters employ yet another mode of zazen, namely, the chanting of dharanis and sutras. A dharani has been described as "a more or less meaningless chain of words or names that is supposed to have a magical power in helping the one who is repeating it at some time of extremity."[20] As phonetic transliterations of Sanskrit words, dharanis have doubtlessly lost much of their profound meaning through the inevitable alteration of the original sounds. But as anyone who has recited them for any length of time knows, in their effect on the spirit they are anything but meaningless. When chanted with sincerity and zest they impress upon the heart-mind the names and virtues of Buddhas and Bodhisattvas enumerated in them, removing inner hindrances to zazen and fixing the heart in an attitude of reverence and devotion. But dharanis are also a symbolic expression in sound and rhythm of the essential truth of the universe lying beyond the realm of the discriminating intellect. To the degree that the discursive mind is held at bay during the voicing of

---

[19] *Shobogenzo*, first chapter, called the "Genjo Koan."

[20] *A Buddhist Bible*, edited by Dwight Goddard (New York: E. P. Dutton, 1952), p. 662.

dharanis, they are valuable as another exercise in training the mind to cease clinging to dualistic modes of thought.

The intoning of sutras, while also a mode of zazen, fulfills yet a further purpose. Since they are the recorded words and sermons of the Buddha, sutras do in some degree make a direct appeal to the intellect. Thus for those whose faith in the Buddha's Way is shallow the repeated chanting of sutras eventually leads to a measure of understanding, and this serves to strengthen faith in the truth of the Buddha's teachings.

In another sense sutra-chanting can be compared to an Oriental ink painting of, say, a pine tree in which most of the picture consists of white space. This empty space corresponds to the deeper levels of meaning of the sutras which the words adumbrate. Just as in the picture our minds are brought to a heightened awareness of the white space because of the tree, so through the reciting of the sutras we can be led to sense the reality lying beyond them, the Emptiness to which they point.

During the chanting of sutras and dharanis, each of which varies in tempo, the chanters may sit, stand, or engage in a succession of kneelings and prostrations or make repeated circumambulations in the temple. Frequently the intoning is accompanied by the steady thumping of the *mokugyo* or punctuated by the sonorous reverberations of the *keisu*. When the heart and mind are truly one with it, this combination of chanting and the throb of percussion instruments can arouse the deepest feelings and bring about a vibrant, heightened sense of awareness. At the very least it provides variety in what could otherwise become a somber and rigorous discipline of unrelieved Zen sitting. In a week's *sesshin* few could endure hour after hour of just sitting. Even if this did not prove to be unbearably difficult, it would still doubtlessly bore all but the most ardent. Zen masters by prescribing various kinds of zazen—that is, sitting, walking, chanting, and manual labor—not only reduce the risk of ennui but actually increase the effectiveness of each type of zazen.

Dogen attached great importance to the proper positions, gestures, and movements of the body and its members during chanting, as indeed in all other modes of zazen, because of their repercussions on the mind. In Tantric Buddhism particular qualities of Buddhas and Bodhisattvas are evoked by the devotee through certain positions of his hands (called mudras) as well as body postures, and it is probably from the Tantric that this aspect of Dogen's teaching derives. In any event, the prescribed postures do induce related states of mind. Thus to chant the Four Vows while kneeling, with the hands in *gassho* (palms together), as practiced in the Soto sect, evokes a reverential frame of mind less readily felt when these same vows are chanted seated or standing, as in the Rinzai sect. Similarly, lightly to touch the tips of the thumbs in seated zazen creates a feeling of poise and serenity not so easily attainable with the hands clenched.

Conversely, each state of mind elicits from the body its own specific response. The act of unself-conscious prostration before a Buddha is thus possible only under the impetus of reverence and gratitude. Such "horizontalizings of the mast of ego" cleanse the heart-mind, rendering it flexible and expansive, and open the way to an understanding and appreciation of the exalted mind and manifold virtues of the Buddha and the patriarchs. So there arises within us a desire to express our gratitude and show our respect before their personalized forms through appropriate rituals. These devotions when entered into spontaneously with a non-discriminating mind endow the Buddha figure with life; what was formerly a mere image now becomes a living reality with the singular power to obliterate in us awareness of self and Buddha at the moment of prostration. Because in this unthinking gesture our immaculate Bodhi-mind shines brightly, we feel refreshed and renewed.

In the light of these observations on the interaction of body and mind, we can now consider in fuller detail the reasons why Zen masters have always stressed an erect back and the classic lotus posture. It is well known that a bent back deprives the mind of its tension so that it is quickly invaded by random thoughts and images, but that a straight back by strengthening concentration lessens the incidence of wandering thoughts and thus hastens samadhi. Conversely, when the mind becomes free of ideas the back tends to straighten itself without conscious effort.

Through a sagging spine and the consequent multiplication of thoughts, harmonious breathing often becomes superseded by quickened or jerky breathing, depending on the nature of the thoughts. This soon reflects itself in nervous and muscular tensions. In these lectures Yasutani-roshi also points out how a slouching back saps the mind's vigor and clarity, inducing dullness and boredom.

This all-important erectness of the spine and parallel tautness of mind are easier to maintain over a long period if the legs are in the full- or half-lotus posture and the attention concentrated in the region just below the navel.[21]

Moreover, since body is the material aspect of mind and mind the immaterial aspect of body, to assemble the hands and arms and the feet and legs into a unity at one central point where the joined hands rest on the heels of the locked legs, as in the full-lotus posture, facilitates the unification of mind. Lastly, the lotus posture, in which the two knees and the seat form a triangular base of great stability, creates a sense of rootedness in the earth, together with a feeling of an all-encompassing oneness, void of the sensation of inner or outer. This is true, however, only when this position can be assumed and maintained without discomfort.

For all these reasons Zen, as the embodiment of the Buddha's essential teaching and practice, has throughout its long history followed the Buddha's method of sitting as the most direct and practical way to attain emptiness of mind and, ultimately, enlightenment.

This is not to imply, however, that zazen cannot be practiced or awakening attained unless one sits in the full- or half-lotus posture. Zazen can in fact be effective even in a chair or on a bench or while kneeling, provided the back is straight.[22] In the last resort what ensures success in the quest for enlightenment is not a particular posture but an intense longing for truth for its own sake, which alone leads one to sit regularly in any fashion and to perform all the affairs of his daily life with devotion and clear awareness. But zazen has always been regarded as fundamental to Zen discipline simply because centuries of experience have demonstrated that it is the easiest way to still the mind and bring it to one-pointedness so that it may be employed as an instrument of Self-discovery. In the long history of Zen, thousands upon thousands have come

[21] *The hara* (see p. 74).
[22] See section IX for the various correct postures.

to awakening through zazen, while few genuine enlightenment experiences have taken place without it.[23] If even the Buddha and Bodhidharma, as Dogen reminds us, had need to sit, surely no aspirant can dispense with zazen. *Kensho* (or satori) is but the first sight of Truth, and whether this is merely a glimpse or a sharp, deep view, it can be enlarged through zazen. Moreover, it is well to remember that unless fortified by *joriki*—that is, samadhi strength, the particular power developed through zazen[24]—the vision of Oneness attained in enlightenment, especially if it is faint to begin with, in time becomes clouded and eventually fades into a pleasant memory instead of remaining an omnipresent reality shaping our daily life. What we must not lose sight of, however, is that zazen is more than just a means to enlightenment or a method for sustaining and enlarging it, but is the *actualization* of our True-nature. Hence it has absolute value. Yasutani-roshi makes this vital point clear in these lectures as well as in his encounters with ten Westerners.

There can be no doubt that for most Westerners, who seem by nature more active and restless than Asians, sitting perfectly still in zazen, even in a chair, is physically and mentally painful. Their unwillingness to endure such pain and discomfort even for short periods of time undoubtedly stems from a deeply entrenched conviction that it is not only senseless but even masochistic to accept pain deliberately when ways can be found to escape or mitigate it. Not unsurprisingly, therefore, do we have the attempt on the part of some commentators, obviously unpracticed in Zen, to show that sitting is not indispensable to Zen discipline. In his *The Way of Zen* (pp. 101, 103) Alan Watts even tries to prove, by citing portions of a well-known dialogue, that the Zen masters themselves have impugned sitting. The following is our translation of the dialogue:

[23] The Sixth Patriarch, Hui-neng (638–713), is the most notable exception. In his autobiography he recounts how he attained enlightenment in his youth upon hearing the Diamond sutra recited by a monk. Evidently he had never practiced formal zazen before.

[24] For a discussion of *joriki,* see pp. 49–50. See also "Samadhi" in the vocabulary section.

Ma-tsu was doing zazen daily in his hut on Nan-yueh Mountain. Watching him one day, Huai-jang, his master, thought, "He will become a great monk," and inquired:

"Worthy one, what are you trying to attain by sitting?"

Ma-tsu replied: "I am trying to become a Buddha."

Thereupon Huai-jang picked up a piece of roof tile and began grinding it on a rock in front of him.

"What are you doing, Master?" asked Ma-tsu.

"I am polishing it to make a mirror," said Huai-jang.

"How could polishing a tile make a mirror?"

"How could sitting in zazen make a Buddha?"

Ma-tsu asked: "What should I do, then?"

Huai-jang replied: "If you were driving a cart and it didn't move, would you whip the cart or whip the ox?"

Ma-tsu made no reply.

Huai-jang continued: "Are you training yourself in zazen? Are you striving to become a sitting Buddha? If you are training yourself in zazen, [let me tell you that the substance of] zazen is neither sitting nor lying down. If you are training yourself to become a sitting Buddha, [let me tell you that] Buddha has no one form [such as sitting]. The Dharma, which has no fixed abode, allows of no distinctions. If you try to become a sitting Buddha, this is no less than killing the Buddha. If you cling to the sitting form you will not attain the essential truth."

Upon hearing this, Ma-tsu felt as refreshed as though he had had drunk an exquisite nectar.

To his own translation Mr. Watts adds (p. 113): "This seems to be the consistent doctrine of all the T'ang masters from Hui-neng [the Sixth Patriarch] to Lin-chi [Rinzai]. Nowhere in their teachings have I been able to find any instructions in or recommendation of the type of zazen which is today the principal occupation of Zen monks." Evidently he overlooked *The Zen Teaching of Huang Po* (as translated by John Blofeld), where we find Huang Po, who died in 850, advising (p. 131): "When you practice mind-control *(zazen* or *dhyana)*, sit in the proper position, stay perfectly tranquil, and do not permit the least movement of your minds to disturb you." Surely this is clear proof that zazen as it is carried on in

Japan today was an established practice even in the T'ang era, as indeed it was in the Buddha's time.

Moreover, to construe the dialogue quoted above as a condemnation of zazen is to do violence to the whole spirit of the koan. Far from implying that sitting in zazen is as useless as trying to polish a roof tile into a mirror—though it is easy for one who has never practiced Zen to come to such a conclusion—Huai-jang is in fact trying to teach Ma-tsu that Buddhahood does not exist outside himself as an object to strive for, since we are all Buddhas from the very first. Obviously Ma-tsu, who later became a great master, was under the illusion at the time that Buddhahood was something different from himself. Huai-jang is saying in effect: "How could you become a Buddha through sitting if you were not a Buddha to begin with? This would be as impossible as trying to polish a roof tile into a mirror."[25] In other words, zazen does not bestow Buddhahood; it *uncovers* a Buddha-nature which has always existed. Furthermore, through the act of grinding the tile Huai-jang is concretely revealing to Ma-tsu that the polishing is itself the expression of this Buddha-nature, which transcends all forms, including that of sitting or standing or lying down.

To guard against their disciples' becoming attached to the sitting posture, Zen masters incorporate mobile zazen into their training. It is emphatically not true, as Mr. Watts states, that today the principal occupation of Zen monks is sitting. Except for a total of six weeks or so in the year when they are in *sesshin,* Japanese Zen monks in training spend most of their time working, not sitting. At Hosshin-ji, which is more or less typical of most Japanese Zen monasteries in this respect, monks usually sit for an hour and a half in the morning and for about two to three hours in the evening. And since they normally sleep about six or seven hours, the other twelve or thirteen hours of the day are spent on such labors as working in the rice fields and vegetable gardens, cutting wood and pumping water, cooking, serving meals, keeping the monastery clean, and sweeping and weeding its extensive grounds. At other times they tend the graves in the cemetery adjoining the monastery and chant sutras and dharanis for the dead both in the homes of

[25] The Sixth Patriarch in his Platform sutra states: "If one did not have the Buddha-mind within oneself, where would one seek the true Buddha?"

devotees and in the monastery. Additionally Zen monks spend many hours walking the streets begging food and other necessities, to learn humility and gratitude, as part of their religious training. All these activities are deemed to be the practice of mobile zazen since they are to be performed mindfully, with total involvement. Huai-hai's famous dictum, "A day of no work is a day of no eating," animates the spirit of the Zen monastery today as strongly as it ever did.

Without zazen, whether it be the stationary or the mobile variety, we cannot speak of Zen training or discipline or practice. The Huai-jang koan and all others point to the Buddha-mind with which we are endowed, but they do not teach *how* to realize the reality of this Mind. The realization of this highest truth demands dedication and sustained exertion, which is to say the pure and faithful practice of zazen. The attempt to dismiss zazen as unessential is at bottom nothing more than a rationalization of an unwillingness to exert oneself for the sake of the truth, with the obvious implication that in fact no real desire for truth exists. In his *Shobogenzo* Dogen takes to task those who would identify themselves with the highest ideals of the Buddha yet shirk the effort required to put them into practice:

> The great Way of the Buddha and the patriarchs involves the highest form of exertion, which goes on unceasingly in cycles from the first dawn of religious truth, through the test of discipline and practice, to enlightenment and Nirvana. It is sustained exertion, proceeding without lapse from cycle to cycle . . .
>
> This sustained exertion is not something which men of the world naturally love or desire, yet it is the last refuge of all. Only through the exertions of all Buddhas in the past, present, and future do the Buddhas of past, present, and future become a reality . . . By this exertion Buddhahood is realized, and those who do not make an exertion when exertion is possible are those who hate Buddha, hate serving the Buddha, and hate exertion; they do not want to live and die with Buddha, they do not want him as their teacher and companion . . .[26]

[26] Quoted in *Sources of Japanese Tradition*, edited by William Theodore de Bary (New York: Columbia University Press, 1961), pp. 250–51.

A BIOGRAPHICAL NOTE ON YASUTANI-ROSHI (1885–1973) / At the age of eighty Zen Master Hakuun[27] Yasutani undertook an extended stay in America to expound the Buddha's Dharma. In so doing he evoked the spirit of the redoubtable Bodhidharma, who in the latter years of his life turned his back on his native land and went forth to distant shores to plant the living seed of Buddhism. Yet for Yasutani-roshi this was but one more remarkable event in a life marked by unique achievements.

After his seventy-fifth birthday he wrote and published five complete volumes of commentaries on the koan collections known, respectively, as the *Mumonkan,* the *Hekigan-roku,* the *Shoyo-roku,* and the *Denkoroku,* and on the *Five Degrees of Tozan* (*Go-i* in Japanese). Altogether this series comprises a feat unique in the modern history of Zen.

Such writing was but one facet of his extensive teaching activity. Besides holding monthly *sesshin* of from three to seven days at his own temple in the suburbs of Tokyo, and periodic sesshin in Kyushu and Hokkaido, the southern and northern extremes of Japan, every week he conducted a number of one-day sesshin (*zazenkai*) in the greater Tokyo area. Among other places these included one of the large universities, several factories, the Self-Defense Academy, and a number of temples.

Twice he has traveled to the West. On his first trip to America, in 1962, he held sesshin of from four to seven days at Honolulu; Los Angeles; Clairmont, California; Wallingford, Pennsylvania; New York; Boston; and Washington, D.C. The following year he repeated his sesshin in America, and expanded his activities to include lectures on Zen in England, France, and Germany.

Husband, father, schoolmaster, and ultimately Zen master, Hakuun Yasutani did not achieve his present distinction by avoiding the pains and joys incident to the life of the ordinary man but in experiencing and then transcending them. In this his life reflects the Mahayana ideal that Self-realization is for the householder no less than the celibate monk.

---

[27] A Zen name meaning "White Cloud." See "clouds and water" in section X.

Yasutani-roshi was born of a pious Buddhist mother and a father who was a pastry-shop owner in a small village. At five he had his head shaved, symbolizing his induction into the Buddhist monkhood, after which his parents, following the custom of devout families of the time, sent him to live in a temple so that he might absorb a religious atmosphere and become influenced in the direction of the priesthood.

He remained at this temple until he was twelve, performing the chores of a neophyte, attending primary school, and receiving an education in the fundamentals of Buddhism from the head priest. Upon his thirteenth birthday he became a novice at a large Soto temple. Then followed two more years of public-school education, five years at a seminary conducted by the Soto sect, and eventually four years at a teachers' training school.

At thirty Hakuun Yasutani married and began to raise a family, which in time numbered five children. Nominally a priest, he took a position as an elementary-school teacher to support his growing family since no temple was then available. He continued to teach for six years, and upon promotion to principal served another four years in the same school.

Despite the burdens of raising a family of five and the demands of his job, throughout the years he had continued, under various teachers, the zazen he had commenced many years earlier—at the age of fifteen, to be exact. While these teachers were generally recognized as among the foremost masters of the Soto sect, the fact that they dealt with satori in vague generalities made its actual realization seem remote and chimerical. Always he felt in want of a genuine master, a Buddha-like figure who could set his feet on the true path. At forty he finally found him in Harada-roshi, and with this meeting his life took a decisive turn.

He relinquished his principalship, became a temple priest in fact as well as name, and began attending sesshin regularly at Harada-roshi's monastery, Hosshin-ji. At his second sesshin he attained *kensho* with the koan Mu.

Yasutani-roshi was fifty-eight when Harada-roshi gave him his seal of approval *(inka shomei)* and named him a Dharma successor. This signal honor implied that his spiritual insight was deep, his moral character high, and his capacity to teach proven.

Like his modest temple, Yasutani-roshi was simple and unaffected. His two meals a day include neither meat, fish, eggs, nor alcohol. He could often be seen trotting about Tokyo in a tattered robe and a pair of sneakers on his way to a zazen meeting, his lecture books in a bag slung over his back, or standing in the crowded second-class interurban trains. In his utter simplicity, his indifference to finery, wealth, and fame, he walked in the footsteps of a long line of distinguished Zen masters.[28]

THE LECTURES / 1 / THEORY AND PRAC-
TICE OF ZAZEN / What I am about to tell you is based upon the teachings of my revered teacher, Daiun[29] Harada-roshi. Although he himself was of the Soto sect, he was unable to find a truly accomplished master in that sect and so went to train first at Shogen-ji and then Nanzen-ji, two Rinzai monasteries. At Nan-zen-ji he eventually grasped the inmost secret of Zen under the guidance of Dokutan-roshi, an outstanding master.

While it is undeniably true that one must undergo Zen training himself in order to comprehend the truth of Zen, Harada-roshi felt that the modern mind is so much more aware that for beginners lectures of this type could be meaningful as a preliminary to prac-tice. He combined the best of each sect and established a unique method of teaching Zen. Nowhere in Japan will you find Zen teach-ing set forth so thoroughly and succinctly, so well suited to the temper of the modern mind, as at his monastery. Having been his disciple for some twenty years, I was enabled, thanks to his favor, to open my Mind's eye in some measure.

[28] Yasutani-roshi died in his temple in Tokyo on March 28, 1973, at the age of eighty-eight. He was about to take his breakfast when he toppled over and, without pain, passed away. A week earlier his strength had begun to fail and he took more rest from his heavy teaching schedule. Three days before he drew his last breath he administered the precepts to twelve persons in a forty-five-minute ceremony called *jukai*. Afterward he confided to a close disciple, "That is my last jukai. I went through it on sheer will power."

[29] A Zen name meaning "Great Cloud." See "clouds and water" in sec-tion x. His other name is Sogaku.

Before commencing his lectures Harada-roshi would preface them with advice on listening. His first point was that everyone should listen with his eyes open and upon him—in other words, with his whole being—because an impression received only through the hearing is rather shallow, akin to listening to the radio. His second point was that each person should listen to these lectures as though they were being given to him alone, as ideally they should be. Human nature is such that if two people listen, each feels only half responsible for understanding, and if ten people are listening each feels his responsibility to be but one tenth. However, since there are so many of you and what I have to say is exactly the same for everybody, I have asked you to come as a group. You must nonetheless listen as though you were entirely alone and hold yourselves accountable for everything that is said.

This discourse is divided into twelve parts, which will be covered in some eight lecture sessions. The first involves the rationale of zazen and direct methods of practice; the next, special precautions; and the following lectures, the particular problems arising from zazen, together with their solution.

In point of fact, a knowledge of the theory or principles of zazen is not a prerequisite to practice. One who trains under an accomplished teacher will inevitably grasp this theory by degrees as his practice ripens. Modern students, however, being intellectually more sophisticated than their predecessors in Zen, will not follow instructions unreservedly; they must first know the reasons behind them. Therefore I feel obligated to deal with theoretical matters. The difficulty with theory, however, is that it is endless. Buddhist scriptures, Buddhist doctrine, and Buddhist philosophy are no more than intellectual formulations of zazen, and zazen itself is their practical demonstration. From this vast field I will now abstract what is most essential for your practice.

We start with Buddha Shakyamuni.[30] As I think you all know, he began with the path of asceticism, undergoing tortures and austerities which others before him had never attempted, including prolonged fasting. But he failed to attain enlightenment by these means and, half-dead from hunger and exhaustion, came to realize

---

[30] The traditional Japanese term is *O-Shaka-sama*. It is both respectful

the futility of pursuing a course which could only terminate in death. So he drank the milk-rice that was offered him by a concerned country girl, gradually regained his health, and resolved to steer a middle course between self-torture and self-indulgence. Thereafter he devoted himself exclusively to zazen for six years[31] and eventually, on the morning of the eighth of December, at the very instant when he glanced at the planet Venus gleaming in the eastern sky, he attained perfect enlightenment. All this we believe as historical truth.

The words the Buddha uttered involuntarily at this time are recorded variously in the Buddhist scriptures. According to the Kegon (Avatamsaka) sutra, at the moment of enlightenment he spontaneously cried out: "Wonder of wonders! Intrinsically all living beings are Buddhas, endowed with wisdom and virtue, but because men's minds have become inverted through delusive thinking they fail to perceive this." The first pronouncement of the Buddha seems to have been one of awe and astonishment. Yes, how truly marvelous that all human beings, whether clever or stupid, male or female, ugly or beautiful, are whole and complete just as they are. That is to say, the nature of every being is inherently without a flaw, perfect, no different from that of Amida or any other Buddha. This first declaration of Shakyamuni Buddha is also the ultimate conclusion of Buddhism. Yet man, restless and anxious, lives a half-crazed existence because his mind, heavily encrusted with delusion, is turned topsy-turvy. We need therefore to return to our original perfection, to see through the false image of ourselves as incomplete and sinful, and to wake up to our inherent purity and wholeness.

The most effective means by which to accomplish this is through zazen. Not only Shakyamuni Buddha himself but many of his disciples attained full awakening through zazen. Moreover, during the 2,500 years since the Buddha's death innumerable devotees in India, China, and Japan have, by grasping this selfsame key, resolved for themselves the most fundamental question of all: What is the

and intimate. The *O* and *sama* are honorifics, and rather than attempt an arbitrary translation of them, I have followed the usual English rendering of this title. (See "Buddha" in section x.)

[31] Other accounts say six years elapsed from the time he left his home until his supreme enlightenment.

meaning of life and death? Even in this day there are many who, having cast off worry and anxiety, have emancipated themselves through zazen.

Between a supremely perfected Buddha and us, who are ordinary, there is no difference as to substance. This "substance" can be likened to water. One of the salient characteristics of water is its conformability: when put into a round vessel it becomes round, when put into a square vessel it becomes square. We have this same adaptability, but as we live bound and fettered through ignorance of our true nature, we have forfeited this freedom. To pursue the metaphor, we can say that the mind of a Buddha is like water that is calm, deep, and crystal clear, and upon which the "moon of truth" reflects fully and perfectly. The mind of the ordinary man, on the other hand, is like murky water, constantly being churned by the gales of delusive thought and no longer able to reflect the moon of truth. The moon nonetheless shines steadily upon the waves, but as the waters are roiled we are unable to see its reflection. Thus we lead lives that are frustrating and meaningless.

How can we fully illumine our life and personality with the moon of truth? We need first to purify this water, to calm the surging waves by halting the winds of discursive thought. In other words, we must empty our minds of what the Kegon (Avatamsaka) sutra calls the "conceptual thought of man." Most people place a high value on abstract thought, but Buddhism has clearly demonstrated that discriminative thinking lies at the root of delusion. I once heard someone say: "Thought is the sickness of the human mind." From the Buddhist point of view this is quite true. To be sure, abstract thinking is useful when wisely employed—which is to say, when its nature and limitations are properly understood—but as long as human beings remain slaves to their intellect, fettered and controlled by it, they can well be called sick.

All thoughts, whether ennobling or debasing, are mutable and impermanent; they have a beginning and an end even as they are fleetingly with us, and this is as true of the thought of an era as of an individual. In Buddhism thought is referred to as "the stream of life-and-death." It is important in this connection to distinguish the role of transitory thoughts from that of fixed concepts. Random ideas are relatively innocuous, but ideologies, beliefs, opinions, and points of view, not to mention the factual knowledge accumulated since birth (to which we attach ourselves), are the shadows which obscure the light of truth.

So long as the winds of thought continue to disturb the water of our Self-nature, we cannot distinguish truth from untruth. It is imperative, therefore, that these winds be stilled. Once they abate, the waves subside, the muddiness clears, and we perceive directly that the moon of truth has never ceased shining. The moment of such realization is *kensho,* i.e., enlightenment, the apprehension of the true substance of our Self-nature. Unlike moral and philosophical concepts, which are variable, true insight is imperishable. Now for the first time we can live with inner peace and dignity, free from perplexity and disquiet, and in harmony with our environment.

I have spoken to you briefly about these matters, but I hope I have succeeded in conveying to you the importance of zazen. Let us now talk about practice.

The first step is to select a quiet room in which to sit. Lay out a fairly soft mat or pad some three feet square, and on top of this place a small circular cushion measuring about one foot in diameter to sit on, or use a square cushion folded in two or even a folded or rolled-up blanket. Preferably one should not wear trousers or socks, since these interfere with the crossing of the legs and the placing of the feet. For a number of reasons it is best to sit in the full-lotus posture. To sit full-lotus you place the foot of the right leg over the thigh of the left and the foot of the left leg over the thigh of the right. The main point of this particular method of sitting is that by establishing a wide, solid base with the crossed legs and both knees touching the mat, you achieve repose and absolute stability. When the body is immobile, thoughts are not stirred into activity by physical movements and the mind is more easily quieted.

If you have difficulty sitting in the full-lotus posture because of the pain, sit half-lotus, which is done by putting the foot of the left leg over the thigh of the right and the right leg under the left thigh. For those of you who are not accustomed to sitting cross-legged, even this position may not be easy to maintain. You will probably find it difficult to keep the two knees resting on the mat and will have to push one or both of them down again and again until they remain there. In both the half- and the full-lotus postures the uppermost foot can be reversed when the legs become tired.

For those who find both of these traditional zazen positions acutely uncomfortable, an alternative position is the traditional Japanese one of sitting on the heels and calves. This can be maintained for a longer time if a cushion is placed between the heels and the buttocks. One advantage of this posture is that the back can be kept erect easily. However, should all of these positions prove too painful, you may use a chair.[32]

Next rest the right hand in the lap, palm upward, and place the left hand, palm upward, on top of the right palm. Lightly touch the tips of the thumbs to each other so that a flattened circle is formed by the palms and thumbs. The right side of the body is the active side, the left the passive. Accordingly, during practice we repress the active side by placing the left foot and left hand over the right members, as an aid in achieving the highest degree of tranquility. If you look at a figure of the Buddha, however, you will notice that the position of these members is just the reverse. The significance of this is that a Buddha, unlike the rest of us, is actively engaged in the task of liberation.

After you have crossed your legs, bend forward so as to thrust the buttocks out, then slowly bring the trunk to an erect posture. The head should be straight; if looked at from the side, your ears should be in line with your shoulders and the tip of your nose in line with your navel. The body from the waist up should be weightless, free from pressure or strain.[33] Keep the eyes open and the mouth closed. The tip of the tongue should lightly touch the back of the upper teeth. If you close your eyes you will fall into a dull and dreamy state. The gaze should be lowered without focusing on anything in particular, but be careful not to incline the head forward. Experience has shown that the mind is quietest, with the least fatigue or strain, when the eyes are in this lowered position.

The spinal column must be erect at all times. This admonition

[32] See section IX for sketches of all these postures, including one widely used in the Southeast Asian Buddhist countries.

[33] The center of gravity of the body-mind should be about two inches below the navel.

is important. When the body slumps, not only is undue pressure placed on the internal organs, interfering with their free functioning, but the vertebrae by impinging upon nerves may cause strains of one kind or another. Since body and mind are one, any impairment of the physiological functions inevitably involves the mind and thus diminishes its clarity and one-pointedness, which are essential for effective concentration. From a purely psychological point of view, a ramrod erectness is as undesirable as a slouching position, for the one springs from unconscious pride and the other from abjectness, and since both are grounded in ego they are equally a hindrance to enlightenment.

Be careful to hold the head erect; if it inclines forward or backward or sideward, remaining there for an appreciable length of time, a crick in the neck may result.

When you have established a correct posture, take a deep breath, hold it momentarily, then exhale slowly and quietly. Repeat this two or three times, always breathing through the nose. After that breathe naturally. When you have accustomed yourself to this routine, one deep breath at the beginning will suffice. After that, breathe naturally, without trying to manipulate your breath. Now bend the body first to the right as far as it will go, then to the left, about seven or eight times, in large arcs to begin with, then smaller ones until the trunk naturally comes to rest at center.

You are now ready to concentrate your mind.[34] There are many good methods of concentration bequeathed to us by our predecessors in Zen. The easiest for beginners is counting incoming and outgoing breaths. The value of this particular exercise lies in the fact that all reasoning is excluded and the discriminative mind put at rest. Thus the waves of thought are stilled and a gradual one-pointedness of mind achieved. To start with, count both inhalations and exhalations. When you inhale concentrate on "one"; when you exhale, on "two"; and so on, up to ten. Then you return to "one" and once more count up to ten, continuing as before. If you lost the count, return to "one." It is as simple as that.

As I have previously pointed out, fleeting thoughts which natu-

---

[34] For additional information on concentrating the mind, see p. 135.

rally fluctuate in the mind are not in themselves an impediment. This unfortunately is not commonly recognized. Even among Japanese who have been practicing Zen for five years or more there are many who misunderstand Zen practice to be a stopping of consciousness. There is indeed a kind of zazen that aims at doing just this,[35] but it is not the traditional zazen of Zen Buddhism. You must realize that no matter how intently you count your breaths you will still perceive what is in your line of vision, since your eyes are open, and you will hear the normal sounds about you, as your ears are not plugged. And since your brain likewise is not asleep, various thoughtforms will dart about in your mind. Now, they will not hamper or diminish the effectiveness of zazen unless, evaluating them as "good," you cling to them or, deciding they are "bad," you try to check or eliminate them. You must not regard any perceptions or sensations as an obstruction to zazen, nor should you pursue any of them. I emphasize this. "Pursuit" simply means that in the act of seeing, your gaze lingers on objects; in the course of hearing, your attention dwells on sounds; and in the process of thinking, your mind adheres to ideas. If you allow yourself to be distracted in such ways, your concentration on the counting of your breaths will be impeded. To recapitulate: let random thoughts arise and vanish as they will, do not dally with them and do not try to expel them, but merely concentrate all your energy on counting the inhalations and exhalations of your breath.

In terminating a period of sitting do not arise abruptly, but begin by rocking from side to side, first in small swings, then in large ones, for about half a dozen times. You will observe that your movements in this exercise are the reverse of those you engage in when you begin zazen. Rise slowly and quietly walk around with the others in what is called *kinhin,* a walking form of zazen.

Kinhin is performed by placing the right fist, with thumb inside, on the chest and covering it with the left palm while holding both elbows at right angles. Keep the arms in a straight line and the body erect, with the eyes resting upon a point about two yards in front of the feet. At the same time continue to count inhalations and exhalations as you walk slowly around the room. Begin walking with the left foot and walk in such a way that the foot sinks into

[35] Shojo Zen (see p. 47).

the floor, first the heel and then the toes. Walk calmly and steadily, with poise and dignity. The walking must not be done absent-mindedly, and the mind must be taut as you concentrate on the counting. It is advisable to practice walking this way for at least five minutes after each sitting period of twenty to thirty minutes.

You are to think of this walking as zazen in motion. Rinzai and Soto differ considerably in their way of doing kinhin. In Rinzai the walking is brisk and energetic, while in traditional Soto it is slow and leisurely; in fact, upon each breath you step forward only six inches or so. My own teacher, Harada-roshi, advocated a gait somewhere between these two and that is the method we have been practicing here. Further, the Rinzai sect cups the left hand on top of the right, whereas in the orthodox Soto the right hand is placed on top. Harada-roshi felt that the Rinzai method of putting the left hand uppermost was more desirable and so he adopted it into his own teaching. Now, even though this walking relieves the stiffness in your legs, such relief is to be regarded as a mere by-product and not the main object of kinhin. Accordingly, those of you who are counting your breaths should continue during kinhin, and those of you who are working on a koan should carry on with it.

This ends the first lecture. Continue to count your breaths as I have instructed until you come before me again.

2 / PRECAUTIONS TO OBSERVE IN ZAZEN / In this second lecture I am going to change your breathing exercise slightly. This morning I told you to count "one" as you inhaled and "two" as you exhaled. Hereafter I want you to count "one" only on the exhalation, so that one full breath [inhalation and exhalation] will be "one." Don't bother counting the inhalations; just count "one," "two," "three," and so forth, on the exhalation.

It is advisable to do zazen facing a wall, a curtain, or the like. Don't sit too far from the wall nor with your nose up against it; the ideal distance is from two to three feet. Likewise, don't sit where you have a sweeping view, for it is distracting, or where you look out on a pleasant landscape, which will tempt you to leave off zazen in order to admire it. In this connection, remember that although your eyes are open you are not actually trying to see. For all these reasons it is wisest to sit facing a wall. However, if you happen to be doing zazen formally in a Rinzai temple, you will have no choice but to sit facing others, as this is the established custom in that sect.

In the beginning, if possible, select a room that is quiet as well as clean and tidy, one which you can regard as special. It may be asked whether it is satisfactory to do zazen on a bed so long as the room is clean and free from noise. For the ordinary healthy person the answer is no; there are any number of reasons why it is difficult to keep the mind in proper tension on a bed. A bedridden person, of course, has no choice.

You will probably find that natural sounds, like those of insects or birds or running water, will not disturb you, neither will the rhythmic ticking of a clock nor the purring of a motor. Sudden noises, however, like the roar of a jet, are jarring. But rhythmic sounds you can make use of. One student of mine actually attained enlightenment by utilizing the sound of the steady threshing of rice while he was doing zazen. The most objectionable sounds are those of human voices, either heard directly or over the radio or television. When you start zazen, therefore, find a room which is distant from such sounds. When your sitting has ripened, however, no noises will disturb you.

Besides keeping your room clean and orderly you should decorate it with flowers and burn incense since these, by conveying a sense of the pure and the holy, make it easier for you to relate yourself to zazen and thus to calm and unify your mind more quickly. Wear simple, comfortable clothing that will give you a feeling of dignity and purity. In the evening it is better not to wear night clothes, but if it is hot and a question of either doing zazen in pajamas or not doing it at all, by all means wear the pajamas. But make yourself clean and tidy.

The room ought not to be too light or too dark. You can put up a dark curtain if it is too light, or you can use a small electric bulb if it is night. The effect of a dark room is the same as closing your eyes: it dulls everything. The best condition is a sort of twilight. Remember, Buddhist zazen does not aim at rendering the mind inactive but at quieting and unifying it in the midst of activity.

A room with plenty of fresh air, that is neither too hot in summer nor too cold in winter, is ideal. Punishing the body is not the purpose of zazen, so it is unnecessary to struggle with extremes of heat or cold. Experience has shown, however, that one can do better zazen when he feels slightly cool; too hot a room tends to make one sleepy. As your ardor for zazen deepens you will naturally become unconcerned about cold or heat. Nevertheless, it is wise to take care of your health.

Next let us discuss the best time for zazen. For the eager and determined any time of day and all seasons of the year are equally good. But for those who have jobs or professions the best time is either morning or evening, or better still, both. Try to sit every morning, preferably before breakfast, and just before going to bed at night. But if you can sit only once—and you should sit at least once a day—you will have to consider the relative merits of morning and evening. Each has its advantages and disadvantages. If you find that either morning or evening is equally good and you ask which I recommend (because you can sit only once a day), I would say the morning, for the following reasons. No visitors come early in the morning, whereas in the evening you are likely to be interrupted. Also, morning—at any rate, in the city—is much quieter than evening since fewer cars are on the streets. Furthermore, because in the morning you are rested and somewhat hungry, you are in good condition for zazen, whereas in the evening, when you are tired and have had your meal, you are likely to be duller. Since it is difficult to do zazen on a full stomach, it is better not to sit immediately after a meal when you are a beginner. Before a meal, however, zazen can be practiced to good advantage. As your zeal grows it won't matter when you sit, before, after, or during a meal.

How long should you do zazen at one sitting? There is no general rule, for it varies according to the degree of one's eagerness as well as the maturity of one's practice. For novices a shorter time is better. If you sit devotedly five minutes a day for a month or two, you will want to increase your sitting to ten or more minutes as your ardor grows. When you are able to sit with your mind taut for, say, thirty minutes without pain or discomfort, you will come to appreciate the feeling of tranquility and well-being induced by zazen and will want to practice regularly. For these reasons I recommend that beginners sit for shorter periods of time. On the other hand, should you force yourself from the beginning to sit for longer periods, the pain in your legs may well become unbearable before you acquire a calm mind. Thus you will quickly tire of zazen, feeling it to be a waste of time, or you will always be watching the clock. In the end you will come to dislike zazen and stop sitting altogether. This is what frequently happens. Now, even though you sit for only ten minutes or so each day, you can compensate for this briefness by concentrating intensely on the counting of each breath, thus increasing its effectiveness. You must not count absent-mindedly or mechanically, as though it were a duty.

In spite of your being able to sit for an hour or more with a feeling of exquisite serenity, it is wise to limit your sitting to periods of about thirty or forty minutes each. Ordinarily it is not advisable to do zazen longer than this at one sitting, since the mind cannot sustain its vigor and tautness and the value of the sitting decreases. Whether one realizes it or not, a gradual diminution of the mind's concentrative intensity takes place. For this reason it is better to alternate a thirty- or forty-minute period of sitting with a round of walking zazen. Following this pattern, one can do zazen for a full day or even a week with good results. The longer zazen continues, however, the more time should be spent in walking zazen. In fact, one might advantageously add periods of manual labor to this routine, as has been done in the Zen temple since olden times. Needless to say, you must keep your mind in a state of clear awareness during such manual labor and not allow it to become lax or dull.

A word about food. It is better to eat no more than eighty percent of your capacity. A Japanese proverb has it that eight parts of a full stomach sustain the man; the other two sustain the doctor. The *Zazen Yojinki* (Precautions to Observe in Zazen), compiled about 650 years ago, says you should eat two-thirds of your capacity. It further says that you should choose nourishing vegetables—of course meat-eating is not in the tradition of Buddhism and it was taboo when the *Yojinki* was written—such as mountain potatoes, sesame, sour plums, black beans, mushrooms, and the root of the lotus; and it also recommends various kinds of seaweed, which are highly nutritious and leave an alkaline residue in the body. Now, I am no authority on vitamins and minerals and calories, but it is a fact that most people today eat a diet which creates too much acid in the blood, and a great offender in this respect is meat. Eat more vegetables of the kind mentioned, which are alkalinic in their effect. In ancient days there was a *yang-yin* diet. The *yang* was the alkaline and the *yin* the acid, and the old books cautioned that a diet ought not be either too *yang* or too *yin*. This is substantially what I have just told you.

There comes a point in your sitting when insights about yourself will flash into your mind. For example, relationships that previously were incomprehensible will suddenly be clarified and difficult personal problems abruptly solved. If you don't jot down things that you want to remember, this could bother you and so interfere with your concentration. For this reason when you are sitting by yourself you may want to keep a pencil and notebook next to you.

3 / ILLUSORY VISIONS AND SENSATIONS / This is the third lecture. Before I begin I will assign you a new way of concentration. Instead of counting your exhalations, as heretofore, count "one" on the first inhalation, "two" on the next inhalation, and so on, up to ten. This is more difficult than counting on the exhalation, because all mental and physical activity is performed on the exhaled breath. For instance, just before pouncing, animals take a breath. This principle is well known in kendo fencing and judo, in which one is taught that by carefully observing his opponent's breathing his attack can be anticipated. While this exercise is difficult, you must try to practice it as another means of concentrating your mind. Until you come before me again you are to concentrate on counting the inhalations of your breath, not audibly but in the mind only. It is not advisable, however, to follow this practice for long. If you are working by yourself, a week would be sufficient.

Makyo are the phenomena—visions, hallucinations, fantasies, revelations, illusory sensations—which one practicing zazen is apt to experience at a particular stage in his sitting. *Ma* means "devil" and *kyo* "the objective world." Hence makyo are the disturbing or "diabolical" phenomena which appear to one during his zazen. These phenomena are not inherently bad. They become a serious obstacle to practice only if one is ignorant of their true nature and is ensnared by them.

The word *makyo* is used in both a general and a specific sense. Broadly speaking, the entire life of the ordinary man is nothing but a makyo. Even such Bodhisattvas as Monju and Kannon, highly developed though they are, still have about them traces of makyo; otherwise they would be supreme Buddhas, completely free of makyo. One who becomes attached to what he realizes through satori is also still lingering in the world of makyo. So, you see, there are makyo even after enlightenment, but we shall not enter into that aspect of the subject in these lectures.

In the specific sense the number of makyo which can appear are in fact unlimited, varying according to the personality and temperament of the sitter. In the Ryogon [Surangama] sutra the Buddha warns of fifty different kinds, but of course he is referring only to the commonest. If you attend a sesshin of from five to seven days' duration and apply yourself assiduously, on the third day you are likely to experience makyo of varying degrees of intensity. Besides those which involve the vision there are numerous makyo which relate to the sense of touch, smell, or hearing, or which sometimes cause the body suddenly to move from side to side or forward and backward or to lean to one side or to seem to sink or rise. Not infrequently words burst forth uncontrollably or, more rarely, one imagines he is smelling a particularly fragrant perfume. There are even cases where without conscious awareness one writes down things which turn out to be prophetically true.

Very common are visual hallucinations. You are doing zazen with your eyes open when suddenly the ridges of the straw matting in front of you seem to be heaving up and down like waves. Or without warning everything may go white before your eyes, or black. A knot in the wood of a door may suddenly appear as a beast or demon or angel. One disciple of mine often used to see visions of masks—demons' masks or jesters' masks. I asked him whether he had ever had any particular experience of masks, and it turned out that he had seen them at a festival in Kyushu[36] when he was a child. Another man I knew was extremely troubled in his practice by visions of Buddha and his disciples walking around him reciting

[36] The southernmost of Japan's main islands.

sutras, and was only able to dispel the hallucination by jumping into a tank of ice-cold water for two or three minutes.

Many makyo involve the hearing. One may hear the sound of a piano or loud noises, such as an explosion (which is heard by no one else), and actually jump. One disciple of mine always used to hear the sound of a bamboo flute while doing zazen. He had learned to play the bamboo flute many years before, but had long since given it up; yet always the sound came to him when he was sitting.

In the *Zazen Yojinki* we find the following about makyo: "The body may feel hot or cold or glasslike or hard or heavy or light. This happens because the breath is not well harmonized [with the mind] and needs to be carefully regulated." It then goes on to say: "One may experience the sensation of sinking or floating, or may alternately feel hazy and sharply alert. The disciple may develop the faculty of seeing through solid objects as though they were transparent, or he may experience his own body as a translucent substance. He may see Buddhas and Bodhisattvas. Penetrating insights may suddenly come to him, or passages of sutras which were particularly difficult to understand may suddenly become luminously clear to him. All these abnormal visions and sensations are merely the symptoms of an impairment arising from a maladjustment of the mind with the breath."

Other religions and sects place great store by experiences which involve visions of God or deities or hearing heavenly voices, performing miracles, receiving divine messages, or becoming purified through various rites and drugs. In the Nichiren sect, for example, the devotee loudly and repeatedly invokes the name of the Lotus sutra, to the accompaniment of vigorous body movements, and feels he has thereby purged himself of his defilements. In varying degree these practices induce a feeling of well-being, yet from the Zen point of view all are abnormal states devoid of true religious significance and therefore only makyo.

What is the essential nature of these disturbing phenomena we call makyo? They are temporary mental states which arise during zazen when our ability to concentrate has developed to a certain point and our practice is beginning to ripen. When the thought-waves that wax and wane on the surface of the mind are partially calmed, residual elements of past experiences "lodged" in the deeper levels of consciousness bob up sporadically to the surface of the mind, conveying the feeling of a greater or expanded reality. Makyo, accordingly, are a mixture of the real and the unreal, not unlike ordinary dreams. Just as dreams are usually not remembered by a person in deep sleep but only when he is half-asleep and half-awake, so makyo do not come to those in deep concentration or samadhi. Never be tempted into thinking that these phenomena are real or that the visions themselves have any meaning. To have a beautiful vision of a Buddha does not mean that you are any nearer becoming one yourself, any more than a dream of being a millionaire means that you are any richer when you awake. Therefore there is no reason to feel elated about such makyo. And similarly, whatever horrible monsters may appear to you, there is no cause whatever for alarm. Above all, do not allow yourself to be enticed by visions of the Buddha or of gods blessing you or communicating a divine message, or by makyo involving prophecies which turn out to be true. This is to squander your energies in the foolish pursuit of the inconsequential.

But such visions are certainly a sign that you are at a crucial point in your sitting, and that if you exert yourself to the utmost, you can surely experience kensho. Tradition states that even Shakyamuni Buddha just before his own awakening experienced innumerable makyo, which he termed "obstructing devils." Whenever makyo appear, simply ignore them and continue sitting wholeheartedly.

4 / THE FIVE VARIETIES OF ZEN / I shall now enumerate the different kinds of Zen. Unless you learn to distinguish between them, you are likely to err on decisive points, such as whether or not satori is indispensable in Zen, whether Zen involves the complete absence of discursive thought, and the like. The truth is that among the many types of Zen there are some which are profound and some shallow, some that lead to enlightenment and some that do not. It is said that during the time of the Buddha there were ninety or ninety-five schools of philosophy or religion in existence. Each school had its particular mode of Zen, and each was slightly different from the others.

All great religions embrace some measure of Zen, since religion needs prayer and prayer needs concentration of mind. The teachings of Confucius and Mencius, of Lao-tzu and Chuang-tzu, all these have their own elements of Zen. Indeed, Zen is spread over many different activities of life, such as the tea ceremony, Noh, kendo, judo. In Japan, starting with the Meiji Restoration, less than a hundred years ago, and continuing up to the present, there have sprung up a number of teachings and disciplines with elements of Zen in them. Among others I recall Okada's System of Tranquil Sitting and Emma's Method of Mind and Body Cultivation. Recently one Tempu Nakamura has been zealously advocating a form of Indian Yoga Zen. All these different methods of concentration, almost limitless in number, come under the broad heading of Zen. Rather than try to specify them all, I am going to discuss the five main divisions of Zen as classified by Keiho-zenji, one of the early Zen masters in China, whose categories, I feel, are still valid and useful. Outwardly these five kinds of Zen scarcely differ. There may be slight variations in the way the legs are crossed, the hands folded, or the breathing regulated, but common to all are three basic elements: an erect sitting posture, correct control of breathing, and concentration (unification) of mind. Beginners need to bear in mind, however, that in the *substance* and *purpose* of these various types there are distinct differences. These differences are crucial to you when you come before me individually to state your aspiration, for they will enable you to define your goal clearly the better that I may assign you the practice appropriate to it.

The first of these types we call *bompu,* or "ordinary," Zen as opposed to the other four, each of which can be thought of as a special kind of Zen suitable for the particular aims of different individuals. Bompu Zen, being free from any philosophic or religious content, is for anybody and everybody. It is a Zen practiced purely in the belief that it can improve both physical and mental health. Since it can almost certainly have no ill effects, anyone can undertake it, whatever religious beliefs he happens to hold or if he holds none at all. Bompu Zen is bound to eliminate sickness of a psychosomatic nature and to improve the health generally.

Through the practice of bompu Zen you learn to concentrate and control your mind. It never occurs to most people to try to control their minds, and unfortunately this basic training is left out of contemporary education, not being part of what is called the acquisition of knowledge. Yet without it what we learn is difficult to retain because we learn it improperly, wasting much energy in the process. Indeed, we are virtually crippled unless we know how to restrain our thoughts and concentrate our minds. Furthermore, by practicing this very excellent mode of mind training you will find yourself increasingly able to resist temptations to which you had previously succumbed, and to sever attachments which had long held you in bondage. An enrichment of personality and a strengthening of character inevitably follow since the three basic elements of mind—that is, intellect, feeling, and will—develop harmoniously. The quietist sitting practiced in Confucianism seems to have stressed mainly these effects of mind concentration. However, the fact remains that bompu Zen, although far more beneficial for the cultivation of the mind than the reading of countless books on ethics and philosophy, is unable to resolve the fundamental problem of man and his relation to the universe. Why? Because it cannot pierce the ordinary man's basic delusion of himself as distinctly other than the universe.

The second of the five kinds of Zen is called *gedo*. Gedo means literally "an outside way" and so implies, from the Buddhist point of view, teachings other than Buddhist. Here we have a Zen related to religion and philosophy but yet not a Buddhist Zen. Hindu yoga, the quietist sitting of Confucianism, contemplation practices in Christianity, all these belong to the category of gedo Zen.

Another feature of gedo Zen is that it is often practiced in order to cultivate various supranormal powers or skills, or to master certain arts beyond the reach of the ordinary man. A good example of this is Tempu Nakamura, the man whom I mentioned earlier. It is reported that he can make people act without himself moving a muscle or saying a word. The aim of the Emma Method is to accomplish such feats as walking barefooted on sharp sword blades or staring at sparrows so that they become paralyzed. All these miraculous exploits are brought about through the cultivation of *joriki*, the particular strength or power which comes with the strenuous practice of mind concentration, and of which I shall speak later in greater detail. Here I will simply remind you that a Zen which aims solely at the cultivation of joriki for such ends is not a Buddhist Zen.

Another object for which gedo Zen is practiced is rebirth in various heavens. Certain sects, we know, practice Zen in order to be reborn in heaven. This is not the object of Zen Buddhism. While the Zen Buddhist does not quarrel with the idea of various strata of heaven and the belief that one may be reborn into them through the performance of ten kinds of meritorious deeds, he himself does not crave rebirth in heaven. Conditions there are altogether too pleasant and comfortable and he can all too easily be lured from zazen. Besides, when his merit in heaven expires he can very well land in hell. Zen Buddhists therefore believe it preferable to be born into the human world and to practice zazen with the aim of ultimately becoming a Buddha.

I will stop here and at the next lecture conclude the five types of Zen.

I have now discussed with you the first two kinds of Zen, namely, bompu and gedo. Before going on to the next three types I am going to give you another method of concentration: experiencing the breath. For the time being stop counting your breaths and instead concentrate intently on following your inhalations and exhalations, trying to experience them clearly. You are to carry on this exercise until you come before me again.

The third type of Zen is *shojo*, literally meaning "Small Vehicle." This is the vehicle or teaching that is to take you from one state of mind [delusion] to another [enlightenment]. This small vehicle is so named because it is designed to accommodate only one's self. You can perhaps compare it to a bicycle. The large vehicle [Mahayana], on the other hand, is more like a car or bus: it takes on others as well. Hence shojo is a Zen which looks only to one's own peace of mind.

Here we have a Zen which is Buddhist but a Zen not in accord with the Buddha's highest teaching. It is rather an expedient Zen for those unable to grasp the innermost meaning of the Buddha's enlightenment, i.e., that existence is an inseparable whole, each one of us embracing the cosmos in its totality. This being true, it follows that we cannot attain genuine peace of mind merely by seeking our own salvation while remaining indifferent to the welfare of others.

There are those, however—and some of you listening to me now may be among them—who simply cannot bring themselves to believe in the reality of such a world. No matter how often they are taught that the relative world of distinctions and opposites to which they cling is illusory, the product of their mistaken views, they cannot but believe otherwise. To such people the world can only seem inherently evil, full of sin and strife and suffering, of killing and being killed, and in their despair they long to escape from it.

The fourth classification is called *daijo*, Great Vehicle [Mahayana] Zen, and this is a truly Buddhist Zen, for it has as its central purpose *kensho-godo*, that is, seeing into your essential nature and realizing the Way in your daily life. For those able to comprehend the import of the Buddha's own enlightenment experience and with a desire to break through their own illusory view of the universe and experience absolute, undifferentiated Reality, the Buddha taught this mode of Zen. Buddhism is essentially a religion of enlightenment. The Buddha after his own supreme awakening spent some fifty years teaching people how they might themselves realize their Self-nature. His methods have been transmitted from master to disciple right down to the present day. So it can be said that a Zen which ignores or denies or belittles enlightenment is not true daijo Buddhist Zen.

In the practice of daijo Zen your aim in the beginning is to awaken to your True-nature, but upon enlightenment you realize that zazen is more than a means to enlightenment—it is the actualization of your True-nature. In this type of Zen, which has as its object satori-awakening, it is easy to mistakenly regard zazen as but a means. A wise teacher, however, will point out from the onset that zazen is in fact the actualization of the innate Buddha-nature and not merely a technique for achieving enlightenment. If zazen were no more than such a technique, it would follow that after satori zazen would be unnecessary. But as Dogen-zenji himself pointed out, precisely the reverse is true; the more deeply you experience satori, the more you perceive the need for practice.[37]

[37] See p. 293.

Saijojo Zen, the last of the five types, is the highest vehicle, the culmination and crown of Buddhist Zen. This Zen was practiced by all the Buddhas of the past—namely, Shakyamuni and Amida[38]—and is the expression of Absolute Life, life in its purest form. It is the zazen which Dogen-zenji chiefly advocated and it involves no struggle for satori or any other object. We call it shikan-taza, and of this I shall speak in greater detail in a subsequent lecture.

In this highest practice, means and end coalesce. Daijo Zen and saijojo Zen are, in point of fact, complementary. The Rinzai sect places daijo uppermost and saijojo beneath, whereas the Soto sect does the reverse. In saijojo, when rightly practiced, you sit in the firm conviction that zazen is the actualization of your undefiled True-nature, *and at the same time you sit in complete faith that the day will come when, exclaiming, "Oh, this is it!" you will unmistakably realize this True-nature.* Therefore you need not self-consciously strive for enlightenment.

Today many in the Soto sect hold that since we are all innately Buddhas, satori is unnecessary. Such an egregious error reduces shikan-taza, which properly is the highest form of sitting, to nothing more than bompu Zen, the first of the five types.

This completes my account of the five varieties of Zen, but unless I now tell you about the three objectives of zazen my presentation of these five types, especially the last two, will be incomplete.

5 / THE THREE AIMS OF ZAZEN / The aims of zazen are three: 1) development of the power of concentration *(joriki)*, 2) satori-awakening *(kensho-godo)*, and 3) actualization of the Supreme Way in our daily lives *(mujodo no taigen)*. These three form an inseparable unity, but for purposes of discussion I am obliged to deal with them individually.

Joriki, the first of these, is the power or strength which arises when the mind has been unified and brought to one-pointedness in zazen concentration. This is more than the ability to concentrate in the usual sense of the word. It is a dynamic power which, once mobilized, enables us even in the most sudden and unexpected situations to act instantly, without pausing to collect our wits, and

[38] See "Amida" in section x.

in a manner wholly appropriate to the circumstances. One who has developed joriki is no longer a slave to his passions, neither is he at the mercy of his environment. Always in command of both himself and the circumstances of his life, he is able to move with perfect freedom and equanimity. The cultivation of certain supranormal powers is also made possible by joriki, as is the state in which the mind becomes like clear, still water.

The first two of the five kinds of Zen I have spoken about depend entirely on joriki. Now, although the power of joriki can be endlessly enlarged through regular practice, it will recede and eventually vanish if we neglect zazen. And while it is true that many extraordinary powers flow from joriki, nevertheless through it alone we cannot cut the roots of our illusory view of the world. Mere strength of concentration is not enough for the highest types of Zen; concomitantly there must be satori-awakening. In a little-known document handed down by the Patriarch Sekito Kisen, the founder of one of the early Zen sects, the following appears: "In our sect, realization of the Buddha-nature, and not mere devotion or strength of concentration, is paramount."

The second of these aims is kensho-godo, seeing into your True-nature and at the same time seeing into the ultimate nature of the universe and "all the ten thousand things" in it. It is the sudden realization that "I have been complete and perfect from the very beginning. How wonderful, how miraculous!" If it is true kensho, its substance will always be the same for whoever experiences it, whether he be the Buddha Shakyamuni, the Buddha Amida, or any one of you gathered in this temple. But this does not mean that we can all experience kensho to the same degree, for in the clarity, the depth, and the completeness of the experience there are great differences. As an illustration, imagine a person blind from birth who gradually begins to recover his sight. At first he can see very vaguely and darkly and only objects close to him. Then as his sight improves he is able to distinguish things a yard or so away, then objects at ten yards, then at a hundred yards, until finally he can recognize anything up to a thousand yards. At each of these stages the phenomenal world he is seeing is the same, but the differences in the clarity and accuracy of his views of that world are as great as those between snow and charcoal.

So it is with the differences in clarity and depth of our experiences of kensho.

The last of the three objectives is *mujodo no taigen*, the actualization of the Supreme Way throughout our entire being and our daily activities. At this point we do not distinguish the end from the means. Saijojo, which I have spoken of as the fifth and highest of the five types of Zen, corresponds to this stage. When you sit earnestly and egolessly in accordance with the instructions of a competent teacher—with your mind fully conscious yet as free of thought as a pure white sheet of paper is unmarred by a blemish— there is an unfoldment of your intrinsically pure Buddha-nature whether you have had satori or not. But what must be emphasized here is that only with true awakening do you directly apprehend the truth of your Buddha-nature and perceive that saijojo, the purest type of Zen, is no different from that practiced by all Buddhas.

The practice of Buddhist Zen should embrace all three of these objectives, for they are interrelated. There is, for instance, an essential connection between joriki and kensho. Kensho is "the wisdom naturally associated with joriki," which is the power arising from concentration. Joriki is connected with kensho in yet another way. Many people may never be able to reach kensho unless they have first cultivated a certain amount of joriki, for otherwise they may find themselves too restless, too nervous and uneasy to persevere with their zazen. Moreover, unless fortified by joriki, a single experience of kensho will have no appreciable effect on your life and will fade into a mere memory. For although through the experience of kensho you have apprehended the underlying unity of the cosmos with your Mind's eye, without joriki you are unable to act with the total force of your being on what your inner vision has revealed to you.

Likewise there is an interconnection between kensho and the third of these aims, *mujodo no taigen*. Kensho when manifested in all your actions is *mujodo no taigen*. With perfect enlightenment (*anuttara samyak-sambodhi*) we apprehend that our conception of the world as dual and antithetical is false, and upon this realization the world of Oneness, of true harmony and peace, is revealed.

The Rinzai sect tends to make satori-awakening the final aim of sitting and skims over joriki and *mujodo no taigen*. Thus the need for continued practice after enlightenment is minimized, and koan study, since it is unsupported by zaren and scarcely related to daily life, becomes essentially an intellectual game instead of a means by which to amplify and strengthen enlightenment.

On the other hand, while the practice advocated in the official quarters of the Soto sect today stresses *mujodo no taigen,* in effect it amounts to little more than the accumulation of joriki, which, as I pointed out earlier, "leaks" or recedes and ultimately disappears unless zazen is carried on regularly. The contention of the Soto sect nowadays that kensho is unnecessary and that one need do no more than carry on his daily activities with the Mind of the Buddha is specious, for without kensho you can never really know what this Buddha-mind is.

These imbalances in both sects[39] in recent times have, unfortunately, impaired the quality of Zen teaching.

This concludes the discussion of the three aims of zazen.

6 / INDIVIDUAL INSTRUCTION / Continue to practice the exercise I gave you last time, namely, concentrating on your incoming and outgoing breaths and endeavoring to experience each breath clearly.

This lecture will deal with *dokusan* (individual instruction), which is the time allotted for bringing all problems pertaining to practice before the roshi in private. This tradition of individual teaching started with the honored Shakyamuni himself and has continued unbroken until today. We know this because one of the great masters of Tendai, Chisha-daishi, in his systematization of all the sutras under Eight Teachings and Five Periods, lists the Secret Teaching, which corresponds to dokusan.

Without this individual guidance we cannot say that our practice

[39] For a poetic description of the differences between Rinzai and Soto, the following from an unpublished manuscript of the late Nyogen Senzaki may be of interest: "Among Zen students it is said that 'Rinzai's teaching is like the frost of the late autumn, making one shiver, while the teaching of Soto is like the spring breeze which caresses the flower, helping it to bloom.' There is another saying: 'Rinzai's teaching is like a brave general who moves a regiment without delay, while the Soto teaching is like a farmer taking care of a rice field, one stalk after another, patiently.'"

of zazen is authentic. Unfortunately, since the Meiji period, nearly a hundred years ago, dokusan has virtually died out in the Soto sect, continuing only in the Rinzai tradition. If we compare zazen to a journey on which some start rapidly and then slow down, others begin slowly and later accelerate their pace, some find one phase of the journey more hazardous than another, and all carry different burdens of luggage (that is, preconceived ideas), we can begin to understand why individual guidance in dokusan cannot be dispensed with.

It may be asked why it is necessary to keep dokusan secret. Since nothing immoral is involved, why can it not be open and in public? First of all, since we are ordinary people, with ego, in the presence of others we are inclined to make ourselves out to be better than we are. We cannot bare our souls and stand naked, as it were. Likewise we hesitate to speak the whole truth for fear of being laughed at. Or if the roshi scolds us, using harsh language, we become more concerned with the effect of this on others than in listening to him openmindedly.

There is yet another reason for privacy in dokusan. After your first experience of kensho you move from koan to koan as your understanding deepens, and were others to be present when you demonstrated these koans, listening to the roshi's replies, they might think, "Oh, so that's the answer!" without fully understanding the import of the koan. Obviously this would hurt their practice, for instead of coming to their own realization and presenting it to the roshi, they would remember that this was an acceptable answer but that was not, and thus, to their own detriment, their koan practice would degenerate to mere intellection. For these reasons you should remain silent when asked about a koan which the questioner has not yet passed. Irresponsible talk may lead to other harmful consequences. Rumors may spread that one is savagely beaten in dokusan, for example, giving Zen an undeservedly bad name. Therefore do not discuss your koans with anybody, not even your best friends or members of your family.

It is precisely this violation of the secrecy which formerly surrounded the koan system that has brought about a steady deterioration in Rinzai teaching. What I am about to say does not apply to laymen, who are generally serious in their practice. But in the monasteries, where there are monks who resent the entire training, being there in the first place only to serve the period required to inherit the resident priesthood of a temple, this problem becomes serious. In monasteries where the discipline is faulty an older monk will often say to a younger one: "What koan are you working on?" When told, the older one will say: "Do you understand it?" "No." "All right, I will tell you the answer," the older monk says, "and you buy me some cakes in return." The roshi can tell whether the answer is authentic or not, but if for some reason he himself becomes lukewarm, he may accept an answer which is not the monk's own. This practice may not be particularly harmful if such a monk spends only two or three years at a monastery before becoming the resident priest of a temple, as his duties there will not require his evaluating another's kensho. But it can happen that there is no opening when he completes this minimal training, so that he may remain at the monastery for perhaps eight or ten years, going through the entire koan system with answers which are not his own. Finally, as is the custom in the Rinzai sect when one completes all the koans, he receives the title of teacher. In this way one with no real understanding becomes "qualified" to guide others. This insidious practice is undermining Zen teaching. Soto scholars studying Zen academically justifiably attack the koan system on just these grounds.

The next point concerns what questions are appropriate during dokusan. All questions should relate to problems growing directly out of your practice. This naturally excludes personal problems. You may feel that the privacy of dokusan offers an excellent opportunity for the discussion of personal or theoretical matters, but you must bear in mind that there are others waiting and that if you take up problems other than those of your practice, you are hindering them. Properly, you may ask about your stomach, for instance, if it is growling, or about your teeth hurting so that you cannot eat, or about visions you may be experiencing. You should not, however, ask about Buddhist doctrine or comparative philosophy or the difference between one sutra and another. You may ask anything so long as it arises directly out of your practice.

The procedure for a new student is to make a monetary offering to the roshi before taking dokusan. Why, it may be asked, all this formality? Dokusan, it cannot be emphasized too strongly, is not a frivolous matter. While everyone is free to practice zazen and to listen to the roshi's commentary at sesshin, the essential character of dokusan is the forming of a karmic bond between teacher and disciple, the significance of which is deep in Buddhism. Dokusan therefore is not to be taken lightly. Moreover, since what passes between the roshi and the student in dokusan concerns problems of a deep and ultimate nature, only the truth must be spoken between them. Very often in public meetings one hesitates to say things which might offend others, but this is not so in dokusan, where the absolute truth must always prevail. For these reasons the proprieties which establish this relationship are not to be slighted.

It is proper to wear ceremonial dress to dokusan, but as this is not insisted upon nowadays you may wear anything which is presentable. When dokusan is announced take a position in line behind the bell outside the zazen hall. When your turn comes and you hear my handbell, strike the bell in front of you twice and come to this room. You should not come dashing in, as that would cause confusion and you would not be in a frame of mind to benefit from dokusan. Neither should you saunter in, for there are others waiting. It was the custom originally to make three prostrations at the threshold, three in front of the roshi, and then three more at the doorway when you left, but this has now been abbreviated to three prostrations altogether, one at each of the places mentioned.

In making your prostrations you should touch the tatami mat with your forehead, your hands extended in front of your head, palms upward. Then, bending your arms at the elbows, raise your hands, palms upward, several inches above your head. This gesture of receiving the feet, the lowliest members of the Buddha's body, symbolizes humility and the grateful acceptance into your life of the Way of the Buddha. Unless you have submerged your ego, you cannot do this. Bear in mind that the roshi is not simply a deputy of the Buddha but actually stands in his place. In making these prostrations you are in fact paying respect to the Buddha just as though he himself were sitting there, and to the Dharma.

Next take a position about a foot in front of me and announce the nature of your practice. Simply say, "I am counting my breaths," "I am doing Mu," or "I am practicing shikan-taza." Make any questions you have brief and to the point. Should I have anything to say to you, I will say it after you have finished. But do not come in and waste time wondering what to talk about; remember, others are waiting to see me. My ringing of this bell is your signal to bow down and leave. After that if you should remember something, you will have to bring it up at the following dokusan, because the next person will already be coming in.

7 / SHIKAN-TAZA / Up to now you have been concentrating on your breaths, trying to experience vividly the inhaled breath as only inhaled breath and the exhaled breath as only exhaled breath. Next I want you to try shikan-taza, which I will shortly describe in detail.

It is neither usual nor desirable to change so quickly from these different exercises, but I have followed this course in order to give you a taste of the different modes of concentration.[40] After these introductory lectures are completed and you come before me singly, I will assign you a practice corresponding to the nature of your aspiration as well as to the degree of your determination.

This lecture will deal with shikan-taza. *Shikan* means "nothing but" or "just," while *ta* means "to hit" and *za* "to sit." So shikantaza is a practice in which the mind is intensely involved in just sitting. In this type of zazen it is all too easy for the mind, which is not supported by such aids as counting the breath or by a koan, to become distracted. The correct temper of mind therefore becomes doubly important. In shikan-taza the mind must be unhurried yet at the same time firmly planted or massively composed, like Mount Fuji let us say. But it must also be alert, stretched, like a taut bowstring. So shikan-taza is a heightened state of concentrated awareness wherein one is neither tense nor hurried, and certainly never slack. It is the mind of somebody facing death. Let us imagine that you are engaged in a duel of swordsmanship of the kind that used to take place in ancient Japan. As you face your opponent

---

[40] If you are working without a teacher, do not change from one exercise to the next until you are able to count from one to ten without losing the count or going beyond ten for, say, fifteen minutes.

you are unceasingly watchful, set, ready. Were you to relax your vigilance even momentarily, you would be cut down instantly. A crowd gathers to see the fight. Since you are not blind you see them from the corner of your eye, and since you are not deaf you hear them. But not for an instant is your mind captured by these sense impressions.

This state cannot be maintained for long—in fact, you ought not to do shikan-taza for more than half an hour at a sitting. After thirty minutes get up and walk around in kinhin and then resume your sitting. If you are truly doing shikan-taza, in half an hour you will be sweating, even in winter in an unheated room, because of the heat generated by this intense concentration. When you sit for too long your mind loses its vigor, your body tires, and your efforts are less rewarding than if you had restricted your sitting to thirty-minute periods.

Compared with an unskilled swordsman a master uses his sword effortlessly. But this was not always the case, for there was a time when he had to strain himself to the utmost, owing to his imperfect technique, to preserve his life. It is no different with shikan-taza. In the beginning tension is unavoidable, but with experience this tense zazen ripens into relaxed yet fully attentive sitting. And just as a master swordsman in an emergency unsheathes his sword effortlessly and attacks single-mindedly, just so the shikan-taza adept sits without strain, alert and mindful. But do not for one minute imagine that such sitting can be achieved without long and dedicated practice.

This concludes the talk on shikan-taza.

8 / THE PARABLE OF ENYADATTA / In the last half of this lecture I will take up the tale of Enyadatta, which comes from the Ryogon (Surangama) sutra.[41] This is an exceptionally fine parable that will, if you reflect carefully upon it, clarify many abstruse points of Buddhism.

This event is said to have occurred at the time of the Buddha.

---

[41] In the journey from India to Japan, Vajradatta, the half-demented villager mentioned in the sutra, was mysteriously transformed into the beautiful maiden Enyadatta.

Whether it is true or legendary I cannot say. In any case, Enyadatta was a beautiful maiden who enjoyed nothing more than gazing at herself in the mirror each morning. One day when she looked into her mirror she found no head relected there. Why not on this particular morning the sutra does not state. At any rate, the shock was so great that she became frantic, rushing around demanding to know who had taken her head. "Who has my head? Where is my head? I shall die if I don't find it!" she cried. Though everyone told her, "Don't be silly, your head is on your shoulders where it has always been," she refused to believe it. "No, it isn't! No, it isn't! Somebody must have taken it!" she shouted, continuing her frenzied search. At length her friends, believing her mad, dragged her home and tied her to a pillar to prevent her harming herself.

The being bound can be compared to undertaking zazen. With the immobilization of the body the mind achieves a measure of tranquility. And while it is still distracted, as Enyadatta's mind was in the belief that she had no head, yet the body is now prevented from scattering its energies.

Slowly her close friends persuaded her that she had always had her head, and gradually she came to half-believe it. Her subconscious mind began to accept the fact that perhaps she was deluded in thinking she had lost her head.

Enyadatta's receiving the reassurance of her friends can be equated with hearing the roshi's commentaries (teisho). Initially these are difficult to understand, but listening to them attentively, every word sinking into your subconscious, you reach the point where you begin to think: "Is that really true? . . . I wonder . . . Yes, it must be."

Suddenly one of her friends gave her a terrific clout on the head, upon which, in pain and shock, she yelled "Ouch!" "That's your head! There it is!" her friend exclaimed, and immediately Enyadatta saw that she had deluded herself into thinking she had lost her head when in fact she had always had it.

In the same way, clouting in zazen is of the utmost value. To be jolted physically by the kyosaku stick or verbally by a perceptive teacher at the right time—if it is too early, it is ineffective—can bring about Self-realization. Not only is the kyosaku valuabe for spurring you on, but when you have reached a decisive stage in your zazen a hard whack can precipitate your mind into an awareness of its true nature—in other words, enlightenment.

When this happened to Enyadatta she was so elated that she rushed around exclaiming: "Oh, I've got it! I have my head after all! I'm so happy!"

This is the rapture of kensho. If the experience is genuine, you cannot sleep for two or three nights out of joy. Nevertheless, it is a half-mad state. To be overjoyed at finding a head you had from the very first is, to say the least, queer. Nor is it less odd to rejoice at the discovery of your Essential-nature, which you have never been without. The ecstasy is genuine enough, but your state of mind cannot be called natural until you have fully disabused yourself of the notion, "I have become enlightened." Mark this point well, for it is often misunderstood.

As her joy subsided Enyadatta recovered from her half-mad state.

So it is with satori. When your delirium of delight recedes, taking with it all thoughts of realization, you settle into a truly natural life and there is nothing queer about it. Until you reach this point, however, it is impossible to live in harmony with your environment or to continue on a course of true spiritual practice.

I shall now point out more specifically the significance of the first part of the story. Since most people are indifferent to enlightenment, they are ignorant of the possibility of such an experience. They are like Enyadatta when she was unconscious of her head as such. This "head," of course, corresponds to the Buddha-nature, to our innate perfection. That they even have a Buddha-nature never occurs to most people until they hear *Shujo honrai hotoke nari*—"All beings are endowed with Buddha-nature from the very first." Suddenly they exclaim: "Then I too must have the Buddha-nature! But where is it?" Thus like Enyadatta when she first missed her head and started rushing about looking for it, they commence their search for their True-nature.

They begin by listening to various teisho, which seem contradictory and puzzling. They hear that their Essential-nature is no different from the Buddha's—more, that the substance of the universe is coextensive with their own Buddha-nature—yet because their minds are clouded with delusion they see themselves confronted by a world of individual entities. Once they establish firm belief in the reality of the Buddha-nature, they are driven to discover it with all the force of their being. Just as Enyadatta was never without her head, so are we never separate from our essential Buddha-nature whether we are enlightened or not. But of this we are unaware. We are like Enyadatta when her friends told her: "Don't be absurd, you have always had your head. It is an illusion to think otherwise."

The discovery of our True-nature can be compared to Enyadatta's discovery of her head. But what have we discovered? Only that we have never been without it! Nonetheless we are ecstatic, as she was at the finding of her head. When the ecstasy recedes, we realize we have acquired nothing extraordinary, and certainly nothing peculiar. Only now everything is utterly natural.

9 / CAUSE AND EFFECT ARE ONE / You cannot hope to comprehend the exalted nature of Zen without understanding this lecture on *inga ichinyo*, the meaning of which is that cause-and-effect are one. This expression comes from Hakuin-zenji's *Chant in Praise of Zazen*. Bear in mind that this lecture will not be an explanation of cause and effect in the broad sense but only in relation to the practice of zazen.

Strictly speaking, you ought not to think of zazen in terms of time. While it is generally true that if you do zazen for a year, it will have an effect equal to a year's effort; and that if you practice zazen for ten years, it will produce an effect proportionate to ten years' effort; yet the results of zazen in terms of enlightenment cannot be measured by the length of your practice. The fact is, some have gained deep enlightenment after only a few years' practice, while others have practiced as long as ten years without experiencing enlightenment.

From the commencement of practice one proceeds upward in clearly differentiated stages which can be considered a ladder of cause and effect. The word *inga*, meaning cause and effect, implies both degree and differentiation, while *ichinyo* signifies equality or sameness or oneness. Thus while there are many stages corresponding to the length of practice, at every one of these different stages the mind substance is the same as that of a Buddha. Therefore we say cause and effect are one. Until satori-awakening, however, you cannot expect to have a deep inner understanding of inga.

Now let us relate this to the parable of Enyadatta, of which I spoke earlier. The time she saw no head reflected in her mirror and rushed about wildly looking for it—this is the first, or bottom, step. When her friends tied her to a pillar and insisted she had a head; when she began to think, "Possibly this is so"; when they whacked her and she yelled "Ouch!" and realized she had a head after all; when she rejoiced at finding it; when finally her joy abated and having a head felt so natural that she no longer thought about it—all these are different steps or degrees of progression—when viewed retrospectively, that is. At every one of these stages she was never without her head, of course, but this she realized only after she had "found" it.

In the same way, after enlightenment we realize that from the very first we were never without Buddha-nature. And just as it was necessary for Enyadatta to go through all these phases in order to grasp the fact that she had always had a head, so we must pass through successive stages of zazen in order to apprehend directly our True-nature. These successive steps are causally related, but the fact that we are intrinsically Buddha, which in the parable is Enyadatta's realization that she had always had a head—this is equality, or undifferentiation.

Thus Dogen-zenji in his *Shobogenzo* states: "The zazen of even beginners manifests the whole of their Essential-nature." He is saying here that correct zazen is the actualization of the Bodhi-mind, the Mind with which we are all endowed. This zazen is saijojo, wherein the Way of the Buddha suffuses your entire being and enters into the whole of your life. Although we are unaware of all this at first, as our practice progresses we gradually acquire understanding and insight, and finally, with enlightenment, wake up to the fact that zazen is the actualization of our inherently pure Buddha-nature, whether we are enlightened or not.

10 / ONENESS AND MANYNESS / When you have kensho you see into the world of oneness, or equality, and this realization can be either shallow or deep; usually a first kensho is shallow. In either case, you still do not understand the world of differentia-

tion, the world that people ordinarily assume they do understand. As you continue your practice on subsequent koans, your awareness of the world of oneness, of non-differentiation, becomes clearer, and since it is through this world of oneness that you are seeing the world of differentiation, this latter also becomes clearer.

At the beginning, the perception of oneness is not distinct—there is still the idea of "something confronting me!" With deepening practice this barrier gradually dissolves. Even so, the feeling that others are actually oneself is still weak, and this is particularly true when these others have qualities we do not like. With a shallow kensho we resist the feeling that such people are indeed oneself. With further training, though, you are able to live a life of equality and to see that even people whom you recognize as having negative characteristics are not less than yourself. When you truely realize the world of oneness, you could not fight another even if he wanted to kill you, for that person is nothing less than a manifestation of yourself. It would not even be possible to struggle against him. One who has realized the world of equality will regard with compassion even people who have homicidal intentions, since in a fundamental sense they and oneself are of equal worth. In the same way, all of nature, mountains and rivers, are seen as oneself. In this deeper realization of oneness you will feel the preciousness of each object in the universe, rejecting nothing, since things as well as people will be seen as essential aspects of yourself. This deeper awareness, mind you, comes only after your practice has fully matured.

Let us take the body as a concrete example of the absolute equality of things. In the realization of the sameness aspect, of each object having equal value, your face and the soles of your feet are not different; one is not high and the other low. Similarly, a law breaker is not inherently evil, nor a law-abiding person a pillar of virtue.

Nevertheless, for society to function harmoniously, people who go against the accepted laws—who kill or steal, for example—must be segregated for the protection of others. This being true, it is clear that there is another aspect, that of relativity—in this case, of moral distinctions.

To understand and act upon differences is not a simple matter. For example, one who truly understood differentiation and could function in accordance with it would never overeat; he would eat only when hungry, and then just enough to satisfy his hunger. The ordinary person, who has not yet awakened, thinks he understands the relative, common world of distinctions, but true understanding can take place only when the aspect of oneness has been realized in depth. Having experienced the world of equality through kensho, one now sees differences in and through the aspect of sameness.

When I first came to America and looked into the faces of the people, they all looked alike. But now I can differentiate faces here quite easily. You can help people only when you are able to recognize and accept the differences among them, seeing each person in the light of his own unique qualities. To do so represents an advanced state of training.

Even after kensho, when you perceive that everything is one and are no longer confronted by an external world, you still cannot live in and through that experience. Somehow you keep returning to the previous state of mind. However, if you continue work on subsequent koans, each time you resolve another koan, that experience is reaffirmed and you return to the world of non-duality with greater clarity. Gradually the clarity and the ability to live in this world of oneness improve.

So there is both suddenness and gradualness in Zen training. The experience of awakening is sudden, but the integration of the experience into your life is gradual.

To awaken quickly is not necessarily advantageous, nor is to take a long time necessarily disadvantageous. When you practice earnestly each day, you are actualizing in your life the aspect of oneness. Though not even striving for enlightenment, one is gradually becoming aware of the world of equality through wholehearted, single-minded zazen.

Hearing this last, you may think, "If through wholehearted zazen in our daily life we are actualizing the kensho state of mind, what need is there to think about kensho?" As you have heard me say many times, when you are involved in zazen to the point of self-transcendence, that is enlightenment manifesting itself. Therefore it is said in Zen, "One minute of sitting, one minute of being a Buddha." Zazen is the cause of which enlightenment is the effect. But since this cause and effect are simultaneous, or one, you are not consciously aware of this enlightenment. *Realizing* this intrinsic enlightenment—suddenly exclaiming, "Oh, this is it!"—is something else again. This latter is a distinct effect, different from "cause and effect are one," and its realization requires the strong faith that one can awaken to his True-nature. This vital point must not be overlooked.

11 / THE THREE ESSENTIALS OF ZEN PRAC-TICE / What I am about to say is especially applicable to daijo Zen, which is specifically directed toward satori, but it also embraces saijojo, though in a lesser degree.

The first of the three essentials of Zen practice is strong faith (*daishinkon*). This is more than mere belief. The ideogram for ·*kon* means "root," and that for *shin*, "faith." Hence the phrase implies a faith that is firmly and deeply rooted, immovable, like an immense tree or a huge boulder. It is a faith, moreover, untainted by belief in the supernatural or the superstitious. Buddhism has often been described as both a rational religion and a religion of wisdom. But a religion it is, and what makes it one is this element of faith, without which it is merely philosophy. Buddhism starts with the Buddha's supreme enlightenment, which he attained after strenuous effort. Our deep faith, therefore, is in his enlightenment, the substance of which he proclaimed to be that human nature, all existence, is intrinsically whole, flawless, omnipotent—in a word, perfect. Without unwavering faith in this the heart of the Buddha's teaching, it is impossible to progress far in one's practice.

The second indispensable quality is a feeling of strong doubt (*daigidan*).[42] Not a simple doubt, mind you, but a "doubt-mass"—and this inevitably stems from strong faith. It is a doubt as to why we and the world should appear so imperfect, so full of anxiety, strife, and suffering, when in fact our deep faith tells us exactly the opposite is true. It is a doubt which leaves us no rest. It is as though we knew perfectly well we were millionaires and yet inexplicably found ourselves in dire need without a penny in our pockets. Strong doubt, therefore, exists in proportion to strong faith.

[42] In Zen, "doubt" implies not skepticism but a state of perplexity, of probing inquiry, of intense self-questioning.

I can illustrate this state of mind with a simple example. Take a man who has been sitting smoking and suddenly finds that the pipe which was in his hand a moment before has disappeared. He begins to search for it in the complete certainty of finding it. It was there a moment ago, no one has been near, it cannot have disappeared. The longer he fails to find it, the greater the energy and determination with which he hunts for it.

From this feeling of doubt the third essential, strong determination (dai-funshi), naturally arises. It is an overwhelming determination to dispel this doubt with the whole force of our energy and will. Believing with every pore of our being in the truth of the Buddha's teaching that we are all endowed with the immaculate Bodhi-mind, we resolve to discover and experience the reality of this Mind for ourselves.

The other day someone who had quite misunderstood the state of mind required by these three essentials asked me: "Is there more to believing we are Buddhas than accepting the fact that the world as it is is perfect, that the willow is green and the carnation red?" The fallacy of this is self-evident. If we do not question why greed and conflict exist, why the ordinary man acts like anything but a Buddha, no determination arises in us to resolve the obvious contradiction between what we believe as a matter of faith and what our senses tell us is just the contrary, and our zazen is thus deprived of its prime source of power.

I shall now relate these three essentials to daijo and saijojo Zen. While all three are present in daijo, this doubt is the main prod to satori because it allows us no rest. Thus we experience satori, and the resolution of this doubt, more quickly with daijo Zen.

In saijojo, on the other hand, the element of faith is strongest. No fundamental doubt of the kind I mentioned assails us and so we are not driven to rid ourselves of it, for we sit in the unswerving faith that we are inherently Buddhas. Unlike daijo Zen, saijojo, which you will recall is the purest type of zazen, does not involve the anxious striving for enlightenment. It is zazen wherein ripening takes place naturally, culminating in enlightenment. At the same time saijojo is the most difficult zazen of all, demanding resolute and dedicated sitting.

However, in both types of zazen all three elements are indispensable, and teachers of old have said that so long as they are simultaneously present it is easier to miss the ground with a stamp of the foot than to miss attaining perfect enlightenment.

12 / ASPIRATION / Even while we all do zazen, our individual aspirations are not identical. These aspirations resolve themselves into four main groups or levels.

The first and shallowest level involves neither faith in Zen Buddhism nor even a cursory understanding of it. One just happens to hear about it and decides he would like to sit with a zazen group or in a sesshin. Nevertheless, that out of millions of deluded people entirely ignorant of Buddhism one particular individual should be led to this 2,500-year-old, unbroken line of teaching is, in the Buddhist view, not a fortuitous but a karmic circumstance and therefore of vast spiritual significance.

The second level of aspiration is a level which goes no deeper than the desire to do zazen in order to improve physical or mental health or both. This, you will recall, falls into the first of the five classifications of Zen, namely, bompu (ordinary) Zen.

At the third level we find people who, no longer satisfied merely to increase their physical and mental well-being, want to tread the path of the Buddha. They recognize how exalted is the Buddhist cosmology, which views existence as not confined to one life-span but endlessly evolving lifetime after lifetime, with the circle of human destiny completed only upon the attainment of Buddhahood. More, they have established faith in the reality of the enlightenment experience, and though the resolve to attain it has not yet been awakened, the desire to pursue the Buddha's Way is clear and real.

The fourth level comprises those determined to realize their True-self. They know this experience to be a living reality, for they have encountered people who have had it, and they are convinced they can likewise attain it. When they come before their teacher they come with an open mind and a humble heart, ready to follow whatever course he prescribes, secure in the knowledge that by so doing they can realize their goal in the shortest time.

I will now quickly recapitulate these four classes of aspirants: those who, having no particular faith in Zen, come to it through fortunate karmic circumstances; those who practice zazen through a desire only to add to their physical or mental health or both; those who practice Zen out of belief in the exalted nature of the Buddha's teaching; and those who have a strong determination to become enlightened.

Hereafter you will come before me one by one and I will ask you what you feel to be the nature of your aspiration, that is, into which of the four classes you fall. Tell me your feelings honestly. Do not add anything through pride, and do not subtract anything out of false modesty. Depending upon what you tell me, I will assign you the zazen most appropriate for you.

There is no definitive practice which applies to everyone. Generally speaking, one who puts himself in the first class is assigned the practice of counting his breaths; one in the second category, the following of his breath; in the third class, shikan-taza; and in the fourth, a koan, usually Mu.[43]

When students come before me individually for the first time, they make all manner of curious replies. Some say: "I think I belong *between* the first and second classes." Others tell me: "I have a chronically bad stomach, so would you assign me a type of zazen that will help this condition?" Or sometimes a person will say: "I am somewhat neurotic; what kind of zazen would be good for that?"

Depending on the type of person and the strength of his determination, I prescribe what I believe to be a suitable practice. With a stolid individual it is usually desirable to spur him on with the kyosaku, whereas a somewhat nervous or sensitive person can do better zazen without it. Only if your appraisal of your feelings is frank can I select for you the most effective practice.

---

[43] It is not wise to assign yourself a koan. Only a teacher who has given you dokusan and therefore knows your temperament, aspiration, and capabilities can, with your help, assign you a suitable koan and, especially in the beginning, give you the necessary guidance.

II / YASUTANI-ROSHI'S COMMENTARY (TEISHO) ON THE KOAN MU /

EDITOR'S INTRODUCTION / Ever since Chao-chou (Joshu), one of the great Chinese Zen masters of the T'ang era, retorted "Mu!"[1] to a monk who had asked whether dogs have the Buddha-nature, the reverberations of the incident have been echoing through the halls of Zen monasteries and temples down through the centuries. Even in this day no koan is assigned novices more often. It is commonly agreed among Japanese masters that it is unsurpassed for breaking asunder the mind of ignorance and opening the eye of truth.

In the *Mumonkan* (The Gateless Barrier), compiled by Zen master Wu-men (Mumon), Mu heads the collection of forty-eight koans. What is the source of Mu's power, what has enabled it to hold first rank among koans for over a thousand years? Whereas such koans as "What is the sound of one hand?" and "What is your Face before your parents' birth?" bait the discursive mind and excite the imagination, Mu holds itself coldly aloof from both the intellect and the imagination. Try as it might, reasoning cannot gain even a toehold on Mu. In fact, trying to solve Mu rationally, we are told by the masters, is like "trying to smash one's fist through

---

[1] Literally, "no," "not," "have not," or "nothing." The *u* in "Mu" is voiced like the *u* in "put."

an iron wall." Because Mu is utterly impervious to logic and reason, and in addition is easy to voice, it has proven itself an exceptionally wieldy scalpel for extirpating from the deepest unconscious the malignant growth of "I" and "not-I" which poisons the Mind's inherent purity and impairs its fundamental wholeness.

Every koan is a unique expression of the living, indivisible Buddha-nature, which cannot be grasped by the bifurcating intellect. Despite the incongruity of their various elements, koans are profoundly meaningful, each pointing to man's Face before his parents were born, to his real Self. To people who cherish the letter above the spirit, koans appear bewildering, for in their phrasing koans deliberately throw sand into the eyes of the intellect to force us to open our Mind's eye and see the world and everything in it undistorted by our concepts and judgments.

Koans take as their subjects tangible, down-to-earth objects such as a dog, a tree, a face, a finger to make us see, on the one hand, that each object has absolute value and, on the other, to arrest the tendency of the intellect to anchor itself in abstract concepts. But the import of every koan is the same: that the world is one interdependent Whole and that each separate one of us is that Whole.

The Chinese Zen masters, those spiritual geniuses who created these paradoxical dialogues, did not hesitate to thumb their noses at logic and common sense in their marvelous creations. By wheedling the intellect into attempting solutions impossible for it, koans reveal to us the inherent limitations of the logical mind as an instrument for realizing ultimate Truth. In the process they liberate the mind from the snare of language, "which fits over experience like a strait jacket," pry us loose from our tightly held dogmas and prejudices, strip us of our penchant for discriminating good from bad, and empty us of the false notion of self-and-other, to the end that we may one day perceive that the world of Perfection is in fact no different from that in which we eat and excrete, laugh and weep.

When Zen master Chung-feng was asked why the teachings of the Buddhas and patriarchs were called koans, he replied: " . . . The koans do not represent the private opinion of a single man, but rather the highest principle . . . This principle accords with the spiritual source, tallies with the mysterious meaning, destroys

birth-and-death, and transcends the passions. It cannot be understood by logic; it cannot be transmitted in words; it cannot be
explained in writing; it cannot be measured by reason . . . For
the essentials of complete transcendence, final emancipation, total
penetration, and identical attainment, nothing can surpass the
koan."[2]

The great merit of koans, which range over the vast area of
the Mahayana teachings, is that they compel us, in ingenious and
often dramatic fashion, to learn these doctrines not simply with
our head but with our whole being, refusing to permit us to sit
back and endlessly theorize about them in the abstract. What Heinrich Zimmer says about certain types of meditation is especially
true of koans, the spirit of which must be demonstrated before
the roshi and not merely explained: "Knowledge is the reward of
action . . . For it is by doing things that one becomes transformed.
Executing a symbolical gesture, actually living through, to the very
limit, a particular role, one comes to realize the truth inherent in
the role. Suffering its consequences, one fathoms and exhausts
its contents . . ."[3]

It must not be supposed, however, that one reaches this point
easily or without a generous measure of frustration and even desperation. In his *Zen Comments on the Mumonkan* (p. 101), contemporary Zen master Shibayama quotes his teacher on the function of
the koan: "Suppose here is a completely blind man who trudges
along leaning on his stick and depending on his intuition. The
role of the koan is to mercilessly take the stick away from him
and to push him down after turning him around. Now the blind
man has lost his sole support and intuition and will not know where
to go or how to proceed. He will be thrown into the abyss of
despair. In this same way, the koan will mercilessly take away all
our intellect and knowledge. In short, the role of the koan is not
to lead us to satori easily, but on the contrary to make us lose
our way and drive us to despair."

The complete solution of a koan involves the movement of the

---

[2] Quoted in *Zen Dust* by Miura and Sasaki, p. 5.
[3] *Philosophies of India,* by Heinrich Zimmer, edited by Joseph Campbell
(Princeton, N. J.: Princeton University Press, 1969), p. 544.

mind from a state of ignorance (delusion) to the vibrant inner awareness of living truth. This implies the emergence into the field of consciousness of the immaculate Bodhi-mind, which is the reverse of the mind of delusion. The determination to struggle with a koan in the first place is generated by faith in the reality of the Bodhi-mind, the struggle itself being the effort of this Mind to cast off the shackles of ignorance and come to its own Self-knowledge.

The present commentary was made by Zen Master Yasutani, without notes, to about thirty-five laymen at a sesshin in 1961. It is reproduced here in translation exactly as he gave it except for minor editing of the few repetitious or awkward expressions which inevitably creep into extemporaneous speech. In its clarity and incisiveness, in the inspiration, encouragement, and guidance it provides the novice and advanced student alike, it stands as a masterly commentary on this time-honored koan.

A vivid, penetrating commentary (apart from the comment accompanying the koan) is invaluable for any aspirant who wishes to utilize a koan as his spiritual exercise. Besides familiarizing him with the backgrounds of the dramatis personae and setting forth in contemporary language obscure terms and metaphorical allusions common to the vernacular of ancient China in which the koans and comments are couched, it thrusts before him in terse, vigorous language the spirit of the koan. One lacking this orientation very likely would find the koan alien if not bizarre.

Since the commentary is not an ordinary lecture or sermon addressed to all and sundry but an integral part of Zen training, it is usually given only at sesshin and essentially for the benefit of those who come to practice zazen.[4] In the monastery the commentary, which takes place at least once and frequently twice a day, is announced by the solemn tolling of the *hansho,* among the largest of the drums, bells, and gongs employed in Zen. At its signal all file into the main hall from the zazen hall and, dividing into two groups facing each other at right angles to the altar, seat themselves

---

[4] Occasionally devotees are permitted to listen to the commentary even though they do not participate in the sesshin. In some monasteries the formal commentary is given at times other than sesshin but primarily for the resident monks.

on the tatami mats in the traditional Japanese sitting position *(seiza)*. The roshi then makes his appearance escorted by an attendant, who carries his book of koans[5] wrapped in a piece of silk ceremonial cloth both as a mark of respect and for protection. All present bow their heads in humility before their teacher as he proceeds to the *butsudan* ("shrine of the Buddhas") to light a stick of incense and place it before the image of the Buddha. Then, led by the roshi, everyone rises, faces the butsudan, and prostrates himself three times. These devotions of gratitude, reverence, and humility toward the Buddha and patriarchs having been completed, the roshi seats himself on a large cushion on a dais facing the butsudan, crosses his legs in the lotus posture, and leads the group in chanting a short selection from a sutra. He is now ready to begin his commentary.

Like the chanted sutra which precedes it, the commentary is an offering to the Buddha, and this in fact is the significance of the roshi's facing the butsudan and not his hearers during the delivery of his commentary. In addressing himself to the Buddha the roshi is in effect saying: "This is my expression of the truth of your teachings. I offer it up to you in the hope you will find it satisfactory."

The commentary is not an erudite discourse on the "meaning" of the koan, for the roshi knows that explanations, no matter how intricate or subtle, cannot lead to that inner understanding which alone enables one to demonstrate the spirit of the koan with certainty and conviction. Zen masters in fact look upon mere definitions and explanations as dry and lifeless, and as ultimately misleading because inherently limited. The one word "Imbecile!" uttered from the guts conveys more than any hundred words defining it. Nor does the roshi burden his listeners with a purely philosophical lecture on Buddhist doctrine or on the metaphysical nature of ultimate reality.

The roshi's object is to relive the spirit and drama of the koan, to bring alive through his charged words and gestures the truth inherent in the roles of the various protagonists. Keenly aware of the different levels of comprehension of his hearers, he pitches his commentary so that each receives according to his capacity to

[5] For the names of these books, see "koan" in section x.

understand, even as he relates the spirit of the koan to his hearers' common life experiences. In Zen parlance, the roshi "strikes against" the koan from his *hara*, trusting that the emitted sparks of truth will illumine the minds of his hearers.

It is from the hara, then, that the roshi must deliver his commentary if it is to glow with the spirit and force of his entire being, and similarly it is in their hara that his hearers must focus their minds if they are to grasp and absorb directly and whole the palpitating truth he is thrusting at them. Listening to the commentary is actually another form of zazen, that is, a state of uninterrupted concentration leading to total absorption. Hence the concentrated mind must not be disrupted by the taking of notes or by otherwise diverting the eyes from their "sitting" stance. In a monastery where the discipline is strict the head monks will reprimand beginners who attempt to make notes or whose eyes wander about the hall to look at other sitters.

Particularly for one whose spiritual exercise is a koan, the commentary, by providing numerous "clues," presents an unparalleled opportunity for gaining direct insight into the koan's essential import. If he has succeeded in exhausting his thoughts through single-minded concentration and has achieved absolute oneness with his koan, one telling phrase uttered by the roshi may be the golden arrow which suddenly and unpredictably finds its mark, tearing asunder the innermost cloak of darkness and suffusing the mind with light and inner understanding. For one whose mind is not yet ripe—in other words, still enveloped in delusive thoughts—the commentary is a rich source of pointers for future practice. But for all, no matter what the state of their minds, a trenchant commentary provides inspiration and encouragement.

Upon completion of his talk the roshi quietly closes his book of koans as all join him in chanting the Four Vows. At no time during or after the commentary does he solicit or encourage questions. Zen teaching frowns on all theoretical questions as not conducive to direct, first-hand experience of the truth. This attitude can be traced back to the Buddha, who held to "a noble silence" whenever asked such questions as "Are the universe and soul finite or infinite? Does the saint exist after death or not?" And Zen Buddhism, which is the quintessence of the Buddha's teaching, likewise refuses to deal with questions that ultimately have no answers, or with questions the answers to which can only be understood by a mind bathed in the light of full consciousness, that is, perfect enlightenment. When abstract, theoretical questions are asked during dokusan (as they sometimes are) the roshi frequently throws them back at the questioner, to try to make him see the source from which they issue and to relate him to that source.

But there are further reasons why abstract questions are viewed with disfavor. A preoccupation with them not only tends to take the place of zazen and the understanding it alone can lead to, but by titillating the intellect they make immeasurably more difficult the stilling and emptying of the mind essential for kensho. The Buddha's classic reply to a monk who threatened to abandon the religious life unless the Buddha answered his questions on whether the saint exists after death or not is worth repeating:

"It is as if a man had been wounded by an arrow thickly smeared with poison, and his friends and companions, his relatives and kinsfolk were to procure for him a physician or surgeon; and the sick man were to say, 'I will not have this arrow taken out until I have learnt whether the man who wounded me belonged to the warrior caste or to the Brahmin caste; . . . learnt whether he was tall, short, or of middle height; was black, dusky, or of yellow skin; was from this or that village or town or city; . . . whether it was an ordinary arrow or a claw-headed arrow . . .' That man would die without ever having learnt this."[6]

And in another dialogue the Buddha stated: "The religious life does not depend on the dogma that the world is eternal or not eternal, infinite or finite, that the soul and the body are identical or different, or the dogma that the saint exists or does not exist after death . . . It profits not, nor has it to do with the fundamentals of religion, nor does it tend to absence of passion . . . to supreme wisdom, and Nirvana.[7]

[6] Majjhima Nikaya 63.
[7] Majjhima Nikaya 72.

THE COMMENTARY / Today I will take up the first case in *Mumonkan*, entitled "Joshu [on the inherent nature of a] dog." I will read the koan proper and then Mumon's comment:

> A monk in all seriousness asked Joshu: "Has a dog Buddha-nature or not?" Joshu retorted "Mu!"

> *Mumon's Comment:* In the practice of Zen you must pass through the barrier gate[8] set up by the patriarchs. To realize this wondrous thing called enlightenment, you must cut off all [discriminating] thoughts. If you cannot pass through the barrier and exhaust the arising of thoughts, you are like a ghost clinging to the trees and grass.

> What then, is this barrier set by the patriarchs? It is Mu, the one barrier of the supreme teaching. Ultimately it is a barrier that is no barrier. One who has passed through it cannot only see Joshu face to face, but can walk hand in hand with the whole line of patriarchs. Indeed, he can, standing eyebrow to eyebrow, hear with the same ears and see with the same eyes.

> How marvelous! Who would not want to pass through this barrier? For this you must concentrate day and night, questioning yourself through every one of your 360 bones and 84,000 pores. Do not construe Mu as nothingness and do not conceive it in terms of existence or non-existence. [You must reach the point where you feel] as though you had swallowed a red-hot iron ball that you cannot disgorge despite your every effort. When you have cast away all illusory thoughts and discriminations, and inside and outside are as one, you will be like a mute who has had a dream [but is unable to talk about it]. Once you burst into enlightenment you will astound the heavens and shake the earth. As though having captured the great sword of General Kuan,[9] you will be able to slay the Buddha should you meet him [and he obstruct you] and dispatch all patriarchs you encounter [should they hinder you]. Facing

[8] In ancient China barrier gates were located on the main road leading to a large town or city, where one had to pass inspection before being allowed to enter; they were roughly comparable to present-day toll stations or immigration-inspection stations.

[9] See p. 85.

life and death, you are utterly free; in the Six Realms of Existence and the Four Modes of Birth you move about in a samadhi of innocent delight.

How then, do you achieve this? Devote yourself to Mu energetically and wholeheartedly. If you continue this way without intermission, your mind will, like a light flashed on in the dark, suddenly become bright. Wonderful indeed!

Mumon's Verse:
A dog, Buddha-nature!—
This is the presentation of the whole, the absolute imperative!
Once you begin to think "has" or "has not"
You are as good as dead.

The protagonist of this koan is Joshu, a renowned Chinese Zen master. I think it would be better to refer to him as the Patriarch Joshu. Inasmuch as my commentary on today's koan will be quite long, I shall omit telling you the facts of Joshu's life. Suffice it to say he was, as you all know, a great patriarch of Zen. While there are numerous koans centering around him, without a doubt this one is the best known. Master Mumon worked zealously on it for six years and finally came to Self-realization. Evidently it made a deep impression on him, for he placed it first in the collection of his forty-eight koans. Actually there is no particular reason why this koan should be first—any of the others could have been placed at the head just as well—but Mumon's feeling for it was so intimate that he naturally put it at the very beginning.

The first line reads: "A monk *in all seriousness* asked Joshu . . ." That is, his question was neither frivolous nor casual but deeply considered.

The next portion, "Has a dog Buddha-nature or not?" raises the question: What is Buddha-nature? A well-known passage in the Nirvana sutra states that every sentient being has Buddha-nature. The expression "every sentient being" means all existence. Not alone human beings, but animals, even plants, are sentient beings. Accordingly, a dog, a monkey, a dragonfly, a worm equally have Buddha-nature according to the Nirvana sutra. In the context of this koan, however, you may consider the term as referring only to animals.

What then is Buddha-nature? Briefly, the nature of everything is such that it can become Buddha. Now, some of you, thinking there is something called *the* Buddha-nature hidden within us, may inquire as to the whereabouts of this Buddha-nature. You may tend to equate it with conscience, which everyone, even the wicked, is presumed to possess. You will never understand the truth of Buddha-nature so long as you harbor such a specious view. The Patriarch Dogen interpreted this expression in the Nirvana sutra to mean that what is intrinsic to all sentient beings is Buddha-nature, and not that all sentient beings have something called *the* Buddha-nature. Thus in Dogen's view there is only Buddha-nature, nothing else.

In Buddhism, "Buddha-nature" is an intimate expression and "Dharma-nature" an impersonal one. But whether we say Buddha- or Dharma-nature, the substance is the same. One who has become enlightened to the Dharma is a Buddha; hence Buddha arises from Dharma. The Diamond sutra says that all Buddhas and their enlightenment issue from this Dharma. Dharma, it follows, is the mother of Buddhahood. Actually there is neither mother nor son, for as I have said, it is the same whether you say Buddha or Dharma.

What is the Dharma of Dharma-nature? Dharma means phenomena. What we ordinarily term phenomena—that is, what is evident to the senses—in Buddhism is called Dharma. The word "phenomena," since it relates only to the observable features without implying what causes them to appear, has a limited connotation. These phenomena are termed Dharma (or Law) simply because they appear neither by accident nor through the will of some special agency superintending the universe. All phenomena are the result of the operation of the law of cause and effect. They arise when causes and conditions governing them mature. When one of these causes or conditions becomes altered, these phenomena change correspondingly. When the combination of causes and conditions completely disintegrates, the form itself disappears. All existence being the expression of the law of cause and effect, all phenomena are equally this Law, this Dharma. Now, as there are multiple modes of existence, so are there multiple dharmas corresponding to these existences. The substance of these manifold dharmas we call Dharma-nature. Whether we say Dharma-nature or use the more personal term Buddha-nature, these expressions refer to one reality. Stated differently, all phenomena are transformations of Buddha- or Dharma-nature. Everything by its very nature is subject to the process of infinite transformation—this is its Buddha- or Dharma-nature.

What is the substance of this Buddha- or Dharma-nature? In Buddhism it is called ku [shunyata]. Now, ku is not mere emptiness. It is that which is living, dynamic, devoid of mass, unfixed, beyond individuality or personality—the matrix of all phenomena. Here we have the fundamental principle or doctrine or philosophy of Buddhism.

For the Buddha Shakyamuni this was not mere theory but truth which he directly realized. With the experience of enlightenment, which is the source of all Buddhist doctrine, you grasp the world of ku. This world—unfixed, devoid of mass, beyond individuality or personality—is outside the realm of imagination. Accordingly, the true substance of things, that is, their Buddha- or Dharma-nature, is inconceivable and inscrutable. Since everything imaginable partakes of form or color, whatever one imagines to be Buddha-nature must of necessity be unreal. Indeed, that which can be conceived is but a picture of Buddha-nature, not Buddha-nature itself. But while Buddha-nature is beyond all conception and imagination, because we ourselves are intrinsically Buddha-nature, it is possible for us to awaken to it. Only through the experience of enlightenment, however, can we affirm it in the Heart. Enlightenment therefore is all.

Once you realize the world of ku you will readily comprehend the nature of the phenomenal world and cease clinging to it. What we see is illusory, without substance, like the antics of puppets in a film. Are you afraid to die? You need not be. For whether you are killed or die naturally, death has no more substantiality than the movements of these puppets. Or to put it another way, it is no more real than the cutting of air with a knife, or the bursting of bubbles, which reappear no matter how often they are broken.

Having once perceived the world of Buddha-nature, we are indifferent to death since we know we will be reborn through affinity with a father and a mother. We are reborn when our karmic relations impel us to be reborn. We die when our karmic relations decree that we die. And we are killed when our karmic relations lead us to be killed. We are the manifestation of our karmic relations at any given moment, and upon their modification we change accordingly. What we call life is no more than a procession of transformations. If we do not change, we are lifeless. We grow and age because we are alive. The evidence of our having lived is the fact that we die. We die because we are alive. Living means birth and death. Creation and destruction signify life.

When you truly understand this fundamental principle you will not be anxious about your life or your death. You will then attain a steadfast mind and be happy in your daily life. Even though heaven and earth were turned upside down, you would have no fear. And if an atomic or hydrogen bomb were exploded, you would not quake in terror. So long as you became one with the bomb what would there be to fear? "Impossible!" you say. But whether you wanted to or not, you would perforce become one with it, would you not? By the same token, if you were caught in a holocaust, inevitably you would be burnt. Therefore become one with fire when there is no escaping it! If you fall into poverty, live that way without grumbling—then your poverty will not be a burden to you. Likewise, if you are rich, live with your riches. All this is the functioning of Buddha-nature. In short, Buddha-nature has the quality of infinite adaptability.

Coming back to the koan, we must approach the question "Has a dog Buddha-nature or not?" with caution, since we do not know whether the monk is ignorant or is feigning ignorance in order to test Joshu. Should Joshu answer either "It has" or "It has not," he would be cut down. Do you see why? Because what is involved is not a matter of "has" or "has not." Everything being Buddha-nature, either answer would be absurd. But this is "Dharma dueling." Joshu must parry the thrust. He does so by sharply retorting "Mu!" Here the dialogue ends.

In other versions of the dialogue between Joshu and the monk the latter continues by inquiring: "Why hasn't a dog Buddha-nature when the Nirvana sutra says all sentient beings do have it?"[10] Joshu countered with: "Because it has ignorance and attachment." What this means is that the dog's Buddha-nature is not other than karma. Acts performed with a delusive mind produce painful results. This

[10] The monk evidently construed Joshu's "Mu!" to mean "has not."

is karma. In plainer words, a dog is a dog as a result of its past karma's conditioning it to become a dog. This is the functioning of Buddha-nature. So do not talk as though there were a particular thing called "Buddha-nature." This is the implication of Joshu's Mu. It is clear, then, that Mu has nothing to do with the existence or non-existence of Buddha-nature but is itself Buddha-nature. The retort "Mu!" exposes and at the same time fully thrusts Buddha-nature before us. Now while you may be unable fully to understand what I am saying, you will not go astray if you construe Buddha-nature in this wise.

Buddha-nature cannot be grasped by the intellect. To experience it directly you must search your mind with the utmost devotion until you are absolutely convinced of its existence, for, after all, you yourself are this Buddha-nature. When I told you earlier that Buddha-nature was ku—impersonal, devoid of mass, unfixed, and capable of endless transformation—I merely offered you a portrait of it. It is possible to *think* of Buddha-nature in these terms, but you must understand that whatever you can conceive or imagine must necessarily be unreal. Hence there is no other way than to experience the truth in your own mind. This way has been shown, with the greatest kindness, by Mumon.

Let us now consider Mumon's comment. He begins by saying: "In the practice of Zen . . ." Zazen, receiving dokusan [that is, private instructions], hearing teisho—these are all Zen practice. Being attentive in the details of your daily life is also training in Zen. When your life and Zen are one you are truly living Zen. Unless it accords with your everyday activities Zen is merely an embellishment. You must be careful not to flaunt Zen but to blend it unpretentiously into your life. To give a concrete example of attentiveness: when you step out of the clogs at the porch or the kitchen or out of the slippers of the toilet room, you must be careful to arrange them neatly so that the next person can use them readily even in the dark. Such mindfulness is a practical demonstration of Zen. If you put your clogs or shoes on absent-mindedly you are not attentive. When you walk you must step watchfully so that you do not stumble or fall. Do not become remiss!

But I am digressing. To continue: ". . . you must pass through the barrier gate set up by the patriarchs." Mu is just such a barrier.

I have already indicated to you that, from the first, there is no barrier. Everything being Buddha-nature, there is no gate through which to go in or out. But in order to awaken us to the truth that everything is Buddha-nature, the Patriarchs reluctantly set up barriers and goad us into passing through them. They condemn our faulty practice and reject our incomplete answers. As you steadily grow in sincerity you will one day suddenly come to Self-realization. When this happens you will be able to pass through the barrier gate easily. The *Mumonkan* is a book containing forty-eight such barriers.

The next line begins: "To realize this wondrous thing called enlightenment . . ." Observe the word "wondrous." Because enlightenment is unexplainable and inconceivable it is described as wondrous. ". . . you must cut off all [discriminating] thoughts." This means that it is useless to approach Zen from the standpoint of supposition or logic. You can never come to enlightenment through inference, cognition, or conceptualization. Cease clinging to all thought-forms! I stress this, because it is the central point of Zen practice. And particularly do not make the mistake of thinking enlightenment must be this or that.

"If you cannot pass through the barrier and exhaust the arising of thoughts, you are like a ghost clinging to the trees and grass." Ghosts do not appear openly in the daytime, but come out furtively after dark, it is said, hugging the earth or clinging to willow trees. They are dependent upon these supports for their very existence. In a sense human beings are also ghostlike, since most of us cannot function independent of money, social standing, honor, companionship, authority; or else we feel the need to identify ourselves with an organization or an ideology. If you would be a man of true worth and not a phantom, you must be able to walk upright by yourself, dependent on nothing. When you harbor philosophical concepts or religious beliefs or ideas or theories of one kind or another, you too are a phantom, for inevitably you become bound to them. Only when your mind is empty of such abstractions are you truly free and independent.

The next two sentences read: "What, then, is this barrier set up by the patriarchs? It is Mu, the one barrier of the supreme teaching." The supreme teaching is not a system of morality but that which lies at the root of all such systems, namely, Zen. Only that which is of unalloyed purity, free from the superstitious or the supernatural, can be called the root of all teachings and therefore supreme. In Buddhism Zen is the only teaching which is not to one degree or another tainted with elements of the supernatural—thus Zen alone can truly be called the supreme teaching and Mu the one barrier of this supreme teaching. You can understand "one barrier" to mean the sole barrier or one out of many. Ultimately there is no barrier.

"One who has passed through it cannot only see Joshu face to face . . ." Since we are living in another age, of course we cannot actually see the physical Joshu. To "see Joshu face to face" means to understand his Mind. ". . . can walk hand in hand with the whole line of patriarchs." The line of patriarchs begins with Maha Kashyapa, who succeeded the Buddha, it goes on to Bodhidharma, the twenty-eighth, and continues right up to the present. ". . . eyebrow to eyebrow . . ." is a figure of speech implying great intimacy. ". . . hear with the same ears and see with the same eyes" connotes the ability to look at things from the same viewpoint as the Buddha and Bodhidharma. It implies, of course, that we have clearly grasped the world of enlightenment.

"How marvelous!" Marvelous indeed! Only those who recognize the preciousness of the Buddha, the Dharma, and the patriarchs can appreciate such an exclamation. Yes, how truly marvelous! Those who do not care for the Buddha and the Dharma may feel anything but marvel, but that cannot be helped.

"Who would not want to pass through this barrier?"—this phrase aims at enticing you to search for truth within yourself. "For this you must concentrate day and night, questioning yourself about Mu through every one of your 360 bones and 84,000 pores." These figures reflect the thinking of the ancients, who believed that the body was constructed in this fashion. In any case, what this refers to is your entire being. Let all of you become one mass of doubt and questioning. Concentrate on and penetrate fully into Mu. To penetrate into Mu means to achieve absolute unity with it. How can you achieve this unity? By holding to Mu tenaciously day and night! Do not separate yourself from it under any circumstances! Focus your mind on it constantly. "Do not construe Mu as nothingness and do not conceive it in terms of existence or non-existence." You must not, in other words, think of Mu as a problem involving the existence or non-existence of Buddha-nature. Then what do you do? You stop speculating and concentrate wholly on Mu—just Mu!

Do not dawdle, practice with every ounce of energy. "[You must reach the point where you feel] as though you had swallowed a red-hot iron ball . . ." It is hyperbole, of course, to speak of swallowing a red-hot iron ball. However, we often carelessly swallow a hot rice-cake which, lodging in the throat, causes considerable discomfort. Once you swallow Mu up you will likewise feel intensely uncomfortable and try desperately to dislodge it. ". . . that you cannot disgorge despite your every effort"—this describes the state of those who work on this koan. Because Self-realization is so tantalizing a prospect they cannot quit; neither can they grasp Mu's significance readily. So there is no other way for them but to concentrate on Mu until they "turn blue in the face."

The comparison with a red-hot iron ball is apt. You must melt down your illusions with the red-hot iron ball of Mu stuck in your throat. The opinions you hold and your worldly knowledge are your illusions. Included also are philosophical and moral concepts, no matter how lofty, as well as religious beliefs and dogmas, not to mention innocent, commonplace thoughts. In short, all conceivable ideas are embraced within the term "illusions" and as such are a hindrance to the realization of your Essential-nature. So dissolve them with the fireball of Mu!

You must not practice fitfully. You will never succeed if you do zazen only when you have the whim to, and give up easily. You must carry on steadfastly for one, two, three, or even five years without remission, constantly vigilant. Thus you will gradually gain in purity. At first you will not be able to pour yourself wholeheartedly into Mu. It will escape you quickly because your mind will start to wander. You will have to concentrate harder—just "Mu! Mu! Mu!" Again it will elude you. Once more you attempt to focus on it and again you fail. This is the usual pattern in the early stages of practice. Even when Mu does not slip away, your concentration becomes disrupted because of various mind defilements. These defilements disappear in time, yet since you have not achieved oneness with Mu you are still far from ripe. Absolute unity with Mu, unthinking absorption in Mu—this is ripeness. Upon your 'attainment to this stage of purity, both inside and outside naturally fuse. "Inside and outside" has various shades of meaning. It may be understood as meaning subjectivity and objectivity or mind and body. When you fully absorb yourself in Mu, the external and internal merge into a single unity. But, unable to speak about it, you will be like "a mute who has had a dream." One who is dumb is unable to talk about his dream of the night before. In the same way, you will relish the taste of samadhi yourself but be unable to tell others about it.

At this stage Self-realization will abruptly take place. Instantaneously! "Bursting into enlightenment" requires but an instant. It is as though an explosion had occurred. When this happens you will experience so much! "You will astound the heavens and shake the earth." Everything will appear so changed that you will think heaven and earth have been overturned. Of course there is no literal toppling over. With enlightenment you see the world as Buddha-nature, but this does not mean that all becomes as radiant as a halo. Rather, each thing *just as it is* takes on an entirely new significance or worth. Miraculously, everything is radically transformed though remaining as it is.

This is how Mumon describes it: "As though having captured the great sword of General Kuan . . ." General Kuan was a courageous general who was invincible in combat with his "blue-dragon" sword. So Mumon says you will become as powerful as he who captures the "blue-dragon" sword of General Kuan. Which is to say that nothing untoward can happen to you. Through Self-realization one acquires self-confidence and an imposing bearing. When one comes before the roshi his manner implies, "Test me in any way you wish," and such is his assurance that he could even thrash the master.

". . . you will be able to slay the Buddha should you meet him and dispatch all patriarchs you encounter." The timid will be flabbergasted when they hear this and denounce Zen as an instrument of the devil. Others, less squeamish yet equally unable to understand the spirit of these words, will feel uneasy. To be sure, Buddhism inspires in us the utmost respect for all Buddhas. But at the same time it admonishes us that eventually we must free ourselves from attachment to them. When we have experienced the Mind of Shakyamuni Buddha and cultivated his incomparable virtues, we have realized the highest aim of Buddhism. Then we bid him farewell, shouldering the task of propagating his teachings. I have never heard of such an attitude in religions teaching belief in God. While the aim of the Buddhist is to become a Buddha, nevertheless, to put it bluntly, you can slay the Buddha and all the patriarchs. You who realize enlightenment will be able to say: "Were the honored Shakyamuni and the great Bodhidharma to appear, I would cut them down instantly, demanding: 'Why do you totter forth? You are no longer needed!' " Such will be your resoluteness.

"Facing life and death, you are utterly free; in the Six Realms of Existence and the Four Modes of Birth you move about in a samadhi of innocent delight." You will be able to face death and rebirth without anxiety. The Six Realms are the realms of maya, namely, hell, the worlds of pretas [hungry ghosts], beasts, asuras [fighting demons], human beings, and devas [heavenly beings]. The Four Modes of Birth are birth through the womb, birth through eggs hatched outside the body, birth through moisture, and birth through metamorphosis. To be born in heaven or hell, since it requires no physical progenitors, is birth through metamorphosis. Who ever heard of a heavenly being that had to undergo the trauma of being born? There are neither midwives nor obstetricians in heaven or hell.

Wherever you may be born, and by whatever means, you will be able to live with the spontaneity and joy of children at play—this is what is meant by a "samadhi of innocent delight." Samadhi is complete absorption. Once you are enlightened you can descend to the deepest hell or rise to the highest heaven with freedom and rapture.

"How, then, do you achieve this?" Through zazen. "Devote yourself to Mu energetically and wholeheartedly." Persevere with all the force of your body and spirit. "If you continue this way without intermission . . ." You must not start and then quit. You must carry on to the very end, like a hen sitting on an egg until she hatches it. You must concentrate on Mu unflinchingly, determined not to give up until you attain kensho. ". . . your mind will, like a lamp flashed on in the dark, suddenly become bright. Wonderful indeed!" With enlightenment the mind, released from the darkness of its infinite past, will brighten immediately. "Wonderful indeed!" is added since nothing could be more wonderful.

The first line of Mumon's verse reads: "A dog, Buddha-nature"—there is no need for "nature." "A dog *is* Buddha"—"is" is superfluous. "A dog, Buddha"—still redundant. "Dog!"—that's enough! Or just "Buddha!" You have said too much when you say "A dog *is* Buddha." "Dog!"—that is all. It is completely Buddha.

"This is the . . . whole, the absolute imperative!" That is to say, it is the authentic decree of Shakyamuni Buddha—it is the correct Dharma. You are this Dharma to perfection! It is not being begrudged—it is fully revealed!

"Once you begin to think 'has' or 'has not' you are as good as dead." What does "you are as good as dead" mean? Simply that your precious Buddha life [of Oneness] will vanish.

III / YASUTANI-ROSHI'S PRI-VATE ENCOUNTERS WITH TEN WESTERNERS /

EDITOR'S INTRODUCTION / The widespread curiosity and practical interest which Zen Buddhism has aroused in the West since World War II—an interest that is surely one of the significant cultural and religious phenomena of our time—has produced a sizable literature in a number of European languages. Some of the more popular of these books in English are summed up by Alan Watts in the preface to his book *The Way of Zen*. He first points out that not even Professor Suzuki has given "a comprehensive account of Zen which includes its historical background and its relation to Chinese and Indian ways of thought," nor written about the "relation of Zen to Chinese Taoism and Indian Buddhism"; that R. H. Blyth's *Zen in English Literature and Oriental Classics* "lacks background information" and "makes no attempt to give an orderly presentation of the subject [Zen]"; and that Christmas Humphreys in his *Zen Buddhism* "does not really begin to put Zen in its cultural context." Whereupon he concludes that the confusion existing among Westerners with respect to Zen is due to this lack of a "fundamental, orderly, and comprehensive account of the subject."

This conclusion is highly misleading. Stimulating as the theoretical approach to Zen may be for the academic-minded and the intellectually curious, for the earnest seeker aspiring to enlightenment it is worse than futile, it is downright hazardous. Anybody who has seriously attempted the practice of Zen after reading such books knows not only how poorly they have prepared him for zazen, but how in fact they have hindered him by clogging his mind with splinters of koans and irrelevant fragments of philosophy, psychology, theology, and poetry which churn about in his brain, making it immeasurably difficult for him to quiet his mind and attain a state of samadhi. Not without good reason have the Chinese and Japanese Zen masters warned of the futility of the artificial, cerebral approach to the illuminating experience of genuine satori.

What does lead to Self-realization is not a knowledge of Chinese, Indian, or other ways of thought but proper methods of practice based on the authentic teachings of the masters. The heart of Zen discipline is zazen. Remove the heart and a mere corpse remains. Despite this, neither the books enumerated by Mr. Watts nor his own books on Zen contain more than a smattering of information— and some not even that—on this vital subject. This espousal of the philosophical, theoretical approach to Zen is all too apparent from the index to a recent anthology of Professor Suzuki's writings. In this book of almost 550 pages only two references to zazen can be found, one a footnote and the other barely three lines in the text.

Certain exponents of Zen, Asians as well as Westerners, have misled their readers in yet another way. In their relish for drama they have underscored out of all proportion the shouting and striking of the ancient Chinese masters even as they have tantalized their readers with such startling, paradoxical quotations as "You must kill the Buddha!" and "Though you can say something about it, I will give you thirty blows of the stick; and if you can't say anything about it, I will give you thirty blows of the stick!" Can they be trying to shock their readers into accepting an iconoclastic and esoteric Zen, to the innermost secrets of which only the select few are privy? And to what purpose, it may be asked, do some writers, less dramatically perhaps but with equally misplaced verve, unearth koans previously unpublished in English, "solving" them for the edification of their less enlightened readers?

On Zen as it is actually practiced today, and in particular of how the master teaches and guides his students and disciples in the day-to-day undramatic and occasionally dreary and discouraging moments of Zen training, or of the nature of the problems which contemporary students bring before him—on this these writers are strangely silent.

It is this distortion of Zen and not the lack of "a systematic, scholarly presentation" that lies at the root of the present confusion. For no insignificant number of Westerners, misdirected by this academic spearhead toward a hypothetical Zen which is the product of theory and speculation and not personal experience, have been repelled by the enigmatic and seemingly nonsensical formulations of the koans and by the apparently cruel or senseless behavior of the ancient Zen masters, with the result that they have rejected Zen as a weird and alien discipline uncongenial to the Western mind. Others, quick to exploit the vaunted freedom of Zen as sanction for cults of libertinism, have been enabled, thanks to the indiscriminate and irresponsible publishing of koans isolated from the body of Zen teaching as a whole, to debase and pervert Zen to such ends.

It is hoped that this disclosure of what actually takes place between a Zen master and his students will not only dispel the entirely erroneous notion that Zen is alien or "mystical," or merely an interesting if somewhat bizarre cultural study, but will also reveal it as an eminently straightforward and practical teaching which when properly understood and practiced is demonstrably capable of liberating man from his deep-seated fears and anxieties so he can live and die with peace and dignity, in our nuclear age no less than in the past.

This compilation of the private instructions and guidance given to ten Westerners—Americans and Europeans—together with their responses and questions, is believed to be the first comprehensive presentation to appear in English, or any other language, of the actual teaching methods of a Zen master in the course of Zen training. Altogether, eighty-five encounters (dokusan) are included. They were gathered over a period of two years and vary from one to twenty-four meetings for an individual student. The dialogue which appears between a set of asterisks is a transcription of one complete encounter with the roshi from the time the student entered his room until he departed. In a general way, the dokusan of a particular student follow each other in the order in which

they occurred, but they are not an unbroken record of every encounter with the roshi. Dokusan which consisted of no more than
a few words of encouragement or dokusan lacking in general interest have been omitted. Where a number of dokusan of one trainee
are involved, a period of a month or two might intervene between
them.

Each of these dokusan took place during the secluded training
period called sesshin (which will be described fully in a later section). While most of them are brief, necessarily so to accommodate
the needs of as many as thirty-five or forty persons three times a
day, their length is ultimately dictated by the requirements of the
individual and not by any arbitrary time limitation.

All the individuals were beginners in the sense that none, with
one exception,[1] had passed his first koan (that is, had the experience
of awakening) and all had trained in Zen for periods ranging from
several weeks to two years. It is possible in individual cases to
discern a developing pattern of understanding but an understanding that has not yet matured into enlightenment.

It might be pointed out that questions concerning theory or
doctrine—for example, "What is the difference between shikan-
taza and koan zazen?"—are not normally dealt with by the roshi
in dokusan, but because these Westerners were foreigners from
non-Buddhist cultures, he answered them.

The material speaks for itself, and any attempt to analyze or
interpret it would not only be superfluous but presumptuous. However, for those readers lacking access to a qualified Zen teacher,
a certain amount of background information relative to dokusan
practice in Japan today, especially as it affects Westerners, may
be found helpful in enabling them to utilize to the fullest in their
own spiritual practice the advice and instructions of the roshi as
it is revealed in these encounters.

Zazen, the formal commentary (teisho), and dokusan together
form the tripod upon which traditional Zen training rests. For the
beginner, this "eyeball to eyeball" encounter with the roshi within

[1] Student H. This has been included so that the reader may compare
the different approach by the roshi for a student on a more advanced
level.

the privacy of his inner chamber can be anything from an inspiring and wonderfully enriching experience, giving impetus and direction to his practice, to a fearful ordeal of mounting frustrations, depending on the strength of his ardor, the point to which his zazen has matured, and, most importantly, on the roshi's own personality and teaching methods.

Once the student enters the roshi's inner sanctum and makes his prostrations as a mark of respect and humility, he is perfectly free to say or do anything so long as it is a genuine expression of his quest for truth and is legitimately connected with his practice. In the beginning, when he has not yet gained control over his wayward thoughts or arrested his egocentricity, it is common for him, especially if he is philosophically inclined, to attempt to engage the roshi in abstract, theoretical discussions. But as time goes by and his mind, through the steady practice of zazen, becomes quieter and more one-pointed, he loses interest in empty discussion and becomes more receptive in a total way to the roshi and his directions.

With further zazen he will gradually begin to experience, if only momentarily, an underlying harmony and unity (especially after periods of samadhi), which will begin to replace the feelings of estrangement and confusion he previously felt. Now when he comes before the roshi and is questioned or tested he will respond with vigor and alacrity where formerly his responses were confused and halting. He may even shout or bellow at the roshi, not out of irritation or resentment but because, freed to a large extent from the mental and emotional constrictions which up to now had bound him, he can increasingly summon up the physical and psychic energies which have been slumbering within him. As his zazen deepens, he may suddenly seize the initiative by grabbing the roshi's baton and striking the mat in response to a pointed question. Or upon being asked to give a concrete demonstration of his understanding of a koan, he may, without recourse to concept or theory, respond with all his being. One able to show his understanding in this manner is hovering on the brink of awakening, although he himself is unaware of it. Only the roshi, with his long years of experience and acutely discerning eye, can gauge the exact degree of his comprehension and give him the necessary direction and encouragement at this critical point.

An accomplished roshi will not scruple to employ every device and stratagem, not excluding jabs with his ubiquitous baton (*kotsu*), when he believes it will jar and rouse the student's mind from a state of dormant unawareness to the sudden realization of its true nature. It not infrequently happens during sesshin that a novice will hesitate to appear at even one daily dokusan. Instead of making a spirited dash for the lineup point when the dokusan bell rings,[2] he sits glued to his seat out of fear of being rebuked for having no ready solution to his koan. If he is not coldly ignored by the head monks (in a monastery) or by the monitors (in a center) as unworthy of even a whacking to encourage him, he may be yanked from his seat and dragged or pushed into dokusan. When, dispirited, he finally appears before the roshi, the roshi may castigate him for his faintheartedness, then summarily dismiss him without asking a question or making a comment. Or he may crack the student with his baton while he is in the act of making his prostrations, and then order him out with a ring of his handbell, leaving him, pained and bewildered, to reflect on the reasons for this peremptory dismissal.

This strategy of placing the student in a desperate situation where he is relentlessly driven from the rear and vigorously repulsed in front often builds up pressures within him that lead to that inner explosion without which true awakening seldom occurs.

However, such extreme measures are by no means universal in Zen. Generally, they are more common in the Rinzai sect than in the Soto, less frequent in the temples than in the monasteries, where the outward discipline is rigid and often harsh. Even so, it is an unusual sesshin that does not resound to shouts of encouragement from the monitors and flailings of the kyosaku. Those who find the use of the kyosaku repugnant are always surprised to learn

---

[2] Those attending their first sesshin are often puzzled and confused by this sight, construing it to be part of some prescribed ritual. Actually it is nothing of the sort. The sudden clanging of the bell for dokusan affords release from the accumulated tension developed during the intensive effort at concentration. Simultaneously there is an uncontrollable urge to race to the roshi to be tested. Occasionally the student who reaches the bell first does not wait for a signal from the roshi but enters the roshi's room at once.

that not only had the kyosaku been relentlessly used on those who achieved kensho at sesshin but that it had actually been asked for by them.

In the *Shobogenzo Zuimonki* Dogen is quoted by one of his disciples as saying that while in China he heard the following from a Zen master concerning zazen: ". . . When I was young I used to visit the heads of various monasteries, and one of them explained to me: 'Formerly I used to hit sleeping monks so hard that my fist just about broke. Now I am old and weak, so I can't hit them hard enough. Therefore it is difficult to produce good monks. In many monasteries today the superiors do not emphasize sitting strongly enough, and so Buddhism is declining. The more you hit them, the better,' he advised me."[3]

That an intense inner energy must be aroused for the tremendous effort of reaching enlightenment, whether it be instigated from the outside by a stick or from the inside by sheer will power, has been taught by all great masters. It was underscored by the Buddha himself in an early sutra in these words: ". . . One should with clenched teeth, and with tongue pressing on palate, subdue, crush, and overpower the mind by the mind, just as if a strong man, having taken a very weak man by the head or shoulders, were to subdue him, crush him, and overpower him. Then the bad harmful thoughts connected with desire, hate, and delusion will pass away, disappear."[4]

The fact that there are Rinzai masters in Japan who seldom employ the kyosaku and Soto masters who persistently use it only proves that, in the last analysis, it is the roshi's own personality together with the training he himself received which determines his methods, and not the circumstance of the sect to which his temple belongs.

In the person of a genuine roshi, able to expound the Buddha's Dharma with a conviction born of his own profound experience of truth, is to be found the embodiment of Zen's wisdom and

[3] Quoted in *Sources of Japanese Tradition,* edited by William Theodore de Bary, p. 254.
[4] The Satipatthana Sutta of the Majjhima Nikaya (translated by Lord Chalmers in *Further Dialogues of the Buddha,* Part 1).

authority. Such a roshi is a guide and teacher whose spirit-heart-mind is identical with that of all Buddhas and patriarchs, separated though they be by centuries in time. Without him Zen's past is lifeless, its future "powerless to be born." Zen, as a transmission from mind to mind, cherishes pulsating, living truth—truth in action. Like sound imprisoned in a record or tape, needing electrical energy and certain devices to reproduce it, so the Heart-mind of the Buddha, entombed in the sutras, needs a living force in the person of an enlightened roshi to re-create it.

In dokusan the roshi fulfills the dual roles traditionally ascribed to a father and a mother. Alternately he is the strict, reproving father who prods and chastens and the gentle, loving mother who comforts and encourages. When the student slackens his effort he is coaxed or goaded, when he displays pride he is rebuked; and conversely, when he is assailed by doubt or driven to despair he is encouraged and uplifted. An accomplished roshi thus combines stern detachment with warm concern, flexibility, and an egolessness that can never be mistaken for weakness or flabbiness, in addition to self-confidence and a commanding air. Because his words are charged with the force and immediacy of his liberated personality, what he says has the power to rejuvenate the student's flagging spirit and reinvigorate his quest for enlightenment despite pain, frustration, or temporary boredom.

But what the student responds to most keenly is the visible evidence of the roshi's liberated mind: his childlike spontaneity, his radiance, his concern. A novice who watches his seventy-eight-year-old roshi demonstrate a koan with dazzling swiftness and total involvement, and who observes the flowing, effortless grace with which he relates himself to every situation and to all individuals, knows that he is seeing one of the finest products of a unique system of mind and character development, and he is bound to say to himself in his moments of despair: "If through the practice of Zen I can learn to experience life with the same immediacy and awareness, no price will be too high to pay."

All the roshi's unique skills and compassion come into full play once he senses that the student's mind is ripe, that is, barren of discriminating thoughts and clearly aware—in other words, in a state of absolute oneness—revealed variously in how the student strikes the dokusan bell, how he walks into the dokusan room, how he makes his prostrations, and the way he looks and acts during dokusan. In a variety of ways the roshi will prod and nudge this mind into making its own ultimate leap to awakening. Up to this point the roshi's main effort has been directed toward cajoling and inspiring the student to apply himself with energy and single-mindedness, and not to give way to weariness or despondency. But now he takes another tack. He shoots sharp questions at him, demanding instantaneous answers, or he jabs him suddenly with his baton, or pointedly slams at the mat, all in an effort to pry apart the student's delusive mind.

In their effect on the mind of the student these prods of the roshi are like darts of rain on parched soil or shafts of light in a dark room, and they serve to advance his mind to the next critical point, the stage where he feels encased in a "block of ice" or immured in a "crystal palace."[5] Now he *virtually* sees the truth, but he cannot break out and take hold of it. The student knows that the roshi is no more able to predict the precise moment of awakening than to "bestow" satori on him. Nor can he himself do any more than strive with might and main to exhaust his thinking and reach a state of infantlike no-mindedness (that is, emptiness of mind).[6] Yet somehow the final breakthrough, the sudden, decisive "somersault" of the mind betokening enlightenment, must occur. At this crucial juncture the temptation, always potential, to antici-pate when awakening, like a bolt from the blue, will take place, for better or worse,[7] becomes irresistible. It is the last desperate maneuver of the retreating ego to disrupt the concentrated mind, plague it with thoughts, and arrest the ultimate leap—signifying complete and total self-abandonment—to freedom. The roshi, aware that the student's mind can be jolted into making this leap by a blow, a phrase, or some sound only if it is empty, will take

[5] These metaphors are often used in Zen to describe the "foretaste" stage. It is possible to remain "stuck" at this point for weeks, months, or even years.

[6] To strive mightily to attain no-mindedness may seem like a contradiction, but the contradiction is a logical, not an existential, one.

[7] Some have an unconscious dread of kensho, believing it may have a deleterious effect on the mind. Needless to say, this is an unwarranted fear.

pains to point out this temptation, cautioning the student not to fall prey to the allurements of the ego.

Enlightenment can take place anywhere, not alone in the dokusan room. Indeed, a number of students experience it while listening to the roshi's formal commentary. Their mind fastens onto a particular phrase which they may have heard from the roshi innumerable times but which now, because the mind is ripe, assumes a fresh and startling significance, serving as the spark to set off the inner explosion heralding the opening of the Mind's eye. Some have come to awakening on a train or bus on their way home from sesshin. Usually, but not always, kensho follows a period of intense concentration and absorption.

In view of the foregoing, the intriguing words with which many koans or *mondo* conclude, "With this the monk suddenly came to enlightenment" or "Then the monk's mind's eye was opened," will be seen to be less imaginary than at first supposed. Puzzled students frequently ask: "How is it possible to achieve satori as quickly and easily as these koans would have one believe?" What is important to observe here is that the master's crucial phrase or blow that broke open the disciple's deluded mind was effective only because it came at a time when the latter's mind was ripe for this type of stimulus, and that this ripeness doubtlessly was the outcome of a long period of zazen and a number of dokusan with the master. In other words, koans in their formulation reveal the precipitating circumstances only; they make no mention of the years of relentless, anxious search for truth which led to this crowning experience.

The proof of the student's awakening lies in his ability to respond instantly in a "live" way to questions that demand a concrete demonstration of the spirit of his koan.[8] What convinces the roshi are not merely the student's words or gestures or silence (which can be equally effective), but the conviction and certainty informing them, that is, the comprehending look in the eye, the decisiveness of the tone of voice, and the spontaneity, freedom, and thoroughness of the gestures and movements themselves. Thus it is possible for two different persons, one just enlightened and the other not

---

[8] For the nature of some of these questions, see pp. 238-39.

yet, to respond with identical words and gestures at dokusan and for the roshi to accept the responses of the one and reject those of the other.

The roshi's acceptance of the student's demonstration is tacit confirmation that the student has had a genuine awakening, even though it be shallow as many first experiences are. Where Zen differs radically from other Buddhist disciplines is precisely in this insistence that the student demonstrate his understanding "beyond all understanding," and not merely verbalize about it. What Zen values are expressive gestures, movements, and phrases which spontaneously issue from the deepest level of the total being, and not arid explanations, however subtle. An experienced roshi can determine with a single question—or if the experience is profound, by merely a glance—the fact of the student's enlightenment, but by requiring him to submit to testing he is able to establish, to the student's as well as to his own satisfaction, the depth and limits of the awakening.

It is frequently claimed that genuine enlightenment ought to be self-validating and therefore no need for testing should arise. But self-deception is as strong here as in other realms of human behavior, even stronger perhaps because of the very nature of enlightenment. It is all too easy for a novice to mistake visions, trances, hallucinations, insights, revelations, ecstasies, or even mental serenity for kensho. The oceanic feeling experienced by certain types of neurotics has likewise been confused with enlightenment since it conveys a sense of oneness with the universe. For all these reasons, and especially because the danger to the personality resulting from such self-deception is real, Zen teaching has always insisted that kensho be tested and confirmed by a master whose own enlightenment has, in turn, been sanctioned by an enlightened master.

If it is possible to deceive oneself about kensho, it is equally possible to experience kensho and not equate it with awakening. Yasutani-roshi relates the story of one of his disciples living in the southern part of Japan whom he saw once a year at sesshin. In the interval between the roshi's yearly visits this man had had an inner realization, but because he had not concomitantly had an emotional upheaval followed by tears of joy, he did not believe that what he had perceived could be kensho. The roshi, upon questioning him in dokusan, felt that his disciple's perception and inner understanding were such as to warrant testing, and he thereupon propounded several "test" questions to him. To this man's surprise he found that he could make full and proper response, and the roshi confirmed his realization. Though admittedly shallow, the kensho was nonetheless real. It should be observed here that the nature of the reaction to one's own enlightenment depends not only on the depth of the enlightenment itself but also on one's emotional and mental makeup.

This kind of testing needs to be distinguished from the testing referred to as "Dharma dueling" (hossen) which anciently took place among Zen monks in China, and in Japan up until about the time of Hakuin, some two hundred years ago. Monks and laymen[9] of varying degrees of spiritual strength would travel about the country in a spiritual pilgrimage, searching for Zen masters and deeply enlightened monks against whom they could pit their Dharma "skill," as a means of deepening and rounding out their own enlightenment and at the same time developing teaching techniques through testing the spiritual strength of their "adversary." The verbal thrusts and counterthrusts that constituted these contests were later written down and compiled into collections of koans which are still widely used by Zen students in Japan.

With the passing of his first koan the student enters a new phase of dokusan. The tense and intense striving, alternating with moods of uncertainty, dejection, and despair, which hitherto characterized his appearance before the roshi, gives way to a relaxed, self-confident, and more nearly equal partnership with the roshi. No more is the roshi father and mother but a wise elder brother. To be sure, the disciple's movements are still groping and unsteady, like those of a puppy which has just opened its eyes on the world and taken its first steps, but the "iron wall and silver mountain" no longer confront him at every turn. Previously, when dokusan was not dreadful it was dreary, but now, moving from koan to koan, swallowing up whole rivers in one gulp and re-creating

[9] Of whom the laymen P'ang (Ho) is the most famous. Many stories and legends have grown up about his fascinating life. For a reference to one of his "Dharma duels," see p. 179; see also "Ho-koji" in section x.

heaven and earth with the lifting of a finger,[10] he experiences an ever-widening sense of power and freedom. For in grasping the spirit of the koans and throwing himself wholeheartedly into the diverse roles created by them, he is able to express vividly and forcefully in concrete situations the truth he has perceived. But perhaps the greatest miracle is his feeling of gratitude toward his teachers, toward Buddhas and Bodhisattvas, toward all who have lent a supporting hand and encouraging word in his hours of need. Now his oft-repeated vow to attain perfect enlightenment for the sake of all humanity takes on fresh and profound meaning.

From what has been said it is clear that the roshi's role in Zen training is transcendent. No one, nothing can take the place of an enlightened master, and fortunate indeed is the student whose karma brings him into contact with one. But wise, compassionate masters are hard to find nowadays—as they probably always have been. Is, then, the practice of Zen without a teacher impossible? By no means. In the material comprising this section the serious-minded student will find answered by an outstanding contemporary roshi virtually every question connected with practice that is likely to arise for him. A thorough reading of this section, therefore, along with the other sections, in which all the steps of practice are clearly set forth, will enable anyone to commence his journey on the road to enlightenment.

A word may be in order as to how this dokusan material was compiled. It was my privilege to be able to act as interpreter for Yasutani-roshi for several years, a circumstance which placed me in the unique position of being privy to the problems of Westerners training in Zen under him in Japan, and to the advice and instructions he gave them. It occurred to me that if these questions and answers could be recorded they would be of incalculable value to students in the West and elsewhere who wished to discipline themselves in Zen yet lacked competent teachers. Furthermore,

[10] A reference to the nineteenth case in the *Blue Rock Records* (and also the third in the *Mumonkan*), commonly called "Gutei's Finger." The introduction to this koan states: "When one speck of dust arises, the great universe is involved. When one blossom opens, the whole world manifests itself."

such a record would go a long way, I felt, toward dispelling the widespread notion that Zen is deliberate mystification or a "sadistic expression of Japanese culture," as some poorly informed critics have termed it.

The use of a tape or other recording device was out of the question since it would have made the students self-conscious and interfered with their dokusan, and therefore would never have been allowed by Yasutani-roshi. On the other hand, for me to have attempted to make notes during dokusan would have been objectionable for the same reasons, and in any case would have been impossible if I were to make an adequate interpretation. I thereupon turned to the idea of jotting down in shorthand at the conclusion of each dokusan, while the dialogue was still fresh in my mind, everything that had transpired. I believe that despite my less than perfect knowledge of Japanese I have rendered a faithful transcription of the substance of the dialogue that passed between Yasutani-roshi and his ten Western students. Whenever I was in doubt I carefully verified my understanding with him. Still, it is possible that here and there I have failed to capture the full nuance or flavor of a comment by the roshi, and for any such omissions I assume responsibility.

It should be pointed out that the decision to publish this dokusan material was not made lightly. Dokusan is normally regarded as a private matter between the roshi and the student, for in order to insure complete frankness between teacher and student, both must know that what transpires in the dokusan room will not be divulged. Nonetheless, Yasutani-roshi consented to the publication of this material upon being assured that it would do much to correct the many misunderstandings that have appeared in books on Zen in English concerning the nature and purpose of dokusan. He did, however, lay down the condition that no solutions to koans be revealed, so that students who later practiced under a roshi might not be handicapped by reading such information. This condition has been respected.

THE ENCOUNTERS / STUDENT A
(WOMAN, AGE 60) /

STUDENT: I feel myself a prisoner of my ego and want to escape. Can I do it through zazen? Would you please tell me the purpose of zazen?

ROSHI: Let us speak of mind first. Your mind can be compared to a mirror,[11] which reflects everything that appears before it. From the time you begin to think, to feel, and to exert your will, shadows are cast upon your mind which distort its reflections. This condition we call delusion, which is the fundamental sickness of human beings. The most serious effect of this sickness is that it creates a sense of duality, in consequence of which you postulate "I" and "not-I." The truth is that everything is One, and this of course is not a numerical one. Falsely seeing oneself confronted by a world of separate existences, this is what creates antagonism, greed, and, inevitably, suffering. The purpose of zazen is to wipe away from the mind these shadows or defilements so that we can intimately experience our solidarity with all life. Love and compassion then naturally and spontaneously flow forth.

*　　*　　*

STUDENT: I am sitting in shikan-taza as you have instructed me. I have pain in my legs, but it is bearable. I am not bothered by many thoughts and my concentration is fairly good. But I really don't know what my aim in sitting is.

ROSHI: The first aim of sitting is to unify the mind. For the average person, whose mind is being pulled in many directions, sustained concentration is virtually impossible. Through the practice of zazen the mind becomes one-pointed so that it can be controlled. This process can be likened to utilizing the sun's rays through a magnifying glass. When the rays of the sun are focused they become, of course, more intense. The human mind too functions more efficiently when it is concentrated and unified. Whether your desire

---

[11] The roshi, like Hui-neng, the Sixth Patriarch, is comparing mind not to the form of a mirror, for mind is formless, but to the mirror's powers of reflection. Hui-neng's verse reads: "Fundamentally no bodhi-tree exists / Nor the frame of a mirror bright. / Since all is voidness from the beginning / Where can the dust alight?"

is to see into your Self-nature or not, you can appreciate the effect on your well-being of mind integration.

STUDENT: Yes, of course. Now, I was sitting quietly doing zazen, and then I had a great deal of pain. I didn't know whether I ought to try to endure the pain or to give up when it got too intense. My real problem, in other words, is this: Should I bring my will to bear or should I sit passively, without forcing myself?

ROSHI: This is an important problem. Eventually you will reach the point where you can sit comfortably, free from strain or pain. But from long habit of misusing our body and mind, in the beginning we must exert our will before we can sit with ease and equilibrium. And this inevitably entails pain.

When the body's center of gravity is established in the region just below the navel, the entire body functions with greater stability. The center of gravity in the average person is in the shoulders. Moreover, instead of sitting and walking with an erect back, most people slump, placing an inordinate strain on all parts of the body.

We likewise misemploy our mind, playing with and harboring all kinds of useless thoughts. This is why we have to make a determined effort to use the body and mind properly. At first it is unavoidably painful, but if you persevere, the pain will gradually give way to a feeling of exhilaration. You will become physically stronger and mentally more alert. This is the experience of all who do zazen regularly and devotedly.

*   *   *

ROSHI: Is there anything you want to ask?

STUDENT: Yes, I have several questions. The first is: Why did you have a sign put above my place saying I should not be struck with the kyosaku? Is it because you feel I am hopeless?

ROSHI: I was under the impression that you, like most Westerners, did not like to be struck. The senior monitor has been striking everyone hard, and I thought if you were struck it might interfere with your zazen. You don't mind being hit?

STUDENT [smiling]: Well, most of the time I don't, if I'm not hit too hard.

ROSHI: Yesterday the young woman sitting opposite you, who happens to be Japanese, was struck with a great deal of force, to spur her on of course. It was the first time she had been hit and she was so surprised and bewildered that she left the sesshin immediately. Fortunately she came back today and told me what had happened, so I had a sign placed over her saying she was not to be struck.

STUDENT: Anyway, I am glad to learn you don't think I am a hopeless case.

This is my next point: Feeling energetic this morning, I began to think: "I must empty my mind of useless thoughts so that wisdom may enter." Then, realizing that this was the work of the ego, I became discouraged. I felt like a donkey that could be made to move only by having a carrot dangled before its eyes.

ROSHI: Do you wish enlightenment?

STUDENT: I don't know what enlightenment is. Yesterday I told you I wanted to banish my ego so that I could become a little wiser. I suppose I am more interested in getting rid of ego than in attaining enlightenment.

ROSHI: Intrinsically there is no ego—it is something we ourselves create. Still, it is this self-created ego that leads us to zazen, so it is not to be despised. Zazen, as you have probably realized, brings about an attrition of the ego. You can also get rid of ego by abiding by the rules of sesshin instead of following your own inclinations. If, for example, you don't want to rise when the bell rings for everyone to get up and walk around, you are catering to your ego and so enhancing it. The same is true of eating. You surrender to your ego each time you decide to forego eating communally and go off to eat by yourself. Now, since ego is rooted in the subconsciousness, the only way to uproot it is by a thoroughgoing enlightenment.

* * *

STUDENT: I am very tired and my legs pain me terrifically. I can't do good zazen any more. I don't know what to do.

ROSHI: Zazen requires considerable energy. If the body is not fit, intense zazen is difficult. Until you recover your strength sit comfortably without straining yourself. When you feel strong again, you can exert yourself. After that it is a matter of determination, of bringing your will to bear. Energy and unswerving determination are both necessary.

* * *

STUDENT: I have been working by myself on the koan "What was the Face you had before you were born?" I believe I have the answer, but would like you to confirm it. I have dwelt, for example, on what I was like before I was born and what my parents were like. I have also thought of what I would be like after I am dead. In fact, in my imagination I have already buried my ashes in a favorite spot. Have I been working on this koan correctly?

ROSHI: No, you have not. What you are giving me is a hypothetical picture of this koan. To deal with it truly you must be able to answer such questions as: If the world were destroyed would the original Face also be destroyed? If so, in what way?

STUDENT: I can't answer such questions.

ROSHI: This koan is no different from Mu. For the time being simply continue with shikan-taza until you reach the point of strongly wanting kensho. Then a koan like "What is my Face before my parents' birth?" or "What is Mu?" would be appropriate.

*   *   *

STUDENT: In speaking of makyo you have said that even psychological insights about oneself are makyo. This is not only confusing but also discouraging. I've had several insights about myself during this sesshin and felt extremely elated. But now I'm confused and don't know what to think.

ROSHI: As your practice progresses many makyo will appear. In themselves they are not harmful, they may even be beneficial in some measure. But if you become attached to or ensnared by them, they can hinder you. In the deepest sense, even the Bodhisattva Kannon might be said to be *attached to* compassion, otherwise he would be a Buddha, free of all attachments. One obsessed by the idea of helping others feels constrained to aid those who might be better off without such aid. Take a person with little money who lives simply. To give him material things unessential to his simple way of life would destroy that life. This would not be kindness at all. A Buddha is compassionate, but he isn't *obsessed* by the desire to save others.

Insights about oneself are valuable, of course, but your aim is to go beyond them. If you stop to congratulate yourself on your insights, your advancement toward realization of your Buddha-nature will be slowed. In the widest sense, everything short of true enlightenment is makyo. Don't become concerned about makyo or elated by them. Don't allow yourself to be diverted by what are essentially transitory experiences. Only continue your practice devotedly.

* * *

STUDENT: About an hour ago during zazen all at once the pain in my legs disappeared and before I knew it tears began to flow and I felt myself melting inside. At the same time a great feeling of love enveloped me. What is the meaning of this?

ROSHI: Zazen done with energy and devotion dispels our sense of alienation from people and things. The ordinary man's thinking is dualistic; he thinks in terms of himself and of that which is antithetical to him, and this is what causes his misery, because it gives rise to antagonism and grasping, which in turn lead to suffering. But through zazen this dichotomy gradually vanishes. Your compassion then naturally deepens and widens, since your feelings and thoughts no longer are focused on a non-existent "I." This is what is happening to you. It is of course highly gratifying, but you must go further. Continue your concentration wholeheartedly.

* * *

STUDENT: My practice is shikan-taza.

ROSHI: Is there anything you want to ask?

STUDENT: Yes, yesterday when I was trying to sit with vigor, as you had urged me to, I felt that my effort was mechanical, because I had to push, so to speak, to achieve that state. Nevertheless, I sat as I was told to sit, and when I was whacked with the kyosaku several times the stick-wielder told me my sitting was very good. I myself felt that my sitting at that time was mechanical. This morning, instead of pushing, I felt myself suddenly being pushed, as it were. My strength arose naturally and I felt that the quality of my sitting was better than that of the sitting in which I had to "push." Yet this morning when I was struck by the monitor I was told: "You're relaxing your effort! Brace up!" I am really confused.

ROSHI: First of all, do not retain in your mind the words of the person trying to encourage you. Listen to what he says and then forget it. Of course the type of sitting where vigor naturally flows forth, without having to "push" for it, is better. Unfortunately, it is not always possible to maintain such vigor. That is why it is necessary to force yourself to sit firmly when energy doesn't come forth spontaneously. Bear in mind that there is a causal relation between your mechanical sitting, as you call it, and the natural, easy sitting you experienced later. In any event, the sitter is not always the best judge of the quality of his sitting. The important thing is not to relax your efforts, not to give way to dullness or tiredness.

*　　*　　*

STUDENT: I had the sensation of an object resting on my forehead between the eyes. It was so strong that automatically my attention became riveted to it. But as you had instructed me to concentrate my mind in the pit of my abdomen, I brought my mind back there. Should I continue that way?

ROSHI: If your mind naturally and spontaneously goes to a point between the eyes, it's all right to direct your concentration there. That is another way of concentrating.

*　　*　　*

ROSHI: Has anything in particular happened to you?

STUDENT: I've had the sensation of the back of my head being pushed up by my breath and of my breath going down to my loins. Is this a makyo? If so, what should I do about it?

ROSHI: Yes, this is also a kind of makyo. These things have no particular significance—they are neither beneficial nor harmful. Don't embrace them, just go on earnestly with your practice. They arise, as I have pointed out, when one is concentrating intensely.

STUDENT: But why do they arise at all?

ROSHI: Countless thoughts, like waves on the sea, are constantly bobbing on the surface of our mind as a result of the functioning of our six senses.[12] Now, in our subconscious are to be found all the residual impressions of our life experience, including those of previous existences, going back to time immemorial. When zazen penetrates so deeply that the surface and intermediate levels of consciousness are stilled, elements of this residuum bubble up to the conscious mind. These we call makyo.

Now, don't be enamored of them when they are pleasant, and don't become afraid when they are weird. If you cling to them—admire or fear them—they can become a hindrance.

*　　*　　*

STUDENT: I have much pain in my legs. What can I do about it?

---

[12] The sixth sense, according to Buddhism, is the discriminating faculty.

ROSHI: If you have too much pain, it is difficult to concentrate. But when your concentration becomes strong, instead of hobbling you, pain will spur you on if you use it bravely.

STUDENT: I have another question. What can I do when I get sleepy?

ROSHI: It depends on the nature of your sleepiness. If it is only drowsiness, you can do the following: swing the body lightly from side to side several times, or rub the eyes. If it is heavy sleepiness because you haven't slept the night before, you can try dipping your face into cold water and vigorously rubbing it. To awaken a flagging spirit, the following is helpful: reflect that death can come at any moment either from sudden accident or serious illness, and resolve to achieve enlightenment without further delay.

* * *

STUDENT: I am afraid I have done badly in this my first sesshin. I have been unable to concentrate at all. My mind has been distracted and disturbed by the shouting of the seniors wielding the kyosaku, by the cracking sound of the kyosaku itself, by the cars and trucks, by the baby crying next door, by the dogs barking. Somehow I had imagined I would come to a quiet temple in idyllic surroundings, but it has turned out quite differently. Besides my disappointment, I am ashamed that I could do no better.

ROSHI: You needn't feel that way. In the beginning everyone finds it difficult to concentrate, because the mind is so easily distracted. Ideally, of course, it is best to go to a quiet place when starting zazen. That is why many Zen monks went and still go to solitary mountain retreats. But it is not well to stay in such an atmosphere for long. As one's powers of concentration develop and grow strong, one is able to do zazen in any kind of surrounding—the noisier the better, in fact. With the cultivation of strong concentrative powers, one can go down to the noisiest part of the Ginza[13] and do zazen.

* * *

STUDENT: I have a long question which will take some time to ask. I know there are many people waiting to see you, but because this is very important for me I hope you will permit me to ask it.

ROSHI: Go right ahead.

[13] The busiest section of downtown Tokyo.

STUDENT: Since the last sesshin I have been attacked in my meditation by a variety of unpleasant thoughts and feelings—and they weren't makyo—about myself, about what I may call my *untrue* nature. In your lecture this morning you said that when we empty our mind of all thoughts, true wisdom enters. You also spoke about just seeing when we looked and just hearing when we listened. I haven't been able to do this, as my ego has always interposed itself. Now, I don't know what kensho is, but if it is looking into one's true nature, it seems to me that what I am doing is just the reverse, namely, looking into my *untrue* nature.

ROSHI: Before zazen we think we are superior beings, but as we come to see ourselves more clearly we are made humble by the knowledge of our evil thoughts and deeds. But such comprehension is itself the reflection of our True-nature. If we are walking in the dark, let us say, and come to a pine tree, we can't see anything of it. Then a sliver of moon appears and we observe pin needles on the ground. As the moon becomes larger we see the trunk of the tree, and then, when the moon is full, the entire tree. Our perception of all this is the reflection of our Real-self.

STUDENT: May I ask another question? I have seen and talked to people who have had, I think, some kind of enlightenment experience. Yet often they seem troubled by what I have been calling the untrue nature. How is this possible?

ROSHI: It is true that there are people who have had a kensho experience and yet who seem to be, morally speaking, inferior to those who have not. How does it happen, you ask. These enlightened people have perceived the truth that all life in its essential nature is indivisible, but because they haven't yet purged themselves of their delusive feelings and propensities, the roots of which are imbedded deeply in the unconscious, they cannot act in accordance with their inner vision. If they continue with zazen, however, gradually their character will improve as they become cleansed of these defilements, and in time they will become outstanding individuals.

On the other hand, those who have never had a kensho experience and yet seem to be modest and unselfish conceal, so to speak, the real condition of their mind. On the face of it, these latter appear more virtuous and steady, but because they have never seen into the truth and therefore still see the universe and themselves as separate and apart, under great stress their seemingly fine character gives way and their behavior leaves much to be desired.

*   *   *

STUDENT [crying]: Just about five minutes ago I had a frightful experience. Suddenly I felt as though the whole universe had crashed into my stomach, and I burst out crying. I can't stop crying even now.

ROSHI: Many strange experiences take place when you do zazen, some of them agreeable, some of them, like your present one, fearful. But they have no particular significance. If you become elated by a pleasant occurrence and frightened by a dreadful one, such experiences may hinder you. But if you don't cling to them, they will naturally pass away.

*   *   *

STUDENT: Yesterday I described my experience of the whole universe rushing headlong into my stomach and of my terrible crying convulsions. After thinking about it I feel that it came about because somehow I was forcing myself. I think if I hadn't forced myself, it would not have happened.

ROSHI: If you want to do zazen in an easy, relaxed manner, that is all right too. We can make this comparison. Three people want to reach the top of a mountain where there is an exceptionally grand view. The first doesn't want to exert himself, he wants to stroll; so of course it will take him a long time to reach the top. The second, in more of a hurry, walks with long strides, swinging his arms as he moves up. The third, in what seems like a leap and a jump, gets to the top quickly and exclaims: "Oh, what a magnificent sight!"

STUDENT: Which way is best?

ROSHI: It all depends on your state of mind. If you have plenty of time, the first way is satisfactory. But if you are eager to reach the top quickly, naturally one of the other ways is better. Needless to say, to move rapidly requires more energy. Furthermore, when you exert yourself with passionate intensity you can expect untoward occurrences, frightening as well as pleasant—in other words, what you have been experiencing.

STUDENT: I would like to thank you very much. I also want to say that as I am returning to the United States next week this will be my last sesshin. While these sesshin have been painful in a number of ways, they have also been enormously revealing. Without this last one in particular I wouldn't understand myself so well as I do, and I wouldn't know how to proceed further. I am very grateful to you for the tremendous help you have given me.

2 / STUDENT B (MAN, AGE 45) /

STUDENT: My koan is Mu.

ROSHI: To realize the spirit of Mu you must, without being sidetracked, travel along an iron rail stretching to infinity. One halt, much less many, will thwart enlightenment. The narrowest separation from Mu becomes a separation of miles. So take care, be vigilant! Don't let go of Mu even for a moment while sitting, standing, walking, eating, or working.

*   *   *

STUDENT: I can't seem to get anywhere with Mu. I don't know what I am supposed to understand or not understand.

ROSHI: If you could truly say "I don't understand" after profound reflection, that would be convincing, since in truth there is nothing to understand. In the deepest sense, we understand nothing. What can be known by philosophers and scientists through reasoning is only a fraction of the universe. If we imagine this fountain pen I am holding to be the entire universe, what is intellectually knowable is the very tip of the pen. Can any philosopher or scientist really say why flowers bloom or why spring follows winter? When we aren't conceptualizing, the deepest part of us is functioning—

STUDENT [interrupting]: Yes, I see that clearly, but—

ROSHI [continuing]: So if you can honestly say, "I don't understand," you understand a great deal. Now go back and work on this koan more intensely.

*   *   *

STUDENT [excitedly]: I know what Mu is! This is Mu in one situation [picking up the roshi's baton]. In another this would be Mu [lifting another object]. Other than that I don't know.

ROSHI: That is not bad. If you really knew what you meant by "I don't know," your answer would be even better. It is obvious that you will think of yourself as an entity standing apart from other entities.

A summary of my morning lecture was given in English to all the foreigners, I understand. Were you present?

STUDENT: Yes, I was.

ROSHI: Then you know how imperative it is to abandon the idea of a "myself" standing in opposition to "others." This is an illusion produced by a false view of things. To come to Self-realization you must directly experience yourself and the universe as one. Of course you understand this theoretically, but theoretical understanding is like a picture: it is not the thing itself but only a representation of it. You must let go of logical reasoning and grasp the real thing!

STUDENT: I can do that—yes, I can!

ROSHI: Very well, tell me at once what the size of the Real You is!

STUDENT [pausing]: Well . . . it depends on the circumstances. In one situation I may be one thing; in another, something else.

ROSHI: Had you realized the truth, you could have given a concrete answer instantaneously.

When I reach out with both arms this way [demonstrating], how far do they extend? Answer at once!

STUDENT [pausing]: I don't know. All I know is that sometimes I feel I am this stick and sometimes I feel I am something else—I'm not sure what.

ROSHI: You are almost there. Don't become lax now—do your utmost!

3 / STUDENT C (MAN, AGE 43) /

[Every student normally states the nature of his practice as soon as he comes before the roshi in dokusan. This student's practice is Mu, but his statement, "My practice is Mu," has been omitted to avoid tiresome repetition.]

STUDENT: I feel Mu is everything and nothing. I feel it is like a reflection of the moon on a lake, with no moon and no lake, only reflection.

ROSHI: You have a keen theoretical grasp of Mu, a clear *picture* of it in your mind; now you need to take hold of it directly. There is a line a famous Zen master wrote at the time he became enlightened which reads: "When I heard the temple bell ring, suddenly there was no bell and no I, just sound." In other words, he no longer was aware of a distinction between himself, the bell, the sound, and the universe. This is the state you have to reach. Don't relax—strive on!

*　　　*　　　*

STUDENT: I have a complaint. Last night while waiting to go to dokusan I was brusquely shoved and pushed and shouted at. I knew this prodding was intended to spur me on, but all the same I felt resentful.

ROSHI: It is because you think of yourself as an "I" that you resent this kind of treatment. If your body and mind were one hundred percent united with Mu, *who* would be resenting? At that point you are like a simpleton, or like a punching bag: whichever way you are pushed you go, because your ego, your willfulness, has been banished. That is the time you directly realize Mu. Upon reaching this stage you are free of all resentments.

*　　　*　　　*

STUDENT: Yesterday I reached the high point of my effort; my zeal, you said, was up to ninety-five percent. But today my burning desire has suddenly left me. I feel completely discouraged. I don't know why.

ROSHI: Don't become discouraged, it is that way with everybody. If you were a piece of machinery, you could function steadily at high speed, but a human being cannot. Consider a person riding a horse. If he is a good rider, he doesn't gallop his horse one moment and slow it down to a walk the next. By keeping it going at a steady trot he is in a better position to elicit a burst of speed when he wants it.

If you relax completely and continue indefinitely at a walk or, what is worse, stop from time to time, it will take you a long time to get to your destination. The trouble may be that consciously or unconsciously you are thinking: "If I don't get kensho at this sesshin, I will get it at the next." But if this were your last sesshin in Japan, you would become desperate and your desperation would sweep you right into enlightenment.

Take these people attending this special sesshin[14] with you. They

---

[14] Yasutani-roshi holds this seven-day sesshin once a year in Hokkaido, the northern island of Japan.

have only one chance a year to attend sesshin, and they feel that if they do not attain kensho this week, they will have to wait another year for the next sesshin. So they do zazen with tremendous energy and devotion. Three of the group have already gotten kensho.

Don't relax your efforts, otherwise it will take you a long time to achieve what you are after.

*   *   *

STUDENT: My mind is freer of thoughts now than it has been for most of this sesshin, but I am still bothered by a few recurring ones. I suppose it's because I have read so much about Zen in the past and reflected on it.

ROSHI: Yes. You will realize your True-nature only after your mind has become as empty of thoughts as a sheet of pure white paper is free of blemishes. It is simply a matter of engrossing yourself in Mu so totally that there is no room for thoughts of any kind, including Mu itself.

*   *   *

ROSHI: Don't be heedless even for an instant. If your are attentive while sitting in zazen yet permit your eyes and mind to wander when you arise, you disrupt your concentrated mind. Are you following what I am saying?

STUDENT: Yes, I am, but all this really has nothing to do with me. I am always attentive.

ROSHI: Well, it is possible to be inattentive without realizing it. Besides, there are degrees of attentiveness. If on a crowded train you are watchful that your wallet is not stolen, that is one kind of mindfulness. But if you are in a situation in which you might be killed at any moment—during wartime let us say—the degree of your attentiveness is far greater.

To become lax even for a second is to separate yourself from Mu. Even when you go to bed continue to absorb yourself in Mu, and when you awaken, awaken with your mind focused on Mu. At every moment your entire attention must be concentrated on penetrating Mu—so much so that you become possessed, like a lover. Only then can you awaken.

*   *   *

ROSHI: You know how to do zazen properly. You also have an excellent mental picture of Mu. But to actually experience Mu, you must discard this portrait of it lodged in your discursive mind.

The roots of ego-strengthening ideas are deep in the subconscious mind, out of reach of ordinary awareness, so they are hard to eliminate. To get rid of them you must become absolutely one with Mu when walking, eating, working, sleeping, excreting. You must not only concentrate your mind but control your eyes as well, for when the eyes aren't riveted down thoughts arise, the mind stirs, and before you know it you have parted from Mu.

As I have said, you know the proper way to concentrate, but your concentration is still weak. You have a tendency to dawdle at times or to busy yourself with extraneous matters. While this is not bad in itself, it is fatal for one aspiring to realize his True-nature, as the mind is constantly being distracted. You will become enlightened only after you have poured the whole force of your being into oneness with Mu.

*   *   *

STUDENT: I struggle with might and main to become one with Mu, but because that which is not Mu is equally strong, Mu doesn't prevail. As a matter of fact, the stronger Mu becomes, the stronger the force opposed to it, so I have come to feel that I am "between two worlds, one dead, the other powerless to be born." Frankly, I am at a loss to know what to do. A greater strength than what I possess is necessary—of this I am convinced.

ROSHI: What you are trying to do can be compared to this [pushing one hand against the other]. Once you realize Mu, you know that nothing can be opposed to it, since everything is Mu.

Now you can begin to appreciate why the kyosaku is used—to help you exert yourself beyond your normal capacity. But as you dislike the kyosaku, I can ask the chief monitor to slap you hard on the back from time to time. With that as a spur you can mobilize greater strength and energy than you have up to now.

*   *   *

ROSHI: Were this a certain large monastery and you came before the roshi in dokusan as you are now doing, he would sharply demand: "Show me Mu!" If you couldn't show him, he would warn you not to return until you could. Dismayed, you would find excuses to stay away from dokusan for fear of being rebuked because you had no answer to Mu yet. On the other hand, if you didn't go voluntarily, you would be yanked off your seat by the head monks and pushed or dragged into dokusan. Not knowing which way to turn, you might out of sheer desperation produce the answer to Mu.

For a variety of reasons we don't employ such measures here. But exert this pressure on yourself. Come before me feeling that, come what may, you will demonstrate the truth of Mu. Now go back to your place and do your best!

*　　　*　　　*

ROSHI: I see you still haven't penetrated Mu . . . Why not? . . . You begin by concentrating intensely, then you slacken off. For a time you hold on to Mu the way I am holding on to my baton [grasping baton tightly with both hands]. Then you relax like this [dropping baton]. That will never do! When you walk only Mu walks, when you eat only Mu eats, when you work only Mu works, and when you come before me only Mu appears. Prostrating yourself, it is Mu that prostrates. Speaking, it is Mu that speaks. Lying down to sleep, it is Mu that sleeps and Mu that awakens. Having reached the point where your seeing, your hearing, your touching, your smelling, your tasting, and your thinking are nothing but Mu, suddenly you directly perceive Mu.

*　　　*　　　*

ROSHI: To come to the realization of Mu you must get into the state of a lover, who has a mind only for his beloved. The ordinary person concerns himself with any number of trivial details: the time of day, his daily dress, random thoughts which enter his mind. But a lover, with his mind centered wholly on his beloved, is in a trancelike state. He is rather like a simpleton in that his mind focuses in but one direction. You will surely become enlightened once you attain to such single-mindedness with respect to Mu.

*　　　*　　　*

STUDENT: At different times you have told me that every single object is Mu, that I am Mu, and so on. What am I supposed to do with these hints? Think about them during my zazen, and if so, in what way?

ROSHI: No, don't think about them in your zazen; these hints are for the moment only. If they open your mind to the direct awareness of Mu, well and good. If not, forget about them and return to questioning "What is Mu?"

STUDENT: A little while back when I was concentrating simply on Mu, my powers of concentration were fairly strong. I could easily focus my mind on Mu without the interference of various thoughts. But ever since you told me I must think of the meaning of Mu, that I must keep querying myself, "What is Mu?" my mind has been opened to a barrage of thoughts which hinder my concentration.

ROSHI: You can reduce "What is Mu?" to simply Mu, for the whole question has by now seeped into you subconscious, and this abbreviated Mu will set the full phrase echoing in your mind.

Your purpose in doing zazen is to experience kensho. Kensho and joriki, which is the Japanese name for the power growing out of zazen, while closely related are nevertheless two different things. There are those who do zazen for years, with strong joriki, yet never awaken. Why not? Because in their deepest unconscious they can't disabuse themselves of the idea that the world is external to them, that they are a sovereign individuality independent of and opposed by other individualities. To renounce such conceptions is to stand in "darkness."[15] Now, satori comes out of this "darkness," not out of the "light" of reason and worldly knowledge. In the intense asking, "What is Mu?" you bring the reasoning mind to an impasse, void of every thought, even as you gradually destroy the tenacious roots of I and not-I in the unconscious mind. This dynamic kind of self-inquiry is the quickest way to Self-realization.

Joriki is, of course, essential, but if your aim is no more than that, you can do zazen for years without coming any closer to your goal of awakening. On the other hand, there are many people whose joriki is comparatively weak and yet who open their mind's eye.

STUDENT: Why, then, should I bother to develop joriki?

ROSHI: Only because you cannot carry on spiritual practice unless your thoughts and emotions are under natural restraint. Once you acquire this natural control through joriki, you are no longer compulsively driven. You are free to experience attractive sights or sounds, let us say, or to ignore them, with no aftermath of remorse or clinging. Nevertheless, until enlightenment your view of the world and your relation to it will be blurred—in other words, still

---

[15] In Zen it is said that "the grand round mirror of wisdom is as black as pitch."

dominated by the idea of "self" and "other"—and you will be misled by your imperfect vision.

Self-realization can come, as I have said, with only a little zazen and correspondingly little joriki, but without joriki it is difficult to redirect one's habitual actions so that they accord with the truth one has experienced. It is only after awakening, when one no longer sees the world and himself as two, that one's potentialities unfold to their fullest, provided always one continues with zazen and the development of joriki.

STUDENT: I can appreciate all that, but my problem still is: How am I to entertain the question "What is Mu?" when I find it entirely meaningless? I can't even formulate the question for myself, much less resolve it. If I were to say to you "What is *baba*?"[16] it would have no meaning for you. I find Mu equally meaningless.

ROSHI: That is *precisely* why Mu is such an excellent practice! To realize your Self-nature you have to break out of the cul-de-sac of logic and analysis. The ordinary question demands a rational answer, but trying to answer "What is Mu?" rationally is like trying to smash your fist through an iron wall. This question forces you into a realm beyond reasoning. But your effort to solve it is not without meaning. What you are really trying to find out is "What is my True-self?" Through the way I have specified you can discover it. If you prefer, you may ask yourself: "What is my True-self?"

STUDENT: Or what am I? or who am I?

ROSHI: Yes, exactly.

* * *

STUDENT [rushing in, panting]: I must tell you what happened to me a short while ago. I practically blacked out.

ROSHI: You mean that everything went black and you couldn't see at all?

STUDENT: Not quite. Everything grew dark, but there were little holes of light in this blackness. This has happened several times. What is the significance of it?

ROSHI: It is a makyo, proving you have reached a critical, halfway point. Makyos do not occur when you are dawdling, neither do they appear when your practice has ripened. Such occurrences indi-

[16] Unwittingly the student chose a word which has several meanings in Japanese.

cate the intensity of your concentration. It is extremely important that you not separate yourself one hair's breadth from your koan. Don't become heedless even for a moment. Don't let a single thing disrupt your concentration. You must now directly realize Mu! Only "one more step!"

STUDENT: My mind is fully concentrated. I've been in deep samadhi. With my heart and soul I've been asking, "What is Mu?"—

ROSHI: Excellent!

STUDENT: But I have this difficulty. All of a sudden my heart begins to beat very fast. At other times my breath disappears from my nose and I feel it in the bottom of my stomach. I don't know whether this is something to worry about or not. Also, when I hear the chief monitor cracking everybody with the kyosaku, shouting at them to concentrate with every last bit of energy, and I hear them snorting and puffing, I don't know whether to continue in my own way, meditating quietly, or to strain and push like the others around me.

ROSHI: I can only repeat: you have reached a crucial point. When I was practicing at Hosshin-ji many years ago, I too reached the stage where my heart began to beat violently and I didn't know what to do. As you know, the kyosaku is used relentlessly at that monastery and everybody is continually urged to do his utmost. When I put the problem to Harada-roshi, he said nothing—nothing at all. This meant that I must feel my own way, for nobody could tell me what to do. If I continued, I felt I might faint. On the other hand, if I slackened my efforts, I knew I would fall back.

I will tell you this: If you sit quietly and mark time you will never come to Self-realization. For enlightenment you have to penetrate Mu with your last ounce of energy; your absorption must be complete and unfaltering. Deep in our subconsciousness the conception "me" and "other" is strong. We think: "I am here; what is not me is out there." This is an illusion; inherently there is no such dichotomy. You know all this theoretically of course, but this "I" is so powerfully imbedded that it can't be uprooted by reasoning. In single-minded concentration on Mu you are not aware of "I" standing against what is "not-I." If the absorption in Mu continues without interruption, the "I-ness" dies out in the subconscious mind. Suddenly "Plap!"—there is no more duality. To experience this directly is kensho.

Don't wobble now. You are at a crucial stage. Sit devotedly!

* * *

ROSHI: You still haven't seen into Mu, have you? . . .

STUDENT: I feel that the bell beside you, the tree out there, and I should be one, but somehow I can't directly realize this oneness. I feel as though I am bound in chains, in a prison from which I can't escape. I just can't break out of duality.

ROSHI: It is just such notions that are thwarting your realization of Mu. Get rid of them! Only through *unthinking* absorption in Mu can you achieve oneness.

Let me ask you a question. When you die does everything around you die too?

STUDENT: I don't know—I haven't had that experience yet.

ROSHI: When you die all things die with you, because you no longer are aware of them; they exist relative to you, don't they?

STUDENT: Yes, I suppose so.

ROSHI: Therefore when you disappear the entire universe disappears, and when the universe vanishes you vanish with it.

Remember, any stimulus can produce the sudden realization of Mu, provided your mind is empty and you are unaware of yourself. Five hours remain before the end of the sesshin. If you concentrate with all your mind you will surely attain enlightenment.

* * *

ROSHI: You look as though you have almost grasped Mu.

Watch this electric fan beside me. I turn it on[demonstrating]. The blades rotate. Where does the rotation come from? Now I shut off the fan. What has happened to the rotation? Isn't that Mu? When I ask students to show me Mu some seize my baton, others hold up a finger, still others embrace me, like this [embracing student].

STUDENT: I know all that, but if I did it, it would be premeditated, not spontaneous.

ROSHI: That is true of course. When you actually experience Mu you will be able to respond spontaneously. But you must stop reasoning and just engross yourself in Mu.

STUDENT: I understand that too, and I am trying to do it.

I had a taste of Mu the other day when I shouted at the monitor for striking me when there was a "Do not strike" sign above me.

ROSHI: That feeling of Mu was wonderful, wasn't it? At the moment you shouted at him there was no duality, no awareness of yourself or him—just the shout. But because that awareness was only partial, it disappeared. Had it been complete, it would have survived.

Don't lose your grip on Mu no matter what happens. Strive on!

*   *   *

STUDENT: I have no particular questions to ask. All I want to say is that I feel very dull today. My mind is fuzzy and I can't concentrate at all.

ROSHI: That's how it is with human beings. Sometimes our mind is sharp and clear, at other times dull and listless. The important thing is not to let this worry or hamper you. Just continue with your zazen resolutely.

*   *   *

ROSHI: Still you haven't come to realization—I wonder why . . .

I have repeatedly told you to abandon reasoning, to stop analyzing, to give up all intellection. Free your mind of notions, beliefs, assumptions. I hit you with my baton [striking student]. You cry, "Ouch!" That "Ouch!" is the whole universe. What more is there? Is Mu different from that? If this were fire and you touched it, you would also cry out and pull your hand away, wouldn't you? Most people *think* of fire as something that provides heat, or as a process that results from combustion, and so forth. But fire is just fire, and when you burn yourself by it and yell, "Ouch!" there is only "Ouch!"

STUDENT: What am I lacking? You are enlightened and I am not. What is the difference between your touching fire and mine?

ROSHI: No difference at all, absolutely none! A verse in the *Mumonkan* reads: "When the sun shines, its rays spread throughout the earth, / When there is rain the earth becomes wet." In this there is neither beauty nor ugliness, neither virtue nor evil, nothing absolute, nothing limited.

STUDENT: I want to see it that way, to accept all life that way, but I can't.

ROSHI: There is nothing to accept. All you need do is *just* see when you look, *just* hear when you listen. But the average man can't do that. He is constantly weaving ideas and embroidering notions about what he experiences. Yet when you touch a red-hot stove and cry, "Ouch!" the simple and obvious fact is "Ouch!" Is there any meaning beyond that?

STUDENT: I understand all this intellectually, but it doesn't help.

ROSHI: Take your understanding as just understanding. You must get rid of all ideas—

STUDENT [interrupting]: I had no ideas until I came here. I was just concentrating on Mu with all my might and not thinking of anything else.

ROSHI: Very well. When you return to your place, stop striving to achieve unity with Mu and profoundly question yourself, "Why can't I realize that when I hear there is nothing more than hearing? Why can't I realize that when I look there is nothing more than seeing?"

STUDENT: I know what I am *supposed* to do, but I can't do it.

ROSHI: There is nothing you are *supposed* to do, nothing you are *supposed* to understand. You have only to grasp the fact that when it rains the ground gets wet, that when the sun shines the world becomes bright. Take understanding as understanding, and as nothing else. If you think, "I *must not* understand" or "I *must* understand," you are adding another "head" to the one you already have.[17] Why can't you accept things as they are without projecting your own values or judgments onto them?

STUDENT: I suppose this is my trouble: subconsciously I am thinking: "I am one individual, you there are another."

ROSHI: But if you disabuse yourself of this fundamental error, in a flash kensho will come and you will exclaim, "Oh, I have it!"

* * *

ROSHI: What is this [tapping student on shoulder with baton]? [No response]

It is Mu—only Mu! When I clap my hands [clapping] it is just Mu. There is nothing you need "figure out" or speculate about. If you try to make even the smallest deduction or the barest analysis, you will never come to the realization of Mu.

STUDENT: I feel that I am pushing against myself all the time.

ROSHI: Cut out speculating about it! Just become completely one with Mu and you will positively come to Self-realization.

---

[17] That is, multiplying thought unnecessarily.

Actually there is no "myself" to push against. Mu is everything, Mu is Nothing. So long as you consciously or unconsciously believe that you are you and everything else is different from you, you will never penetrate Mu. You are close to kensho. Only one more step! Be alert! Don't separate yourself from Mu by so much as the thickness of a thin sheet of paper!

*   *   *

STUDENT: As a result of the explanation you gave me yesterday, I no longer associate "I" with my body or actions. But when I ask myself, "Who is it that knows all that?" I conclude that *I* am the knower. Am I back where I started?

ROSHI: The following is vital for you, so listen carefully.

Your mind, like a mirror, reflects everything: this table, this mat—whatever you see. If you don't perceive anything, the mirror reflects itself. Now, everybody's mind is different. How my mind reflects objects differs from the way yours does. Whatever is in your mind is the reflection of your mind, therefore it is you. So when you perceive this mat or this table you are perceiving yourself. Again, when your mind is devoid of all conceptions—opinions, ideas, points of views, values, notions, assumptions—your mind is reflecting itself. This is the condition of undifferentiation, of Mu.

Now, all this is merely a picture. What you have to do is directly grasp the truth yourself so that you are able to say, "Ah, of course!" This is awakening.

*   *   *

ROSHI: You still haven't taken hold of Mu—that is too bad.

STUDENT: I haven't, I am sorry to say.

ROSHI: Mu is nothing you can feel or taste or touch or smell. And if it has shape or form, it is not Mu. What you have in your mind is merely a picture of Mu. You must discard it—

STUDENT [interrupting]: I can assure you I have no pictures in my mind!

ROSHI: Mu is beyond meaning and no-meaning. It cannot be known either by the senses or by the discursive mind. Get rid of your false notions, and Awakening will abruptly come to you. But you must apply yourself more fervently. You must cling to Mu more tenaciously, like a hungry dog with its bone. Concentrate Mu! Mu! Mu! with all your heart.

*   *   *

ROSHI: I can tell from the way you walk in here that you are still not one with Mu. You are wobbling—your mind is distracted. If you were one with Mu, you would come before me with an unhurried yet firm gait, wholly absorbed, as though you were carrying the most precious treasure in the world.

STUDENT: Anyway, I am no longer in duality as I used to be. When I laugh I don't think *"I am laughing"* but *"just laughing."* The same when I feel pain, and the same with everything else.

ROSHI: That is all right, but if you want to realize your True-nature, you must not pause to indulge in self-congratulation. If you do, you will separate yourself from Mu and land in the very duality you are trying to escape from. For enlightenment all you need do is achieve total oneness with Mu, nothing more. You must empty your mind of all delusive notions and become like a sleep-walker carrying a fragile treasure that could be broken with one misstep. There must be no wobbling, not the slightest.

STUDENT: I feel I am not far from enlightenment, but somehow I can't summon up that last push.

ROSHI: The realization of your Self-nature can be compared to this [placing the palm of one hand over the palm of the other]. This top hand is like a large stone. It represents the average person's mind, a mind dominated by delusive thought. The bottom hand represents enlightenment. In reality these are merely two aspects of the One. Now, in order to turn over the top hand you must use tremendous force, for this mind is heavy with delusion. "Force" means unremitting concentration. If you merely "raise" this mind on top slightly and then let it "drop" again, you will never experience your True-nature. You have to overturn it in one fell swoop, like this [demonstrating with a fast, vigorous movement]! And lo and behold! there is the mind of enlightenment, vivid and spotless!

Don't relax—do your utmost!

* * *

ROSHI: You have something to say, haven't you?

STUDENT: Yes.

ROSHI: Go right ahead.

STUDENT: You told me to ask myself: "Why can't I just see when I am looking? Why can't I just hear when I am listening? Why can't I understand that when I get hit with your baton and cry,

'Ouch!' that 'Ouch!' is the whole universe?" My answer is that I see this baton, for example, as a baton in its limited aspect and as no more. I see this mat as just a mat. I hear a sound as a sound but as nothing else.

ROSHI: You are looking at things one-sidedly. Suppose I cover my head with my robe and raise my hands in the air. If you see only my hands, you are likely to think there are just two objects. But if I uncover myself, you see that I am also a person, not merely two hands. In the same way, you must realize that to view objects as separated entities is only half the truth.

Now let us go a step further. Consider this electric fan beside me. It is related to its stand, its stand to the table, the table to the floor, the floor to the room, the room to the house, the house to the ground, the ground to the sky, the sky to the universe. So this fan doesn't exist merely by itself, it is related to the whole universe, and when it moves the universe moves. Of course what I have just told you is not the expression of reality but only an explanation of it.

Again, take a circle with a nucleus. Without the nucleus there is no circle, without the circle, no nucleus. You are the nucleus, the circle is the universe. If you exist, the universe exists, and if you disappear, the universe likewise disappears.[18] Everything is related and interdependent. This box on the table has no independent existence. It exists in reference to my eyes, which see it differently from yours and differently again from the next person's. Accordingly, if I were blind, the box would cease to exist for me.

Let us take another example. Suppose you eat sugar while you are sick. It tastes bitter, so you say, "It is bitter," but someone else says, "It is sugar, it is sweet." For you the sugar is nonetheless bitter. The bitterness of the sugar, then, also is relative to your taste; its quality depends on you.

All existence is relative, yet each of us creates his own world; each perceives according to the state of his own mind.

STUDENT: I understand all that theoretically. I can appreciate that

[18] Compare: "Because I am, heaven overhangs and earth is upheld. Because I am, the sun and the moon go round. The four seasons come in succession, all things are born, because I am, that is, because of Mind." (Eisai-zenji in the *Kozen-Gokoku-Ron.*)

if the sun disappears, I disappear, but I can't conceive that I am the sun or the whole universe.

ROSHI: But you are. If when you die the universe dies with you, you and the universe are not separate and apart. Enlightenment is no more than the realization that the world of discrimination and the world of undifferentiation are not two. When you directly and positively experience this, you are enlightened.

STUDENT: What, then, is Mu? Is it the realization of the undifferentiated?

ROSHI: To realize the undifferentiated is a necessary first step, but the realization is incomplete if it goes no further. After you have seen into your True-nature—that is, become enlightened— you see all objects as temporary phenomena undergoing endless change, but you see them in and through the aspect of sameness. You then understand that without the undifferentiated there can be no individual existences.

I can illustrate what I am saying with this paper fan. One side has many stripes, as you see; the other is pure white. The white side can be called the undifferentiated, the side with the stripes, the discriminated. What makes the stripes appear as stripes is the white, or undifferentiated, side of the fan. Conversely, what makes the white side meaningful is the stripes. They are two aspects of the One. But while the discriminated aspect is subject to ceaseless transformation, that which is undifferentiated is changeless.

Since you are a philosophically minded person, hereafter don't try to become one with Mu, but simply dwell upon what I have just told you until suddenly you perceive your Self-nature. Is this clear? That will be your practice from now on.

4 / STUDENT D (WOMAN, AGE 40) /

STUDENT: I am doing shikan-taza.

ROSHI: I noticed you last night sitting with your hands clenched in your lap and straining hard. In shikan-taza it is unnecessary to strain.

STUDENT: Everybody around me was straining and pushing, so I thought I should too.

ROSHI: Most of them are novices working on their first koan. If they do not strain, whatever concentrative strength they develop dissipates itself quickly, so they must struggle constantly to maintain it. It is like learning to write the Chinese ideograms. At first you have to bear down with force as you painfully form the characters, but later, when you have learned how to make them, you can of course write effortlessly. You are experienced at zazen, so you need not strain yourself.

STUDENT: I must admit there are times when my concentration is strong without forcing myself. But for satori isn't it necessary to do zazen forcefully?

ROSHI: Shikan-taza is practiced in the faith that such zazen is itself the actualization of your pure Buddha-nature, so it is unnecessary to strive self-consciously for satori.[19] You must sit with a mind which is alert and at the same time unhurried and composed. This mind must be like a well-tuned piano string: taut but not overtight. Also remember that in a sesshin you are helped by everyone else through this communal sitting, so you need not strain yourself.

Last night I observed you laughing and crying. Did you experience anything unusual?

STUDENT: I was absolutely without will. I felt as though I had crushed everything, nothing remained, and I was joyous.

ROSHI: Tell me, have you ever had anxieties about death?

STUDENT: No, I have not.

ROSHI: People who are troubled by the thought of dying often have their anxieties relieved by an experience like yours.

Did your way of looking at things change at all?

STUDENT: No. After it was over I felt no different, I regret to say [smiling wanly].

ROSHI: Did the feeling of opposition, of yourself standing against the external world, disappear at all, even momentarily?

STUDENT: My feeling was only one of tremendous elation, because I felt that everything had been reduced to nothing.

ROSHI: After that did your former state of mind return?

STUDENT: Yes.

ROSHI: All right, just sit diligently without straining yourself.

---

[19] Compare: "Enlightenment and practice are one."—Dogen.

5 / STUDENT E (MAN, AGE 44) /

STUDENT: I am doing shikan-taza.

ROSHI: Is there anything you wish to say or ask?

STUDENT: Yes. When I was struck by a certain one of the monitors I had a most unfavorable reaction. I felt that, in a sadistic way, he really enjoyed striking me, so I couldn't raise my hands in gratitude to him as with the others. I therefore request that I not be struck by him any more during this sesshin. I don't mind being hit by the other monitors, since their strikings are stimulating and encouraging, but when this certain person hits me the effect is just the opposite.

ROSHI: When you are struck you should not think, "So-and-so has hit me in such-and-such a way," nor otherwise try to evaluate your reaction. Only raise your hands, palms together, in gratitude. There are many people who find it disagreeable to be hit and who cannot do good zazen if they are. When they request it, a sign is placed above their sitting place saying they are not to be struck. This can be done in your case if you wish.

STUDENT: I don't mind being struck by the others. To test my reaction, I signaled one of the other monitors to strike me. When he did I had no adverse reaction such as I had with this particular person. In fact, I found it easy to raise my hands palm to palm. But it was quite different with the other man.

ROSHI: Of course the monitors should take care to hit only the soft part of the shoulder, not the bone. This being summer, they should not hit too hard, because everyone is wearing light clothing. As a matter of fact, when we had new sticks made yesterday they were purposely made out of soft wood so that they would not hurt. But of course one can be struck too hard.

STUDENT: I don't know but that my reaction might not be a kind of makyo. Naturally I will do whatever you suggest, but I thought I ought to tell you about it.

ROSHI: The important thing is not to make a problem of it.

* * *

STUDENT: I am practicing as you have instructed me. I have no questions. I came because this is my last dokusan and I want to thank you for your kindness.

ROSHI: Even though you have no questions to ask, it is well to come to dokusan, for this reason: there is a tendency to become lax sitting by yourself. Coming before me tightens up your practice so that you can resume it with greater energy and detemination.

6 / STUDENT F (WOMAN, AGE 45) /

STUDENT: When I come here before you I get a tight feeling all over. I wonder what's wrong.

ROSHI: This is a matter of mind. Don't think or worry about yourself during zazen. Just practice with a calm, deeply concentrated mind, free from strain. Then your tightness will disappear and you will feel relaxed.

Are you able to do shikan-taza well?

STUDENT: No, not well at all.

ROSHI: In that case you should go back to the exercise of following the breath until you are able to do it well, after which you may return to shikan-taza.

STUDENT: I tried to, but it was too painful. I felt considerable pain in my chest when I did that. You see, for years I have had trouble with my breathing.

ROSHI: Resume counting the breath then. Can you do that easily?

STUDENT: Yes, I think so.

ROSHI: When you can concentrate on that exercise without pain or discomfort, try the exercise of following or experiencing the breath. After you have mastered that, return to shikan-taza.

STUDENT: Would you please tell me again how to count the breath and how to follow the breath?

ROSHI: There are various ways to count the breath, as I have previously explained, but the best way is this: On the first exhalation count silently to yourself "one," on the second exhalation, "two," and so on, up to ten. Then go back to one and again count up to ten. Whenever you lose track of the count, go back to one and start gain.

Following the breath is done this way: With the mind's eye you try to visualize the incoming breath, that is, to become one with it, and then you do the same with the exhaled breath. That is all there is to it.

* * *

STUDENT: Last night you told everybody: "When you go to bed continue to count your breath, those of you who are counting your breath, and thus the counting will go on in your subconscious mind." However, I find that I rather naturally forget the counting when my breathing is rhythmic, and when it is not rhythmic I have to count my breath in order to bring it into harmonious rhythm again. Should I continue the counting even when it is more natural for me to stop it?

ROSHI: Continue the counting when you go to bed and you will fall asleep naturally. But counting the breath is not a natural state of mind. It is only the first step toward concentrating the mind. The next step is following the breath, that is, trying to see each inhalation and each exhalation clearly. This is more difficult, because you don't have the counting itself to fall back on when your mind begins to wonder. The idea is to unify your mind through progressive steps of concentration until you reach the point where you can practice shikan-taza, which, as you know, involves neither counting the breath nor following it. It is the purest form of zazen, and the breathing is natural. But shikan-taza is also the most difficult zazen, since you have no crutches to lean on. When your practice has matured and your concentration is fairly strong, you can begin it.

If you carefully notice the pictures of the Buddha in the Nirvana posture, you will see that he is resting on his right side, with his hand under his head, the limbs of his body together. This is the best position in which to sleep. The point is, in going to bed you should not lie down with a sigh of relief, exclaiming: "Oh, I'm glad the day is over, now I can forget all about zazen." This is a wrong attitude.

To answer your question directly, you needn't continue the counting if you can concentrate your mind without it.

STUDENT: I am afraid I didn't make myself clear. What I mean is this: When my breathing becomes rhythmic I forget to count. Is it all right not to?

ROSHI: Yes. Similarly, experience your breath only as long as you need to. After that do pure zazen. This involves neither counting the breath nor following it but just breathing naturally.

7 / STUDENT G (MAN, AGE 25) /

STUDENT: What is the relation between zazen and the precepts? I would like to understand that better.

ROSHI: Regardless of the sect, Buddhist teaching and practice has three basic features. They are *kai*, or precepts; *jo*, or zazen; and *e*, or satori-wisdom. In the Bommo sutra the relation between the three is explained. The precepts are likened to the foundation of a house. If one lives improperly, thereby creating unrest and disturbance in himself and others, the foundation of his effort at spiritual realization is undermined. Zazen is the living space, the rooms. It is the place where one finds his repose. Satori-wisdom is comparable to the furnishings. The three are interrelated. In zazen one naturally observes the precepts, and through zazen comes to satori-wisdom. Thus all aspects of Buddhism are embraced within these three.

*   *   *

STUDENT: I was doing shikan-taza before I came here—at least I think it was that. Would you please tell me what shikan-taza is?

ROSHI: If you come to the next sesshin and hear all the general lectures, you will learn about shikan-taza in detail. I will tell you a little about it now.

Shikan-taza is the purest kind of zazen, the practice emphasized by the Soto sect of Zen. Counting the breath and following the breath are expedient devices. A person who can't walk well requires support and all these other methods are such supports. But eventually you must dispense with them and just walk. Shikan-taza is zazen in which your mind, intensely involved in just sitting, has nothing to lean on; therefore it is a very difficult practice. In counting or experiencing the breath with the mind's eye, you soon know it if you are not doing them properly, but in shikan-taza it is easy to become lax as you have no gauges by which to check yourself.

How you sit in shikan-taza is of vital importance. The back must be absolutely straight, the body taut but not tense. The center of gravity should be in the region just below the navel. If you can, sit with your legs crossed in the full- or half-lotus posture and you will have absolute stability and equilibrium as well as the dignity and grandeur of a Buddha.

*   *   *

STUDENT: How can one realize his Self-nature? I know so little about the subject.

ROSHI: First of all you must be convinced you can do so. The conviction creates determination, and the determination, zeal. But if you lack this conviction to start with, if you think, "*Maybe* I can get it, maybe I can't," or what is even worse, "This is beyond me," you won't awaken to your True-nature no matter how often you come to sesshin or how long you practice zazen.

*   *   *

STUDENT: What is the difference between koan zazen and shikan-taza?

ROSHI: Koan zazen has two aims: awakening and the actualization of it in your daily life. Koans are like candy used to coax a reluctant child. With shikan-taza, on the other hand, you must practice for five, ten or even more years alone, because you receive no such encouragement. In shikan-taza you sit with the conviction that your essential nature is no different from the Buddha's, so there is no *purposeful* striving for kensho. Still, you must believe that your sitting will one day eventuate in awakening.

In koan zazen, with enlightenment you realize that zazen, when correctly practiced, is the actualization of the Buddha-nature, and in this respect it ends where shikan-taza does—that is, when shikan-taza culminates in enlightenment.

Particularly in shikan-taza your concentration must be absolutely single-minded. Your mind, like that of a person aiming a gun, must be sharply focused, without a random thought intervening. The slightest deflection would be fatal.

STUDENT: Earlier you said that shikan-taza involves correct concentration and proper sitting posture. So does yoga. Is there is no difference, then?

ROSHI: I don't know much about yoga. I understand that the aim of yoga as it is generally practiced these days is the cultivation of physical and mental health or the attainment of a long life, and that there are various postures which will accomplish these ends. Higher forms of yoga no doubt involve enlightenment of one kind or another, but this enlightenment necessarily is different from Buddhist enlightenment. The difference essentially is in the aim. In shikan-taza you are not self-consciously striving for satori. Rather you are practicing zazen in the unswerving faith that your zazen is the actualization of your intrinsically undefiled Mind, and that one day you will directly perceive the nature of this Buddha-mind.

*   *   *

ROSHI: Are you able to count your breath well?

STUDENT: I can do it, but I don't know how well. What do you mean by "well"?

ROSHI: Doing it well means having a clear and distinct impression of each number as you count it. It also means not losing the count.

STUDENT: I can do it without losing count, but it is not always clear.

ROSHI: It is hard at first, since the tendency is to do it mechanically. You must absorb yourself completely in the counting. I know a man who teaches the abacus, which, as you know, is a calculating device. He is an expert at it, yet he finds it difficult to count his breath well. If you apply yourself with energy and devotion to this exercise, gradually you will be able to do it with ease.

*   *   *

STUDENT: I am counting my breath.

ROSHI: Are you able to count with clarity and precision?

STUDENT: No, I am not. I want to ask you whether I can count my breath and do shikan-taza at the same time.

ROSHI: No, you cannot. You can count your breath for half the period of your sitting and do shikan-taza the other half, but you can't do them simultaneously.

STUDENT: I have been trying to do just that—unsuccessfully, I might add. I also tried counting my breath only, but was unable to do even that.

ROSHI: You must not count absent-mindedly, as though in a daze. You must pour your whole heart into it. You must experience each number clearly and sharply. Did you lose count sometimes?

STUDENT: Yes, sir. Perhaps my trouble is that I don't see the connection between counting the breath and Buddhism.

ROSHI: The purpose in counting the breath is to still the ceaseless waves of thought set in motion by habits of thinking that have persisted for a long time. With their quieting, the mind becomes one-pointed and we can then directly perceive our Essential-nature. Counting the breath is a necessary first step. Another method is to keep questioning, "What is my True-nature?" or "Where is my True-nature?" But unless you have the firm conviction that you can discover your True-nature in this wise, your practice will degenerate into a mere mechanical repetition and your effort will be wasted.

You said you could not see the connection between counting the breath and Buddhism. The Buddha taught that only by direct apprehension of our Self-nature can we actually know who and what we are. The fundamental purity and clarity of the mind is obscured by the ceaseless waves of thought which pitch and toss about in it; consequently we falsely see ourselves as individual existences confronted by a universe of multiplicities. Zazen is a means of stilling these waves so that our inner vision can be brought into accurate focus, and counting the breath is one type of zazen.

* * *

STUDENT: You have said that I should put more energy into my sitting. I have tried to, but I can't concentrate for more than fifteen minutes before my mind begins to wander. Toward the end of the last sesshin I was able to concentrate fairly well, but when I sat by myself I fell apart and couldn't for the life of me concentrate.

ROSHI: It is difficult to sit alone, especially in the beginning; that is why we have sesshin. Communal zazen is easier because there is mutual support and reinforcement. When you practice zazen rather than listen to lectures about it, for the first time you really taste Zen and through this experience come to true Self-understanding. So sit devotedly. Your concentration will become stronger and you will feel better mentally and physically.

* * *

STUDENT: I would like to ask you once more about breathing. You have explained to me how I should count my breaths, but you haven't yet explained how I should follow them. Would you do so, please?

ROSHI: After you give up counting your breaths the next step is following them. Here you simply follow each inhalation with your mind's eye without allowing your attention to become diverted. When you exhale, do the same. That is all there is to it. "Follow" simply means to experience or become one with.

STUDENT: What about the stomach? Should it go in and out? I have heard that the stomach instead of moving up and down should move in and out.

ROSHI: Of course there are various breathing techniques. What you are describing is, I think, the way to breathe in certain types of yoga. It may be satisfactory, but it is not the kind of breathing advocated here.[20] Don't try to manipulate your breathing; just keep your mind in the region below the umbilicus. Your mind is at the spot where you put your attention. If you concentrate on your finger your mind is at your finger; if on your leg, at that place. With your mind concentrated below the navel your vital energy gradually becomes stabilized in that region.

Feel here [pointing to his lower abdomen].

[Student places his hand where the roshi has indicated.]

When I put pressure there it was hard, wasn't it?

STUDENT: It certainly was!

ROSHI: With your mind concentrated in that area over a long time, your energy easily and naturally settles there, because the center of gravity no longer is in the vicinity of the head and shoulders, and you can exert pressure in that region at will. Since we are anchored down as it were, we don't get angry and fly off the handle; our thoughts and emotions are under natural control.

STUDENT: I have another question. Is it so that in the Soto sect your walking is in harmony with your breathing?

ROSHI: Yes. With one complete inhalation and exhalation you move the left foot approximately half the length of the right, and with the next breath you move the right foot half the length of the left. The Rinzai way is to walk very fast.

STUDENT: But at these sesshin the method seems to be halfway between the Soto and the Rinzai.

ROSHI: That's right. Here we use the system of my teacher, Harada-roshi, who, having had extensive training in Rinzai and being himself from the Soto sect, combined the two.

*   *   *

ROSHI: Have you any questions?

STUDENT: All I can say is that I am confused.

ROSHI: What is your confusion?

STUDENT: I don't see the connection between counting the breaths and shikan-taza.

ROSHI: They are two different things, why look for a connection? Is your difficulty that you find counting your breaths too mechanical and uninteresting?

STUDENT: Yes, I suppose that's it.

[20] See p. 35.

ROSHI: There are many like you. Instead of counting your breaths or doing shikan-taza, it may be better for you to ponder a question like "What am I?" or "Where did I come from?" or "Buddhism teaches that we are all innately perfect; in what way am I perfect?" The technical Zen designation for such questions is *Honrai no Memmoku*, "What was my Face before my parents were born?"

STUDENT: Is that a koan?

ROSHI: Yes. Hereafter stop counting your breaths and devote yourself earnestly to this koan.

* * *

ROSHI: Have you any questions?

STUDENT: I have no questions, but I would like to tell you something. Last night I said to myself, "Fortunately I don't have to strive for enlightenment, because I am already enlightened."

ROSHI: While it is true that innately you are a Buddha, until you have concretely perceived your Buddha-nature you are speaking in borrowed phrases when you speak of enlightenment. The purpose of your practice is to lead you to this experience.

STUDENT: I would like to sit only with a feeling of genuine gratitude and not have to think about a koan.

ROSHI: Very well, try sitting in shikan-taza. If you do it sincerely, you will experience this feeling of gratitude. It is a fact that when you sit in the lotus posture as the Buddha sat and concentrate single-mindedly, a gradual unfoldment of your Buddha-heart takes place. This is the expression of living Buddhism, from which grows true gratitude. Moreover, even though you have no desire for enlightenment, through earnest and zealous sitting you will develop your powers of concentration and gain control over your mind and emotions, with the result that your physical and mental health will improve considerably.

* * *

STUDENT: Before I came to this temple I used to think: "If I go to a sesshin and do zazen, I will accumulate good karma." Now that I am here I don't see where I am acquiring any merit at all.

ROSHI: Whether you are aware of it or not, you are creating good karma all the time you are here. Sitting embraces the three fundamental elements of Buddhism, namely, the precepts, the power of concentration, and satori-wisdom. It is obvious, of course, how concentration is strengthened and mind stability developed;

it may be less obvious to you how your eye of true wisdom is gradually being opened as your intrinsically pure nature is cleansed of its delusions and defilements in sincere and wholehearted sitting. As for the precepts, clearly one can't kill or steal or lie during zazen. In a profounder sense, however, observance of the precepts is grounded in zazen, because through zazen you are gradually ridding yourself of the basic delusion which leads man to commit evil, namely, the delusion that the world and oneself are separate and distinct. Inherently there is no such bifurcation. The world doesn't stand outside me—it *is* me! This is the realization of your Buddha-nature, out of which observance of the precepts naturally and spontaneously arises. To be sure, when you have realized your Real-self, all this will make sense to you, but without that experience what I have just said is hard to understand.

STUDENT: I have no intention of trying to become enlightened!

ROSHI: That is all right too. To sit for the purpose of strengthening one's concentrative powers is also worth while.

STUDENT: I think I am better off not seeking enlightenment.

ROSHI: Zazen is the expression of living Buddhism. Since you are innately a Buddha, your sitting, if it is ardent and single-minded, is the actualization of your Buddha-nature. That is true, to be sure.

STUDENT: I guess we can't disagree on anything, can we [laughing]?

ROSHI: Now go back to your place and apply yourself more seriously.

* * *

STUDENT: Can you tell me what is most essential in shikan-taza?

ROSHI: The quality of your sitting is of vital importance. The back must be straight and the mind taut—ever watchful. A sagging body creates a sagging mind, and vice versa. The mind must be thoroughly alert, yet not tense. If you look at the picture of Bodhidharma painted by Sesshu and carefully study the eyes, you will see what I mean. Bodhidharma is doing shikan-taza. This is the degree of alertness required: If you were sitting in one corner of a room doing shikan-taza and a door on the other side was quietly opened half an inch, you would know it instantly.

* * *

STUDENT: This will be my last sesshin, as I have to return to the United States next month. Will it be all right to train under a Soto priest there?

ROSHI: Yes, but I would advise you not to be guided by him with respect to satori unless you are sure he is enlightened himself. Very few Soto priests these days have realized their True-nature and therefore they pooh-pooh the experience, saying in effect: "Since in possessing the Buddha-mind we are all inherently enlightened, why is satori necessary?" But this argument is specious, because until they have directly perceived their Buddha-mind they don't really know that they possess it.

STUDENT: Then, is it possible for me to carry on my practice without a teacher?

ROSHI: Whether you have no teacher in America or only a mediocre one, you can continue to discipline yourself in Zen by following what you have learned at this temple. Any teacher, even an unenlightened one, is able to supervise your practice. He can check your posture, for instance, and your breathing, and can guide you in other respects. But he ought not try to pass on satori unless he himself has had it and it has been verified by his teacher.

STUDENT: Oh yes, that reminds me of something I wanted to ask you. This morning in your lecture you spoke about the necessity of having one's enlightenment confirmed by one's teacher because only in this way could correct Zen be transmitted. I don't quite understand this. Why is it necessary to be authenticated by anyone?

ROSHI: Starting from the time of the Buddha Shakyamuni, correct Buddhism has been transmitted from master to disciple. Where the master's enlightenment has been authentic and sanctioned by *his* master, he has been able to sanction the enlightenment of his disciples by using his own experience of enlightenment as a guide.

You ask why this is necessary. It is necessary, first of all, in order to insure the transmission of true Buddhism from master to disciple. If this hadn't been done, there would be no authentic Zen today. But the truth is, you can never be sure by yourself that what you take to be kensho actually is kensho. With a first experience it is quite possible to misjudge it.

STUDENT: But isn't enlightenment self-authenticating?

ROSHI: No, it isn't. In fact, there are many examples of persons who became teachers without having enlightenment at all. It is like a person searching alone for diamonds in the mountains. If he has never seen a real diamond, he may think when he finds glass or quartz or some other mineral that he has found a genuine diamond. If he could verify his find through somebody who has had experience with diamonds, he could be sure. Failing that, he could easily make a mistake regardless of how brightly his stones glittered.

STUDENT: This business of the transmission from the Buddha down to the present time—it isn't really true, is it? It's myth, isn't it?

ROSHI: No, it is true, If you don't believe it, that's too bad.

8 / STUDENT H (WOMAN, AGE 37) /

STUDENT: I am pregnant and probably won't be able to attend any more sesshin until after the birth of my child a couple of months away. How should I continue to do zazen in my own home during the rest of my pregnancy?

ROSHI: Continue to concentrate on your present koan. When a solution comes to you, put it on the shelf, so to speak, as you did with the other koans, and go back to shikan-taza until you come before me again, at which time you can demonstrate your understanding of the spirit of the koan.

Sit comfortably at all times, with your mind profoundly absorbed yet flexible, and without strain in the region of the stomach. The last is important. It is well known in Japan that zazen has an exceedingly beneficial effect on the mind and spirit of the foetus. It is even better if you place a picture of Kannon before you when you start zazen. Thus the virtues of this Bodhisattva which you are reflecting upon will impress themselves upon the mind of your unborn baby.

*   *   *

STUDENT: My koan is "From where you are, stop the distant boat moving across the water."

ROSHI: Demonstrate your understanding of the spirit of it.

[The student demonstrates.]

That is good, but try it this way [demonstrating].

Do you understand the true spirit of this?

STUDENT: Yes, the boat and I are not two.

ROSHI: That is right. When you become one with the boat it

ceases to be a problem for you. The same is true of your daily life. If you don't separate yourself from the circumstances of your life, you live without anxiety. In summer you adapt yourself to heat, in winter to cold. If you are rich, you live the life of a rich man; if you are poor, you live with your poverty. Were you to go to heaven, you would be an angel; were you to fall into hell, you would become a devil. In Japan you live like a Japanese, in Canada like a Canadian. Lived this way, life isn't a problem. Animals have this adaptability to a high degree. Human beings also have it, but because they imagine they are this or that, because they fashion notions and ideas of what they *ought* to be or how they *ought* to live, they are constantly at war with their environment and themselves.

The purpose of this koan, then, is to teach you how to be at one with every aspect of your life.

9 / STUDENT I (MAN, AGE 30) /

ROSHI: This is your first sesshin, isn't it?

STUDENT: Yes.

ROSHI: Tell me why you want to practice zazen.

STUDENT: I want to know the meaning of human existence, why we are born and why we die.

ROSHI: That is an excellent motivation. There are various ways to resolve this problem. Before I go into them, however, let me explain what kensho is. It is seeing into your True-nature and directly realizing that you and the universe are basically One. Once you have perceived this, you will know down to your bowels the meaning of human existence and thereby acquire the peaceful mind that arises from such a revolutionary insight.

The road to such knowledge is through zazen. As you know, there are many ways to practice. You have been counting your breath, following your breath, and doing shikan-taza. It is possible to come to awakening through these exercises alone, but the quickest way is through a koan.

In ancient days there was no koan system, yet many people came to Self-realization. But it was hard and took a long time. The use of koans started about a thousand years ago and has continued down to the present. One of the best koans, because the simplest, is Mu. This is its background: A monk came to Joshu, a renowned Zen master in China hundreds of years ago, and asked: "Has a dog Buddha-nature or not?" Joshu retorted, "Mu!" Literally, the expression means "no" or "nothing," but the significance of Joshu's answer does not lie in the word. Mu is the expression of the living, functioning, dynamic Buddha-nature. What you must do is discover the spirit or essence of this Mu, not through intellectual analysis but by search into your innermost being. Then you must demonstrate before me, concretely and vividly, that you understand Mu as living truth, without recourse to conceptions, theories, or abstract explanations. Remember, you can't understand Mu through ordinary cognition; you must grasp it directly with your whole being.

This is how to practice: If possible, sit with your legs in the full- or half-lotus posture. If you can sit neither full- nor half-lotus, sit with your legs crossed in the most comfortable way. If even crossing your legs is impossible, use a chair. Your back must be straight. After taking several deep breaths and slowly exhaling, swing the body from side to side, first in large arcs and then in smaller ones, until the body comes to rest at center. Then breathe naturally. You are now ready to begin zazen.

First repeat the word "Mu," not audibly but in your mind. Concentrate on becoming one with it. Do not think of its meaning. I repeat: just concentrate wholeheartedly on becoming one with Mu. At first your efforts will be mechanical, but this is unavoidable. Gradually, however, all of you will become involved.

Since the human mind is accustomed from childhood to functioning centrifically, like the rays of a light bulb which fan outward, your aim at first is to bring your mind to a focus. After you are able to concentrate on Mu, then question yourself: *"What* is Mu?[21] *What* can it be?" You must ask the question right from the guts! When the questioning reaches the point of gripping you like a vise so that you can think of nothing else, suddenly you will perceive your True-nature and will exclaim: "Oh, now I know!" With true enlightenment the problem of suffering and death is resolved.

*   *   *

[21] See also p. 153.

ROSHI: Do you have anything you wish to say?

STUDENT: Yes. When the bell rang for everybody to get up and walk around, an old woman began to sob. I don't know why he did it, but the monitor began cracking her with the kyosaku. At that point I suddenly began thinking of the meaning of life and why human beings suffer. Without realizing it, I began to cry too, and then the tears just gushed forth. I haven't cried that way since I was a child of seven. What does this mean?

ROSHI: Many changes take place in your body-mind when you do zazen with zeal and devotion. Your emotions become more sensitive, your thinking sharper and clearer, your will stronger. Above all, you experience a feeling of gratitude. Because your emotions have already become more sensitive and responsive, when you heard this woman crying you began to cry yourself. She probably didn't know why she was crying either. She was struck at that time to encourage her to put forth her best effort.

What happened shows me that you are doing zazen with zeal and sincerity.

10 / STUDENT J (WOMAN, AGE 33) /

STUDENT: My last teacher assigned me the koan Mu two years ago. I've been practicing it, but frankly, I don't know what I'm doing. I just seem to be repeating it mechanically. I was told to become one with it and in that way I would get kensho, but I am not even sure I know what kensho is. Before I came to this temple I had difficulty both in making myself understood and in understanding what was said to me, as there was never adequate interpretation available. I suppose that is why I am so badly informed.

ROSHI: It is useless to repeat Mu mechanically.

Kensho is the direct awareness that you are more than this puny body or limited mind. Stated negatively, it is the realization that the universe is not external to you. Positively, it is experiencing the universe as yourself. So long as you consciously or unconsciously think in terms of a distinction between yourself and others, you are caught in the dualism of I and not-I. This I is not indigenous to our True-nature, being merely an illusion produced by the six senses. But because this illusory ego-I has been treated as a real entity throughout this existence and previous ones, it has come to occupy the deepest level of the subconscious mind. Your single-hearted concentration on Mu will gradually dispel this I-concept from your consciousness. With its complete banishment you suddenly experience Oneness. This is kensho.

The traditional Rinzai way of handling this koan is to let you struggle with it willy-nilly. You repeatedly ask yourself: "What is Mu? What can it be?" The first answer that comes to your mind you bring before the roshi, who promptly brushes it aside. "No, that's not Mu! Search further!" he commands. Next time you present what amounts to virtually the same answer. Now the roshi may scold: "I told you that is not Mu. Bring me Mu!" You try again and again, but every solution you can conceive or imagine the roshi rejects. Such encounters usually last only a minute or two. Eventually, after months or years of exhaustive reasoning, your mind reaches the point where it is emptied of all thought-forms and you come to the sudden realization of Mu.

With students thirsting for truth this method was effective. But nowadays students have less ardor as well as less stick-to-it-iveness. What is even worse, incompetent teachers pass students who have not truly experienced the spirit of the koan, in order to encourage them to stay on. My own teacher, Harada-roshi, who had studied and practiced Rinzai Zen for many years, sought, out of the greatest kindness, to eliminate this anguished struggle of past days by telling his students in advance that any conception of Mu, no matter how subtle or ingenious, is unavailing and that therefore they must bend every effort to becoming one with Mu. But the danger here is of lapsing into a mechanical repetition of it. Quite apart from all this, however, there are people for whom the koan Mu is distasteful. Regardless of how hard they try to embrace it, it never grips them. You may be such a person.

STUDENT: I find it completely distasteful.

ROSHI: In that case it is better to change your koan. I might assign you *Sekishu*, "What is the sound of one hand?" or *Honrai no Memmoku*, "What was my Face before my parents' birth? or just "What am I?" or "Who am I?" whichever would be most absorbing for you.

STUDENT: The last would be the most meaningful.

ROSHI: Very well. Henceforth this will be your koan.

STUDENT: Do I treat it the same as Mu?

ROSHI: Yes, but you must not ask the question mechanically, like a stamping machine. When eating, ask yourself, *"What* is eating?"* with an intense yearning to resolve the question. When listening, inquire of yourself, *"Who* is listening?"* When seeing, *"Who* is seeing?"* While walking, *"Who* is walking?"*

* * *

[Hereafter the statement "My koan is 'Who am I?' " at the opening of each dokusan of this student will be omitted.]

ROSHI: Do you have any questions?

STUDENT: Yes. When I question myself, "Who am I?" I say to myself, "I am bones, I am blood, I am skin." Where do I go from there?

ROSHI: Then ask yourself, "What is it that has this blood? What is it that has these bones? What is it that has this skin?"

STUDENT: It seems to me that I have to do two things: to become one with eating, for instance, as well as to ask myself, "Who is eating?" Is that right?

ROSHI: No, only question yourself as to who is eating. Your mind must become one mass of profound questioning. This is the quickest way to the realization of your True-nature. Asking, "Who am I?" is really no different from asking, "What is Mu?"

STUDENT: To be honest, I have no burning desire for kensho. I wonder why. This bothers me.

ROSHI: People who have been compelled to face painful life situations, such as the death of a beloved one, for example, are frequently precipitated into asking the most searching questions about life and death. This questioning gives rise to an acute thirst for Self-understanding so that they can alleviate their own as well as mankind's sufferings. With true enlightenment, disquiet and anxiety are replaced by inner joy and serenity. Listening to the Buddha's teachings in my lectures, you will develop within you a longing for Self-realization, which will grow deeper and deeper.

* * *

STUDENT: Last night during zazen I was often troubled by the thought that my desire for enlightenment is weak. Why, I kept asking myself, do I not strive more intensely like so many around me? At one o'clock this morning I was ready to quit, though only four hours earlier I had determined to sit up in zazen all night. In the kitchen, where I went for a drink, I saw the old cook-nun washing clothes. Watching her, I felt ashamed of my own feeble efforts.

The other day you told me that those who have the strongest desire for enlightenment are people who have suffered in life. You said that they keenly wish kensho so as to relieve their own suffering as well as the suffering of others. The fact is that in my teens I experienced considerable suffering. Perhaps that is why I felt so compassionate toward others and why my friends and acquaintances often came to me for advice and help.

Some years later when I heard about Zen I began to practice it, after a fashion, in the United States. Then a few years ago I came to Japan, having given up my work in America, and began the traditional practice of Zen. The sympathy and compassion I had always felt toward people before I undertook zazen have dried up in me. I have experienced so much pain in Zen that I no longer think of saving anybody but myself. I hate having to suffer! So my life in Zen, far from making me sensitive to the sufferings of others and kindling in me a desire to save them, has destroyed whatever altruistic feelings I possessed, leaving me cold and selfish.

ROSHI: As I observe your face and manner, I see neither insensitivity nor selfishness—on the contrary, I see much that is Kannon-like. I am sure that most people who come in contact with you sense your natural warmth and feel well-disposed toward you. What you have described to me, rather than making you out to be cold-hearted and selfish, reveals a deepening of your natural sympathies, but all this lies outside your consciousness. One who thinks of himself as kindhearted and sympathetic is truly neither.[22] That you no longer are consciously aware of these emotions only shows how deeply entrenched they have become.

There are many people who spend all their time giving aid to the needy and joining movements for the betterment of society. To be sure, this ought not to be discounted. But their root anxiety, growing out of their false view of themselves and the universe,

---

[22] Compare with Lao-tzu's "The truly virtuous is not conscious of his virtue. The man of inferior virtue, however, is ever consciously concerned with his virtue and therefore he is without true virtue. True virtue is spontaneous and lays no claim to virtue." (From the *Tao Teh Ching*, quoted by Lama Govinda in his *Foundations of Tibetan Mysticism*, p. 235.)

goes unrelieved, gnawing at their hearts and robbing them of a rich, joyous life. Those who sponsor and engage in such social betterment activities look upon themselves, consciously or unconsciously, as morally superior and so never bother to purge their minds of greed, anger, and delusive thinking. But the time comes when, having grown exhausted from all their restless activity, they can no longer conceal from themselves their basic anxieties about life and death. Then they seriously begin to question why life hasn't more meaning and zest. Now for the first time they wonder whether instead of trying to save others they ought not to save themselves first.

I assure you that you have not made a mistake in deciding to tread this path, and one day it will become clear to you. It is not selfishness to forget about saving others and to concentrate only on developing your own spiritual strength, though it may seem to be. The solemn truth is that you can't begin to save anybody until you yourself have become whole through the experience of Self-realization. When you have seen into the nature of your True-self and the universe, your words will carry conviction and people will listen to you.

STUDENT: But I become tired and discouraged so easily—the Way is terribly long and hard.

ROSHI: The Buddha's Way calls for energetic devotion and perseverance. When you stop to consider, however, that philosophers have been struggling for two or three thousand years to resolve the problem of human existence, without success, but that through asking, "Who am I?" you can succeed where they have failed, have you cause to be discouraged? What activity or work in life is more urgent or compelling than this? By comparison everything else fades into insignificance.

STUDENT: I feel that way too; that's why I came to Japan to train in Zen.

ROSHI: You are different from most here. They come for a sesshin because they hear Zen is remarkable and they want to grab it as quickly as they can and go about their business; therefore they strain themselves. They attack zazen with the fury of a sudden storm where the rain comes down in torrents and is swiftly carried away. But you, having made tremendous sacrifices for the sake of entering upon the Way of the Buddha, need not torture yourself.

Your practice ought to be like rain gently dropping from the sky and seeping deep into the earth. With this state of mind you can sit patiently for four or five years, or even more, until you realize Truth in its fullness.

STUDENT: Is it because philosophers ask, "Why?" and "How?" that they have been unable to resolve the problem of human existence?

ROSHI: Their investigations take them away from themselves into the realm of diversity—this is how philosophers and scientists work—whereas the question "Who am I?" precipitates you into an awareness of your fundamental solidarity with the universe.

STUDENT: I am ready to do whatever you say.

ROSHI: I feel that your training up to now has not been entirely suited to your temperament. However, you must not think that the time you have spent in Zen has been wasted; it has been valuable in more ways than you are aware. I also feel that, for the time being at least, you ought not to be struck with the kyosaku.

STUDENT: I can't tell you how nervous it has made me. In the last place I was doing zazen I spent ninety-five percent of the time fighting my reaction to it.

ROSHI: Had it been possible for you to communicate with your last teacher the way you and I are now able to, thanks to this interpretation, a different practice might well have been assigned you. In any case, hereafter question yourself, "Who am I?" with sharp yet unruffled penetration.

*   *   *

ROSHI: Have you anything to say?

STUDENT: Yes. A few days after the last sesshin I suddenly realized in a new way that seeking excitement and pleasure and trying to avoid pain, which has been the story of my life, was senseless, since it was always followed by an aching hollowness. Now even though this insight had come to me with great force, along with an exhilaration which persisted throughout the day, within a week the old feeling of the flatness and meaninglessness of life, together with a craving for excitement, returned. Is this natural or unnatural—?

ROSHI: To wish for a fuller, happier life than your present one is natural and commendable. What is not commendable is to despise your present state while yearning for a more exalted one.

In giving yourself over wholly to whatever you are doing at the moment, you can achieve a deeper and richer state of mind— Am I answering your question?

STUDENT: I haven't come to the crux of it yet. When I feel this way I want to get away from myself, to run off to a movie or to stuff myself with loads of rich food. My question is, should I indulge these desires or fight to repress them and continue with my zazen?

ROSHI: Your question is a vital one. It is unwise either to repress your feelings severely or to indulge them wildly. There are people who, when they feel as you do, either get riotously drunk or eat themselves sick. Of course you are not that kind of person. The point is, it is all right to go to a movie occasionally if you go to one you enjoy and not to just any movie. Likewise, when you have an irresistible urge to treat yourself to a feast, eat food that you not only enjoy but that is nourishing as well, and don't overeat so that you are sick the next day. If you exercise moderation and judgment, you won't feel remorseful afterwards, reproaching yourself for having foolishly wasted valuable time which you could have utilized more profitably in zazen. You will be taken out of your doldrums and given a lift, and will be able to resume your practice with greater zest. But if you have feelings of self-disgust, they will give rise to a host of thoughts which will interfere with your practice. As your zazen deepens, however, all this will cease to be a problem to you.

* * *

STUDENT: If I understood you correctly, at one time you told me to keep my mind in my palm, another time to focus it in the region below the navel, and again, when I become sleepy, to place it between my eyes. I am confused. I don't even know what my mind is, so how can I put it in any of these places?

ROSHI: When I told you to put your mind in the palm of your hand, what I meant was to focus your *attention* at that point. You must not constantly change the focal point of your concentration. Both Dogen and Hakuin recommend focusing the mind in the palm of the hand. If you want to increase the intensity of your zazen, you can do so by directing your attention to your hara. A good way to overcome sleepiness is to concentrate your attention between your eyes.

STUDENT: But what is mind, anyway? I mean, I know what it is theoretically, because I have read many of the sutras and other books on Buddhism. But can I really find out what mind is by asking "Who am I?"

ROSHI: A theoretical understanding of mind is not enough to resolve the question "Who am I?" and through it the problem of birth-and-death. Such understanding is merely a portrait of reality, not reality itself. If you persistently question yourself, "Who am I?" with devotion and zeal—that is to say, moved by a genuine desire for Self-knowledge—you are bound to realize the nature of Mind.

Now mind is more than your body and more than what is ordinarily called mind. The inner realization of mind is the realization that you and the universe are not two. This awareness must come to you with such overwhelming certainty that you involuntarily slap your thigh and exclaim: "Oh, of course!"

STUDENT: But I don't know who it is that is asking, "Who am I?" and not knowing this—or who it is that is being asked—how can I find out who I am?

ROSHI: The one asking the question is You and You must answer. The truth is, they are not two. The answer can only come out of persistent questioning with an intense yearning to know. Up to the present you have been wandering aimlessly, uncertain of your destination, but now that you have been given a map and have your bearings, don't stop to admire the sights—march on!

*   *   *

STUDENT: You have said that we are all inherently perfect—without a flaw. I can believe that in our mother's womb we are, but after birth we are anything but perfect. The sutras say that we are all beset by greed, anger, and folly. I believe that, because it is certainly true of myself.

ROSHI: A blind man, even while blind, is fundamentally whole and perfect. The same is true of a deaf-mute. If a deaf-mute suddenly regained his hearing, his perfection would no longer be that of a deaf-mute. Were this saucer on the table to be broken, each segment would be wholeness itself. What is visible to the eye is merely the form, which is ever-changing, not the substance. Actually the word "perfect" is superfluous. Things are neither perfect nor imperfect, they are what they are. Everything has absolute worth, hence nothing can be compared with anything else. A tall man is tall, a short man is short, that is all you can say. There is a koan where in reply to the question "What is the Buddha?" the master answers: "The tall bamboo is tall, the short bamboo is short." Kensho is nothing more than directly perceiving all this in a flash.

* * *

STUDENT: I am still having trouble putting my mind in the palm of my hand.

ROSHI: What is the matter?

STUDENT: It is a strain for me to focus my attention there while exhaling; my concentration becomes disrupted.

ROSHI: You must not strain yourself. Instead of trying to put your mind somewhere, simply concentrate on the question "Who am I?"

STUDENT: When I prostrate myself before you or before the image of the Buddha, or when I am chanting the sutras or walking, I have no inclination to ask myself, "Who am I?" Is it all right not to at these times?

ROSHI: You must ask the question at all times. While walking you must question, "Who is walking?" When prostrating yourself you must question, "Who is prostrating?"

STUDENT: Or else "Who am I?"

ROSHI: Yes. It amounts to the same thing.

* * *

STUDENT: In addressing everybody last night you said that when we went to bed we should not separate ourselves from our koan but continue the questioning even during sleep. I find that I forget my koan quickly when I am sleeping because I dream a lot. The dream world seems to be another world from that of "Who am I?" Dreaming is such a waste of time and energy. How can I avoid it?

ROSHI: Generally, active people who have little time for sleep dream only occasionally, whereas those who sleep long hours have many dreams. Also, those who have much time on their hands tend to dream a great deal, as do those who sleep on their back. One way to stop yourself from dreaming, of course, is to sleep less, but if you don't get enough rest, you are likely to nap during zazen. You will notice in pictures of the reclining Buddha that he is resting on his right side. For many reasons this is a good position for sleeping.

STUDENT: In my work—either doing laundry or cleaning up—I often find myself daydreaming. What can I do about that?

ROSHI: While cleaning continue to question, "Who am I?" No other thoughts will enter your mind if the questioning is sufficiently intense. It is only because you separate yourself from your koan that daydreams occur.

* * *

ROSHI: Is there anything you wish to say or ask?

STUDENT: From five this morning up to now [3 P.M.] I have been steadily asking myself, "Who am I?" Sometimes the question has absorbed me, but most of the time I have been just plain bored. Why do I get bored?

ROSHI: Probably because you are not yet convinced that through such questioning you can perceive your True-nature and thus attain lasting peace of mind. When those who have experienced a great deal of pain in life hear the truth of Buddhism and begin to practice zazen, they usually want to get kensho quickly in order to relieve their own sufferings as well as those of others.

STUDENT: Part of the reason I find it so hard to concentrate is that the new monitor we have is roaring at us all and clouting everyone so hard.

ROSHI: You need only ask yourself, "*Who* is listening to all this shouting?" Don't make a problem of it, it is no concern of yours.

STUDENT: It is impossible for me to be indifferent to it. On either side of me the sitters are being struck so hard that I shudder every time I hear the kyosaku. I tried to ask myself, "*Who* is listening to all this horrible shouting?" but I was so upset I couldn't continue.

ROSHI: These people around you are close to kensho, that is why they are being struck so hard—to spur them on to a last desperate effort. If you don't want to be hit because it interferes with your zazen, I can have a "Do not strike" sign placed over you.

STUDENT: Yesterday when Mr. K_____ struck me it was helpful, as he knows how and when to strike, but this man hits without rhyme or reason and his shouting is so frightening it makes me sick in my stomach.

ROSHI: Of course some of the wielders of the kyosaku are more capable than others. Mr. K_____, having had long experience, is quite accomplished. Do you wish a sign placed over you?

STUDENT: The funny thing is that half of me wants to be hit, because I think I'll get kensho quicker that way, and half of me dreads it. If Mr. K_____ returns, I would like him to strike me occasionally.

ROSHI: We can have a sign put over your place, and when you wish to be struck you can signal with your hands raised over your head, palms together. But don't concern yourself with what happens around you, only concentrate on your own problems.

From now on you can reduce "Who am I?" to "Who?" since the whole question has sunk into your subconscious.

* * *

ROSHI [sharply]: Who are you? [No answer.] Who are you!

STUDENT [pausing]: I don't know.

ROSHI: Good! Do you know what you mean by "I don't know"?

STUDENT: No, I don't.

ROSHI: You are You! You are *only* You—that is all.

STUDENT: What did you mean by "Good!" when I answered, "I don't know"?

ROSHI: In the profoundest sense, we can know nothing.

STUDENT: Yesterday when you told me you were going to ask me who I am, I concluded that I must have some answer prepared, so I thought of various responses, but just now when you asked, "Who are you?" I couldn't think of a single thing.

ROSHI: Excellent! It shows your mind is emptied of all ideas. Now you can respond with your whole being, not with just your head. When I said I would ask you who you are, I didn't want you to reason out an answer but only to penetrate deeper and deeper into yourself with "Who am I?" When you come to the sudden inner realization of your True-nature, you will be able to respond instantly without reflection.

What is this [suddenly striking tatami mat with baton]?

[No answer]

Probe further! Your mind is almost ripe.

* * *

STUDENT: I have been asking and asking, "Who am I?" until I feel there is just no answer to this question.

ROSHI: You won't find an entity called "I."

STUDENT [heatedly]: Then why am I asking the question!

ROSHI: Because in your present state you can't help yourself. The ordinary person is forever asking, "Why?" or "What?" or

"Who?" There are many koans in which a monk asks, "What is Buddha?" or "Why did Bodhidharma come from India to China?" The aim of the master's response is to break open the monk's deluded mind so that he can realize his question is an abstraction.

STUDENT: I have been reading the English translation of the Bassui letters[23] during your morning lecture, as you suggested I do. At one point Bassui says: "*Who* is the Master that moves the hands?"

ROSHI: There is no real answer to "Who?" "What?" or "Why?" Why is sugar sweet? Sugar is sugar. Sugar!

STUDENT: You told me earlier, "You are You!" All right, I am I—I accept that. Isn't this enough? What more need I do? Why must I keep struggling with this question?

ROSHI: Because this understanding is external to you—you don't really know what you mean by "I am I." You must come up against this question with the force of a bomb, and all your intellectual notions and ideas must be annihilated. The only way to resolve this question is to come to the explosive inner realization that everything is [ultimately reducible to] Nothing. If your understanding is merely theoretical, you will forever ask, "Who?" "What?" and "Why?"

*   *   *

STUDENT: In questioning, "Who am I?" I have come to the conclusion that I am this body, that is, these eyes, these legs, and so forth. At the same time I realize that these organs do not exist independently. If I were to take out my eye and place it in front of me, for example, it could not function as an eye. Neither could my leg function as a leg if it were separated from my body. For walking, my legs need not only my body but also the ground, just as my eyes need objects to perceive in order to perform the act of seeing. Furthermore, what my eyes see and what my legs walk on are part of the universe. Therefore I am the universe. Is this correct?

ROSHI: You are the universe all right, but what you have just given me is an abstraction, a mere reconstruction of reality, not reality itself. You must directly grasp reality.

STUDENT: But *how* do I do that?

ROSHI: Simply by questioning, "Who am I?" until abruptly you

[23] See p. 172 ff.

perceive your True-nature with clarity and certainty. Remember, you are neither your body nor your mind. And you are not your mind added to your body. Then what are you? If you would grasp the real You and not merely a figment, you must constantly ask yourself, "Who am I?" with absolute devotion.

*   *   *

STUDENT: Last time you said I was not my mind and not my body. I don't understand. If I am neither of these nor a combination of them, what am I?

ROSHI: Were you to ask the average person what he is, he would say, "My mind" or "My body" or "My mind and body," but none of this is so. We are more than our mind or our body or both. Our True-nature is beyond all categories. Whatever you can conceive or imagine is but a fragment of yourself, hence the real You cannot be found through logical deduction or intellectual analysis or endless imagining.

If I were to cut off my hand or my leg, the real I would not be decreased one whit. Strictly speaking, this body and mind are also you but only a fraction. The essence of your True-nature is no different from that of this stick in front of me or this table or this clock—in fact every single object in the universe. When you directly experience the truth of this, it will be so convincing that you will exclaim, "How true!" because not only your brain but all your being will participate in this knowledge.

STUDENT [suddenly crying]: But I am afraid! I am afraid! I don't know why, but I am afraid!

ROSHI: There is nothing to fear. Just deepen and deepen the questioning until all your preconceived notions of who and what you are vanish, and at once you will realize that the entire universe is no different from yourself. You are at a crucial stage. Don't retreat—march on!

*   *   *

STUDENT: You said earlier that I am not my body and not my mind. I have always thought of myself as a mind and a body. It frightens me to think differently.

ROSHI: It is true that the majority of people think of themselves as a body and a mind, but that doesn't make them any the less mistaken. The fact is that in their essential nature all sentient beings transcend their body and their mind, which are not two but one.

The failure of human beings to perceive this fundamental truth is the cause of their sufferings.

As I said in my lecture this morning, man is forever seeking and grasping. Why? He grasps for the world because intuitively he longs to be rejoined with that from which he has been estranged through delusion. It is in consequence of this alienation that we find the strong overcoming the weak and the weak accepting enslavement as an alternative to death. Yet when undeluded, human beings naturally gravitate toward one another. Those with strong natures want to cherish and protect the weak, while the latter long to be cherished by them. So we have the Buddha, who is spiritually powerful, embracing us who are weak, and we bow down before him in grateful acceptance of his overwhelming compassion. Like a mother caressing her infant, here there is no separateness, only harmony and oneness. Everything in nature seeks this unity. If you carefully observe the pod of a lotus, you will see that when drops of rain or dew overflow the little combs they merge.

But because we delude ourselves into accepting the reality of an ego-I, estrangement and strife inevitably follow. The Buddha in his enlightenment perceived that ego is not indigenous to man's nature. With full enlightenment we realize we possess the universe, so why grasp for what is inherently ours?

You have only to persevere in questioning, "Who am I?" if you wish to experience the truth of what I have been saying.

STUDENT: Thank you for your full explanation.

* * *

STUDENT: My eyes are strange. They feel as though they are looking not outward but inward, asking, "Who am I?"

ROSHI: Excellent!

[Suddenly] *Who are You?*

[No answer]

You are You! I am I!

There is a koan in the *Hekigan-roku* [Blue Rock Record] where a monk named Etcho asks, "What is Buddha?" and the master answers, "You are Etcho!"[24]

Do you understand?

[No answer]

[24] Case No. 7.

You must take hold of this directly. You are coming closer. Concentrate as hard as you possibly can.

*   *   *

STUDENT: I had several questions, but I don't feel like asking them.

ROSHI: Good! Unless you are bothered or worried by something it is better not to ask questions, for there is no end to them. They take you farther and farther away from your Self, whereas the question "Who am I?" brings you to the radiant core of your being.

STUDENT: I'm not worried about anything right now.

ROSHI: Don't separate yourself from "Who am I?" All questions will answer themselves once you realize your Self-nature.

*   *   *

ROSHI: Is there anything you wish to say?

STUDENT: No, but would you tell me through the interpreter what you said at four thirty this morning when you addressed all the sitters?

ROSHI: What I said was substantially this: Man fancies himself to be the most highly evolved organism in the universe, but in the view of Buddhism he stands midway between an amoeba and a Buddha. And because he falsely sees himself as no more than this puny body,[25] just a speck in the universe, he is constantly endeavoring to enlarge himself through possessions and power. But when he awakens to the fact that he embraces the whole universe, he ceases his grasping, for he no longer feels a lack within himself. In the Lotus sutra the Buddha relates that with enlightenment he realized that he possessed the universe, that all its beings were his children, and that he needed nothing more than his begging bowl. He was, in truth, the richest man in the world.

So long as you think of yourself as this small body you will feel restless and discontented. But when through enlightenment you actually experience the universe as identical with yourself, you will attain lasting peace.

[25] Compare with the Buddha's oft-quoted statement: "Verily, I declare unto you that within this very body, mortal though it be and only a fathom high, but conscious and endowed with mind, is the world and the waxing thereof and the waning thereof, and the way that leads to the passing away thererof." (From the Anguttara-Nikaya II, Samyutta-Nikaya I.)

STUDENT: Before I entered upon the practice of Zen I was constantly trying to acquire possessions, but now I desire only peace of mind.

ROSHI: And that, after all, is the only thing worth attaining. True peace and joy can be achieved only with enlightenment, so do your utmost!

* * *

STUDENT: You have told me that when a person becomes enlightened and perceives that he is the whole universe, he ceases grasping for things. Well, I have lived with people who have had an enlightenment experience, yet instead of becoming less grasping and selfish and egotistical they sometimes become more so.[26] If that is what enlightenment does for one, I don't want it!

ROSHI: With a first enlightenment the realization of oneness is usually shallow. Yet if one has genuinely perceived, even though dimly, and continues to practice devotedly for five or ten more years, his inner vision will expand in depth and magnitude as his character acquires flexibility and purity.

One whose actions are still dominated by ego cannot be said to have had a valid enlightenment. Furthermore, an authentic experience not only reveals one's imperfections, but it simultaneously creates the determination to remove them.

STUDENT: But the Buddha after his enlightenment didn't practice constantly, did he?

ROSHI: His practice was his ceaseless teaching and preaching. The Buddha is unique. He was enlightened long before he was born into this world. He came in order to teach us, who are ignorant, how to become enlightened, how to live wisely, and how to die in peace. He endured various austerities, not because he needed to but in order to demonstrate vividly to us that mortification of the flesh is not the true path to emancipation. He was born, he lived, and he died in this world only as an example for all humanity.[27]

---

[26] See footnote 26, p. 300.

[27] Compare: "In the Lotus Sutra [Ch. XV and XVI] the Buddha, in reply to a query by the Bodhisattva Maitreya, states, '. . . The world thinks that Lord Shakyamuni after going out from the home of the Shakyas arrived at the highest perfect enlightenment. But the truth is that many hundred

STUDENT: But don't we ordinary people need self-discipline?

ROSHI: We do, of course. Self-discipline consists in the observance of the precepts, and this is the foundation of zazen. Furthermore, self-indulgence—that is, overeating, oversleeping, and the like— is as bad as self-torture. Both spring from ego and therefore disturb the mind, so they are equally a hindrance to enlightenment.

STUDENT: Though I haven't yet experienced my True-nature, I am aware of my imperfections and am determined to rid myself of them. How is that?

ROSHI: Let me go back to what you said earlier about having lived with people who were Self-realized and yet who appeared selfish and conceited. Such people usually do not practice devotedly after kensho, though they may appear to. They put in a certain number of hours at zazen, but it is only a matter of form. If we indicate it percentage-wise, their involvement after kensho is about twenty or thirty percent; consequently their illumination gradually becomes clouded and in time their experience becomes a mere memory. On the other hand, those who throw themselves into zazen one hundred percent become acutely sensitive to their short-comings and develop the strength and determination to triumph over them despite the fact that they are not yet enlightened.

*   *   *

STUDENT: I am a little edgy this morning. Hearing the stick makes me uneasy.

ROSHI: Did you do zazen all night?

STUDENT: I stayed up till 2 A.M., but I'm not tired.

ROSHI: Many think that when they are tired effective zazen is impossible. But this is a mistaken idea. When you are tired so is your "foe"—that is, the mind of ignorance—and when you are energetic so is it. In reality they are not two.

STUDENT: Would you please tell me through the interpreter what you said in your lecture this morning?

thousand myriads of *kotis* of aeons ago I arrived at supreme perfect enlight-enment . . . The Tathagata who was perfectly enlightened so long ago has no limit to the duration of his life, being everlasting. Never extinct, he makes a show of extinction for the sake of those he leads to salvation." (Quoted in *Honen the Buddhist Saint,* by Coates and Ishizuka, Chion-in, Kyoto, 1925, p. 98.)

ROSHI: This is what I said in essence: There are now five or six hours left to the end of this sesshin. You needn't worry that this is insufficient for enlightenment—on the contrary, it is more than enough. Kensho requires but a minute—no, an instant!

To use the analogy of a battle, last night you were engaging the "enemy" in hand-to-hand combat, fighting whichever way you could. This is now the last attack, the mopping-up operation. However, you must not think that straining and pushing are indispensable for enlightenment. All you need do is empty your mind of the delusive notion of "self" and "other."

Many have come to realization simply by listening to the tinkling of a bell or some other sound. Usually when you hear a bell ringing you think, consciously or unconsciously, "I am hearing a bell." Three things are involved: I, a bell, and hearing. But when the mind is ripe, that is, as free of discursive thoughts as a sheet of pure white paper is unmarred by a blemish, there is just the sound of the bell ringing. This is kensho.

STUDENT: While listening to sounds I have been asking, "Who is listening?" Is this wrong?

ROSHI: I see your problem. In asking, "Who is listening?" you are at first conscious of the question as well as the sound. When the questioning penetrates deeper, you cease to be aware of it. So when a bell rings it is only the bell listening to the sound of the bell. Or to put it another way, it is the sound of yourself ringing. This is the moment of enlightenment.

Consider these flowers in the bowl on this table. You look at them and exclaim: "Oh, how beautiful these flowers are!" That is one kind of seeing. But when you see them, not as apart from you but as yourself, you are enlightened.

STUDENT: That is hard for me to understand.

ROSHI: It is not difficult to understand in a purely intellectual way. Upon hearing the foregoing explanation one can truthfully say: "Yes, I understand." But such understanding is merely intellectual recognition, and quite different from the experience of enlightenment, where you directly experience the flowers as yourself.

It is better that I say no more or these explanations will become a hindrance to you. Go back to your place and concentrate intensely on your koan.

*   *   *

ROSHI: Would you like to say something?

STUDENT: Yes. Last time you used terms like "enemy" and "battle." I don't understand. Who is my enemy and what is the battle?

ROSHI: Your enemy is your discursive thinking, which leads you to differentiate yourself on one side of an imaginary boundary from what is not you on the other side of this non-existent line. Or to put it in terms that may be more meaningful, your enemy is your own personal ego. When you have stopped thinking of yourself as a separated individuality and have realized the Oneness of all existence, you have dealt your ego a mortal blow.

The end of the sesshin is approaching. Don't lose your grip!

IV / BASSUI'S DHARMA TALK ON ONE-MIND AND LETTERS TO HIS DISCIPLES /

EDITOR'S INTRODUCTION / In the year 1327, toward the close of the Kamakura era—the strife-torn, anxiety-ridden period of Japanese history that produced so many notable religious figures—the Rinzai Zen master Bassui Tokusho was born. Having had a vision that the child she was carrying would one day become a fiend who would slay both his parents, his mother abandoned him at birth in a field, where a family servant secretly rescued and reared him.

At seven Bassui's sensitive religious mind began to evince itself. At a memorial service for his late father he suddenly asked the officiating priest: "For whom are those offerings of rice and cakes and fruit?" "For your father, of course," replied the priest. "But Father has no shape or body now,[1] so how can he eat them?" To this the priest answered: "Though he has no visible body, his soul will receive these offerings." "If there is such a thing as a soul," the child pressed on. "I must have one in my body. What is it like?"

To be sure, these are not unusual questions from a thoughtful, sensitive child of seven. For Bassui, however, they were only the beginning of an intense, unremitting self-inquiry which was to continue well into manhood—until, in fact, he had achieved full enlight-

---

[1] In Japan the dead are usually cremated.

enment. Even during his play with other children he was never free of these uncertainties as to the existence of a soul.

His preoccupation with a soul naturally led him to think about hell. In an agony of fear he would exclaim: "How awful to be consumed by the flames of hell!" and tears would well up. When he was ten, he relates, he was often awakened by brilliant flashes of light which filled his room, followed by an all-enveloping darkness. Anxiously he sought for some explanation of these weird occurrences, but the replies that were forthcoming scarcely allayed his fears.

Again and again he questioned himself: "If after death the soul suffers the agonies of hell or enjoys the delights of paradise, what is the nature of this soul? But if there is no soul, what is it within me which this very moment is seeing and hearing?"

His biographer[2] relates that Bassui would often sit for hours "stewing" over this question in a state of such utter self-forgetfulness that he no longer knew he had a body or a mind. On one such occasion—at what age we are not told—Bassui suddenly directly realized that the substratum of all things is a viable Emptiness, and that there is in essence nothing which can be called a soul, a body, or a mind. This realization caused him to break into deep laughter, and he no longer felt himself oppressed by his body and mind.

In an effort to learn whether this constituted true awakening, Bassui questioned a number of well-known monks, but none could give him a satisfying answer. "At any rate," he told himself, "I no longer have doubts about the truth of the Dharma." But his basic perplexity as to the one who sees and hears had not been dispelled, and when he saw in a popular book one day "Mind is host and body guest," every one of his quiescent doubts was suddenly resurrected. "I have seen that the foundation of the universe is Voidness; still what is this *something* within me which can see and hear?" he desperately asked himself anew. In spite of every effort, he could not rid himself of this obsessive doubt.

Nominally Bassui was a samurai, having been born into a samurai

[2] One Myodo, a disciple of Bassui, who on May 5, 1387, the year Bassui died, published the biography from which this introductory material was taken.

family. Whether he actually pursued the duties of a samurai his biographer does not reveal, but it seems safe to conclude that Bassui's continuous search for Zen masters would have given him little opportunity, and presumably as little taste, for the life of a samurai.

At all events, we do know that Bassui had his head shaved at twenty-nine, symbolizing his initiation into the Buddhist monkhood. For the ceremonial rites of a monk or priest, however, he had little use, believing that a monk should live a simple life dedicated to attaining the highest truth so as to lead others to liberation, and not engage in ceremony and luxurious living, not to mention political intrigue, to which the priesthood of his day was only too prone. On his numerous pilgrimages he stubbornly refused to remain even overnight in a temple, but insisted on staying in some isolated hut high up on a hill or mountain, where he would sit hour after hour doing zazen away from the distractions of the temple. To stay awake he would often climb a tree, perch among the branches, and deeply ponder his natural koan, "Who is the master?" far into the night, oblivious to wind and rain. In the morning, with virtually no sleep or food, he would go to the temple or monastery for an encounter with the master.

So strong was Bassui's distaste for the ceremonialism of the temple that many years later, after had had become master of Kogaku-ji,[3] he always insisted on calling it Kogaku-an instead, the suffix -an meaning "hermitage" as opposed to the more grandiose -ji meaning "temple" or "monastery."

In the course of his spiritual journeys Bassui eventually met the Zen master through whom his Mind's eye was to be completely opened—Koho-zenji, a great Zen roshi of his day. The lesser masters from whom Bassui had sought guidance had all sanctioned his enlightenment, but Koho, sensing Bassui's keen, sensitive mind and the strength and purity of his yearning for truth, did not give him his stamp of approval but merely invited him to remain. On his part, Bassui recognized in Koho a great roshi but declined to

---

[3] Literally, "Monastery Facing the Mountain," that is, Mount Fuji. Mount Fuji is symbolic of True-mind, so Kogaku-ji connotes grappling with one's True-mind.

stay in his temple, taking a solitary hut in the nearby hills and for the next month coming daily to see Koho.

One day Koho, sensing the ripeness of Bassui's mind, asked him: "Tell me, what is Joshu's Mu?" Bassui started to reply: "Mountains and rivers, grass and trees, are equally Mu," and Koho stopped him with: "Don't use your mind!"

All at once, his biographer relates, Bassui felt as though he had "lost his life root, like a barrel whose bottom had been smashed open." Sweat began to stream from every pore of his body, and when he left Koho's room he was in such a daze that he bumped his head several times along the walls trying to find the outer gate of the temple. Upon reaching his hut he wept for hours from his very depths. The tears overflowed, "pouring down his face like rain." In the intense combustion of this overwhelming experience Bassui's previously held conceptions and beliefs, we are told, were utterly annihilated.

The following evening Bassui came to tell Koho what had happened. Hardly had he opened his mouth when Koho, who had despaired of ever finding a true successor among his monks, declared, as though addressing all his followers: "My Dharma will not vanish. All may now be happy. My Dharma will not disappear."

Koho formally conferred *inka* on his disciple and gave him the Zen name "Bassui"—"high above average." Bassui remained for two months near Koho, receiving his instructions and guidance. But Bassui, who had a strong and independent mind, wished to mature his profound experience through "Dharma combat" with accomplished masters so as to integrate his experience thoroughly into his conscious mind and into his every act, and to develop his capacity to teach others. So he left Koho and continued to live an isolated life in forests, hills, and mountains not far from the temples of famous masters. When not engaging them in "Dharma combat" he would carry on his zazen for hours at a time.

Wherever he stayed zealous aspirants quickly discovered his whereabouts and sought his guidance, but feeling himself still deficient in the spiritual strength necessary to lead others to liberation, he resisted their efforts to make him their teacher. When their entreaties became importunate he would pick up his meager belongings and vanish in the night. Apart from the entreaties of would-be disciples, however, he deliberately curtailed his stay in any one place so as not to become attached to it.

At length—now fifty—Bassui built himself a hut deep in a mountain near the town of Enzan in Yamanashi Prefecture. As had happened in the past, word spread through the nearby village of the presence in the mountain of a Bodhisattva, and seekers again began literally to beat a path to his hut. Now, his enlightenment having ripened and feeling himself capable of leading others to emancipation, he no longer turned away from these seekers but willingly accepted all who came. Soon they became a sizable flock, and when the governor of the province offered to donate land for a monastery and his followers to build it, Bassui agreed to become its roshi.

Although Bassui disliked the designation "temple" or "monastery," Kogaku-ji at its apogee, with more than a thousand monks and lay devotees, could hardly be described as a hermitage. Bassui was a rigid disciplinarian, and of the thirty-three rules he promulgated for the behavior of his disciples, interestingly enough, the first prohibited the imbibing of alcohol in any form.

Just before he passed away, at the age of sixty, Bassui sat up in the lotus posture and, to those gathered around him, said: "Don't be misled! Look directly! What is this?" He repeated this loudly and then calmly died.

The teaching methods of every great master inevitably grow out of his own personality, his spiritual problem as he experienced it, and the mode of zazen which gave birth to his enlightenment. For Dogen, whose religious strivings came to a focus in a problem totally different from Bassui's and whose full awakening came without a koan of any kind, shikan-taza became the prime teaching method. Bassui's natural koan, on the other hand, was "Who is the master?"[4] and therefore, as we see in the following letters, he urges his disciples to employ this mode of zazen. Moreover,

[4] The Japanese word which we have rendered as "master" is *shujin-ko*. In Japanese a husband (that is, the head of the house), a proprietor, a landlord, an employer are all *shujin*. *Ko* is a term implying great respect; it was used when addressing a lord in ancient Japan. "Master" in this sense, therefore, means the head, the center of power, the controlling force.

since Bassui, like Dogen, could not wholly satisfy his deep inner longing for liberation through shallow enlightenment, the goal he holds out in these letters is nothing short of full awakening.

Bassui was not a prolific writer. Besides his Dharma talk on One-mind and these letters, he wrote a single large volume called *Wadei-gassui*, setting forth the principles and practices of Zen Buddhism, and a smaller work. Just when Bassui wrote "One-mind" and the letters is unknown, since none of them bears a date, but presumably they were written after he had become master of Kogaku-ji. Evidently his correspondents were disciples who either were too sick or lived too far away to come to Kogaku-ji for sesshin and personal instruction. Only such extenuating circumstances and the manifest ardor and sincerity of his correspondents could have persuaded Bassui to instruct them by letter instead of by traditional methods.

True, some of the letters are repetitious, but this is inevitable since Bassui is giving the same teaching in essence to each of his correspondents. Yet it is by just such repetition that Bassui, master that he is, superbly clarifies and hammers home his theme of One-mind. There is little in Zen literature written by outstanding masters which is so squarely aimed at practice or is as inspiring as these writings. Bassui speaks as directly to the reader of today as he did to his correspondents of the fourteenth century, guiding and inspiring him at every turn. Added to this is a pungent sense of paradox coupled with a profound simplicity which has made the Dharma talk and these letters immensely popular in Japan right down to the present day. Takusuizenji, a well-known Zen master of the Tokugawa period (1603–1868), who, like Joshu, is said to have lived to the ripe age of one hundred and twenty (and who himself was the writer of a number of Zen letters), warmly praised both these writings as valuable not only for devotees but even for Zen masters.

It is hoped that with this translation, the first into English, they will find equal favor with English-speaking readers eager to understand and practice Zen.

THE TALK / If you would free yourself of the sufferings of samsara, you must learn the direct way to become a Buddha. This way is no other than the realization of your own Mind. Now what is this Mind? It is the true nature of all sentient beings, that which existed before our parents were born and hence before our own birth, and which presently exists, unchangeable and eternal. So it is called one's Face before one's parents were born. This Mind is intrinsically pure. When we are born it is not newly created, and when we die it does not perish. It has no distinction of male or female, nor has it any coloration of good or bad. It cannot be compared with anything, so it is called Buddha-nature. Yet countless thoughts issue from this Self-nature as waves arise in the ocean or as images are reflected in a mirror.

To realize your own Mind you must first of all look into the source from which thoughts flow. Sleeping and working, standing and sitting, profoundly ask yourself, "What is my own Mind?" with an intense yearning to resolve this question. This is called "training" or "practice" or "desire for truth" or "thirst for realization." What is termed zazen is no more than looking into one's own Mind. It is better to search your own Mind devotedly than to read and recite innumerable sutras and dharani every day for countless years. Such endeavors, which are but formalities, produce some merit, but this merit expires, and again you must experience the suffering of the Three Evil Paths. Because searching one's own mind leads ultimately to enlightenment, this practice is a prerequisite to becoming a Buddha. No matter whether you have committed either the ten evil deeds or the five deadly sins, if you turn back your mind and enlighten yourself, you are a Buddha instantly. But do not commit sins and expect to be saved by enlightenment [from the effects of your own actions], for neither enlightenment nor a Buddha nor a patriarch can save a person who, deluding himself, goes down evil ways.

Imagine a child sleeping next to its parents and dreaming it is being beaten or is painfully sick. The parents cannot help the child no matter how much it suffers, for no one can enter the dreaming mind of another. If the child could awaken itself, it could be freed of this suffering automatically. In the same way, one who realizes that his own Mind is Buddha frees himself instantly from the sufferings arising from [ignorance of the law of] ceaseless change of birth-and-death. If a Buddha could prevent it, would he allow even one sentient being to fall into hell?[5] Without Self-realization one cannot understand such things as these.

What kind of master is it that this very moment sees colors with the eyes and hears voices with the ears, that now raises the hands and moves the feet? We know these are functions of our own mind, but no one knows precisely how they are performed. It may be asserted that behind these actions there is no entity, yet it is obvious they are being performed spontaneously. Conversely, it may be maintained that these *are* the acts of some entity; still the entity is invisible. If one regards this question as unfathomable, all attempts to reason [out an answer] will cease and one will be at a loss to know what to do. In this propitious state deepen and deepen the yearning, tirelessly, to the extreme. When the profound questioning penetrates to the very bottom, and that bottom is broken open, not the slightest doubt will remain that your own Mind is itself Buddha, the Void-universe. There will then be no anxiety about life or death, no truth to search for.

In a dream you may stray and lose your way home. You ask someone to show you how to return or you pray to God or Buddhas to help you, but still you can't get home. Once you rouse yourself from your dream-state, however, you find that you are in your own bed and realize that the only way you could have gotten home was to awaken yourself. This [kind of spiritual awakening] is called "return to the origin" or "rebirth in paradise." It is the kind of inner realization tht can be achieved with some training. Virtually all who like zazen and make an effort in practice, be they laymen or monks, can experience to this degree. But even such [partial] awakening cannot be attained except through the practice of zazen. You would be making a serious error, however, were you to assume that this was true enlightenment in which there is no doubt about the nature of reality. You would be like a man who having found copper gives up the desire for gold.

Upon such realization question yourself even more intensely in

[5] What is implied here is that Buddhas are not supernatural beings who can prevent one from falling into hell by conferring enlightenment, but that enlightenment, through which alone one can be saved from the sufferings of such a fate, is attainable solely through one's own efforts.

this wise: "My body is like a phantom, like bubbles on a stream. My mind, looking into itself, is as formless as empty-space, yet somewhere within sounds are perceived. Who is hearing?" Should you question yourself in this wise with profound absorption, never slackening the intensity of your effort, your rational mind eventually will exhaust itself and only questioning at the deepest level will remain. Finally you will lose awareness of your own body. Your long-held conceptions and notions will perish, after absolute questioning, in the way that every drop of water vanishes from a tub broken open at the bottom, and perfect enlightenment will follow like flowers suddenly blooming on withered trees.

With such realization you achieve true emancipation. But even now repeatedly cast off what has been realized, turning back to the subject that realizes, that is, to the root bottom, and resolutely go on. Your Self-nature will then grow brighter and more transparent as your delusive feelings perish, like a gem gaining luster under repeated polishing, until at last it positively illumines the entire universe. Don't doubt this! Should your yearning be too weak to lead you to this state in your present lifetime, you will undoubtedly gain Self-realization easily in the next, provided you are still engaged in this questioning at death, just as yesterday's work half done was finished easily today.

In zazen neither despise nor cherish the thoughts that arise; only search your own Mind, the very source of these thoughts. You must understand that anything appearing in your consciousness or seen by your eyes is an illusion, of no enduring reality. Hence you should neither fear nor be fascinated by such phenomena. If you keep your mind as empty as space, unstained by extraneous matters, no evil spirits can disturb you even on your deathbed. While engaged in zazen, however, keep none of this counsel in mind. You must only become the question "What is this Mind?" or "What is it that hears these sounds?" When you realize this Mind you will know that it is the very source of all Buddhas and sentient beings. The Bodhisattva Kannon [Avalokitesvara] is so called because he attained enlightenment by perceiving [that is, grasping the source of] the sounds of the world about him.

At work, at rest, never stop trying to realize who it is that hears. Even though your questioning penetrates the unconscious, you won't find the one who hears, and all your efforts will come to naught. Yet sounds can be heard, so question yourself to an even profounder level. At last every vestige of self-awareness will disappear and you will feel like a cloudless sky. Within yourself you will find no "I," nor will you discover anyone who hears. This Mind is like the void, yet it hasn't a single spot that can be called empty. Do not mistake this state for Self-realization, but continue to ask yourself even more intensely, "Now who is it that hears?" If you bore and bore into this question, oblivious to anything else, even this feeling of voidness will vanish and you won't be aware of anything—total darkness will prevail. [Don't stop here, but] keep asking with all your strength, "What *is* it that hears?" Only when you have completely exhausted the questioning will the question burst; now you will feel like a man come back from the dead. This is true realization. You will see the Buddhas of all the universes face to face and the patriarchs past and present. Test yourself with this koan: "A monk asked Joshu: 'What is the meaning of Bodhidharma's coming to China?' Joshu replied: 'The oak tree in the garden.' "[6] Should this koan leave you with the slightest doubt, you need to resume questioning, "What is it that hears?"

If you don't come to realization in this present life, when will you? Once you have died you won't be able to avoid a long period of suffering in the Three Evil Paths.[7] What is obstructing realization? Nothing but your own half-hearted desire for truth. Think of this and exert yourself to the utmost.

THE LETTERS / 1 / TO A MAN FROM KUMASAKA / You ask me to write you how to practice Zen on your sickbed. Who is he that is sick? Who is he that is practicing Zen? Do you know who you are? One's whole being is Buddha-

[6] *Mumonkan* No. 37. For more about Joshu, see p. 77 and "Joshu" in section x.

[7] According to Buddhist teaching, enlightenment can be attained only with a human body. What is meant here and in the preceding passage is that if one loses his human form, and with it the opportunity for enlightenment and higher states of consciousness, one will have to undergo long suffering in subhuman states of existence.

nature. One's whole being is the Great Way. The substance of this Way is inherently immaculate and transcends all forms. Is there any sickness in it? Man's own Mind is the essential substance of all Buddhas, his Face before his parents' birth. It is the matter of seeing and hearing, of all the senses. One who fully realizes this is a Buddha, one who does not is an ordinary human being. Hence all Buddhas and patriarchs point directly to the human mind so man can see his own Self-nature and thereby attain Buddhahood. For the best relief for one perplexed by shadows is to see the real thing.

Once a man was invited to the home of a friend. As he was about to drink a cup of wine offered him, he believed he saw a baby snake inside his cup. Not wishing to embarrass his host by drawing attention to it, he bravely swallowed it. Upon returning home he felt severe pains in his stomach. Many remedies were applied but in vain, and the man, now grievously ill, felt he was about to die. His friend, hearing of his condition, asked him once more to his home. Seating his friend in the same place, he again offered him a cup of wine, telling him it was medicine. As the ailing man raised his cup to drink, once again he saw a baby snake in it. This time he drew his host's attention to it. Without a word the host pointed to the ceiling above his guest, where a bow hung. Suddenly the sick man realized that the "baby snake" was the reflection of the hanging bow. Both men looked at each other and laughed. The pain of the sick man vanished instantly and he recovered his health.

Becoming a Buddha is analogous to this. The Patriarch Yoka said: "When you realize the true nature of the universe you know that there is neither subjective nor objective reality. At that very moment karmic formations which would carry you to the lowest hell are wiped out." This true nature is the root-substance of every sentient being. Man, however, can't bring himself to believe that his own Mind is itself the Great Completeness realized by the Buddha, so he clings to superficial forms and looks for truth outside this Mind, striving to become a Buddha through ascetic practices. But as the illusion of an ego-self does not vanish, man must undergo intense suffering in the Three Worlds. He is like the one who became sick believing he had swallowed a baby snake. Various remedies were of no avail, but he recovered instantly upon realizing the basic truth.

So just look into your own Mind—no one can help you with nostrums. In a sutra the Buddha said: "If you would get rid of your foe, you have only to realize that that foe is delusion." All phenomena in the world are illusory, they have no abiding substance. Sentient beings no less than Buddhas are like images reflected in water. One who does not see the true nature of things mistakes shadow for substance. That is to say, in zazen the state of emptiness and quiet which results from the diminution of thought is often confused with one's Face before one's parents were born. But this serenity is also a reflection upon the water. You must advance beyond the stage where your reasons is of any avail. In this extremity of not knowing what to think or do, ask yourself: "Who is the master?" He will become your intimate only after you have broken a walking stick made from a rabbit's horn or crushed a chunk of ice in fire. Tell me now, who is this most intimate of yours? Today is the eighth of the month. Tomorrow is the thirteenth!

2 / TO THE ABBESS OF SHINRYU-JI / In order to become a Buddha you must discover who it is that wants to become a Buddha. To know this Subject you must right here and now probe deeply into yourself, inquiring: "What is it that thinks in terms of good and bad, that sees, that hears?" If you question yourself profoundly in this wise, you will surely enlighten yourself. If you enlighten yourself, you are instantly a Buddha. The Mind which the Buddhas realized in their enlightenment is the Mind of all sentient beings. The substance of this Mind is pure, harmonizing with its surroundings. In a woman's body it has no female form, in a man's body it has no appearance of male. It is not mean even in the body of the lowly, nor is it imposing in the body of the noble. Like boundless space, it hasn't a particle of color. The physical world can be destroyed, but formless, colorless space is indestructible. This Mind, like space, is all-embracing. It does not come into existence with the creation of our body, nor does it perish with its disintegration. Though invisible, it suffuses our body, and every single act of seeing, hearing, smelling, speaking, or moving the hands and legs is simply the activity of this Mind. Whoever searches for Buddha and Truth outside this Mind

is deluded; whoever directly perceives that his intrinsic nature is precisely that of a Buddha is himself a Buddha. There has never been a Buddha who has not realized this Mind, and every last being within the Six Realms of Existence is perfectly endowed with it. The words of a sutra "In Buddha there is no discrimination" confirms this.

Everyone who has realized this Mind and attained to Buddhahood wants to make it known to mankind. But men, clinging stupidly to superficial forms, find it hard to believe in this purposeless Dharma-kaya, this pure, true Buddha. To give it a name Buddhas resort to such metaphors as "Treasure Gem of Free Will," "Great Path," "Amitabha Buddha," "Buddha of Supreme Knowledge," "Jizo," "Kannon," "Fugen," "One's Face before one's parents were born." The Bodhisattva Jizo[8] is the guide through the Six Realms of Existence, [he being the symbol of the power which] controls the six senses. Every epithet of a Buddha or a Bodhisattva is simply a different designation for the One-mind. If one believes in his own Buddha-mind, it is the same as believing in all Buddhas. Thus in a sutra we read: "The Three Worlds are but One-mind; outside this Mind nothing exists. Mind, Buddha, and sentient beings are One, they are not to be differentiated."

Since the sutras deal only with this Mind, to realize it is to accomplish at one stroke the reading and understanding of all the sutras. One sutra says: "The teachings of the sutras are like a finger pointing to the moon." These teachings are the sermons that have been preached by all the Buddhas. "Pointing to the moon" is pointing to the One-mind of sentient beings. Just as it is said that the moon shines upon both sides of the earth, in the same way the One-mind illumines the inner and outer world. When it is said, then, that great merit can be derived from reciting the sutras, this means what has just been said and nothing more.[9] Again, it is said that through services for the Buddha one can attain Buddhahood, but to attain Buddhahood simply means to realize this Mind. Thus

[8] Jizo has always occupied a special niche in the hearts of Japanese Buddhists, and perhaps that is why Bassui, rather gratuitously it would seem, singles out this Bodhisattva.

[9] Namely, that the sutras say that they themselves are not truth but are like an arrow pointing to the truth.

the merit of realizing this One-mind in a single-minded instant is infinitely greater than that of reciting the sutras for ten thousand days, just as perceiving one's own Mind in a moment of single-mindedness is incomparably greater than hearing for ten thousand years why this is so. But just as one must progress from shallow to deep by degrees, so is it a blessing for beginners, either deluded or obtuse, to recite sutras enthusiastically or to invoke the names of Buddhas. For them it is like getting onto a raft or boat as a first step. But if they do not yearn to reach the shore of realization, contenting themselves to remain forever on the raft, they only deceive themselves. Shakyamuni Buddha underwent many austerities yet failed to attain Buddhahood. After this he did zazen for six years, giving up everything else, and at last realized this One-mind. Following his perfect enlightenment he spoke about the Mind he had realized for the sake of all mankind. These talks are called sutras and are the words flowing from the realized Mind of the Buddha.

This Mind is latent in everyone, it is the master of the six senses. The effects and causes of all transgressions vanish in a flash, like ice put into boiling water, when one awakens to this Mind. Only after gaining such direct Insight can you affirm that your own Mind is itself Buddha. The Mind-essence is intrinsically bright and un-blemished, in it there is no distinction of Buddha and sentient beings. But its clarity is hidden by delusive thoughts just as the light of the sun or the moon is obscured by clouds. Yet such thoughts can be dispelled by the power of zazen, in the same way that clouds can be dissipated by a blast of wind. Once they vanish, the Buddha-nature reveals itself, just as the moon makes its appearance when clouds disappear. This light has ever been present; it is not newly obtained outside oneself.

If you would free yourself from being driven within the Six Realms of Existence or from [the sufferings of] birth-and-death, you must dispel your delusive feelings and perceptions. To dispel them you must realize this Mind. To realize this Mind you must do zazen. How you practice is of the utmost importance. You must penetrate your koans to the very core. The foundation of every koan is one's own Mind. The deep yearning for the realization of Mind we call "desire for truth" or "thirst for realization." He is wise who deeply fears falling into hell.[10] Only because the terrors of hell are so little known to them do men have no desire for the teachings of the Buddha.

There was a Bodhisattva who attained enlightenment by concentrating intently on every sound he heard, so Shakyamuni Buddha called him Kannon.[11] If you would know the substance of the Mind-Buddha, the very instant you hear a sound search for this one who hears. Thus you will unfailingly come to the realization that your own Mind is no different from Kannon's. This Mind is neither being nor non-being. It transcends all forms and yet is inseparable from them.

Do not try to prevent thoughts from arising and do not cling to any that have arisen. Let them appear and disappear as they will, don't struggle with them. You need only unremittingly and with all your heart ask yourself, "What is my own Mind?" I keep urging this because I want to bring you to Self-realization. When you persistently try to understand what is beyond the domain of intellect, you are bound to reach a dead end, completely baffled. But push on. Sitting or standing, working or sleeping, probe tirelessly to your deepest self with the question "What is my own Mind?" Fear nothing but the failure to experience your True-nature. This is Zen practice. When the intense questioning envelops every inch of you and penetrates to the very bottom of all bottoms, the question will suddenly burst and the substance of the Buddha-mind be revealed, just as a mirror [concealed] in a box can reflect [its surroundings] only after the box is broken apart. The radiance of this Mind will light up every corner of a universe free of even a single blemish. You will be liberated at last from all entanglements within the Six Realms, all effects of evil actions having vanished. The joy of this moment cannot be put into words.

[10] What is implied in this and the following sentence is that the plane of existence or state of consciousness called hell is excruciatingly painful, and that it is the dread of falling into such a miserable life which gives rise to a deep yearning for Self-realization. For it is enlightenment that takes the terror out of hell.

[11] Kannon is a simplification of Kanzeon, which means "hearer (or regarder) of the cries of the world." Sometimes Bassui uses the term Kanzeon and sometimes Kannon. To avoid confusion we have adhered throughout to Kannon.

Consider a person suffering intensely in a dream where, having fallen into hell, he is being tortured. Once he awakens, his suffering ceases, for he is now liberated from this delusion. In the same way, through Self-realization one frees himself from the sufferings of birth-and-death. For enlightenment, not nobility of birth or wide learning but only strong determination is essential. Buddhas bear the same relation to sentient beings as water does to ice. Ice, like stone or brick, cannot flow. But when it melts it flows freely in conformity with its surroundings. So long as one remains in a state of delusion he is like ice. Upon realization he becomes as exquisitely free as water. So you will understand there is no difference between ordinary beings and Buddhas except for one thing—delusion. When it is dissolved they are identical.

Don't allow yourself to become discouraged. If your desire for truth is wanting, you may be unable to attain enlightenment in this life. But if you carry on your Zen practice[12] faithfully, even while dying, you will unquestionably achieve enlightenment in your next existence. But don't dawdle. Imagine yourself on your death-bed at this very moment. What alone can help you? What alone can prevent you from falling into hell because of your transgressions? There is fortunately a broad path to liberation. From your very roots ask this one question: "What is my Buddha-mind?" If you would see the substance of all Buddhas in a trice, realize your own Mind.

Is what I say true or false? Ask yourself this instant: "What is my own Buddha-mind?" Upon your enlightenment the lotus will blossom in a roaring fire and endure throughout eternity. Man inherently is no different from the lotus. Why can't you grasp this?

3 / TO LORD NAKAMURA, GOVERNOR OF AKI PROVINCE / You asked me how to practice Zen with reference to this phrase from a sutra: "Arouse the Mind without its abiding anywhere." There is no express method for attaining enlightenment. If you but look into your Self-nature directly, not allowing yourself to be deflected, the Mind flower will come into bloom. Therefore the sutra says: "Arouse the Mind without its abiding

12 That is, asking: "What is the true substance of my Mind?"

anywhere." Thousands of words spoken directly by Buddhas and patriarchs add up to this one phrase. Mind is the True-nature of things, transcending all forms. The True-nature is the Way. The Way is Buddha. Buddha is Mind. Mind is not within or without or in between. It is not being or nothingness or non-being or non-nothingness or Buddha or mind or matter. So it is called the abodeless Mind. This Mind sees colors with the eyes, hears sounds with the ears. Look for this master directly!

A Zen master [Rinzai] of old says: "One's body, composed of the four primal elements,[13] can't hear or understand this preaching. The spleen or stomach or liver or gall bladder can't hear or understand this preaching. Empty space can't understand it. Then what does hear and understand?" Strive to perceive directly. If your mind remains attached to any form or feeling whatsoever, or is affected by logical reasoning or conceptual thinking, you are as far from true realization as heaven is from earth.

How can you cut off at a stroke the sufferings of birth-and-death? As soon as you consider how to advance, you get lost in reasoning; but if you quit you are adverse to the highest path. To be able neither to advance nor to quit is to be a "breathing corpse." If in spite of this dilemma you empty your mind of all thoughts and push on with your zazen, you are bound to enlighten yourself and apprehend the phrase "Arouse the Mind without its abiding anywhere." Instantly you will grasp the sense of all Zen dialogue as well as the profound and subtle meaning of the countless sutras.

The laymen Ho asked Baso: "What is it that transcends everything in the universe?" Baso answered: "I will tell you after you have drunk up the waters of the West River in one gulp."[14] Ho instantly became deeply enlightened. See here, what does this mean? Does it explain the phrase "Arouse the Mind without its abiding anywhere," or does it point to the very one reading this? If you still don't comprehend, go back to questioning. "What is hearing now?" Find out this very moment! The problem of birth-

[13] Namely, solids (earth), liquids (water), heat (fire), gas (air).

[14] The West River is a large river in China. Another version of this koan states: "Ho replied to Baso: 'I have already drunk up the waters of the West River in one gulp.' 'Then I have already told you!' retorted Baso."

and-death is momentous, and the world moves fast. Make the most of time, for it waits for no one.

Your own Mind is intrinsically Buddha. Buddhas are those who have realized this. Those who haven't are so-called ordinary sentient beings. Sleeping and working, standing and sitting, ask yourself, "What is my own Mind?" looking into the source from which your thoughts arise. What is this subject that right now perceives, thinks, moves, works, goes forth, or returns? To know it you must intensely absorb yourself in the question. But even though you do not realize it in this life, beyond a doubt you will in the next because of your present efforts.

In your zazen think in terms of neither good nor evil. Don't try to stop thoughts from arising, only ask yourself: "What is my own Mind?" Now even though your questioning goes deep, you will get no answer, and eventually you will reach a cul-de-sac, your thinking totally checked. You won't find anything within that can be called "I" or "Mind." But who is it that understands all this? Continue to probe more deeply yet and the mind that perceives there is nothing will vanish; you will no longer be aware of questioning but only of emptiness. When awareness of even emptiness disappears, you will realize there is no Buddha outside Mind and no Mind outside Buddha. Now for the first time you will discover that when you do not hear with your ears you are truly hearing, and when you do not see with your eyes you are truly seeing Buddhas of the past, present, and future. But don't cling to any of this, just experience it for yourself!

See here, what is your own Mind? Everyone's Original-nature is not less than Buddha. But since men doubt this and search for Buddha and Truth outside their Mind, they fail to attain enlightenment, being helplessly driven within cycles of birth-and-death, entangled in karma both good and bad. The source of all karma bondage is delusion, that is, the thoughts, feelings, and perceptions [stemming from ignorance]. Rid yourself of them and you are emancipated. Just as ash covering a charcoal fire is dispersed when the fire is fanned, so these delusions vanish once you realize your Self-nature.

In zazen neither loathe nor be charmed by any of your thoughts. With your mind turned inward, look steadily into their source and the delusive feelings and perceptions in which they are rooted will evaporate. This is not yet Self-realization, however, though your mind becomes bright and empty like the sky and you have awareness of neither inner nor outer and all the ten quarters seem clear and luminous. To take this for realization is to mistake a mirage for reality. Now even more intensely search this mind of yours that hears. Your physical body, composed of the four basic elements, is like a phantom, without reality, yet apart from this body there is no mind. The empty-space of the ten quarters can neither see nor hear; still, something within you does hear and distinguish sounds. Who or what is it? When this question totally ignites you, distinctions of good and evil, awareness of being or emptiness, vanish like a light extinguished on a dark night. Though you are no longer consciously aware of yourself, still you can hear and know you exist. Try as you will to discover the subject hearing, your efforts will fail and you will find yourself at an impasse. All at once your mind will burst into great enlightenment and you will feel as though you have risen from the dead, laughing loudly and clapping your hands in delight. Now for the first time you will know that Mind itself is Buddha. Were someone to ask, "What does one's Buddha-mind look like? I would answer: "In the trees fish play, in the deep sea birds are flying." What does this mean? If you don't understand it, look into your own Mind and ask yourself: "What is he, this master who sees and hears?"

Make the most of time—it waits for no one.

4 / TO A DYING MAN / Your Mind-essence is not subject to birth or death. It is neither being nor nothingness, neither emptiness nor form-and-color. Nor is it something that feels pain or joy. However much you try to know [with your rational mind] that which is now sick, you cannot. Yet if you think of nothing, wish for nothing, want to understand nothing, cling to nothing, and only ask yourself, "What is the true substance of the Mind and of this one who is now suffering?" ending your days like clouds fading in the sky, you will eventually be freed from your painful bondage to endless change.

5 / TO THE LAYMAN IPPO (HOMMA SHOKEN) /
You are meeting *him* face to face, but who is *he*? Anything you
say will be wrong. And if you hold your tongue, you will be equally
wrong. Who is *he*, then? On top of a flagpole a cow gives birth
to a calf. If you come to Self-realization at this point, you need
do nothing further. If you cannot, look inward to behold your
Buddha-nature. Everyone is perfectly endowed with this Buddha-
nature. Its substance is the same in ordinary human beings as in
Buddhas, with not the slightest difference in degree. But because
man can't bring himself to believe this, he binds himself to delusion
with the rope of unreality by saying: "The realization of my Self-
nature is beyond me. It is better that I recite sutras, bow down
before Buddhas, and enter the Way gradually through the grace
of all Buddhas." Most of those who hear this accept it as true. It
is as though one blind man were leading many blind men in the
wrong direction. These people do not really believe sutras and
Buddhas—on the contrary, they set no store by them. [For if they
truly accepted them, they would know that] merely reciting the
sutras is no more than looking at them from the outside, and speaking of "Buddha" but another way of speaking of the essence of
Mind. A sutra says: "Mind, Buddha, and sentient beings, these
are not to be discriminated from one another." Accordingly, a
man who does not believe in the reality of his own Mind but says
he believes in Buddha is like one who puts trust in a symbol while
spurning the real thing. How then can he realize this Mind? One
who wants only to recite sutras is like a hungry man who refuses
food offered in the belief that he can allay his hunger by merely
looking at a menu. Each sutra is but a catalogue of the Mind-nature.
One of the sutras says: "The teachings of the sutras are like a
finger pointing to the moon." Can the Buddha have intended that
you acknowledge the finger and not perceive the moon? Everybody
contains within himself the [substance of the] sutras. If you catch
even a glimpse of your Self-nature, it is the same as reading and
understanding all the sutras simultaneously, none excepted, without so much as holding one in your hand and reading a word.
Isn't this real sutra-"reading"? Look, that green bamboo grove
over yonder is precisely your own Mind, and this mass of yellow
flowers is nothing less than the supreme wisdom of the universe!
  As for the practice of bowing down before Buddhas, this is merely

a way of horizontalizing the mast of ego in order to realize the Buddha-nature. To attain Buddhahood one must come to Self-realization through his own efforts no matter what his talents or capabilities may be. Unfortunately, most who understand this and practice zazen begin to dawdle along the way and thus never come to complete realization. Then there are those who take the state of no-thoughts and no-awareness, where all reflection and discrimination stop for a time, to be true realization; others think it sufficient Zen practice to remember every single koan; still others insist that the true way of the Zen devotee is not to violate the precepts, or else to dwell in forests to escape from the problem of good and evil in the world; while still others maintain that the right way is to avow that there is no truth to be realized, or that there is no other truth to grasp than that of drinking tea when tea is offered or eating when food is served, or of shouting *"Katsu!"* when asked about Buddhism, or of leaving suddenly with a flourish of the kimono sleeve, pretending to repudiate everything, while calling anyone who practices zazen seriously and seeks out accomplished Zen masters a bore. If such individuals can be called truth-seekers, then a child of three can be said to understand Zen. Again, there are those who think that when one's mental functions have ceased, leaving one like a decayed tree or cold stone, one has attained no-mindness; while still others maintain that in the practice of Zen a decisive point has been reached when one feels a deep void with awareness of neither inner nor outer, the entire body having become shining, transparent, and clear like a blue sky on a bright day.

This last appears when the True-nature begins to manifest itself, but it cannot be called genuine Self-realization. Zen masters of old would call it the "deep pit of pseudo-emancipation." Those who reach this stage, believing they have no more problems in [the study and practice of] Buddhism, behave haughtily through lack of wisdom; engage eagerly in debates on religion, taking delight in cornering their opponents but becoming angry when cornered themselves; appear perpetually discontented while no longer believing in the law of causation; go about telling jokes in a loud, jabbering voice; deliberately disturb and ridicule those who study and strive earnestly, calling them clods whose practice is not Zen. This is as though a lunatic were to laugh at a sane person. The conceit of these idiots knows no bounds and they fall into hell as quick as an arrow. The first patriarch, Bodhidharma, said: "One who thinks only that everything is void but is ignorant of the law of causation falls into everlasting, pitch-black hell." These would-be teachers sometimes sound like Zen masters, but they are unable to free themselves of their delusive feelings and perceptions. Most beginners mistake the barest manifestation of truth for Self-realization. An ancient Zen master [Rinzai] said: " 'The body of the True-nature' and 'the ground of the True-nature,' these, I know for certain, are shadows [that is, concepts]. You must find the subject that casts the shadows. It is the very source of all Buddhas."

Certain people say: "In the practice and study of Zen we acquire various ideas about it,[15] and such notions [we are told] are a kind of mind illness; for this reason Self-realization through Zen is difficult. But what if we don't realize our Self-nature, or understand [the Truth] through reading the sutras? Need we fear retribution if we don't sin? What if we never attain Buddhahood? As long as we don't tread the Three Evil Paths, why need we strive for Buddhahood?"

Answer: The source of all sin is delusion. Without Self-realization it can't be destroyed. In the bodies of human beings are six sense-roots, in each of which lurks a seducer.[16] These six seducers each carry three kinds of poison;: greed, anger, and folly. There are no human beings free from these three poisons. They are the causes of which the Three Evil Paths are the effects. Necessarily the effects flow from the causes. One who says, "I am free of sin" is ignorant of this law. Even one who commits no sin in this life has these three poisons *a priori*. What, then, of those who add new transgressions?

Question: If all human beings are heir to these three poisons,

[15] That is, conceptions about satori, Mu, ku, etc.

[16] Our sense impressions are called seducers because until we have learned to control our minds and realized the Truth, we are prey to their never-ceasing seductions, to their efforts to tempt us away from our True-nature through alluring sights, sounds, and other distractions. Greed, anger, and folly are the inevitable outcome of attachment to the objects of the senses. (See also "Six Realms of Existence" and "ego" in section x.)

is it correct to say that even Buddhas, patriarchs, and holy sages cannot avoid treading the Three Evil Paths?

Answer: When one realizes his Self-nature the three poisons are transmuted [in such a way that greedy actions turn] into observance of the precepts, [anger into] mind stability, and [folly into] wisdom. Buddhas, patriarchs, and holy sages are all enlightened, so how could they possibly sin [that is, act with greed, anger, or folly]?

Question: Granting that through enlightenment the three poisons are transmuted [in such a way that greedy actions turn] into observance of the precepts, [anger into] mind stability, and [folly into] wisdom, how can one rid the mind of the malady of delusion?

Answer: Realization of the Self-nature is the sole cure for all [mind] illness. Do not rely on any other remedy. Have I not already quoted to you: "Find the subject which casts the shadows, it is the very source of all Buddhas"? Your Buddha-nature is like the jewel-sword of the Vajra king: whoever touches it is killed.[17] Or is it like a massive, raging fire: everything within reach loses its life. Once you realize your True-nature, all evil bent of mind arising from karma extending over innumerable years past is instantly annihilated, like snow put into a roaring furnace. No thought of Buddha or Truth remains. How, then, can any mind illness persist? Why can't the karmically begotten delusions and the manifold discriminative thoughts and notions of the unenlightened mind be quelled? Simply because true Self-realization has not taken place. You can no more stop yourself from being driven within the Six Realms of ceaseless change without [first] realizing your Self-nature than you can stop water from boiling without quenching the fire beneath it.

Fortunately, you believe there is a truth specially transmitted outside the scriptures and scholastic teachings. Then why bother about the meaning of these scriptures? Renounce forthwith all such reflections and see the master directly. What is the master who at this very moment is seeing and hearing? If you reply, as most do, that it is Mind or Nature or Buddha or one's Face before birth or one's Original Home or Koan or Being or Nothingness or Emptiness or Form-and-Color or the Known or the Unknown or Truth

---

[17] Compare with this statement attributed to God in the Old Testament: "For there shall no man see me, and live." (Exodus 33:20)

or Delusion, or say something or remain silent, or regard it as Enlightenment or Ignorance, you fall into error at once. What is more, if you are so foolhardy as to doubt the reality of this master, you bind yourself though you use no rope. However much you try to know it through logical reasoning or to name or call it, you are doomed to failure. And even though all of you becomes one mass of questioning as you turn inward and intently search the very core of your being, you will find nothing that can be termed Mind or Essence. Yet should someone call your name, something from within will hear and respond. Find out this instant who *it* is!

If you push forward with your last ounce of strength at the very point where the path of your thinking has been blocked, and then, completely stymied, leap with hands high in the air into the tremendous abyss of fire confronting you—into the ever-burning flame of your own primordial nature—all ego-consciousness, all delusive feelings and thoughts and perceptions will perish with your ego-root and the true source of your Self-nature will appear. You will feel resurrected, all sickness having completely vanished, and will experience genuine peace and joy. You will be entirely free. For the first time you will realize that walking on water is like walking on ground and walking on ground like walking on water; that all day long there is speaking, yet no word is ever spoken; that throughout the day there is walking, yet no step is ever taken; that while the clouds are rising over the southern mountains their rain is falling over the northern range; that when the lecture gong is struck in China the lecture begins in Korea; that sitting alone in a ten-foot-square room you meet all the Buddhas of the ten quarters; that without seeing a word you read the more than seven thousand volumes of the sutras; that though you acquire all the merits and virtues of good actions, yet in fact there are none.

Do you want to know what the Mind is? The layman Ho asked Baso: "What is it that transcends all things in the universe?" Baso answered: "I will tell you after you have swallowed all the water of the West River in one gulp." Upon hearing this, Ho became deeply enlightened. Now, how do you swallow all the water of the West River in one gulp? If you grasp the spirit of this, you will be able to go through ten thousand koans at one time and perceive that walking on water is like walking on ground and walking on ground like walking on water. If you imagine I am describing something supernatural, you will one day have to swallow a red-hot iron ball before Yama-raja. But if it is not supernatural, what is it? Face up to this!

6 / TO A MONK IN SHOBO HERMITAGE (AT HIS URGENT REQUEST) / In my boyhood this question perplexed me: Aside from this physical body, what replies, "I am so-and-so," when asked, "Who are you?" This perplexity having once arisen, it became deeper year by year, resulting in my desire to become a monk. Then I made this solemn vow: Now that I have determined to be a monk, I cannot search for truth for my own sake. Even after winning the supreme Truth I will defer Buddhahood[18] until I have saved every sentient being.[19] Furthermore, until this perplexity has been dissolved I will not study Buddhism or learn the rituals and practices of a monk. So long as I live in the human world I will stay nowhere except with great Zen masters, and in the mountains.

After I entered a monastery my perplexity increased. At the same time a strong resolve arose from the bottom of my heart and I thought: Shakyamuni Buddha has passed already and Miroku, the future Buddha, has not yet appeared. During this period when authentic Buddhism has declined to the point where it is about to expire,[20] may my desire for Self-realization be strong enough to save all sentient beings in this Buddha-less world. Even should

[18] That is, the highest perfected state. (See "Buddha" in section x.)

[19] The vow of a Bodhisattva. (See "Bodhisattva" in section x.)

[20] Like many others of his time, Bassui believed he was in the beginning of the period of the destruction of the true Law as prophesied by the Buddha himself. The Mohasannipata Candragarbha sutra quotes the Buddha as saying that in the first five hundred years after his Parinirvana his disciples would attain emancipation according to the right Law; in the second five hundred they would only be sure of attaining samadhi; in the third five hundred, of reading and reciting the sutras; in the fourth five hundred, of building temples and pagodas; and in the fifth five hundred, of the destruction of the Law. If the date of the Buddha's Parinirvana is accepted as around 476 B.C., Bassui's birth, in 1327, would have been within the fourth period.

I suffer the pangs of everlasting hell as a result of this sin of attachment [to saving], so long as I can shoulder the sufferings of sentient beings, I will never become discouraged or forsake this eternal vow. Furthermore, in practicing Zen I will not idle away my time thinking of life and death or waste even a minute in trifling good works. Nor will I blind others to the truth by trying to minister to them so long as my own [spiritual] strength is insufficient to lead them to Self-realization.

These resolutions became part and parcel of my thinking, bothering me to some extent in my zazen. But I could not do otherwise. I constantly prayed[21] to Buddhas for strength to carry out these resolutions, which I made the standard of my conduct in both favorable and unfavorable circumstances, under the watchful but friendly eyes of heavenly beings.[22] Thus it has been up to the present.

It is really pointless to tell you about these delusive states of mine, but as you make bold to ask I write here of my aspirations as a novice.

7 / TO THE NUN FURUSAWA / You have written me that the object of Zen practice [you believe] is the manifestation of Mind-in-itself. But how does it manifest itself? What can be seen with the eyes or be known by reason cannot be called Mind-in-itself. You must begin your zazen by looking into your own mind. As your thoughts diminish you will become aware of them, but it is a mistake to struggle to stop them from arising. Neither loathe nor cherish your thoughts, only realize the source from which they stem. By constantly questioning whence thoughts arise, the time will come when your mind, unable to answer, will be free of even a ripple of thought. Yet even now you will find no answer. But still ask, "What *is* this Mind?" to the very rock bottom and the questioning mind will suddenly vanish and your body feel

---

[21] Petitionary prayer is not unknown in Zen. Beginners often pray to Buddhas and patriarchs for strength to purge themselves of evil and delusion so they may carry on their spiritual practice successfully. Dogen's *hotsugammon* is an example of a widely used petition in Zen.

[22] That is, devas. See "Six Realms of Existence."

as though it were without substance, like the empty space of the ten quarters.

This is the first stage to which Zen beginners attain and they are encouraged to some extent. But if they mistake this for the manifestation of Mind-in-itself (or Truth-in-itself), they are like one who takes fish eyes for pearls. Those who persist in such error become haughty, malign Buddhas and patriarchs, and ignore the law of causation. So they have to struggle with evil spirits in this life and tread thorny paths in the next. But with favorable karmic relations they will eventually attain enlightenment. Men, however, who cannot perceive the truth of all this, who do not believe their own Mind is Buddha and who look for Buddha, or Truth, outside this Mind, are infinitely worse off than non-Buddhists who attach themselves to the phenomenal world.

As I have already written you, when some insight comes to you go to a competent Zen master and openly demonstrate to him what you have perceived, exactly as it came to you. If it is faulty and needs to be dissolved, let it be done like boiling water destroying ice. At last, like a bright moon shining in an empty sky through clouds that have broken open, your Face before your parents' birth will be revealed, and for the first time you will understand what is meant by "The saw dances the Sandai." Sandai is a kind of dance. Just consider: a saw dances the Sandai! What does this mean? Tackle it resolutely but without reasoning, for it has no meaning in the usual sense. You will be able to comprehend it only upon Self-realization.

You next mentioned that you are going to fast. Fasting is a non-Buddhist practice; don't do it. Renunciation of your wrong views which discriminate gain from loss, good from bad—this is true fasting. Relinquishment of delusion in the wholehearted practice of Zen—this is self-purification. To desire abnormal experiences[23] is as misguided as wanting to appear different from ordinary people. You have but to keep your mind steadfast yet flexible, concerning yourself with neither good nor evil in others and not obstructing them. If you remind yourself that this world is but a dream in which there is no grief to avoid and no joy to look for, your mind will become visibly serene. Not only this, but your illnesses will

[23] Presumably hallucinations or fantasies arising from prolonged fasting.

disappear as your delusive feelings and perceptions fall away. You must even discard whatever you realize through enlightenment. What is more, you must not attach yourself to or be repelled by visions of any kind, for they are all illusional. Don't involve yourself in such fantasies but only inquire: "What is the master who sees all this?"

I have fully answered the questions you have raised. Should you not realize your True-self in this lifetime even though you practice Zen exactly as I now advise you, you will unquestionably meet a perfectly enlightened Zen master in your next life and attain Self-realization a thousand times over through one Sound [of Truth].

I dislike writing you in such detail, but since you have written me from a sickbed to which you have long been confined, this is the only way I can answer so you will readily understand.

8 / FIRST LETTER TO THE ZEN PRIEST IGUCHI / I have read your presentation at length, but it misses the point of the koan. The Sixth Patriarch said: "The flag doesn't move, the wind doesn't move, only your mind moves."[24] To realize this clearly is to perceive that the universe and yourself are of the same root, that you and every single thing are a unity. The gurgle of the stream and the sigh of the wind are the voices of the master. The green of the pine, the white of snow, these are the colors of the master, the very one who lifts the hands, moves the legs, sees, hears. One who grasps this directly without recourse to reason or intellection can be said to have some degree of inner realization. But this is not yet full enlightenment.

An ancient Zen master [Rinzai] said: "You should not cling to the idea that you are Pure-essence." And again: "Your physical body, composed of the four basic elements, can't hear or understand this preaching. The empty space can't understand this preaching. Then what is it that hears and understands?" Meditate fully and directly on these words. Take hold of this koan as though wielding the jewel-sword of the Vajra king. Cut down whatever appears in the mind. When the thoughts of mundane matters arise, cut them off. When notions of Buddhism arise, likewise lop them

[24] *Mumonkan* No. 29.

off. In short, destroy all ideas, whether of realization, of Buddhas, or of devils, and all day long pursue the question "What is it that hears this preaching?" When you have eradicated every conception until only emptiness remains, and then cut through even the emptiness, your mind will burst open and that which hears will manifest itself. Persevere, persevere—never quit halfway—until you reach the point where you feel as though you have risen from the dead. Only then will you be able to wholly resolve the momentous question, "What is it that hears this preaching?"

I am afraid it may be inconvenient for you to write me often, so I am writing you this [detailed] letter. After you have read it drop it into the fire.

9 / SECOND LETTER TO THE ZEN PRIEST IGUCHI / I have read your letter carefully.

Having long admired you for your determination to come to Self-realization, I was highly gratified to learn that you have not forgotten the Great Question. Your answer has been noted in all respects. Here I want to tell you to make this your koan: "What is the substance of my Fundamental-nature?" In your search for the master that hears and speaks, though thousands of thoughts arise don't entertain them but only ask, *"What* is it?" Every thought and all self-awareness will then disappear, followed by a state not unlike a cloudless sky. Now, Mind itself has no form. What is it, then, that hears and works and moves about? Delve into yourself deeper and deeper until you are no longer aware of a single object. Then beyond a shadow of a doubt you will perceive your True-nature, like a man awakening from a dream. Assuredly at that moment flowers will bloom on withered trees and fire flame up from ice. All of Buddhism, all worldly concerns, all notions of good and evil, will have disappeared, like last night's dream, and your fundamental Buddha-nature alone will manifest itself. Having come to such inner understanding, you must not then cherish the notion that this Mind is fundamentally Buddha-nature. If you do you will be creating for yourself another thought-form.

Only because I regard your desire for Self-realization so highly do I write in such detail.[25]

[25] At first blush this statment may seem to be at variance with others

Thank you for sending the five hundred packets of caked rice and the pound of tea.

10 / THIRD LETTER TO THE ZEN PRIEST IGUCHI / I have read your letter with particular care. I am much pleased to hear about your Zen practice. But if I answer you at any length, you are bound to make your own interpretations of what I write and that will become somewhat of a hindrance to your Self-realization.

Try to perceive directly the subject that is presently inquiring. Buddhas and patriarchs say that this subject is inherently Buddha-mind. Yet this Mind is without substance. In your physical body what can you call Mind or Buddha? Now intensely ask yourself, "What is *this* which can't be named or intellectually known?" If you profoundly question, "What is it that lifts the hands, moves the legs, speaks, hears?" your reasoning will come to a halt, every avenue blocked, and you won't know which way to turn. But relentlessly continue your inquiry as to this subject. Abandon intellection and relinquish your hold on everything. When with your whole heart you long for liberation for its own sake, beyond every doubt you will become enlightened.

With the passage of time one's thoughts are stilled and one experiences a void like that of a cloudless sky. You must not, however, confuse this with enlightenment. Putting aside logic and reason, question yourself even more intensely in this wise: "Mind is formless, and so right now am I. What, then, is hearing?" Only after your search has permeated every pore and fiber of your being will the empty space suddenly break asunder and your Face before your parents were born appear. You will feel like a man who abruptly awakens from a dream. At such time go to a reputable Zen master and ask for his critical examination. While you may not come to Self-realization in this life, you will surely become

in these letters wherein Bassui says it is unwise to write in detail. Bassui is always afraid of saying too much, of burdening his correspondents with ideas which may hang in their minds and thus prove a hindrance to enlightenment. As this point Bassui is implying that he is so moved by Priest Iguchi's ardor that, despite his better judgment, he has written him this type of letter.

enlightened in your next, Zen masters have taught, if on your death-bed your mind is barren of every thought and you only ask, "What is this Mind?" dying unconcerned, like fire expiring.

I have written as you have asked me to but reluctantly. Once you have read this letter burn it. Don't reread it but only search deeply for the one hearing. My words will seem like so much nonsense when you experience enlightenment yourself.

11 / FOURTH LETTER TO THE ZEN PRIEST IGUCHI / I am glad to learn how ardently you are practicing zazen. What you have reported to me is a little like a Zen experience, but it is essentially what you have understood with your intellect. The Great Question cannot be resolved by the discursive mind. Even what becomes clear through realization is delusion of a kind. In a previous letter, I wrote you that only when you have come back from the dead, so to speak, will that which hears manifest itself. Your persistent inquiry, "What is it that hears?" will eventually lead you to awareness of nothing but the questioning itself. You must not, however, be misled into thinking this is the subject which hears.

You say that in working on this koan you feel as though you have taken hold of a sword and cut away every idea in your mind, including the impression of emptiness, and that questioning alone remains. But *what* is doing all this? Delve to your inmost being and you will discover it is precisely that which hears.

Even though you experience your Self-nature again and again, and understand Buddhism well enough to discourse upon it, your delusive thoughts will survive, inevitably precipitating you into the Three Evil Paths in your next life, unless their root is severed through perfect enlightenment. If, on the other hand, still unsatisfied, you persevere in your self-inquiry even to your deathbed, you will unquestionably come to full enlightenment in your next existence.

Don't allow yourself to become discouraged and don't fritter away your time, just concentrate with all your heart on your koan. Now, your physical being doesn't hear, nor does the void. Then what does? Strive to find out. Put aside your rational intellect, give up all techniques [to induce enlightenment], abandon the desire for Self-realization, and renounce every other motivation. Your mind will then come to a standstill, and you won't know what to do. No longer possessing the desire to attain enlightenment or to use your powers of reason, you will feel like a tree or a stone. But go further yet and question yourself exhaustively for days on end, and you will surely attain deep enlightenment, cutting away the undermost roots of birth-and-death and coming to the realm of the non-self-conscious Mind. The undermost roots of birth-and-death are the delusive thoughts and feelings arising from the self-conscious mind, the mind of ego. A Zen master [Rinzai] once said: "There is nothing in particular to realize. Only get rid of [the idea of a] Buddha and sentient beings."[26] The essential thing for enlightenment is to empty the mind of the notion of self.

To write in such detail is unwise, but as you have written me so often I feel obliged to reply in this way.

12 / TO A NUN / I have read your letter carefully. It is gratifying to see how eagerly you are practicing Zen, putting it before everything else.

You say you once thought you ought to have gone west to the capital but that you now see it was a mistaken idea, that the capital is everywhere, and that therefore you need do no more than question yourself one-pointedly, "What *is* it?" But this is not enough, for though you have found the capital to be everywhere you have not seen the Ruler face to face. The Ruler is your Face before your parents were born.

When you "pierce" the question somewhat, your mind becomes like the void; [ideas of] Buddhas, sentient beings, past or present, are no more. A tranquility not unlike the serenity of moonlight flooding the countryside suffuses the heart, but this can't be put into words. Such serenity is the outcome of some Zen practice, yet the mind is still sick, for the Self is still topsy-turvy, and this inversion is the root source of delusion. What is meant by cutting away the root is breaking through this serene state of mind.

One who lacks a genuine thirst for Self-realization digs up old

---

[26] In other words, of a Buddha *as opposed to* sentient beings.

koans and, reasoning out "answers," considers himself enlightened. You must not become attached to anything you realize, you must only search directly for the subject that realizes. Thus like something burnt to a crisp or slashed to bits, your preconceived notions will all be annihilated. You will perceive the master only after you have probed "What is it?" with your last ounce of strength and every thought of good and evil has vanished. Not until then will you feel like one who has actually been resurrected.

Tokusan said: "Even though you can say something about *it*, I will give you thirty blows of the stick . . ."[27]? Can you avoid the stick? If you can, you understand the import of "The East Mountain strides over the water."[28]

I am afraid I have written too much, but I have done so because I admire your determination to become enlightened. These ideas are not mine but what I have learned from the teachings of the ancient Zen masters.

[27] The koan in its entirety reads: "Even though you can say something about it, / I will give you thirty blows of the stick. / And if you can't say anything about it, / I will also give you thirty blows of the stick."

[28] This is from Yun-men's (Ummon's) *Collected Sayings*. A monk asked Yun-men: "Where do Buddhas come from?" [that is, "What is the Buddha-mind?"]. Yun-men replied: "The East Mountain strides over the water."

PART TWO / ENLIGHTENMENT

V / EIGHT CONTEMPORARY ENLIGHTENMENT EXPERI- ENCES OF JAPANESE AND WESTERNERS /

EDITOR'S INTRODUCTION / In recent years stories of the enlightenments of ancient Chinese Zen monks have found their way into English. While their laudable aim is to inspire and instruct modern readers, paradoxically they often have the opposite effect. A contemporary Asian or Westerner surveying the paths to Self-realization that these ancient worthies trod is all too likely to say to himself: "It's all very well for these people, they could attain satori because they were monks isolated from the hurly-burly of the world, celibates unburdened by the affections and responsibilities of wife and children. Life in their day was relatively simple. Theirs was not a highly organized industrial society making insatiable demands on the individual. The spirit of their day and mine is vastly different. What meaning can their enlightenment have for me?"

No such objections can be raised to the following eight accounts. These Asians and Westerners are living among us today, neither as monks nor unworldly solitaries but as business and professional men and women, artists, and housewives. All have trained in Zen under a modern master and realized their Self-nature in one degree or another. Their stories bear witness that what man has done man can do, that satori is no impossible ideal.

The majority of these enlightenment stories first appeared in

Japanese Buddhist publications, from which they were translated into English, the remainder having been solicited specifically for this book. They have been pruned in such a way as to eliminate irrelevant background material without sacrificing either the thread of events which was significant in propelling these people into their awakening, or their varied and intimate reactions to zazen and the elements of Zen training. By not rigidly limiting these accounts to the circumstances of the enlightenment itself, we believe we have added to their value as human documents.

Each of these stories bears in its caption the age and occupation of the individual at the time of his or her enlightenment. All were written soon after the experience with the exception of number three, which was not set to paper until almost twenty years later. Account number two is the editor's own experience and number eight that of his wife.

More often than not the ordinary mystical experience of expanded consciousness comes purely by chance, and since it is unconnected with a proven discipline, a discipline for sustaining and enlarging it, it effects little or no transformation of personality or character, eventually fading into a happy memory.

Kensho is no such haphazard phenomenon. Like a sprout which emerges from a soil which has been seeded, fertilized, and thoroughly weeded, satori comes to a mind that has heard and believed the Buddha-truth and then uprooted within itself the throttling notion of self-and-other. And just as one must nurture a newly emerged seedling until maturity, so Zen training stresses the need to ripen an initial awakening through subsequent koan practice and/or shikan-taza until it thoroughly animates one's life. In other words, to function on the higher level of consciousness brought about by kensho, one must further train oneself to *act* in accordance with this perception of Truth.

This special relationship between awakening and post-awakening zazen is brought out in a parable in one of the sutras. In this story enlightenment is compared to a youth who, after years of destitute wandering in a distant land, one day discovers that his wealthy father had many years earlier bequeathed him his fortune. To actually take possession of this treasure, which is rightly his, and become capable of handling it wisely is equated with post-kensho zazen, that is, with broadening and deepening the initial awakening.

The perceptive reader will observe that these enlightenments vary in their clarity and depth, that some individuals, in Zen parlance, have actually taken hold of the "Ox," while others have barely seen his "tracks." Although examples can be found of profound enlightenment having been attained after only a few years' exertion and of shallow kensho having resulted from a lengthy effort at zazen, in the majority of cases the more extensive the zazen prior to awakening—the more wholehearted and pure—the broader and firmer the enlightenment which follows.

What manner of people were these who, like the carp in the Chinese fable that leapt up the waterfall in a mighty thrust to become a dragon, could rise to a higher level of consciousness, to a wholly new awareness of the indivisibility of all life and the basic emptiness of all things? Certainly none was gifted with extraordinary intellect, nor were any endowed with supranormal powers. Suffering they had each known, but it was no more than what is experienced in the lifetime of an ordinary person. If they were exceptional in any way it was simply in their courage to "go they knew not where by a road they knew not of," prompted by a faith in their real Self.

The seeker who does not find is still entrapped by his illusion of two worlds: one of perfection that lies beyond, of peace without struggle,[1] of unending joy; the other the everyday meaningless world of pain and evil which is scarcely worth relating himself to. Secretly he longs for the former even as he openly despises the latter. Yet he hesitates to plunge into the teeming Void, into the abyss of his own Primal-nature, because in his deepest unconscious he fears abandoning his familiar world of duality for the unknown world of Oneness, the reality of which he still doubts. The finders, on the other hand, are restrained by neither fears nor doubts. Casting both aside, they leap because they can't do

---

[1] "Peace of mind is not absence of struggle but absence of uncertainty and confusion." From an article on "Yoga and Christian Spiritual Techniques" by Anthony Bloom.

otherwise—they simply must and no longer know why—and so they triumph.

The bulk of these enlightenments came in sesshin, a vehicle of spiritual discipline whose exact counterpart can be found nowhere in Buddhism except Zen. Sesshin in one form or another goes back to the time of the Buddha, when monks would train themselves in seclusion during the several months of the rainy season. The purpose of sesshin, as the word implies, is to enable one to collect and unify his normally scattered mind so that he can focus it like a powerful telescope inward in order to discover his true Self-nature. During sesshin the basic teaching devices and methods of Zen—that is, zazen, teisho (the formal commentary), and doku-san (private instruction)—are coordinated into a meaningful whole during seven days[2] of seclusion. Kensho is not of course confined to sesshin, but since sesshin is unquestionably its most potent incubator, the progressive steps involved in this unique form of mind-maturation are worth describing at some length if the reader is to have a clear insight into this incubation process.

In a monastery, sesshin actually begins with certain ceremonies the evening before formal zazen begins. In the dimly lit *zendo,* which is to be the hub of all activities for one week, solemn head monks assemble the participants for the purpose of assigning places, instructing newcomers how to enter and leave the zendo unobtrusively, how to handle their utensils and bowls silently during meals, how to walk in kinhin, and how to get on and off their sitting cushions quietly.

With the conclusion of these formalities everyone is summoned to the main hall, ablaze with lights, by the ponderous beats of the giant monastery drum. Dressed in formal sitting attire, the participants line up in two rows facing each other across the hall, kneel in the traditional Japanese posture, then bow to each other as a sign of mutual respect and identification with one another's aspiration. There is an air of suppressed excitement and hushed expectancy when, a few minutes later, the roshi and his principal aides in full ceremonial dress enter. As they pass between the two

---

[2] This refers to monastery sesshin. Temple or other types of sesshin are frequently less than seven days.

ranks to take their seats at the head of the hall, all bow again, this time with heads touching the tatami mats, out of deep respect for their teachers.

After welcoming everyone the roshi speaks in effect as follows:

During sesshin you are not to talk with one another, as speaking disrupts the concentrated mind and thus hinders your own practice and that of others.

Each must devote himself single-mindedly to his own zazen to the exclusion of everything else, including a concern with his neighbors' problems. If you have pressing questions, speak to the head monks out of earshot of the others.

Your eyes should always rest unfocused in front of you while sitting, standing, walking, or working—at a distance of about one yard when sitting and about two yards in the other positions. When your eyes dart about and fix themselves on something or other, this contact creates an impression, which in turn gives rise to a thought. Thoughts multiply and then like flies buzz about in the mind, making concentration difficult if not impossible. Do not therefore divert your eyes for any reason whatever.

During sesshin dispense with social amenities of every sort. Don't greet one another "Good morning" or bid one another "Good night," and don't compliment or criticize each other. Further, you mustn't make a point of stepping aside to allow others to go ahead, nor should you push ahead of them. In all your activities you should move neither hastily nor sluggishly but naturally, like flowing water.

It is advisable in sesshin to eat no more than half of what you normally eat, and if you follow this caution your zazen will be more effective. However, zazen is not asceticism and it is unwise to abstain altogether from food, as your mind might become disturbed by pangs of hunger or you might find yourself becoming too weak to do zazen. If you have no desire to eat during certain meals because you are striving particularly hard, you may of course refuse food.

Do not eat too rapidly or so slowly that everybody has to wait for you. Ideally all should finish at approximately the same time so as not to upset the established rhythm of the sesshin. Be careful not to rattle your bowls when you uncover them and when you put them away, and munch the pickled radishes as quietly as possible; such sounds often prove intrusive to beginners.

For some reason, many people imagine it is more difficult for women to come to Self-realization than for men. On the contrary, women usually attain kensho quicker because their minds are less prone to play with ideas than are men's. But both men and women, if they expunge every thought from their minds and become self-less, can equally attain enlightenment during one week of sesshin. Many have done so in the past and a few determined ones will do it during this sesshin.

Lastly, bear in mind that sesshin is a cooperative endeavor in which there is mutual support and stimulation only if all participate jointly in sesshin activities and do not follow their own inclinations. To indulge your own desires at the expense of this common effort is an expression of ego and hence inimical to our purpose, both individual and collective.

The roshi then concludes by exhorting all to do their utmost.

Tea and cakes are now served, first to the roshi, next to the head monks, and then to those assembled. The roshi sips his tea first and is followed by the others. Again he is the first to eat his cake, after which everyone joins him.

This ritual is not without significance. It symbolizes the joining of all hearts and minds in this common undertaking. At the same time it is an expression of the students' confidence in their teacher, by whom they agree to be led, and of their faith in the Dharma which he expounds. This ceremony over, the roshi and his aides depart, and once more all bow to them as before.

The nine-o'clock bell tolls and everyone retires to bed. In six hours the great venture begins . . .

Clang, clang! . . . 3 A.M. . . . sesshin's begun! . . .

Slightly dazed newcomers rub sleepy eyes, fumble with quilts . . . seasoned hands alertly fold and store bedding, go to the toilet, brush teeth, dash cold water on their faces, dress, mount the *tan* (zazen platform) in a quick movement, adjust their sitting cushions, begin zazen . . . no time, no effort wasted . . . lethargic beginners clumsily climb onto the *tan* and their cushions . . . adjusting, wriggling, readjusting . . .

Minutes later the roshi silently enters . . . walking in the rear he inspects backs, to his comprehending eye more eloquently revealing the mind's tension or slackness than the face . . .

A sagging spine arches with a light crack of his stick, another straightens merely with whispered advice or encouragement . . . each sitter as Roshi passes by greets him with gassho, the universal gesture of humility, respect, and gratitude . . .

Roshi may relate to the now wall-gazing sitters an inspiring anecdote of an ancient Zen worthy or a noteworthy contemporary . . . "After all," he concludes, "he was only human; if he could awaken, so can you.". . . jaws grimly set, the struggle is on . . .

Clang! clang! . . . kinhin . . . forty-five minutes have elapsed . . . old-timers flip off their cushions in one swirl, cat-land on their feet, fall in line and slowly circle the zendo, hands folded across chest, with measured steps, concentrated mind . . . Clang! . . . kinhin finishes . . . some quickly mount the *tan,* others head for the toilet . . . Clang! clang! clang! . . . the next sitting period commences . . . the pungent smell of a new stick of incense[3] drifts through the zendo . . .

Some twenty minutes later the *godo,* Roshi's chief deputy, slips softly from the·*tan* . . . he goes for the kyosaku, symbol of Manjusri's delusion-cutting sword, resting in the shrine in the center of the zendo, under the figure of Manjusri. He grips it at each end, bows low before this zendo guardian . . .

Silently the godo stalks around the zendo, appraising the telltale postures . . . no sound but the barely audible undertone of puffing and wheezing from novices straining desperately with bodies instead of minds to corral stampeding thoughts . . .

Smash! . . . his kyosaku lands full force on a corner of the *tan* . . . a murmur like wind soughing through cornstalks sweeps through the startled, slightly frightened newcomers . . . silence . . . a deafening silence . . .

Slam! wham! . . . flailing away at sitters whose slouching backs signal wilting minds, the godo roars: "Only fifteen minutes to dokusan! Brace up! Concentrate, concentrate! Don't separate yourselves a hair's breadth from your koan! . . . You must bring Roshi an answer, not a blank!"

Slumped bodies shore up . . . the puffing and straining loudens. Clang! clang! . . . dokusan!

---

[3] The sitting period of forty-five minutes is measured by the combustion of a particular length of incense.

"Move!" the godo yells . . . the tension broken, all but a reluctant few eagerly race to the lineup . . .

"Do you want the truth or don't you!" he barks at the laggards, jerking one or two from the *tan* and egging them on toward the dokusan line with his kyosaku, coldly ignoring others.

In most monastery and temple sesshin the kyosaku plays a vital and often crucial role, which reaches a dramatic climax just before dokusan. The essential purpose of the kyosaku is to arouse every vestige of dormant energy in the sitters to enable them to break through their protective shell of self-delusion and come to true Self-understanding. No single element of Zen training, however, has been more vociferously criticized, none less understood, by Asians and Westerners alike, than the use of this stick. Condemned as a "sadistic expression of Japanese culture" and as a "flagrant perversion of Buddhism," it is in fact neither. Along with Zen itself, the kyosaku is an import from China.[4] It is probably a hardier descendant of a small rod used even in the Buddha's day to awaken dozing monks and constructed so as to whistle when shaken beside the ear.[5] In China at some point the Zen masters evidently felt their disciples needed to be stimulated with something more than pleasant sounds or an occasional slap of the hand or blow of the fist, and in response to this need the forefather of the kyosaku was born.

Kyosaku are made in varying sizes, shapes, and weights, those constructed of hard wood being used in the winter when monks and laymen are heavily clad, those of soft wood in the summer when they are wearing light clothing. The end of the kyosaku that comes in contact with the body is flattened like a paddle to a width of perhaps three inches, while the handle end is rounded to permit a firm grip. In some monasteries and temples it measures as much as four and a half feet in length, in others no more than two and a half.

The kyosaku may be applied to rouse a sleepy sitter, to enliven

[4] For a brief description of the use of the kyosaku (called *keisaku* in the Rinzai tradition) in a latter-day Chinese Zen monastery, see John Blofeld's *The Wheel of Life*, p. 167.

[5] This piece of information was given me by Yasutani-roshi.

a weary one, or to spur on a striving one, but it is never used as chastisement or out of personal pique. This is clear from the fact that the one struck raises his hands in gassho to show his gratitude to the godo, who in turn acknowledges this gesture with a bow, in a spirit of mutual respect and understanding. In the monastery the heaviest blows of the kyosaku are mostly reserved for the earnest and the courageous and not wasted on the slackers or the timid. The adage that a poor horse can't be made to run fast no matter how hard or how often he is whipped is well understood in the zendo.

In Soto monasteries and temples sitters face the wall and not each other as they do in the Rinzai sect, so the godo applies the kyosaku from the rear, at his own discretion,[6] and occasionally without any warning.[7] In the hands of a sensitive, enlightened godo, able to strike when the iron is hot, or for that matter to make the iron hot by striking, the kyosaku is unequaled for raising one's concentrative effort to its greatest intensity. Just as a whip sensitively used on a racing horse can drive him to even greater speed without harm, so the kyosaku perceptively applied to the back of a striving sitter can, without paining him, elicit that superhuman burst of energy which leads to the dynamic one-pointedness of mind indispensable for kensho. Even at less critical moments, particularly in midafternoon or evening, when a slumping, exhausted body has slackened the mind's tautness, opening the way to invading hordes of thoughts, a well-timed blow across the shoulders will knock them all from the head, simultaneously releasing unsuspected stores of energy.[8]

It cannot be emphasized too strongly that administering the kyosaku is not a matter of simply striking one with a stick. In this act compassion, force, and wisdom are joined. In a first-rate monastery or temple the godo is invariably a man of strong spirit yet

[6] Sitters frequently ask for the kyosaku by signaling with their hands in gassho above their head.

[7] Usually, however, it is preceded by a warning tap on the shoulder. In Rinzai the striking is from the front, so one always knows when he is going to be struck.

[8] Each shoulder is struck twice on points corresponding to acupuncture meridians.

with a compassionate heart. Indeed, if his kyosaku is to be a spur and not a thorn, he must be identified with the deepest spiritual aspiration of the sitters. Well has it been said that love without force is weakness, force without love brutality.

There is no denying, however, that for those Westerners unable to disabuse themselves of the notion that beatings with a stick under any circumstances are an affront to their dignity the kyosaku will always remain a menace rather than a welcome goad.

Dokusan is followed by sutra-chanting, announced by the sharp C-r-a-ck! of the wooden clappers. At this signal all file outdoors along an open canopied passageway, to be greeted by the first cold breath of dawn, and then proceed to the main hall. There laymen take their place on one side, monks on the other. Dokusan and two hours of zazen have brought the mind to a clarity and one-pointedness where every posture and movement of the body during prostrations and the chanting take on fresh meaning and significance. The rhythmic beat of the *mokugyo,* the deep ring of the large, bowl-shaped gong, the flickering candles on the butsudan (Buddhist altar), and the fresh scent of incense all play their part in further whetting the mind.

After chanting comes the first meal, at five thirty, consisting of rice gruel, a side dish of a few vegetables, and pickled radishes. This simple fare is for the nourishment of the body, to give it strength to pursue the Buddha's Way, and not for enjoyment. But one does not eat immediately. First, with the ting-a-ling of the head monk's handbell the mealtime recitation commences with an expression of faith in the Unified Three Treasures—that is, Vairochana Buddha (symbolizing transcendental Buddha-Knowledge); the Dharma (or law of cause and effect); and the Sangha (comprising Buddhas everywhere). The chanting then ceases temporarily while each person removes the cloth around the four nested lacquer bowls and chopsticks which are supplied him for the sesshin and sets them out in front of him.

Ting-a-ling! The chanting resumes with an avowal of faith in the person and life of the Buddha Shakyamuni, in his Dharma, and in the great exemplars of his teaching, namely, the Bodhisattvas Manjusri, Samantabhadra, and Avalokitesvara, in addition to the patriarchs. Now the rice gruel is ladled out from a large wooden tub and the vegetables served.

Before anything is touched, however, there is another round of chanting in which each recalls that the food about to be eaten comes of the labors of many people, and that each is entitled to receive it only if his aspiration is pure and his effort sincere. If taken, it is to be received with gratitude, not greedily, and without preference or aversion.

Now only one more ritual remains before the meal is actually eaten. Each takes from his rice bowl some half dozen grains of rice and places them in a special receptacle, which is passed to all for this purpose. This symbolic offering is for the hungry unseen spirits of this and other worlds who through their greed have condemned themselves to miserable existences. The meal when finally eaten is consumed in silence so that concentration, whether on a koan, counting the breath, or on the eating itself, may continue uninterrupted.

Three times in all monk-waiters come with the large tub of gruel. Those wanting more proffer their rice bowls, waiting with hands in gassho while being served. Wordlessly they rub their hands together to signal "Enough." If no further servings are desired, each simply nods his head and bows from the waist, hands folded across the chest, when the waiters come by. Not all heed the roshi's injunction to eat sparingly; monks who are obviously more intent on filling their bellies than emptying their minds take even a third bowl of rice.

Food once touched with the chopsticks must be eaten and not discarded. Not a scrap is to be wasted. At the conclusion of the meal hot water is passed around, and each one, using a pickled radish for the purpose, cleans his bowls of every particle, after which, if he is thirsty, he drinks the water, not forgetting, however, to deposit the last dregs in a common container passed for the same hungry spirits. The meal finishes with a chant, the substance of which is an expression of thanks for the nourishment just received and a pledge to use this strength for the spiritual welfare of all beings.[9]

[9] These are Hosshin-ji Soto rituals, differing slightly from Rinzai. Incidentally, Zen monasteries usually serve polished white rice, not brown.

Not alone food but every object is to be used with due regard for its proper function and not wasted or needlessly destroyed. This is one of the inviolable rules of the Zen monastery and care must be taken especially during sesshin not to transgress it. The reasons are more spiritual than economic. To squander is to destroy. To treat things with reverence and gratitude, according to their nature and purpose, is to affirm their value and life, a life in which we are all equally rooted. Wastefulness is a measure of our egocentricity and hence of our alienation from things, from their Buddha-nature, from their essential unity with us. Further, it is an act of indifference to the absolute worth of the wasted object, however humble. Thus, breaking a glass heedlessly at any time, leaving a light burning when it is no longer needed, using more water than is required for a particular task, permitting a book to remain overturned after it has been read—these are all wanton acts in the deepest religious sense and therefore harmful to our spiritual progress. For this reason they are roundly condemned.

Following the morning meal, most monasteries and temples schedule *samu* (physical work), which during sesshin takes the form of sweeping, dusting, scrubbing the floors and toilets, sweeping the walks, raking leaves, weeding the gardens, and working in the kitchen.[10] Since the time when Huai-hai (Hyakujo) first instituted it, more than a thousand years ago, manual labor has been an essential ingredient of Zen discipline. It is recorded of Huai-hai that one day his monks, feeling he had grown too feeble to work, hid his gardening tools. When they refused to heed his entreaties to return them, he stopped eating, saying: "No work, no eating." The same spirit was expressed in modern times by Gempo Yamamoto-roshi, former abbot of Ryutaku-ji, who died in June of 1961 at the age of ninety-six. Almost blind and no longer able to teach or work about the monastery, he decided it was time to die, so he stopped eating. When asked by his monks why he refused his food, he replied that he had outlived his usefulness and was only

[10] In monasteries where there is a large amount of manual labor the year round—for example, in those which raise their own rice as well as vegetables—*samu* is dispensed with during sesshin so as to permit more time for sitting.

a bother to everybody. They told him: "If you die now [January] when it is so cold, everybody will be uncomfortable at your funeral and you will be an even greater nuisance, so please eat!" He thereupon resumed eating, but when it became warm he again stopped, and not long after quietly toppled over and died.

What is the significance of such work in terms of Zen training? First, it points up that zazen is not merely a matter of acquiring the ability to concentrate and focus the mind during sitting, but that in the widest sense zazen involves the mobilization and dynamic utilization of joriki (the power generated by zazen) in our every act. Samu, as a mobile type of zazen, also provides the opportunity to quiet, deepen, and bring the mind to one-pointedness through activity, as well as to invigorate the body and thereby energize the mind.

The object here, as in every other type of zazen, is the cultivation first of mindfulness and eventually mindlessness. These are simply two different degrees of absorption. Mindfulness is a state wherein one is totally aware in any situation and so always able to respond appropriately. Yet one is aware that he is aware. Mindlessness, on the other hand, or "no-mindness" as it has been called, is a condition of such complete absorption that there is no vestige of self-awareness.

Any action arising from these states of mind can be neither rushed nor desultory, neither strained nor lax, can have no false movements nor waste any energy. All labor entered into with such a mind is valued for itself apart from what it may lead to. This is the "meritless" or "purposeless" work of Zen. By undertaking each task in this spirit, eventually we are enabled to grasp the truth that every act is an expression of the Buddha-mind. Once this is directly and unmistakably experienced, no labor can be beneath one's dignity. On the contrary, all work, no matter how menial, is ennobling because it is seen as the expression of the immaculate Buddha-nature. This is true enlightenment, and enlightenment in Zen is never for oneself alone but for the sake of all.

This ideal is stressed throughout sesshin. Four times a day in fact—at the close of the formal lecture, at the end of sutra-chanting in the morning and in the afternoon, and the last thing in the evening—the Four Vows are recited three times in unison:

All beings, without number, I vow to liberate.
Endless blind passions I vow to uproot.
Dharma gates,[11] without number, I vow to penetrate.
The Great Way of Buddha I vow to attain.

Samu finished, there follows a formal talk of about an hour's length (an example of which is to be found in section II). Then, around eleven, comes the main meal of the day, usually white rice mixed with barley and supplemented by fresh vegetables and soy-bean-paste soup. After lunch all but the most ardent, who continue to sit in the zendo, relax for an hour, as provided by the sesshin schedule, not forgetting, however, to absorb themselves in their koan or other exercise.

With the exception of the talk and manual work, the afternoon and evening are a repetition of the morning timetable. Some monasteries and temples allow a hot bath in the afternoon or evening, and for beginners with aching legs and strained bodies this relief is inexpressibly welcome. At four in the afternoon a light repast, mainly made up of leftovers from the midday meal, is served. Unlike the first two meals, which are preceded by and end with chanting, this "medicine"[12] is consumed in complete silence.

At Hosshin-ji, noted for its strict sesshin, on the fourth night and every night thereafter, beginning at eight, there is a unique discipline for combatting the seductive visions of sleep which begin to tug at the fatigued, faltering mind at this hour. With the clang of the large zendo bell there is a sudden outburst of "Mu-ing" by all who are striving with this koan. At first weak and uncertain, this ground swell gathers depth, force, and momentum under the energetic prodding of the free-swinging kyosaku of the godo and his aides, who shout: "Voice Mu from the hara, not from the throat!" When these cries of "Mu!" reach a crescendo of deep bellows, as they eventually do, suddenly they are turned off by

[11] That is, levels of truth.
[12] *Yakuseki*, literally "medicine stone." Buddhist monks in ancient China ate only two meals a day. In the winter to keep themselves warm and to relieve the pangs of hunger, they would place a warm stone, regarded as a panacea for all stomach disorders, over their bellies. From this the third meal, when it came to be eaten, was known as "medicine."

the clanging of the same bell, usually about thirty minutes later. Now silent zazen resumes, but the air has become electric.

Zazen ends at a quarter to nine and the final chanting of the day follows, a short sutra and the Four Vows, now recited with lusty enthusiasm. With bodies and minds aroused and bursting with energy, sleep is out of the question and practically everyone files out of the zendo into the cool night air with his sitting cushion under his arm. Instead of wearily shuffling off to bed as on previous nights,[13] each buoyantly strides off to a solitary spot, often the monastery cemetery, there to continue his zazen far into the night.

Particularly on the last night of a sesshin, with the shouting and clouting fiercest, none but the obviously ill or palpably timid would dare retire to bed at nine when virtually the entire zendo has taken up quarters for the night in the cemetery and nearby hills, rending the still air with desperate cries of "Mu!" And during the severest yearly sesshin, the *rohatsu*, in December, which commemorates the Buddha's enlightenment, *yaza* (zazen after 9 P.M.) is the rule each night.

The last day of sesshin, especially if it has been preceded by all-night zazen, tends to become anticlimactic. The roshi therefore admonishes everyone that this is the most critical day of all and that to relax now when the mind has reached its peak of concentration is in effect to throw away six days of solid effort. On this seventh day the kyosaku and its companion shouting are dispensed with—as though the godo were saying, "I can do no more, it is now entirely up to you"—and after (or because of) six days of periodic commotion this day of silent yet dynamic zazen is frequently the most rewarding.

Before the formal close of a sesshin the roshi, addressing everyone, will say in effect:

> A sincere effort at sesshin is never wasted even though it does not terminate in enlightenment. Getting kensho can be compared to a person's hitting the bull's-eye on the hundredth shot. Who can say that the ninety-nine misses are unrelated to the final success?

[13] In most monasteries laymen who come for sesshin do not sleep with the monks in the zendo but are given sleeping quarters in a separate building.

Some have come to enlightenment even during the drinking of tea which ends the sesshin and others on the train going home, so remain attentive at all times. Concentrate unremittingly on your koan if that is your practice, or if you are doing shikan-taza, perform every task single-mindedly. Don't fritter away the joriki you have accumulated during sesshin in vain, empty talk, but conserve and strengthen it through all your daily tasks.

In some monasteries and temples a special ceremony is held, in the presence of all participants, to permit those who have attained kensho to express their gratitude to the roshi and the head monks. The sesshin formally ends with the chanting of the Hannya Shingyo (Heart of Wisdom sutra) and the Four Vows. Afterward all join once more in drinking tea and eating cake to thank the roshi and the head monks as well as each other for the aid and support received during the sesshin.

In spite of the spectacular use of the kyosaku, the wild scrambling before dokusan, and the exciting exchanges which often occur in dokusan itself, the real drama of a sesshin lies not in these displays but in zazen: in the solitary search into the vast, hidden world of one's own mind, in the lonely trek through winding canyons of shame and fear, across deserts of ecstatic visions and tormenting phantasms, around volcanoes of oozing ego, and through jungles of folly and delusion in a ceaseless struggle to gain that oneness and emptiness of body and mind which ultimately lead to the lightning-and-thunder discovery that the universe and oneself are not remote and apart but an intimate, palpitating Whole.

Whether awakening follows or not, one cannot seriously participate in a sesshin and not return home chastened in heart, strengthened in mind, and with a startlingly fresh vision of an old familiar world.

The central theme of sesshin is sustained self-effort, for in the last analysis one is liberated not by his fellows, not by the roshi, not even by the Buddha, and certainly not by any supernatural being, but by one's own unfaltering, indefatigable exertions.

In Zen's emphasis on self-reliance, in its clear awareness of the dangers of intellectualism, in its empirical appeal to personal experience and not philosophic speculation as the means of verifying ultimate truth, in its pragmatic concern with mind and suffering, and in its direct, practical methods for body-mind emancipation, Westerners will find much that is congenial to their temperament and *Weltanschauung.*

At a time when "things are in the saddle and riding mankind" as never before, when the tensions of fear, anxiety, and estrangement are devastating the minds of modern men, the fact that ordinary people through enlightenment can discover meaning and joy in life, as well as a sense of their own uniqueness and solidarity with all mankind, surely spells hope for human beings everywhere.

THE EXPERIENCES / 1 / MR. K. Y., A JAPANESE EXECUTIVE, AGE 47 / NOVEMBER 27, 1953:

Dear Nakagawa-roshi:

Thank you for the happy day I spent at your monastery.

You remember the discussion which arose about Self-realization centering around that American. At that time I hardly imagined that in a few days I would be reporting to you my own experience.

The day after I called on you I was riding home on the train with my wife. I was reading a book on Zen by Son-o, who, you may recall, was a master of Soto Zen living in Sendai during the Genroku period [1688–1703]. As the train was nearing Ofuna station I ran across this line: "I came to realize clearly that Mind is no other than mountains and rivers and the great wide earth, the sun and the moon and the stars."[14]

I had read this before, but this time it impressed itself upon me so vividly that I was startled. I said to myself: "After seven or eight years of zazen I have finally perceived the essence of this statement," and couldn't suppress the tears that began to well up. Somewhat ashamed to find myself crying among the crowd, I averted my face and dabbed at my eyes with my handkerchief.

Meanwhile the train had arrived at Kamakura station and my wife and I got off. On the way home I said to her: "In my present exhilarated frame of mind I could rise to the greatest heights."

[14] A quotation from Dogen's *Shobogenzo,* originally found in *Zenrui No. 10,* an early Chinese Zen work.

Laughingly she replied: "Then where would I be?" All the while I kept repeating that quotation to myself.

It so happened that that day my younger brother and his wife were staying at my home, and I told them about my visit to your monastery and about that American who had come to Japan again only to attain enlightenment. In short, I told them all the stories you had told me, and it was after eleven thirty before I went to bed.

At midnight I abruptly awakened. At first my mind was foggy, then suddenly that quotation flashed into my consciousness: "I came to realize clearly that Mind is no other than mountains, rivers, and the great wide earth, the sun and the moon and the stars." And I repeated it. Then all at once I was struck as though by lightning, and the next instant heaven and earth crumbled and disappeared. Instantaneously, like surging waves, a tremendous delight welled up in me, a veritable hurricane of delight, as I laughed loudly and wildly: "Ha, ha, ha, ha, ha, ha! There's no reasoning here, no reasoning at all! Ha, ha, ha!" The empty sky split in two, then opened its enormous mouth and began to laugh uproariously: "Ha, ha, ha!" Later one of the members of my family told me that my laughter had sounded inhuman.

I was now lying on my back. Suddenly I sat up and struck the bed[15] with all my might and beat the floor with my feet, as if trying to smash it, all the while laughing riotously. My wife and youngest son, sleeping near me, were now awake and frightened. Covering my mouth with her hand, my wife exclaimed: "What's the matter with you? What's the matter with you?" But I wasn't aware of this until told about it afterwards. My son told me later he thought I had gone mad.

"I've come to enlightenment! Shakyamuni and the patriarchs haven't deceived me! They haven't deceived me!"[16] I remember crying out. When I calmed down I apologized to the rest of the family, who had come downstairs frightened by the commotion.

Prostrating myself before the photograph of Kannon you had

[15] This is not a Western but a traditional Japanese "bed," which consists of a quilted mattress two or three inches thick spread over the regular tatami mats.

[16] See footnote 3, p. 290.

given me, the Diamond sutra, and my volume of the book written by Yasutani-roshi, I lit a stick of incense and did zazen until it was consumed half an hour later, though it seemed only two or three minutes had elapsed.

Even now my skin is quivering as I write.

That morning I went to see Yasutani-roshi and tried to describe to him my experience of the sudden disintegration of heaven and earth. "I am overjoyed, I am overjoyed!" I kept repeating, striking my thigh with vigor. Tears came which I couldn't stop. I tried to relate to him the experience of that night, but my mouth trembled and words wouldn't form themselves. In the end I just put my face in his lap. Patting me on the back he said: "Well, well, it is rare indeed to experience to such a wonderful degree. It is termed 'Attainment of the emptiness of Mind.' You are to be congratulated!"

"Thanks to you," I murmured, and again wept for joy. Repeatedly I told him: "I must continue to apply myself energetically to zazen." He was kind enough to give me detailed advice on how to pursue my practice in the future, after which he again whispered in my ear, "My congratulations!" and escorted me to the foot of the mountain by flashlight.

Although twenty-four hours have elapsed, I still feel the aftermath of that earthquake. My entire body is still shaking. I spent all of today laughing and weeping by myself.

I am writing to report my experience in the hope that it will be of value to your monks, and because Yasutani-roshi urged me to.

Please remember me to that American. Tell him that even I, who am unworthy and lacking in spirit, can grasp such a wonderful experience when time matures. I would like to talk with you at length about many things, but will have to wait for another time.

P.S. That American was asking us whether it is possible for him to attain enlightenment in one week of sesshin. Tell him this for me: don't say days, weeks, years, or even lifetimes. Don't say millions or billions of *kalpa*. Tell him to vow to attain enlightenment though it take the infinite, the boundless, the incalculable future.

MIDNIGHT OF THE 28TH: [These diary entries were made during

the next two days.] Awoke thinking it 3 or 4 A.M., but clock said it was only 12:30.

Am totally at peace at peace at peace.

Feel numb throughout body, yet hands and feet jumped for joy for almost half an hour.

Am supremely free free free free free.

Should I be so happy?

There is no common man.[17]

The big clock chimes—not the clock but Mind chimes. The universe itself chimes. There is neither Mind nor universe. Dong, dong, dong!

I've totally disappeared. Buddha is!

"Transcending the law of cause and effect, controlled by the law of cause and effect"[18]—such thoughts have gone from my mind.

Oh, you *are!* You laughed, didn't you? This laughter is the sound of your plunging into the world.

The substance of Mind—this is now luminously clear to me.

My concentration in zazen has sharpened and deepened.

MIDNIGHT OF THE 29TH: I am at peace at peace at peace. Is this tremendous freedom of mine the Great Cessation[19] described by the ancients? Whoever might question it would surely have to admit that this freedom is extraordinary. If it isn't absolute freedom or the Great Cessation, what is it?

4 A.M. OF THE 29TH: Ding, dong! The clock chimed. This alone *is!* This alone *is!* There's no reasoning here.

Surely the world has changed [with awakening]. But in what way?

The ancients said the enlightened mind is comparable to a fish swimming. That's exactly how it is—there's no stagnation. I feel no hindrance. Everything flows smoothly, freely. Everything goes

[17] That is, Buddhahood is latent in everyone.

[18] This is a reference to the second case of *Mumonkan,* the koan commonly known as Hyakujo's Fox.

[19] A designation for the state of mind flowing from a deep realization that, since inherently we suffer no lack, there is nothing to seek outside ourselves.

naturally. This limitless freedom is beyond all expression. What a wonderful world!

Dogen, the great teacher of Buddhism, said: "Zen is the wide, all-encompassing gate of compassion."

I am grateful, so grateful.

2 / MR. P. K., AN AMERICAN EX-BUSINESS-MAN, AGE 46 / DIARY EXTRACTS /

NEW YORK, APRIL 1, 1953: . . . Belly aching all week, Doc says ulcers are getting worse . . . Allergies kicking up too . . . Can't sleep without drugs . . . So miserable wish I had the guts to end it all.

APRIL 20, 1953: Attended S_____'s Zen lecture today. As usual, could make little sense out of it . . . Why do I go on with these lectures? Can I ever get satori listening to philosophic explanations of *prajna* and *karuna*[20] and why A isn't A and all the rest of that? What the hell is satori anyway? Even after four of S_____'s books and dozens of his lectures, still don't know. I must be awfully stupid . . . But I know this, Zen philosophy isn't ridding me of my pain or restlessness or that damn "nothing" feeling . . .

Only last week a close friend complained: "You're forever spouting Zen philosophy, but you've hardly become more serene or considerate since you've begun studying it. If anything, it's made you supercilious and condescending . . ."

JUNE 1, 1953: Talked with K_____ about Zen and Japan until two this morning . . . Like S_____ he's Japanese and has practiced Zen but they have little else in common . . . Before meeting K_____ I imagined that people with satori all functioned like S_____, now I see satori's not so simple, it apparently has many facets and levels . . . Why am I hung up on satori? . . .

Pelted K_____ all night with: "If I go to Japan to train in Zen, can you assure me I'll be able to find some meaning in life? Will I absolutely get rid of my ulcers and allergies and sleeplessness?

---

[20] Sanskrit words meaning satori-wisdom and compassion, respectively.

My two years of attending Zen lectures in New York have neither mitigated my constant frustration nor, if I'm to believe my friends, lessened my intellectual conceit."

K_____ kept repeating: "Zen's not philosophy, it's a healthy way to live! . . . If you really want to learn Buddhism in Japan and not just talk about it, your whole life will be transformed. It won't be easy, but you can rely on this: once you enter upon the Buddha's Way with sincerity and zeal, Bodhisattvas will spring up everywhere to help you. But you must have courage and faith, and you must make up your mind to realize the liberating power of your Buddha-nature no matter how much pain and sacrifice it entails . . ."

This is the transfusion of courage I've needed.

SEPTEMBER 3, 1953: Quit business, sold apartment furniture and car . . . Friends' unanimous judgment: "Your're mad throwing up ten thousand a year for pie in the sky!". . . Maybe. Or maybe they're the mad ones, piling up possessions and ulcers and heart disease . . . I suspect some of them may even envy me . . . If I didn't need to, I wouldn't be doing it, of this I'm positive, but I *am* frightened a little. Hope it's true about life at forty . . . Bought ticket for Japan.

TOKYO, OCTOBER 6, 1953: How the features and mood of Japan have changed in seven years! The ghastly rubble and despairing faces have virtually disappeared . . . Good to be back this time as a seeker instead of a carpetbagger with the Occupation . . . Wonder what really brought me back? Was it the dignity of the Japanese, their patient endurance in the face of their untold sufferings that I marveled at? Was it the unearthly silence of Engaku Monastery and the deep peace it engendered within me whenever I strolled through its gardens or beneath its giant cryptomerias? . . .

NOVEMBER 1, 1953: In Kyoto almost a month now . . . P_____, the American professor whom I'd met at one of S_____'s lectures in New York, is teaching the history of philosophy at a Japanese university . . . He and I have already called on five or six Zen teachers and authorities . . . Talk talk talk! Some of these Zen men are curiously verbose for a teaching that boasts of mind-to-mind transmission and an abhorrence of concepts. Professor M_____, when I reminded him of this, said: "In the beginning you have to utilize concepts to get rid of concepts." That sounds like fighting fire with oil . . . Feeling restless again. All of yesterday toured the curio shops buying art objects. Is this what I returned to Japan for?

NOVEMBER 2, 1953: Letter arrived today from Nakagawa-roshi, master of Ryutaku Monastery, saying yes, P_____ and I could spend two days there . . . Will such a trip prove productive? Not if S_____ and the Zen professors in Kyoto are right: "Zen monasteries are too traditional and authoritarian for modern intellectually minded people.". . . Anyway, it'll be a novel experience to converse with a roshi in English and may turn out a pleasant holiday . . . P_____'s wife piled us up with heavy blankets and lots of American groceries. Her Japanese friend says Zen monasteries are notoriously cold and austere . . . What does one do in a monastery anyway? . . .

NOVEMBER 3, 1953: Arrived at monastery at dusk . . . During 6½-hour train trip P_____ and I busied ourselves framing questions to test the roshi's philosophical knowledge of Zen. "If he has an intellectual grasp of Zen," we decided, "and is not just an old-fashioned religious fanatic, we'll stay the full two days, otherwise let's leave tomorrow.". . .

Nakagawa-roshi received us in his simple, unpretentious quarters . . . How young-looking he is, so unlike the bearded patriarch of our imaginings . . . And so cordial and affable, he personally made us hot whipped green tea, delicious and soothing, and even joked with us in surprisingly good English . . .

"Your long train journey must have tired you, would you like to lie down and rest?". . . "No, we're a little tired, but if you don't mind we've prepared a number of questions on Zen we'd like to ask you.". . . "If you don't care to rest, the attendant will take you to the main hall where you can sit and meditate until I dispose of some urgent business; afterwards we can talk if you like.". . .

"But we've never meditated in our lives, we wouldn't know how to sit cross-legged.". . . "You may sit any way you like, but you must not talk. The monk attendant will provide you with sitting cushions and show you where to sit; he will call you when I can see you again.". . .

Sat—no, wriggled—wordlessly for two miserable hours in dark hall next to P_____ . . . Concentration impossible, thoughts chasing each other like a pack of monkeys . . . Excruciating pain in legs, back, and neck . . . Desperately want to quit, but if I do before P_____ does, he'll never stop ragging me, nor will the roshi have a good opinion of American fortitude . . . At last monk came and mercifully whispered: "You may see Roshi now.". . . Looked at watch, 9:30 . . .

Hobbled into the roshi's room to be greeted with his inscrutable smile and a large bowl of rice with pickles . . . He watched us intently while we gobbled down the food, then benignly asked: "Now what would you like to know about Zen?". . . We're so exhausted that we can only answer weakly: "Not a thing!". . . "Then you'd better go to sleep now because we get up at 3:30 in the morning . . . Pleasant dreams.". . .

NOVEMBER 4, 1953: "Wake up, wake up, it's already 3:45! Didn't you hear the bells and gongs, don't you hear the drums, the chanting? Please hurry.". . .

What a weird scene of refined sorcery and idolatry: shaven-headed black-robed monks sitting motionlessly chanting mystic gibberish to the accompaniment of a huge wooden tom-tom emitting otherworldly sounds, while the roshi, like some elegantly gowned witch doctor, is making magic passes and prostrating himself again and again before an altar bristling with idols and images . . . Is this the Zen of Tanka, who tossed a Buddha statue into the fire? Is this the Zen of Rinzai, who shouted, "You must kill the Buddha"?[21] . . . The Kyoto teachers and S_____ were right after all . . .

---

[21] Eradicating from the mind the notion of a Buddha as opposed to an ordinary being, ridding oneself of the idea that Shakyamuni Buddha is God or a super-being, obliterating the subtle pride which arises from kensho and leads one to think, "Now I'm a Buddha"—this is killing the Buddha.

After breakfast the roshi led us on an inspection tour of the monastery, set within a horseshoe of rolling hills in the quivering silence of a cultivated forest of pine, cedar, and bamboo and graced by an exquisite lotus pond—a veritable Japanese Shangri-la . . . And what a view of Mount Fuji, the majestic sentinel in the sky! . . . If only he doesn't mar it all by insisting we bow down before those images in the halls . . .

O my prophetic soul! . . . he's brought us into the founder's room and is lighting incense and fervently prostrating himself before a weird statue of Hakuin . . . "You too may light incense and pay your respects to Hakuin.". . . P_____ looks at me and I at him, then he explodes: "The old Chinese Zen masters burned or spit on Buddha statues, why do you bow down before them?" . . . The roshi looks grave but not angry. "If you want to spit you spit, I prefer to bow.". . . We don't spit, but neither do we bow.

NOVEMBER 6, 1953: P_____ left for Kyoto today, and the roshi invited me to stay on . . . For all his religious fanaticism and unphilosophical mind he's a warm, regular guy and I like him . . . No use fooling myself though, it's going to be rough getting up at 3:30 in the cold, living on a diet of mainly rice, and trying to meditate cross-legged . . . Can I do it? Do I want to? . . . Still, there's something about all this that's deeply satisfying . . . Anyway, I'm glad he invited me to stay and I've accepted . . .

NOVEMBER 8, 1953: Roshi says I can meditate by myself in founder's room instead of in the cold zendo. I can sit, kneel Japanese style

---

"Wash your mouth when you utter the name Buddha!" is another widely misunderstood Zen expression. It comes from the thirtieth case of *Mumonkan* in the comment of Mumon: "Don't you know that one has to rinse his mouth for three days after uttering the word 'Buddha'?" This is not a reference to Shakyamuni Buddha the person but to Buddha-nature or Buddha-mind. Everything is complete and perfect in itself. A stick is a stick, a shovel a shovel. Use a shovel and you know its shovelness in a direct, fundamental way. But describe it as "Buddha" or "Buddha-mind" and you needlessly "sully" it, that is, add to the name "shovel" one more concept.

or use a chair and wear as much clothing as I please if I'm cold . . . Have no idea how to meditate, though . . . When I told Roshi this he cryptically advised: "Put your mind in the bottom of your belly, there's a blind Buddha there, make him see!". . . Is that all there is to meditation? Or is the roshi deliberately letting me stew in my own juice? . . . Carefully inspected Hakuin's features today; they're less grotesque, even faintly interesting.

NOVEMBER 10, 1953: Each morning been climbing the hill back of the main hall for a wide-screen view of Mount Fuji . . . Yesterday skipped my meditation because of a headache and Fuji looked somber and lifeless . . . Today after a couple of hours of good meditation in a chair it's grand and soaring again. A remarkable discovery: *I* have the power of life and death over Fuji! . . .

NOVEMBER 23, 1953: During tea with Roshi in his room today he suddenly asked me: "How would you like to attend the rohatsu sesshin at Harada-roshi's monastery? The discipline is especially severe during this sesshin. But he is a famous roshi, a much better teacher for you than I.". . . "If you think so, sure, why not?". . . "But my old teacher,[22] whom you met the other day, is against it: he does not approve of Harada-roshi's harsh methods for inducing satori. A Zen student he thinks should ripen slowly, then like fruit which falls from the tree when ripe, come naturally to enlightenment . . . Let me meditate further on it.". . .

NOVEMBER 25, 1953: Two interesting visitors at the monastery this morning, one a master called Yasutani, the other a layman named Yamada, his disciple, who said he'd been practicing Zen for some eight years. Wanted to ask him whether he had satori yet, but decided it might prove embarrassing . . .

Asked Yasutani-roshi if he thought I could get satori in one week of sesshin . . . "You can get it in *one day* of sesshin if you're genuinely determined to and you surrender all your conceptual thinking."

NOVEMBER 27, 1953: "How is your zazen coming along?" Roshi

[22] Gempo Yamamoto-roshi, who was retired at the time.

suddenly asked me today . . . "That Buddha in my belly is hopelessly blind.". . . "He is not really blind, he only seems so because he's sound asleep . . . How would you like to try the koan Mu?" . . . "All right, if you think I should, but what do I do with it?" . . . "You know its background I suppose . . ." "Yes.". . . "Then just keep concentrating on Joshu's answer until you intuitively realize its meaning.". . . "Will I then be enlightened?". . . "Yes, if your understanding is not just theoretical.". . . "But how do I concentrate?". . . "Put your mind in your hara and focus on nothing but Mu."

NOVEMBER 28, 1953: Roshi called me into his room this morning and beckoned me to follow him to the little altar-shrine in back . . . "Do you see the letter I put into the hands of Kannon? You have become karmically linked with the man who wrote it; let us gassho before Kannon out of gratitude.". . . I did a gassho unthinkingly, quickly asked: "What's the letter say, who wrote it? And what do you mean 'karmically linked'?". . . The roshi, outwardly solemn but inwardly animated, merely said: "Come to my room and I will explain.". . .

With his usual grace he knelt Japanese style, put the kettle on the charcoal fire for tea, then decisively announced: "I've decided to take you to the rohatsu sesshin at Hosshin-ji. This letter has decided me.". . . "Tell me what it's all about.". . . "Do you remember Yamada-san, the man who came here with Yasutani-roshi the day before yesterday? It's from him. He had a deep satori the very day after he left and he tells about it in this letter."[23] . . .

"Did you say he got satori? Please translate it for me right now.". . . "There isn't time. Hosshin-ji is far from here, on the shore of the Japan Sea, and we must be ready to leave tomorrow. I will translate it for you on the train.". . .

NOVEMBER 29, 1953: As our third-class train bounced along in the night Roshi slowly, carefully translated Yamada's letter . . . What a vivid, stirring experience, and he no monk but a layman! . . . "Do you really believe it's possible for me to get satori during

[23] See pp. 215–17.

this sesshin?". . . "Of course, provided you forget yourself completely.". . . "But what is satori anyway? I mean—"

"Stop!". . . Roshi threw up his hand, flashing his inscrutable smile. "When you get it you will know, now no more questions please. Let us do zazen and then try to get some sleep before we come to Hosshin-ji.". . .

NOVEMBER 30, 1953: Arrived hungry and exhausted at Hosshin-ji in late afternoon . . . Skies leaden, air cold and damp . . . But Harada-roshi was cordial and warm, greeting me with outstretched hands . . . Later he introduced me to the assistant roshi and four head monks . . . Though somewhat reticent, they glow with a strong inner flame . . .

Roshi and I retired to the small room we're to share . . . "You'd better get some rest before the battle begins.". . . "Battle?". . . "Yes, a battle to the death with the forces of your own ignorance . . . I will call you when everyone assembles in the main hall for final instruction from Harada-roshi, in about an hour.". . .

Like lobsters in conclave, Harada-roshi, the assistant roshi, and four head monks in robes of scarlet brocade and arching ceremonial headdress sat on large silk cushions at one end of the hall, while four young monks, each with a black-lacquer tray on which were placed gold-colored cups, stood poised at the other end ready to serve them. Sandwiched between in rows facing each other across the room knelt some fifty grim lay people attired in somber traditional robes . . . Their eyes were glued to the floor in front of them, and none stirred to look at Harada-roshi when he spoke except me . . .

Why's everybody so tense and grim? Why do they all look as though they're steeling themselves for some terrible ordeal? True, Roshi said this would be a battle, but surely that was only a figure of speech—how does one fight his own mind? Isn't Zen *wu wei*, non-striving? Isn't the all-embracing Buddha-nature our common possession, so why strive to acquire what is already ours? . . . Must ask Harada-roshi about this first chance I get . . .

Back in our room Roshi summarized Harada-roshi's instructions: 1) You must not talk or bathe or shave or leave the premises during the week. 2) You must concentrate only on your own practice without diverting your eyes for any reason. 3) You as a beginner have as good a chance as old hands to attain enlightenment at this sesshin. And Roshi added pointedly: "But you must work hard, terribly hard."

DECEMBER 1, 1953: Raining incessantly, zendo uncomfortably cold and damp . . . Wore long johns and wool shirt and two sweaters and wool robe and two pairs of wool socks but couldn't stop shivering . . . Godo's bellowing and roaring more of a distraction than his wallops with kyosaku . . . Tortured by pain in legs and back . . . thoughts racing wildly . . . Flopped from *agura* to *seiza* to *hanka*, manipulating my three cushons in every conceivable way, but couldn't escape pain . . .

At my first dokusan Harada-roshi drew a circle with a dot in the center. "This dot is you and the circle is the cosmos. Actually you embrace the whole cosmos, but because you see yourself as this dot, an isolated fragment, you don't experience the universe as inseparable from yourself . . . You must break out of your self-imprisonment, you must forget philosophy and everything else, you must put your mind in your hara and breathe only Mu in and out . . . The center of the universe is the pit of your belly! . . .

"Mu is a sword which enables you to cut through your thoughts into the realm that is the source of all thoughts and feelings . . . But Mu is not only a means to enlightenment, it is enlightenment itself . . . Self-realization is not a matter of step-by-step progress but the result of a leap. Until your mind is pure you cannot make this leap.". . .

"What do you mean by 'pure'?". . . "Empty of all thoughts." . . . "But why is it necessary to struggle for enlightenment if we already have the enlightened Buddha-nature?". . . "Can you show me this enlightened nature of yours?". . . "Well, no, I can't, but the sutras say we have it, don't they?". . . "The sutras are not your experience, they are Shakyamuni Buddha's. If you realize your Buddha-mind, you'll be a Buddha yourself."

DECEMBER 2, 1953: At 5 A.M. dokusan told Harada-roshi the pain in my legs was agonizing. "I can't go on.". . . "Do you want a chair?" He looked at me tauntingly . . . "No, I won't use a chair even if my legs drop off!". . . ."Good! With that spirit you're bound to become enlightened.". . .

Terrific whack by the kyosaku just when my concentration was beginning to jell and I fell apart . . . damn that godo! "Straighten your back, sit firmly, center your energy in your hara!" he cries. But how the devil do I put my energy into my hara? When I try, my back is stabbed with pain . . . Must ask Harada-roshi about this . . .

Throughout one round of sitting my thoughts've been entangled in the Mokkei[24] pictures I saw at the Daitoku-ji exhibition last month. That crane's so haunting, the secret of all existence lies in its eyes. It's self-creating, emerging from formlessness to form. I must reverse the process, merging again into formlessness, into non-time. I must die to be reborn . . . Yes, that's the inner meaning of Mu! . . .

Clang, clang! the dokusan bell . . . Harada-roshi listened impatiently, then roared: "Don't think of Mokkei's crane, don't think of form or formlessness or anything else. Think only Mu, *that's* what you're here for!"

DECEMBER 3, 1953: Pain in legs unbearable . . . Why don't I quit? It's imbecilic trying to sit with this gruesome pain and taking these senseless wallops of the kyosaku plus Godo's insane shouting, it's masochism pure and simple . . . Why did I leave Ryutaku-ji, why did I ever leave the United States? . . . But I can't quit now, what will I do? I must get satori, I must . . .

What the devil is Mu, what can it be? . . . Of course! It's absolute prayer, the Self praying to itself . . . How often as a student had I wanted to pray, but somehow it'd always seemed pointless and even silly to petition God for strength to cope with predicaments which He in his omniscience and omnipotence had allowed to arise in the first place . . .

Tears welling up, how blissful is prayer for its own sake! . . . What do these tears mean? They're a sign of my helplessness, a tacit admission that my intellect, my ego, has reached the limit of its power . . . Yes, tears are nature's benediction, her attempt

[24] A great Chinese Zen monk painter (Mu Ch'i) who lived in the tenth century. Most of his paintings in Japan are national treasures.

to wash away the grime of ego and soften the harsh outlines of our personalities made arid and tense through an egotistic reliance on the invincibility of reason . . .

. . . What marvelous insights, I feel so good about them! I know I've progressed. I won't be surprised if satori hits me this very night!

Crack! Crack! "Stop dreaming! Only Mu!" cried the godo, walloping me . . .

Dokusan! . . . "No, no, no! Didn't I tell you to concentrate simply on Mu? . . . Banish these thoughts! . . . Satori's not a matter of progress or regress, haven't I told you it's a leap? . . . You are to do this and only this: put your mind in the bottom of your belly and inhale and exhale Mu. Is that clear?". . . Why's he so harsh all of a sudden? . . . Even the hawks in the screen behind him have begun to glower at me.

DECEMBER 4, 1953: My God, my Buddha, a chair's standing at my place! I am so grateful! . . . Roshi came and whispered: "Harada-roshi ordered the head monk to give you a chair because he felt you would never get satori sitting with a bent back and constantly shifting your position . . . Now you have no obstacles, so concentrate on Mu with all your heart and soul.". . . Concentration quickly tightened, thoughts suddenly disappeared. What a marvelous feeling this buoyant emptiness . . .

Suddenly the sun's streaming into the window in front of me! The rain's stopped! It's become warmer! At last the gods are with me! Now I can't miss satori! . . . Mu, Mu, Mu! . . . Again Roshi leaned over but only to whisper: "You are panting and disturbing the others, try to breathe quietly.". . . But I can't stop. My heart's pumping wildly, I'm trembling from head to toe, tears are streaming down uncontrollably . . . Godo cracks me but I hardly feel it. He whacks my neighbor and I suddenly think: "Why's he so mean, he's hurting him.". . . More tears . . . Godo returns and clouts me again and again, shouting: "Empty your mind of every single thought, become like a baby again. Just Mu, Mu! right from your guts!"—crack, crack, crack! . . .

Abruptly I lose control of my body and, still conscious, crumple into a heap . . . Roshi and Godo pick me up, carry me to my room and put me to bed . . . I'm still panting and trembling . . .

Roshi anxiously peers into my face, asks: "You all right, you want a doctor?". . . "No, I'm all right I guess.". . . "This ever happen to you before?". . . "No, never.". . . "I congratulate you!". . . "Why, have I got satori?". . . "No, but I congratulate you just the same.". . . Roshi brings me a jug of tea, I drink five cups . . .

No sooner does he leave than all at once I feel my arms and legs and trunk seized by an invisible force and locked in a huge vice which slowly begins closing . . . Spasms of torment like bolts of electricity shoot through me and I writhe in agony . . . I feel as though I'm being made to atone for my own and all mankind's sins . . . Am I dying or becoming enlightened? . . . Sweat's streaming from every pore and I have to change my underclothing twice . . . At last I fall into a deep sleep . . .

Awoke to find a bowl of rice and soup and beans next to my sleeping mat . . . Ate ravenously, dressed, entered the zendo . . . Never in my life have I felt so light, opened, and transparent, so thoroughly cleansed and scoured . . . During kinhin didn't walk but bobbed like a cork on water . . . Couldn't resist looking out at the trees and flowers, vivid, dazzling, palpitating with life! . . . The wind soughing through the trees was the loveliest of music! . . . How deliciously fragrant the fumes of incense! . . .

Later at dokusan Harada-roshi said: "Your trembling came because you are beginning to throw off you delusions, it is a good sign. But don't pause for self-congratulation, concentrate harder yet on Mu.". . .

DECEMBER 5, 1953: . . . Am still aglow . . . Satori will hit me any moment now, I know it, I feel it in my marrow . . . Won't my Zen friends in the United States be envious when I write I have satori! . . . Don't think of satori, you fool, think only of Mu! . . . Yes, Mu, Mu, Mu! . . . Damn it! I've lost it! . . . My excitement about satori has triggered off hundreds of thoughts—which leave me dispirited . . . It's no use, satori's beyond me . . .

DECEMBER 6, 1953: Body tired this morning but mind's sharp and clear . . . Mu'd in monastery garden all night sans sleep . . . miserably cold . . . Stayed up only because at dokusan Harada-roshi had chided: "You'll never open your Mind's eye unless you develop the strength and determination to do zazen all night. Some of the sitters have been up every single night in zazen.". . .

Around midnight prostrated myself before statue of Buddha in main hall and desperately prayed: "O God, O Buddha, please grant me satori and I'll be humble, even bowing willingly before you . . ." But nothing happened, no satori . . . Now I see the Old Fox was hoaxing me, probably trying to pry me loose from my attachment to sleep . . .

Shouting and clouting by Godo and his assistants getting fiercer and fiercer, the din and tumult of the last three nights beyond belief. All but a handful of the fifty-odd sitters have been bellowing "Mu!" continuously during the last half hour while the head monks lambasted them, shouting: "Voice Mu from the bottom of your belly, not from the top of your lungs!" . . . and later the shrill "Mu-ing" throughout the night in the cemetery and hills, like that of cattle being readied for slaughter . . . I'll bet it kept the whole countryside awake . . .

This walloping doesn't enliven me one bit. Godo must have clouted me fifteen minutes straight last night, but it produced only a sore back and bitter thoughts . . . Why hadn't I grabbed his stick and given him a dose of his own medicine? Wonder what would have happened if I had . . .

At dokusan told Harada-roshi: "The trouble is I can't forget myself, I'm always aware of myself as subject confronting Mu as object . . . I focus my mind on Mu, and when I can hang onto it I think: 'Good, now you've got it, don't let go.' Then I tell myself: 'No, you mustn't think "Good," you must think only Mu.' So I clench my hands, bear down with every nerve and muscle and eventually something clicks, I know I've reached a deeper level of consciousness because no longer am I aware of inside or out, front or back. Exhilarated, I think: 'Now I'm getting close to satori, every thought's vanished, satori'll hit me any moment.' But then I realize I can't be close to satori so long as I'm still thinking of it . . . So, discouraged, my hold on Mu loosens and Mu's gone again . . .

"Then I have this problem. You've told me to make my mind as barren of preconceptions as an infant's, with no self-will or ego. But how can I be free of ego when the godo cracks me furiously and urges me to strive harder and harder and to bear down on

Mu? Isn't such purposeful striving on my part an expression of ego? Instead of banishing ego it seems to me I'm bolstering it.". . .

"The mind of ego and the mind of Purity are two sides of the same reality . . . Don't think, 'This is ego,' 'This is not ego.' Just concentrate on Mu, that's the way to realize the mind of Purity . . . It's like a man who is starving; he doesn't think, 'I'm hungry, I must get food.' So completely absorbed in his hunger is he that he finds something to eat without pondering . . . If you self-consciously think, 'I want satori, I must get satori,' you'll never attain it. But when from the bottom of your heart you have a deep yearning for Self-realization, satori will come if, absorbing yourself wholly in Mu, you concentrate your mind and strength in your hara . . . Mu must occupy your entire mind, resounding in your hara . . . Don't try to anticipate satori, it comes unexpectedly. When your mind is emptied of every thought and image, anything can enlighten it: the human voice, the call of a bird . . . But you must have stronger faith. You must believe you have the capacity to realize your True-nature, and you must believe that what I am telling you is true and will lead to what you seek.". . .

Dokusan with the Old Lion's always a shot in the arm . . . So once again charged into Mu, quickly exhausted my energies, and got struck not by satori but by a barrage of thoughts . . . I'm stymied . . . If I push hard, I soon tire and my body and mind wilt. But if I don't dig in, Godo whacks me or else yanks me off my seat and shoves me into dokusan. When I appear before Harada-roshi he asks, "Why do you come when you can't show me Mu?" or else he bawls me out for my half-heartedness . . . Are they trying to drive my *thoughts* out of my mind or to drive *me* out of my mind? They're deliberately trying to create an artificial neurosis . . . Why don't I quit?

. . . Crash, bang! . . . the whole zendo is shaking, what's happened? . . . Shouldn't have, but turned my head to see . . . The Old Lion has just broken the longest kyosaku in the zendo across the back of Manjusri's shrine . . . "You're all lazy!" he yells. "You have within your grasp the most precious experience in the world, yet you sit dreaming. Wake up and throw your lives into the struggle, otherwise satori will elude you forever!". . . What strength of spirit, what power in that frail five-foot-three, 84-year-old body!

DECEMBER 7, 1953: Too exhausted to sit up with the others last night. Might just as well have, though, their raucous "Mu-ing" throughout the night kept me awake anyway . . . Roshi says this last day is crucial and not to weaken . . . But my do-or-die spirit's gone, the race is over and I'm just an also-ran . . .

Watched, chagrined and envious, as the three "winners" marched around the zendo, bowed down before Harada-roshi, the assistant roshi, and the head monks to show their reverence and gratitude . . . One of the fortunate had sat next to me. He'd been struck repeatedly and had blubbered all of yesterday and today . . . Evidently he'd been crying from sheer joy when all along I imagined he was in pain.

DECEMBER 8, 1953: Together with Nakagawa-roshi had tea with Harada-roshi after sesshin . . . His forbidding sesshin manner's gone, he's gentle and radiant as the sun . . . After a pleasant chat he invited us to stay for the formal ceremonies that afternoon commemorating the Buddha's enlightenment . . .

. . . Watched in utter fascination as Harada-roshi, the assistant roshi, and ten senior monks, attired in their ceremonial robes, again and again prostrated themselves before the Buddha, chanted sutras, tossed their sutra books in the air, beat drums, rang bells, struck gongs, and circumambulated the main hall in a series of rituals and ceremonies to honor Shakyamuni Buddha and celebrate his immortal enlightenment . . . These ceremonies glow with the living Truth which these monks have obviously all experienced in some measure . . . Yes, through these rituals they are reaffirming their link with their great Buddhist tradition, enriching it and allowing it to enrich them so they may extend its chain into the future . . . If I likewise embrace this tradition, I can forge my own link with Buddhism and its tremendous resources for enlightening the human mind . . . Now I know why I tired so quickly of church and synagogue services in the United States. The priests and rabbis and ministers obviously had no intimate experience of the God they preached so glibly about, that's why their sermons and ceremonies were stale and lifeless.

JANUARY 9, 1954: Back in Kyoto, tired, half frozen, and sore but inwardly alive . . .

JANUARY 20, 1954: Good to return to Ryutaku-ji . . . In Kyoto, P_____ and I merely talked Zen, with each other and with the professors, here I practice it . . . Though painful, practice is rejuvenating . . . My mind's a swamp of stagnant opinions, theories, impressions, images. I've read and thought too much, experienced without feeling. I need to recover the freshness of my jaded sensibilities, to face myself honestly, nakedly. And this I can best do through zazen in the monastery.

APRIL 8, 1954: My second Hosshin-ji sesshin is over . . . Harada-roshi said he'd accept me as a disciple if I remain at his monastery as a lay monk . . . "If you can cope with monastery life and gain enlightenment, you'll be master of your life instead of its slave." . . . After consultations with Nakagawa-roshi, decided to stay on indefinitely . . .

OCTOBER 1, 1956: . . . In just two months three years will have elapsed since I first came to Hosshin-ji . . . So much water has flowed under the stone bridge, or should I say so many stone bridges have flowed over the motionless water? . . . Have toiled with the monks in the heat of summer and shivered with them on snowy *takuhatsu*, felled trees, planted rice, cultivated the gardens, cleaned the outhouses, and worked in the kitchen with them. I've shared their heroic, dedicated moments, joined in their petty intrigues . . .

Sitting, sitting, sitting, one painful sesshin after another, then more zazen morning after morning, night after night, and night into morning . . . Dazzling insights and alluring visions have filed through my mind, but true illumination, satori, still eludes me . . . Tangen-san my wise monk-guide-interpreter-friend, solemnly assures me that just doing zazen wholeheartedly each day brings greater rewards in serenity, clarity, and purity than does a quickly attained kensho which is unnurtured by further zazen . . . Is this a consolation prize or another of Zen's paradoxes which needs the personal experience of enlightenment to be understood? . . . He insists I've gained in fortitude and purity, though I see little evidence of it . . .

Every one of my allergies has disappeared, my stomach pains me only occasionally, I sleep well . . . The dark fears which formerly haunted me, my cherished dreams and hopes, all these have withered away, leaving me lighter and with a clearer sense of the real . . . But I'm still the hungry dog next to the tank of boiling fat that is satori: I can't taste it and I can't leave it.

NOVEMBER 15, 1956: Is it worth struggling with the cold sparse diet through another long winter, waiting, waiting, waiting? . . . A number of my friends, the older serious monks, will soon be leaving for temples of their own . . . I must find a master whom I can communicate with easily outside the tense atmosphere of the monastery . . . Those same intuitions which once told me I needed to stay at Hosshin-ji now warn me it is time to leave.

NOVEMBER 23, 1956: Left Hosshin-ji today carrying enough presents and advice to last me a long time . . . The heart-warming farewells have dissipated whatever chill remained from those icy Obama winters.

NOVEMBER 25, 1956: Nakagawa-roshi took me to Yasutani-roshi . . . "He will be a good teacher for you, he is in Harada-roshi's line, his disciples are chiefly laymen, you need not stay in a monastery but can live in Kamakura and attend his sesshin in the Tokyo area."

DECEMBER 3, 1956: Joined my first sesshin at Yasutani-roshi's mountain temple . . . An ideal place for zazen, it nestles high in the hills away from the noises of the city . . . A scant eight participants, probably because the sesshin's only three days and hard to get to . . . Atmosphere's real homey, the roshi eats with us family style . . . And what a charming twist: the godo's a 68-year-old grandmother, the cook and leader of the chanting a 65-year-old nun, between them they manage the entire sesshin! Each sits like a Buddha and acts like one—gentle, compassionate, and thoroughly aware . . .

What a huge relief not to be driven by a savage kyosaku or verbally belted by the roshi at dokusan . . . The manual work after breakfast is stimulating and the afternoon bath immensely soothing . . . Am completely at ease with Yasutani-roshi. His manner's gentle yet penetrating, he laughs easily and often.

At dokusan he told me: "For enlightenment you must have deep faith. You must profoundly believe what the Buddha and the patriarchs from their own firsthand experience declared to be true, namely, that everything, ourselves included, intrinsically is Buddha-nature; that like a circle, which can't be added to or subtracted from, this Self-nature lacks nothing, it is complete, perfect . . . Now why if we have the flawless Buddha-nature are we not aware of it? Why if everything in essence is wisdom and purity itself is there so much ignorance and suffering in the world? . . . This is the 'doubt-mass' which must be dispersed . . . Only if you deeply believe that it was neither a mistake nor deception when the Buddha affirmed that we are all inherently Whole and Self-sufficient can you tirelessly probe your heart and mind for the solution to this paradox.". . .

"This is what perplexes me no end: Why haven't I attained kensho after three years of backbreaking effort when others who have labored neither as long nor as hard have got it? Some I know have come to kensho at their very first sesshin with little or no previous zazen.". . .

"There have been a few rare souls whose minds were so pure that they could gain genuine enlightenment without zazen. The Sixth Patriarch, Eno, was such a one; he became enlightened the first time he heard the Diamond sutra recited. And Harada-roshi has related the case of a young girl student of his who got kensho during his introductory lectures the very moment he drew a circle and declared the cosmos to be indivisibly One . . . But most have to do zazen tirelessly to win enlightenment . . .

Now don't feel anxious about awakening, for such anxiety can be a real hindrance . . . When you enter the world of enlightenment you take with you, so to speak, the results of all your efforts and this determines the quality of it; accordingly, your kensho will be wider and deeper by reason of the zazen you have done . . . In most cases a kensho quickly attained is shallow . . . Do zazen with zeal and Self-realization will take care of itself.". . .

Another time he instructed me: "Zen Buddhism is based on the highest teachings of Shakyamuni Buddha . . . In India, the very birthplace of the Buddha, it has practically ceased to exist, and as far as we know it is virtually extinct in China, where it was brought from India by Bodhidharma . . . Only in Japan does it still live, though it's declining steadily; today there are probably no more than ten true masters in all Japan . . . This unique teaching must not be lost, it must be transmitted to the West . . . Great minds in the United States and Europe have interested themselves in Buddhism because it appeals not only to the heart but to the intellect as well. Buddhism is an eminently rational religion . . .

"Zen you know from your own experience is not easy, but its rewards are in proportion to its difficulties . . . Remember, Bodhidharma had to suffer hardship after hardship, and both Eisai and Dogen, who brought Zen to Japan from China, had to overcome countless obstacles . . . Everything valuable has a high price . . . It is your destiny to carry Zen to the West . . . Don't quail or quit in spite of the pain and hardships.

JULY 27, 1958: August 1 is my D-Day, the start of a one-week summer sesshin, my twentieth with Yasutani-roshi . . . Sat two sesshin this month, one at Yasutani-roshi's temple and one at Ryutaku-ji, besides day and night zazen in my own room, all in preparation for this Big Push . . . My mind has a rare clarity and incisiveness. I must, I will break through . . . For the first time I'm truly convinced I can.

AUGUST 1, 1958: . . . Sesshin's under way! . . . Quickly my concentration became strongly pitched . . . Boring into Mu, thinking only Mu, breathing Mu . . .

AUGUST 3, 1958: First two days passed quickly, uneventfully . . .

AUGUST 4, 1958: Reached a white heat today . . . Monitors whacked me time and again . . . their energetic stick wielding is no longer an annoyance but a spur . . . Raced to the lineup with each clang of the dokusan bell to be first to see the roshi . . . Hardly aware of pain in legs . . . Was so eager to confront him that once or twice charged into his dokusan room without waiting for his signal . . . When he asked me to show him Mu, I spontaneously seized his fan, fanned myself, picked up his handbell, rang it, and then left . . .

At next dokusan he again asked for Mu. Quickly raised my hand as though to smack him. Didn't intend to really hit him, but the roshi, taking no chances, ducked . . . How exhilarating these un-premeditated movements—clean and free . . .

Animatedly the roshi warned: "You are now facing the last and toughest barrier between you and Self-realization. This is the time one feels, in the words of an ancient master, as though he were a mosquito attacking an iron bowl. But you must bore, bore, bore, tirelessly . . . Come what may, don't let go of Mu . . . Do zazen all night if you feel you may lose Mu in your sleep.". . .

"Mu'd" silently in temple garden till clock struck one . . . Rose to exercise stiff, aching legs, staggered into a nearby fence. Suddenly I realized: the fence and I are one formless wood-and-flesh Mu. Of course! . . . Vastly energized by this . . . pushed on till the 4 A.M. gong.

AUGUST 5, 1958: Didn't intend to tell Roshi of my insight, but as soon as I came before him he demanded: "What happened last night?" . . . While I talked, his keen darting eyes X-rayed every inch of me, then slowly he began quizzing me: "Where do you see Mu? . . . How do you see Mu? . . . When do you see Mu? . . . How old is Mu? . . . What is the color of Mu? . . . What is the sound of Mu? . . . How much does Mu weigh?". . .

Some of my answers came quickly, some haltingly . . . Once or twice Roshi smiled, but mostly he listened in serene silence . . . Then he spoke: "There are some roshi who might sanction such a tip-of-the-tongue taste as kensho, but—"

"I wouldn't accept sanction of such a picayune experience even if you wanted to grant it. Have I labored like a mountain these five years only to bring forth this mouse? I'll go on!". . .

"Good! I respect your spirit."

Threw myself into Mu for another nine hours with such utter absorption that I completely vanished . . . I didn't eat breakfast, Mu did. I didn't sweep and wash the floors after breakfast, Mu did. I didn't eat lunch, Mu ate . . . Once or twice ideas of satori started to rear their heads, but Mu promptly chopped them off . . .

Again and again the monitors whacked me, crying: "Victory is yours if you don't relinquish your hold on Mu!". . .

Afternoon dokusan! . . . Hawklike, the roshi scrutinized me as

I entered his room, walked toward him, prostrated myself, and sat before him with my mind alert and exhilarated . . .

"The universe is One," he began, each word tearing into my mind like a bullet. "The moon of Truth—" All at once the roshi, the room, every single thing disappeared in a dazzling stream of illumination and I felt myself bathed in a delicious, unspeakable delight . . . For a fleeting eternity I was alone—I alone was . . . Then the roshi swam into view. Our eyes met and flowed into each other, and we burst out laughing . . .

"I have it! I know! There is nothing, absolutely nothing. I am everything and everything is nothing!" I exclaimed more to myself than to the roshi, and got up and walked out . . .

At the evening dokusan Roshi again put to me some of the previous questions and added a few new ones: "Where were you born? . . . If you had to die right now, what would you do?". . . This time my answers obviously pleased him, for he smiled frequently. But I didn't care, for now I *knew* . . .

"Although your realization is clear," Roshi explained, "you can expand and deepen it infinitely . . .

"There are degrees of kensho . . . Take two people gazing at a cow, one standing at a distance, the other nearby. The distant one says: 'I know it's a cow, but I'm not sure of its color.' The other says unequivocally: 'I know it's a *brown* cow.' . . .

"Henceforth your approach to koans will be different," the roshi said, and he explained my future mode of practice . . .

Returned to the main hall . . . As I slipped back into my place Grandmother Yamaguchi, our part-time godo, tiptoed over to me and with eyes aglow whispered: "Wonderful, isn't it! I'm so happy for you!" . . . I resumed my zazen, laughing, sobbing, and muttering to myself: "It was before me all the time, yet it took me five years to see it." . . . A line Tangen-san had once quoted me rang in my ears: "Sometimes even in the driest hole one can find water."

AUGUST 9, 1958: Feel free as a fish swimming in an ocean of cool, clear water after being stuck in a tank of glue . . . and so grateful.

Grateful for everything that has happened to me, grateful to everyone who encouraged and sustained me in spite of my immature personality and stubborn nature.

But mostly I am grateful for my human body, for the privilege as a human being to know this Joy, like no other.

3 / MR. K. T., A JAPANESE GARDEN DESIGNER, AGE 32 / Although I was born into a family of the Soto Zen sect, I was twenty-eight before I formally started zazen. What led me to take this step was the fear of death when I began to spit blood after contracting tuberculosis, and uncertainties which had begun to plague me about life itself. I did not experience monastery life, but I did attend sesshin a number of times until I came to Self-realization and it was confirmed by the master. During this period I did zazen with a group and took dokusan under Taji-roshi every Sunday.

How well I remember my first sesshin! It was at a temple called Nippon-ji, in Nokogiriyama, Chiba Prefecture, and the master was Harada-roshi. The first day, I recall, I was tense. The second day I could no longer taste the meals. I had much pain in my legs and could make neither head nor tail of the roshi's teisho. Sometimes I was downright bored. On top of this, the sesshin regulations were strict and the general atmosphere cold and oppressive. Then I began to feel rebellious. "Zazen must be a kind of hypnosis. I will find out if the techniques of this religion really lead to truth," I told myself, and dropped the idea of returning home.

For three days I was obliged to attend the general lectures on zazen, as they were compulsory for all beginners. Following this I appeared voluntarily before the master for dokusan. Facing him, I felt that I was confronting an iron wall, but I was fascinated by the unique quality of his voice, which sounded very much like my late grandfather's. I went to dokusan several times just to listen to that voice and look at his unusual face. At these times I keenly felt his strong character and personality, his confidence in his own teaching, his dignity, his overwhelming forcefulness; and by comparison I felt insignificant and hollow. "If through being deceived I can reach his level of development, I won't mind the deception," I concluded, and decided to sit faithfully as he instructed.

The fourth and fifth days passed. The pain in my legs persisted, but my mind had now become more stable, even though I was experiencing visions of one kind and another. Gradually I began to feel enthusiastic about sitting. Came the sixth day. In the ante-room where I was kneeling awaiting my turn to go to dokusan I had a small joyful experience. Just in front of my knees I saw a large post and the leg of a small table overlapping. At that moment I felt the post to be the roshi and the small leg to be myself. Suddenly this insight came to me: The post as a post is occupying all of heaven and earth, and the leg of the table as the leg of a table is doing the same. The roshi as roshi and I as I fill the entire cosmos. Is there emptiness anywhere? With that I laughed heartily from the bottom of my belly.

Briskly entering the roshi's room at dokusan, I presented him my experience. "What is the value of such a blank insight? Don't dream! he said brusquely, and dismissed me. Though it may have been a hallucination, the joy of that moment has never left me. Thereafter whenever I came before the roshi I wasn't afraid of him.

After this first sesshin at Nippon-ji I attended one sesshin three years later at Hosshin-ji, but I was unsuccessful in attaining enlightenment. One night during the summer of that year while single-mindedly devoting myself to the practice of my koan, Mu, I experienced a state in which I felt as though I were looking at the vast, utterly transparent sky, and the next moment was able to penetrate the world of Mu with an awareness that was clear and sharp. At once I went to see Taji-roshi and asked him to receive me in dokusan. He confirmed my realization after I had made prompt reply to: "How old is Kannon?" "Cut the word Mu into three," and other tests. Whereupon he instructed me as follows:

"There is a tremendous difference between shallow and deep realization, and these different levels are depicted in the Ten Ox-herding Pictures.[25] The depth of your enlightenment is no greater than that shown in the third picture, namely, that of *seeing* the Ox. In other words, you have only caught a glimpse of the realm 'beyond the manifestation of form.' Your kensho is such that you can easily lose sight of it if you become lazy and forego further practice. Furthermore, though you have attained enlightenment you remain the same old you—nothing has been added, you have

[25] See section viii.

become no grander. But if you continue with zazen, you will reach the point of grasping the Ox, that is, the fourth stage. Right now you do not, so to speak, 'own' [26] your realization. Beyond the stage of grasping the Ox is the stage of taming it, followed by riding it, which is a state of awareness in which enlightenment and ego are seen as one and the same. Next, the seventh stage, is that of forgetting the Ox; the eighth, that of forgetting the Ox as well as oneself; the ninth, the grade of grand enlightenment, which penetrates to the very bottom and where one no longer differentiates enlightenment from non-enlightenment. The last, the tenth, is the stage in which, having completely finished one's practice, one moves, as himself, among ordinary people, helping them wherever possible, free from all attachment to enlightenment. To live in this last stage is the aim of life, and its accomplishment may require many cycles of existence. You have now set foot on the path leading to this goal, and for this you should be grateful."

Before receiving instructions from my first teacher I did zazen in my own way. Picking up the first koan in *Hekigan-roku,* I reflected on the question of the emperor: "What is the highest truth of the holy doctrine?" and then Bodhidharma's answer: "*Kakunen musho,* boundless expanse and nothing that can be called holy." [27] But I couldn't understand this. Still, reminding myself of a Japanese proverb, "If you read a book a hundred times you are bound to come to understand it," I sat down to zazen, devotedly reciting in my mind Bodhidharma's answer, "*Kakunen musho.*" After two days of this I experienced the same state I mentioned earlier, of looking at a vast clear sky. This, I now feel, helped bring about my later realization.

The following incident is also worth mentioning in this connection. As a Japanese-style fencing champion in my school days, I

---

[26] This condition can be compared to that of a newly hatched chick, whose life, while real enough, is still fragile and tentative.

[27] This question was addressed to Bodhidharma by Emperor Wu of Liang (502–49), a renowned Buddhist patron. The emperor next asked: "Who are you? Are you not a holy man?" To this Bodhidharma retorted: "I don't know." One of the points of the koan is to grasp the spirit of this "I don't know."

competed against five students in the intercollegiate matches. The first three were comparatively weak and I tried to beat them by figuring out techniques in advance, but was defeated by all three. When I faced my fourth opponent I was overwhelmed by a feeling of responsibility to uphold the reputation of my school, as well as bitterness at having been defeated three times. I was desperate. Without thinking, I instinctively leapt at my adversary and then returned to my place not knowing whether I had won or lost. Later I was told by a friend that I had achieved a splendid victory. My fifth opponent, who was by far the strongest, I defeated in the same way.

In these two contests I experienced moments which I call the naked expression of enlightenment, in which I acted in response to my direct feeling and deepest mind, without considering victory or defeat, opponent or myself, and with no awareness of even engaging in a match. Faced with a situation involving life or death, one can act instantly, intuitively, free from illusion or discrimination, and yet not be in a trance. It is a matter of training oneself, through the principles of Zen, to act wholeheartedly in every circumstance.

When we live inattentively we are apt to fall into partial discrimination. This is a state of mind in which egocentricity is fostered and human suffering enhanced. Therefore, whenever I become aware that I am relapsing, I remind myself that heaven and earth have the same root. Everything is One. The visual form of things is no different from the emptiness which is their essential nature.

Having read many books about Zen prior to enlightenment, I had the illusory notion that if I could attain enlightenment I would acquire supernatural powers, or develop an outstanding personality all at once, or become a great sage, or that all suffering would be annihilated and the world become heavenlike. These false ideas of mine, I now see, hindered the master in guiding me.

Before awakening I was very much worried about my physical condition, about death, about the unsatisfactory condition of society, and many other things, but after enlightenment they no longer upset me. Nowadays whatever I do I am completely at one with it. I accept pleasant things as wholly pleasant and distasteful things as completely distasteful, and then immediately forget the reaction of pleasantness or distastefulness.

I feel that through the experience of enlightenment the human mind can expand to the infinity of the cosmos. True greatness has nothing to do with fortune, social status, or intellectual capacity but simply with enlargement of mind. In this sense I am constantly endeavoring to become great.

As is well known, worldly knowledge and powers of subtle reasoning are not prerequisites for training in Zen. Buddhist tradition has it that the famous Sixth Patriarch, Eno, the most excellent of masters in ancient China, was able to attain perfect enlightenment because, being illiterate, he was not given to reading and speculating about truth; thus he could directly grasp the source of Mind. Since olden times the Japanese have said that not through intellection but by devoted sitting can we see into the ultimate nature of Mind and in the same way deepen and expand this vision endlessly.

There are certain trees which, because they spring up rapidly, never develop the strength to withstand a strong gale. Similarly, in Zen there are those who attain enlightenment quickly but who, since they give up practice, never become spiritually strong. Of prime importance in Zen, therefore, are calm and steadfast application of zazen in one's daily life and a staunch determination not to stop short of perfect enlightenment.

4 / MR. C. S., A JAPANESE RETIRED GOVERN-MENT WORKER, AGE 60 / My experience of kensho was simple and unspectacular, lacking the drama of many another. Indeed my enlightenment itself is shallow, but since I've been asked to write this account I offer it for what interest it may have.

I came to Zen out of no such lofty ambition as kensho. The insecurity and utter confusion in this country right after the recent war drove me to the point where I often thought of committing suicide. To quiet my apprehensive, turbulent mind I decided to do zazen. Since my sole aim was the cultivation of mind stability, I did not even know the word kensho when I began zazen. The roshi instructed me first to practice counting my breath, then following my breath with my mind's eye, and finally to do shikan-taza, the last being concentration without an object in mind.

On the way to Yasutani-roshi's temple to attend my first sesshin I thought (knowing nothing of what a sesshin entails): "How pleasant it will be to relax with the roshi, even perhaps to drink sake with him." It was dusk when I got to the temple and all I could hear were the sounds of the bush warbler and the trickle of water from a broken pipe. I could see bluish-green bamboo in the grove and the red blooms of the camellia. The surroundings, at once serene and beautiful, affected me profoundly. I had brought several books with me and beamed in anticipation of being able to read quietly during the sesshin and to compose poems inspired by all this natural beauty.

But when the sesshin began the following day it turned out to be something I had never imagined. It was, as a matter of fact, torture. It so happens that several of the joints of my legs are permanently stiff from two automobile accidents. This, together with the fact that I was almost sixty at the time, made sitting with my legs crossed in the lotus posture excruciating. (Still, thinking about it afterward, I know that whatever I gained came to me through this pain.) I experienced the worst in my legs at dawn of the second day. Feeling that death itself could not be worse, I told myself: "All this pain comes from zazen, and you can escape it if you wish. But if you were dying and in agony, you would be unable to escape the suffering, so bear this pain in the same spirit and die if need be!"[28] I fought this torment with every ounce of strength.

Gradually I felt the pain in my legs less and less as the sesshin progressed, and my mind began to expand until, imperceptibly, it reached a sublime state. I couldn't say whether I was unconscious of my existence or conscious of my non-existence. My only awareness was of both thumbs touching each other lightly. The sliding screen doors in front of me turned stark white and a purified brightness descended upon everything. I felt as though I were in paradise.

[28] It is interesting to read of the Catholic abbess St. Teresa counseling her nuns: "Strive like strong men until you die in the attempt, for you are here for nothing else than to strive." Quoted by E. Allison Peers in the preface (p. 16) to his translation of *The Autobiography of St. Teresa of Avila.*

My dominant feeling was gratitude, yet I wasn't aware of anyone's feeling grateful. Involuntarily I began to cry softly, then the tears streamed down my cheeks. Tears, tears, tears—a veritable river of tears! Even as I sat before the bell awaiting my turn to go before the roshi I couldn't control my silly sobbing. I was ashamed of showing a tear-stained face to the roshi, believing that tears were no part of zazen, and after a strong effort managed to control the weeping. After the sesshin I mentioned this crying episode to the roshi. He told me that while I hadn't yet reached the point of kensho, nevertheless I had attained to a significant degree of ego attrition, of which this crying was an indication. This I was happy to hear, and on that note ended my first sesshin.

With this experience I knew I had established the basis for transforming my life. It is often said that Zen is not theory but practice. The truth of this was unmistakably brought home to me. Sitting in solitude like a mountain—this alone is required. With this first sesshin there grew within me a resolve to cultivate and deepen what I had barely tasted in order to acquire the equanimity so essential to cope with the confusions of this troubled world. By practicing zazen according to the roshi's instructions my powers of concentration steadily grew stronger, and each day became a day of thanks. In my home there were now no quarrels, and I was cheerful as I walked to the office each morning. I was content with my life, which could be called serene and peaceful. Yet from time to time I was troubled by the question: What is the purpose of human life? I knew that without kensho I could never establish the inner certainty I now lacked.

SHIKAN-TAZA: I began zazen with counting my breaths, then I followed them with my mind's eye, and after that the roshi assigned me shikan-taza, the purest kind of zazen. Generally speaking, through a koan one can get kensho more quickly than through shikan-taza, where a gradual ripening of the mind takes place.[29] The roshi had often encouraged me with these words: "Instead of trying to get kensho forcibly through a koan, sit patiently while natural ripening takes place." So I sat steadily, firmly convinced

[29] For a more precise statement on koan zazen and shikan-taza, see p. 56.

that the time would come when my mind, now like an astringent persimmon, would become ripe and sweet. The more zazen I did, the clearer my mind became. Each time I sat down to zazen I would first regulate my breath, after which I would slip into deep concentration. As my practice progressed I often experienced a condition in which I was no longer aware of my body and mind or of anything else. When I told the roshi about this he urged me not to linger in this world of the eighth class of consciousness,[30] the state of purity and stability, but bravely to break through beyond. I felt, however, as though I were facing a "silver mountain" or an "iron wall." I could neither advance nor retreat.

Sometime later, during another sesshin, I recall an incident when I got up alone one night and began to sit facing one of the sliding paper doors, which dimly reflected the bright evening sky. With a determined effort, made easier by the deep solitude of midnight, I rapidly got into a state of profound concentration. My mind attained to such clarity that I felt the next morning would surely bring kensho, contrary to even the roshi's expectations. But in spite of my dogged sitting I couldn't reach no-mindness, and being by nature rather dull-witted anyway, I soon became seduced by the croaking of the frogs, whose voices were highly melodious, the like of which I'd seldom heard. This evening the chorus rang out sharply in the stillness. "That's it, that's all, that's all, that's it," they seemed to be singing and mocking. A strange laugh bubbled up from deep within me. It became impossible for me to do pure zazen, and I gave up trying.

At the following spring sesshin Mrs. Y_____, who was sitting next to me came to kensho and shed tears of gratitude and joy. Straightway I decided that I would be the next. But in spite of my struggles I could find no weapon in shikan-taza to break down the "iron wall" confronting me. At dokusan the last words of the roshi were always: "Now push on!" What I wanted, however, was a tool with which to push on, so I almost begged him to assign me the koan Mu. This he did after the spring sesshin, presenting me at the same time with a sitting cushion and a Buddhist amice to encourage me to strive on. Now all the "tools" were at hand save one: the unshakable will to get kensho at any price. As I

[30] See also "consciousness" in section x.

walked home after the sesshin, I made this vow: Either I get kensho at the next sesshin or else!

THE KOAN MU: Though I had been given Mu practically at my own request, I couldn't do good zazen with it. Having practiced shikan-taza over a long time and grown accustomed to holding my mind like a flowing stream or a drifting cloud, with no focal point, I found Mu a formidable burden. Yet I sorely needed this tool to demolish the "silver mountain." So I concentrated fiercely, trying to merge myself with Mu, and gradually grew accustomed to it.

In early autumn of 1955 I was again in sesshin. Somehow I felt this sesshin would be crucial for me; I knew that on me alone depended success or failure.

At 4:30 A.M. of the first day the roshi, during his inspection round, told us: "Conditions at this sesshin are ideal; the weather is neither hot nor cold and it is quiet. You have a splendid opportunity." I took his words to heart and gripped Mu like a heavy hiking stick to forge my way through the narrow mountainous pass opening into kensho.

First day . . . Second day . . . Third day . . . Time passed quickly. My first attempts to grasp Mu failed—I simply could not break through. Bewildered and frustrated because I could not budge my mind out of the serene clarity into which it had settled, I strove desperately to cut through this mind-state with the sharp sword of Mu, now driven by an overwrought impatience, but to no avail.

Earlier this year at the spring sesshin I had also reached this realm of the eighth consciousness and had failed to penetrate beyond it. It was now apparent to me that I had never exerted myself to my very limits, and that if I was ever to get kensho, nothing less than a superhuman effort could do it. This often led me to continue my sitting even after the bell had rung signaling a round of walking. But I still could not break out of this "cave of Satan" even with Mu and the superhuman effort I was making. I just couldn't crack this impasse.

Kensho demands enormous psychic and physical vitality, but I was now sixty and had lost much of my former energy and resilience. Still, I refused to give up, continuing with Mu without sliding back.

On the fourth day, on my way to the outhouse, in the silence of twilight I spied an old loquat tree. Its branches seemed possessed of a strange, indescribably solemnity. "What I am seeing is absolute truth!" I told myself. My mind, I knew, had progressed in awareness, and I returned to my sitting with renewed vigor. In the evening at dokusan I told Roshi what I had felt about the tree and asked him what it meant. "You have reached a decisive point—there is only one more step! This is the last evening of the sesshin. Do zazen all night." Fired by the roshi's "one more step!" I was now ready for an all-night, all-out attack on Mu.

OPENING MY MIND'S EYE: Customarily all lights are put out at 9 A.M., but this night, with the roshi's permission, I kept one small light burning. Mr. M_____, the senior monitor, joined me in my sitting, and with his spiritual strength added to mine I felt vastly stronger. Centering my energy in my hara, I began to feel exhilarated. Intently I watched the still shadow of my chin and head until I lost awareness of them in a deepening concentration. As the evening wore on, the pain in my legs became so grueling that even changing from full- to half-lotus didn't lessen it. My only way of overcoming it was to pour all my energy into single-minded concentration on Mu. Even with the fiercest concentration to the point of panting "Mu! Mu! Mu!" there was nothing I could do to free myself of the excruciating pain except to shift my posture a little.

Abruptly the pains disappear, there's only Mu! Each and every thing is Mu. "Oh, it's *this!*" I exclaimed, reeling in astonishment, my mind a total emptiness. "Ting-a-ling, ting-a-ling"—a bell's ringing. How cool and refreshing! It impels me to rise and move about. All is freshness and purity itself. Every single object is dancing vividly, inviting me to look. Every single thing occupies its natural place and breathes quietly. I notice zinnias in a vase on the altar, an offering to Monju, the Bodhisattva of Infinite Wisdom. They are indescribably beautiful!

At the next dokusan Roshi tested me and confirmed my understanding of Mu.

A full kensho-awakening usually generated not only astonishment but also profound joy, but I neither wept nor laughed with joy.

In most cases it transforms one's fundamental outlook on life and death and offers a new and penetrating insight into the words "Life is vain and transitory." But my experience carried in its wake no such insights, for it was but a touch of enlightenment.

I was born in September 1895, and so in September 1955 was just sixty years old. In Japan the sixtieth birthday is celebrated as the day of rebirth. I am happy that the opening of my Mind's eye this very month coincided with the first steps of my new, second life. Eight years have passed since I first began zazen. It is said in Japan that it takes eight years for the persimmon tree to bear fruit. In like manner, my efforts have borne fruit. But the flavor is for others to judge.

5 / MRS. A. M., AN AMERICAN SCHOOL-TEACHER, AGE 38 / Of Jewish and Gentile parentage, I was born in Germany, where I led the idyllic childhood of an elf in Grimms' fairy tales. My father, a Jew, earned the respect of everyone in our sleepy medieval town, not only for his learning as a doctor of laws but also for his unlimited generosity. My mother, of Lutheran German background, was loved by rich and poor alike for her understanding, her charity, and her joy of life. Completely sheltered from financial and other worries, I grew up in childish innocence.

The words "God" and "religion" were never discussed in my family, as my parents thought it best to leave the choice of Judaism or Christianity to us children when the time was ripe. My early exposure to the Old and New Testaments came in the class in religion at school, where the Lutheran translation of the Bible made a profound impression on me.

Hitler rose to power and everything changed. My childhood dreams blew up in smoke and I was faced with the stark reality of persecution. Brick by brick the Nazis knocked the security from the wall surrounding my ego. The love and respect we had enjoyed disappeared and we knew only loneliness and anxiety.

Friendless, I withdrew into myself and spent most of my time reading. Voraciously I went through my father's vast library, looking for stories of romantic hue, of *Weltschmerz*, in which I imagined myself the heroine.

The climax of persecution for my family came on the infamous ninth of November, 1938, when our home along with other Jewish houses was destroyed by hordes of drunken storm troopers, my father brutally beaten and dragged off to a concentration camp. My mother was in Berlin at the time, and my sister and I were left in desolation, shivering in the attic of our once so beautiful home. In my soul's despair I uttered the first real prayer of my life: "God help us!"

Penniless but with pioneer spirit my family landed by boat in San Pedro, California, on January 24, 1939. Miraculously we had escaped from the clutches of the Nazis and, thanks to the affidavits of my mother's sisters in Los Angeles, now embarked hopefully on a new life.

I pinched pennies for four years and was able to attend the University of California at Los Angeles. Eventually I obtained my master's degree in education and became a full-fledged language teacher.

Now married, on September 3, 1955, my first child, a beautiful blue-eyed girl, was born. With the little money we had and with my husband's GI rights we purchased a tract house near both our schools.

Between home and school my life moved on an even keel. In 1957 my son was born and in 1960 my second daughter. My leisure time I spent reading books on philosophy and religion. The story of Yogananda of India impressed me deeply. Later I became even more profoundly interested in the wisdom of the Orient through a series of lectures I heard on the philosophy of East and West. Zen literature followed, and finally my husband and I formulated a definite plan to visit Japan and India "after our children are a little more mature," in order to seek enlightenment ourselves.

In the meantime one of my teacher friends interested me in joining a group in depth psychology. Somewhat familiar with the Freudian unconscious, I now became acquainted with Jung's viewpoint regarding the possibility of full inner development between the ages of thirty-five and forty. I practiced meeting life's challenges minute by minute, with some success. The only thing, however, which kept me from greater achievement was the lack of a purpose greater than myself. "What am I living for?" I asked myself again and again. I had all material advantages: good health, professional success, a lovely family, leisure time, no financial worries, yet I could find no deep inner satisfaction.

When my husband suggested a vacation in Hawaii in the summer of 1962, I said: "Why not?" In spite of the fact that we were roaming about the beach at Waikiki with three children and two surfboards, both of us were actually looking for something more spiritual. Fortunately my husband discovered a zazen group which was meeting at a private residence in Honolulu. "Why wait till we visit Japan?" we decided. "Let's get accustomed to sitting now. We probably need years of conditioning anyway."

Much to our delight we found that a roshi, an enlightened sage from Japan, was stopping in Hawaii to lead a sesshin before embarking on a tour through the United States. This group of serious zazen participants was small and they welcomed us to join. A little embarrassed by our ignorance of Buddhism, my husband and I took turns at home every other evening with the children while each of us went to do zazen and learn about Buddhism for two weeks prior to the sesshin. The pain of the half-lotus posture chagrined me, because I had been athletic all my life and imagined I could do this comfortably with no training. "Am I ready for this?" I questioned myself. "I came to Hawaii for relaxation, not meditation." A neurotic fatigue crept through my whole body and I can't remember when I have ever been so tired.

Before the sesshin formally opened, Yasutani-roshi's preliminary lectures on zazen were distributed to us. They concluded with a classification of the four distinct grades of aspiration, which ranged from mental and physical health to enlightenment. "I am interested in kensho, but would consider myself fortunate if he assigns me the counting of my breaths," I convinced myself. "Perhaps a novice like me will merely learn to entangle her legs correctly and sit up straight." With awe I looked around the room at the other participants sitting perfectly erect, legs in half-lotus posture, breathing in deep concentration in front of a white curtain.

Time passed quickly. Yasutani-roshi arrived and we were all invited to come on Sunday for zazen and tea. When I saw the little light man, seventy-seven yet bearing himself like fifty-seven, with the sparkling magnetism of youth in his eyes, all doubts vanished. "This is my master, for whom I was going to search all over India and Japan," I told myself, and was filled with a strange feeling of joy.

That same evening at the Soto Mission Yasutani-roshi spoke on the koan Mu and how to penetrate it. His pantomime was so vivid that I understood without knowing a word of Japanese. It seemed to me to be like the anguished joy of bearing a baby, and I was ready for the labor.

The night before sesshin I couldn't sleep. I knew I was going on the trip of my life, and my heart beat with the wild anticipation I feel before climbing a mountain. The next morning I arose at four, sat two sittings without much trouble, and boldly announced to Yasutani-roshi that I was in the fourth category of aspiration, hoping to reach kensho. To my surprise, he asked no further questions but straightway assigned me the koan Mu. Almost at once I regretted my decision!

For two days I worked on Mu half-heartedly, scared to death to face the roshi at dokusan, because to me he represented the strict disciplinarian father of my youth. On top of this, I could never remember the simple Japanese words for "My koan is Mu."

The third day everything changed. Our interpreter, the serenely smiling, "floating" Tai-san, became the angel of vengeance. "This is no tea party," his voice thundered, "but a sesshin! Today I will teach you the meaning of sesshin!" Whereupon he began cracking everyone with his kyosaku, a flat board used on the shoulders of sleepy monks to rouse them to full concentration. I was anything but sleepy—I was absolutely panic-stricken. That whole day I saw myself walking on the edge of an abyss with water gushing wildly below. Every breath was Mu. "If you let go even once you will fall," I cautioned myself, "so keep going as though you were starting on a long hike up a steep mountain."

That night I had a strange dream. A table with four cups, clover-leaf fashion, was set for a Japanese tea ceremony. Just as I was lifting my cup, a winged Tai-san descended upon me like an angel with a fiery sword, and with a loud Mu! whacked me. I awoke with a start and immediately fell into zazen, this time in a lying position stretched out on my bed, hands over my belly. "You'll never get anywhere in this panic," I tried to quiet myself. "You must relax. Picture a quiet mountain scene at night beneath the star-studded infinite." Slowly, deeply I inhaled and exhaled, and a wondrous peace enveloped me. My belly seemed to expand into a balloon, and a fog which had shortly before enveloped me slowly began to lift until a sweet nothingness invaded my whole being. I heard the sound of flowing water and slowly came out of my trance. At dokusan I was told that I was on the verge of the great experience of enlightenment.

The fourth day the tension rose to an even higher pitch. Tai-san told the story of a monk so determined to reach kensho that he meditated with a stick of incense in one hand and a knife in the other. "Either I am enlightened by the time the incense is burned out or I shall kill myself," he vowed. With the pain of the burning stub of incense he became enlightened. Tai-san then made the rounds with his kyosaku, reducing everyone, even my husband, to tears.

"I shall reach kensho at this sesshin," I promised myself and sat three sittings in half-lotus. Then I broke down and sobbed bitterly; even in dokusan I could not stop crying. I went upstairs to rest, and when I got up to wash my face I had the strange sensation of water gushing right through me and blinked my eyes. It sounded like the water I had heard the night I experienced voidness.

The morning of the fifth day I stayed home to take care of the children. I should mention that neither my husband nor I attended sesshin full time. We took turns going to the 4 A.M. sitting and went home for almost all meals. I stayed overnight once, my husband not at all.

A little embarrassed at dokusan that afternoon, I confessed that I had not done zazen at home because of too many interruptions. I was told that two people had already reached kensho and that if I exerted myself to the utmost, I could also get kensho. So that night my husband allowed me to stay overnight.

With Mu I went to bed, with Mu I arose the sixth day. "Don't get nervous," Tai-san cautioned, "just concentrate." I listened to these words of wisdom, but was too tired to meditate. My energies were drained. After breakfast I lay down to rest, doing Mu in a horizontal position, when suddenly a glow appeared in front of my eyes as though sunshine were hitting them directly. I clearly heard sounds I had not heard since I was a little girl sick in bed: my mother's footsteps and the rustling of her boxes. Having had so many strange experiences already at this sesshin, I paid no further heed but continued my concentration on Mu throughout the entire morning's sitting. As I was awaiting dokusan a familiar aroma tantalized my nostrils; it was the tempting smell of my mother's cooking. My eyes glanced at a red cushion on a brown table, the same colors of my grandmother's living-room furniture. A door slammed, a dog barked, a white cloud sailed through a blue sky— I was reliving my childhood in makyo, hallucinations.

At noon, with the roshi's permission, my husband told me that he had achieved kensho. "Now or never!" I told myself. "A pumpkin wife cannot be married to an enlightened husband!" I vividly recalled the story of the youth with the knife and incense. "Death or deliverance!" became my watchword.

I inhaled deeply and with each exhalation concentrated with all my might on Mu. I felt as though I were all air and would levitate any second. I "crawled" into the belly of a hideous, hairy spider. "Mu! Mu! Mu!" I groaned, and I became a big, black Mu. An angel, it seemed, touched me ever so softly on the shoulder, and I fell backwards. Suddenly I realized that my husband and Taisan were standing behind me, but I could not move; my feet were absolutely numb. They practically carried me outside, and I sobbed helplessly. "I was already dead," I said to myself. "Why did they have to bring me back to life?" At dokusan the roshi told me that this was but a foretaste of kensho, it was not yet realization.

Then I took a little walk and suddenly the whole experience of the last few days seemed utterly ridiculous to me. "That stupid roshi," I remember thinking, "he and his Oriental hocus-pocus. He just doesn't know what he's talking about." At dinner, half an hour later, as I was fumbling with my chopsticks, I felt like getting up and handing him a fork. "Here, old boy, let's get used to Western ways." I giggled at my own joke. Throughout the evening chanting I could hardly keep a straight face. After the roshi's final words I wanted to pick up my bag and walk out, never to return, so unreal did it all seem.

In his first lecture the roshi had told us that Mu was like a red-hot ball stuck in the throat which one can neither swallow nor spit out. He was right, so right. As I look back, every word, every move was part of the deliberate plan of this venerable teacher. His name, "White Cloud" [Hakuun], indeed fits him. He is the greatest, whitest cloud I have ever experienced, a real antidote to the dark atomic mushroom.

Now I was in bed, doing zazen again. All night long I alternately breathed Mu and fell into trances. I thought of the monk who had reached kensho in just such a state of fatigue. Eventually I must have dozed off in complete exhaustion. Suddenly the same light angel touched me on the shoulder. Only this time I awoke with a bright "Ha!" and realized I was enlightened. The angel was my kind tired husband tapping me on the shoulder to waken me to go to sesshin.

A strange power propelled me. I looked at the clock—twenty minutes to four, just in time to make the morning sitting. I arose and calmly dressed. My mind raced as I solved problem after problem. I arrived at the sesshin before four o'clock and accepted an offer of coffee with such a positive "Yes" that I could not believe my own ears. When Tai-san came around with his "sword" I told him not to bother hitting me. At dokusan I rushed into the little cottage my teacher was occupying and hugged and kissed him and shook Tai-san's hand, and let loose with such a torrent of comical verbosity that all three of us laughed with delight. The roshi tested and passed me, and I was officially ushered through the first barrier of the gateless gate.

A lifetime has been compressed into one week. A thousand new sensations are bombarding my senses, a thousand new paths are opening before me. I live my life minute by minute, but only now does a warm love pervade my whole being, because I know that I am not just my little self but a great big miraculous Self. My constant thought is to have everybody share this deep satisfaction.

I can think of no better way to end this account than with the vows I chanted at sesshin every morning:

> All beings, without number, I vow to liberate;
> Endless blind passions I vow to uproot;
> Dharma gates, beyond measure, I vow to penetrate;
> The Great Way of Buddha I vow to attain.

6 / MR. A. K., A JAPANESE INSURANCE AD-JUSTER, AGE 25 / I first began to think seriously about life

and death at the age of twelve when my eight-year-old brother died of a kidney disease. I grieved so much over his death that I collapsed at his funeral. Deep within me was a feeling of contrition so strong that I remember crying out: "Forgive me, forgive me!"

Four years later my only other brother drowned. This was such a profound shock that I began to question over and over: "Why is life so uncertain and miserable? Are we born only to die?" I was overwhelmed by a feeling of utter helplessness. School study was sheer drudgery, and every day was a day of misery. "Why are we born, why do we die?"—this question obsessed me like an eternal nightmare.

In hopes of ending my wretchedness I began avidly to read the bible of one of the postwar religions in Japan, called *The Truth of Life*. After the death of my younger brother my parents had become followers of this sect for a short time. It urged: "Live a life of gratitude with a smile. Be meek and always respond with 'Yea.'" This was all very well, but how one cultivated meekness and gratitude was not made clear. It further claimed that man, as the son of God, is without flaw, and that through his identity with God he could realize this innate perfection. "But why," I questioned, "should man, who they insist is born free, be tied even to God, eternally enslaved by him? This can't be the way to peace of mind." Disillusioned, I dropped this religion out of my life, convinced that it was no more than an opiate.

I was just seventeen when, in August 1949, I came to Sosei-ji, a Soto temple, to ask the abbot what Buddhism was. He was pleased to see me and said: "It cannot be explained in a sentence, but let me tell you the reply given by a renowned Zen master to the same question. When the Chinese poet Hakurakuten asked Zen Master Dorin about the mysteries of Buddhism, he was told:

> 'Avoid evil,
> Practice good,
> Keep the heart-mind pure—
> This is what all Buddhas teach.'[31]

"Remember," the abbot continued, "zazen is the most direct way to understand Buddhism, but choosing a good teacher is para-

[31] For the full conversation, see "Hakurakuten" in section x.

mount." In November of that year I attended my first *zazenkai*, conducted by Yasutani-roshi.

To my surprise, I found the roshi to be a simple old man with no apparent dignity, wearing the shabbiest of robes. In a quiet voice he spoke about counting the breath in zazen while facing a wall, but such questions as "What is the meaning of life?" or "How can we get rid of suffering?" he didn't deal with at all. However, I began to count my breath in the manner he instructed, though it went against my grain. "Zen can't be real," I told myself, "it must be a fake!"

But for some reason I went again when the next zazen meeting rolled around and continued to go. Upon learning of kensho, through which experience the roshi claimed human suffering could be dissolved, I made up my mind to get kensho so that I could disprove the roshi. My skepticism persisted for two years until I was finally persuaded by a senior member of the zazenkai to join a three-day sesshin. He had told me: "If you don't come back a wiser, stronger man, you can knock my block off." The roshi gave me Mu as my first koan. While half of me strove resolutely for kensho, the other half held back in fear of the fierce blows of the kyosaku. I went to no more sesshin until the next year, when I attended five in succession. By now every one of my doubts as to the validity of Zen had vanished, but for all my striving I could not reach the point of kensho.

Each time I returned from a sesshin I found that I had grown calmer and better able to deal with my daily life. Despite this gain, however, I felt that with no kensho I had spent another year in vain.

It was now my graduation year, 1954, and the fear that I would have no time for zazen in business life fired my determination to get kensho before I finished school. In this state of mind I joined the March sesshin. On the third day I was struck with peculiar force by this remark of the roshi: "Mu is nothing but Mu!" It was a simple statement that I had often heard from him, but now it hit me like lightning. "Then why on earth have I been imagining otherwise?" A heavy load suddenly fell from my shoulders, but because this was not yet realization, I fell into darkness again. At afternoon dokusan I had nothing to say to the roshi and returned to my place disheartened. With this insight, however, I became convinced that kensho was entirely possible for me.

Repeatedly I had urged my mother to accompany me to a zazen meeting, and she had steadfastly refused. Now she went and very quickly attained kensho. I was dumbfounded. Her experience so set me on fire that at the following month's sesshin I redoubled my efforts. With strong encouragement from the roshi, who urged, "Only one more step!" I fiercely applied myself to my koan. But in my deepest unconscious (I now see) I was still conceiving Mu as something outside me; that's why the world of kensho never appeared. Bitterly disappointed, I told myself: "You have sat and sat, yet you haven't succeeded. There must be something wrong with you."

Deeply discouraged, I talked myself into believing I lacked the intrinsic potentiality for enlightenment; still I continued to attend sesshin after sesshin, for reasons which were obscure to me at the time. But I could no longer pour myself into zazen. Then I began to think in this wise: "Since the universe and I are one, to understand the meaning of the universe I must understand myself. But I won't be able to understand myself until once and for all I end my habit of seeking Mu outside myself."

By the following year I had recovered a good deal of my former spirit and was able to sit with a calm, vigorous mind. This encouraged me to participate in subsequent sesshin. Returning to my regular life after each such sesshin, I was astonished to find myself so changed. Every day was a day of gratitude, and when I went to bed at night after a hard day's work, I felt grateful to be alive, though I didn't know why. By now I had a considerable theoretical knowledge of enlightenment, but when I reflected that it had not brought me awakening, a restless discontent took hold of me. I knew that deep down I still feared death and shrank from life. I was suspended between a feeling of gratitude on the one hand and anxiety and frustration on the other.

One hot August evening as I sat with my parents at home during a period of zazen, I suddenly experienced myself as a ripple spreading endlessly throughout the universe. "I've got it! There is no universe apart from me"—this repeatedly flashed into my mind. While it was no more than an insight, it convinced me I was nearing kensho, and I began to sit more earnestly. My habit of reasoning about Mu, however, persisted. "What a curse thought is!" I would exclaim in chagrin. "It confuses the mind, creates disputes between men by setting them apart from each other, it creates war itself. Stop thinking! Stop analyzing!"

Not long after this I went to a zazen meeting at which Yasutani-roshi delivered a teisho on the "Three Gates of Oryu," a koan from *Mumonkan*. At one point he was saying: "How does your hand compare with the hand of a Buddha? Reaching out in your sleep for your dislodged pillow, instinctively you recover it. One's whole being is no different from this timeless hand. When you truly realize this, you will spontaneously burst into laughter."

Hearing these lines, my mind became enormously cleansed, and I trembled with joy. But since I had not yet gained true freedom, I decided to say nothing of this during dokusan. Considerably heartened, however, I renewed my efforts to penetrate deeper into my koan.

The one-week August sesshin had arrived. Owing to the pressure of business, I could not get to the temple until noon of the second day. My strategy for this sesshin was to sit determinedly, like a ball of fire, during sitting periods, and to relax completely during rest periods. At the opening of the third day the roshi had reminded everyone: "Every year at this great sesshin at least one person gets kensho." Then and there I made up my mind that if anybody got kensho it would be me.

The fourth day had come. Again and again I was walloped by the kyosaku, once so hard that my mind and body became momentarily paralyzed. This day I "fought" the hardest. But in spite of everything, I still could not come to kensho. Now it was the fifth day; only a day and a half remained to me. On the sixth day I threw my last ounce of energy into the "battle," allowing nothing whatever to sidetrack me. After the morning chores, and just before the roshi's talk, a university student sitting near me (who got kensho at this sesshin), suddenly yelled out: "You foolish, foolish, stupid guy!" referring to himself. "Go on, on! One more step, only one! The summit! Die if need be, die!" The strength of his desperation flowed into me and I began to concentrate as though my very life depended on it.

My mind was empty as an infant's as I listened to the roshi's lecture. He was reading from an ancient koan: "Not even a sage can impart a word about that Realm [of Silence] from which thoughts issue . . . A piece of string is eternal and boundless . . . The bare white Ox[32] before you is pure, vivid . . ."[33]

As the roshi spoke in a calm, quiet voice, I felt every one of his words filter into the deepest recesses of my mind. "Not even a sage can utter a word about that Realm from which thoughts issue," the roshi repeated, adding, "No, not even a Buddha." "Of course! Of course!" I repeated breathlessly. "Then why have *I* been searching for such a word?" All at once everything became sheer brilliance, and I saw and knew that I am the only One in the whole universe! Yes, I am that only One!

Though not entirely confident the roshi would confirm this as kensho, I decided to present my realization to him at the afternoon dokusan, anyway. "Show me more clearly!" he demanded.

Returning to my place in the main hall of the temple, I again attacked zazen. About seven in the evening I suddenly heard these words explode over my head: "Thirty minutes to dokusan! Make up your mind to come to Self-realization! This is your last chance!" Again and again the blows of the stick rained down on me. My concentration became utterly desperate. At last it dawned on me: *there is Nothing to realize!*

At dokusan the roshi tested me with: "Show me Mu! How old is Mu? Show me Mu when you are taking a bath. Show me Mu on a mountain." My responses were instantaneous, and he confirmed my kensho. Prostrating myself outside the roshi's doorway as I left his room, I overflowed with a joy which beggared description.

I cannot close this account without expressing my deep gratitude to Yasutani-roshi, who led me, so stubborn and willful, to open my Mind's eye, and to all others who directly or indirectly have helped me.

[32] That is, Mind. See section VIII.
[33] These lines are from the commentary on Case 94 in *Hekigan-roku.*

7 / MRS. L. T. S., AN AMERICAN ARTIST, AGE
5 1 / I had come to Zen and the Pendle Hill [Pennsylvania] sesshin
obliquely and inevitably. As I look back over my shoulder at the
apparent meandering of my path to the moment of realization, I
see that it led straight to the sound of that tiny kinhin bell. As a
sculptor, as a wife and mother, as a drunk, and finally as a member
of Alcoholics Anonymous, I had good pretraining.

I suppose the first step in this life was the knowing, at about
fifteen, that I must be an artist. This knowing coincided with a
total rejection of Christianity (as I saw it) and an earnest groping
for truth within myself. In a few years I discovered stone, and
again I knew that carving was my way—slow and hard—as the
inner groping was slow and hard.

I was determined to experience as much as possible, so marriage
and family followed. But in time my zest for living became throttled.
Life was too much for me, it began to pinch and bruise. Then I
discovered blessed alcohol, which subtly dulled my pain and un-
shackled my soaring spirit.

Stone rested silently, untouched. My husband and children, demanding my love, were pushed aside. No sculpture. No wholehearted acceptance of family. Just pain and guilt and inadequacy.
And slowly alcohol took over and controlled my life. I no longer
knew my center.

Life was a bad dream. Struggling from one twenty-four hours
to the next, I was controlled by fear and guilt and the secret bottle.
I would not believe that *I* could not find a way out. So eight years
of psychiatry and attempts at every method of self-discipline I knew
of followed. But I was still trapped.

One morning, which seemed no different from all the other terrible mornings, I phoned Alcoholics Anonymous for help. With this
act I was at last freed to truly look at myself, and with the help
of all the other alcoholics who had lived through the same hell,
to *be* myself. I stopped drinking. I learned that there is something
infinitely more powerful than my small human mind. And I knew
that I must find it, know it, see it, *be it.*

My search had begun!

A few weeks later, idly looking at books on a bargain counter,
I picked up *How to Know God,* a translation by Swami Prabhavananda

and Christopher Isherwood of Patanjali's *Aphorisms*. I was stunned! Patanjali had known and taught, perhaps two thousand years ago, what I had just discovered for myself. This book I read and reread and studied and puzzled over for two months on the deck of our schooner as we sailed up the Atlantic coast and down again on a vacation trip. All footnote material was tracked down, books ordered and devoured.

The deep need for a teacher was answered by my finding Swami Pramananda, who agreed to help me. He guided and directed me, started me in disciplined meditation, helped me sort out hallucinations from reality, prepared me for the great plunging effort at Pendle Hill.

In the course of my reading I had found references to Zen in Huxley's *Perennial Philosophy*. This I knew was for me. I continued to read, to practice *kriya* meditation, though not to sit in the Zen way.

Entirely unexpectedly I was given an opportunity to go to Japan for a few months to supervise the construction of an exhibit I had designed. There I ruthlessly, persistently chased Zen. And there I was shown, as ruthlessly, that the only place to chase it was within myself. I was told to sit.

I sat. I sat at sesshin at Engaku-ji, Ryutaku-ji, and briefly at Nanzen-ji. I sat at Ryosen-an in Daitoku-ji.

It happened this way. Before leaving America I had heard of Engaku-ji, so there I went. When I arrived in a cold November rain, I had no idea what to do, no introduction to anyone, no understanding of Japanese. Not knowing which way to turn, I stood irresolute, absolutely alone in a gray, deserted landscape, with rain soaking through my raincoat, running down my neck, dripping into my shoes. A dark figure ran out in the rain. Helplessly we looked at each other. Words tumbled out, Japanese and English. He beckoned me to follow and led me to a door where he knocked and called. A figure appeared. It was a young Englishwoman, who, after a brisk conversation in Japanese with my guide, asked what she could do for me.

She took me to the head monk and arranged for me to stay (they were in sesshin), taught me how to get through the meals, requested an interview with the roshi, and interpreted for me— was my guide and good friend. Her final gift was to introduce me to an American Zen student, who arranged by telephone for me to go to Ryutaku-ji for more sitting.

So it went—on and on—kindness from so many people, and painful, painful sitting. Wherever I sought help in Japan, from a roshi, a monk, or a lay student, I found it. The compassion of all these people for my floundering ignorance has been infinite, and I am so grateful.

The ting of that tiny bell at the Pendle Hill sesshin was the shock, the force that crumbled walls that had been gently eroding through four years of zazen, and before that five years of *kriya* yoga every day, every night. Patiently, stubbornly, I had sat, sat, sat. Sometimes a long time, sometimes a few minutes, but always, always every day. Sitting patiently had become so familiar that I accepted it as naturally and uneventfully as breathing.

When I arrived at the Pendle Hill sesshin I had never seen Yasutani-roshi before. His monk interpreter I had met at Ryutaku-ji, where I had attended a sesshin four years earlier. I was braced for the physical misery of four and a half days of zazen, but I also knew well that the reward was clarity and peace. After attending the sesshin in Delaware conducted by Nakagawa-roshi in 1961, I had jotted down: "I feel that I've been turned inside out, shaken, and rinsed in pure, clear water."

So this Pendle Hill sesshin began. About forty strangers sat together, some merely curious, some very earnest. Yasutani-roshi divided the group, according to their expressed purpose for being there, into several smaller groups. He spoke privately to each of the groups, explaining the discipline they were to follow during the next four and a half days. I was one of those who sought enlightenment, and to this group he gave the koan Joshu's Mu.

I began to sit with Mu.

The first day Mu was no hot iron ball—in fact it was a heavy lump of lead in my belly.

"Melt that lead!" the roshi commanded. But it would not melt, so next day I hammered with Mu, and came to know that its center was a brilliant, crystalline light, like a star or a diamond, so brilliant that it outlined and illuminated physical objects, dazzled my eyes, filled me with light. My body felt weightless. I thought: "This is

Mu." But the roshi counseled: "Hallucinations. Ignore them. Concentrate harder."

By the end of that day there was no light, just drowsiness, infinite weariness, and Mu. Before going to bed I wrote a note to myself: "Now I am *determined*. If others can do it I can too! And I *will!* I will exhaust every bit of strength and stubborn determination." Then I slept, with Mu blanketing dreams, Mu moving in and out with each breath.

The third day my eyes would not stay open—with each breath they closed. When I fought this off, my mind was immediately filled with problems of my family and marriage. It was a terrible struggle against both sleep and mental torment. With each breath I was determined to get hold of Mu, but it went down and down and disappeared in nothingness.

"Go deeper," the roshi said. "Question 'What is this Mu?' to the very bottom."

Deeper and deeper I went . . .

My hold was torn loose and I went spinning . . .

To the center of the earth!

To the center of the cosmos!

To the *Center*.

I was There.

With the sound of the little kinhin bell I suddenly *knew*.

Too late to see the roshi that night, I rushed to the first dokusan in the morning.

Questions . . .

Sharp voices . . .

Laughter . . .

Movement . . .

The roshi said: "Now you understand that seeing Mu is seeing God."

I *understood*.

[After miscellaneous koan zazen at the Brewster, New York, sesshin several weeks later:]

I feel clean.

I feel free.

I feel ready to live every day with zest, by *choice!*

I am delighted by the adventure of each moment.

I feel as though I have just awakened from a restless, disjointed dream. Everything looks different!

The world no longer rides heavily on my back. It is under my belt. I turned a somersault and swallowed it.

I am no longer restless.

At last I have what I want.

8 / MRS. D. K., A CANADIAN HOUSEWIFE, AGE 35 /

CANADA AND THE UNITED STATES: The early years of my life were quiet and uneventful. No tragedy touched me, and my parents were devoted to the bringing up of myself and my two sisters. It could almost be called an ideal childhood by most Western standards. Even from the first, though, there were recurrent periods of despair and loneliness which used to seep up from no apparent source, overflowing into streams of tears and engulfing me to the exclusion of everything else. At these times the painful feeling of being entrapped was overpowering, and simply to be a human being a wretched and ignominious lot.

Once in my early teens I was lent some books of Hindu stories which provoked my intensest interest. They spoke unabashedly of a multiplicity of lives and of the soul's freedom, of man's spiritual self and the possibility of life without a physical body. Most of the details of this reading evaporated in the face of something stirring much deeper in my being and I felt happy to learn that such understanding did exist. The Indian myths of limitless time touched my deepest concerns, and I vowed that one day I would visit India for myself.

After my enrollment at university I began in earnest to study religious literature, even trying some simple meditation. The years at university taught me the joy and stimulation of intellectual discovery, but they were at the same time pervaded by a mounting restlessness. At length I graduated and commenced graduate studies. Toward the end of that first year my life took an unexpected turn. After a few indecisive months I went to the United States to marry an American whom I had met in Canada.

Within a few months our marriage took place and almost immediately after I awoke to find myself a widow. The violent, self-inflicted death of my husband was a shock more severe than anything I had ever experienced. The circumstances and implications of it precipitated me into the innermost depths of my being, where the foundations shook with a truly terrifying intensity. I could not divest myself of a deep sense of human responsibility for it. Perception, maturity, wisdom—all these I sorely lacked.

Frequently at this time I would be seized by a total numbness, and always there was fear, a deep pervasive fear, which lasted long, obstructing my breathing and inhibiting my eating. Often at night I would find myself seated cross-legged on the floor, rocking back and forth and hitting my head against the tiles, almost delirious with grief and despair.

One afternoon, returning from an errand and stepping into my apartment, where I lived alone, the profoundest misery seized me and in helplessness I slumped to the floor. "I am dying," I sobbed, "I have killed all my gods. I have no key to resurrection. I am totally alone." Stark fear and utter despair possessed me, and I lay on the floor for I don't know how long until from the pit of my abdomen a cry came forth: "If there is any being in the entire universe who cares whether I live or die, help me, oh help me!"

Gradually an idea took form and I began to write. I had a very dear friend who had recently renounced the world. She was now living in an *ashram*[34] in South India, and I begged her to direct her meditations toward me, for I needed help badly and no longer felt capable of helping myself. Quickly she replied that she and others in the ashram were sending as much spiritual support as they could. Her response so touched me that I decided to leave the West as soon as I could for India.

It was many months more before this was possible. All my energies were now harnessed into winding up my husband's estate and selling my belongings. At last I sailed, exhausted, to India, intending to stay there until I had found an enlightened teacher. Exactly three years had passed since I had come to the United States.

INDIA AND BURMA: One hot afternoon two months after my departure from New York I entered the compound of the large ashram

[34] The Sri Aurobindo Ashram, in Pondicherry. An *ashram* is a spiritual retreat or religious community.

where my friend was living. Silently I was ushered into her tiny room, and such was my relief when she came to greet me, gentle and smiling, that I fell into a fit of tears, my arms became paralyzed, and I began to faint. Without my fully realizing it, the years in the United States had been so fraught with inner tension and struggle that I could not spontaneously adjust to this tranquility. The tautness of mind and body continued for a long time from force of habit.

The ashram, set on the shores of the Bay of Bengal, was rejuvenating. But metaphysical speculation and philosophical discussion are strong in India and I had always been quick to succumb to them. While part of me was stimulated by them, my deepest instincts warned me that they would in the end prove unavailing. A regimen which encouraged so much study and reading, it seemed to me, was at that particular time the very thing I should not have. I felt a growing need for closely guided meditation.

My mounting dissatisfaction with what I took to be haphazard meditation at the ashram coincided with the visit of an American Buddhist who had practiced Zen in Japan for a number of years. What impressed me most about this American was the serenity with which he mingled with and absorbed himself in all the varied circumstances he encountered in the ashram and his compassionate interest in the lives of all whom he encountered, including my own, so full of desperate and uneven strivings. I determined to go to Japan if I could get his help. This he unstintingly gave, together with the assurance of helping me find a Zen teacher there.

Following my departure from the ashram I traveled up and down India, visiting at other ashrams, exploring archaeological sites, and absorbing the rich lore and pervasive religious atmosphere of Buddhist and Hindu holy places: the shrines, temples, and caves with which India abounds. An overwhelming intensity of spiritual vision informs her architecture and mighty cave sculpture, so that it is impossible to step into these caves without being swept up by this religious fervor. Standing before the giant rock-cut Buddhas, I fairly trembled in awe, and my resolution to follow the Buddha's path was given the most powerful impetus.

I had long hoped to visit Burma, which I had pictured as being second only to Tibet in its unique concern with religion as the foundation of daily life. So when my American friend wrote that of all the Southeast Asian Buddhist countries the meditation centers of Burma were reputed to be the best, suggesting that I join him in the center of a famous Burmese master (Mahasi Sayadaw) in Rangoon for five weeks of intensive meditation, I jumped at the chance.

Now began my first formal practice of meditation under the guidance of a teacher, and in every direction it proved to be extremely painful. The hot season had already settled in when I reached Rangoon, and I early contracted a fever together with a racking cough, both of which lasted almost until I left and considerably debilitated me. In addition to the frightful heat and the lethargy it fostered, there was the unremitting strain of sitting alone in a small bare cubicle on a wooden-plank bed hour after hour struggling against the searing pains in knees and back from cross-legged sitting. For the beginner, lacking the invisible support of others sitting alongside him, and the more visible support of a varied timetable, as in Zen in Japan, sitting alone is unbearably difficult and one soon finds oneself seeking means to escape from the tedium and pain.

The meditation itself consisted of concentration on the rising and falling of the breath, the attention being focused on the diaphragm. When the mind wandered (which it repeatedly did), it was to be recalled by the words "thinking, thinking, thinking" until it had been re-established in the diaphragm. Every other distraction was similarly treated. "Coughing, coughing" when one coughed, "hearing, hearing" when any sound captured the attention. An hour's sitting alternated with an hour's walking, which was done for the most part at a funereal pace back and forth outside each person's quarters in perfect silence. The hands were held behind the back and the mind was concentrated on nothing only the movements of each step. "Lifting, lifting" when the foot was raised, "moving" when it was carried forward, "putting" when it was placed on the ground.

Each day at noon we met with our preceptor, a senior monk, who examined us on our progress. He asked minute questions and called for detailed accounts of sitting time. When I complained to him that my frequent mental wanderings were due to boredom, he laughed and told me to think "bored, bored, bored" until the boredom vanished. To my surprise this worked.

Like everyone else, I had to sign a pledge upon entering the center to observe the Buddhist precepts[35] and to refrain from eating after twelve noon or sleeping more than five hours a night. Food was brought to my door twice before noon in tiffin carriers, and I ate it alone while meditating "lifting lifting, putting putting, chewing chewing, swallowing swallowing." In just this way the tiniest detail of every action, mental as well as physical, had to be attended to with total attention.

Here in the center, for the first time in my life, I was relegated to a position socially below men, and further, as a laywoman devotee, to the lowest stratum of all in a structure which placed monks at the top, nuns next, then laymen, and finally laywomen. Nevertheless, I was enormously grateful for this opportunity to practice meditation even from such a lowly position, and later came to see that it was only my ego which had led me to consider my position in the first place.

At the end of five weeks my concentration and health had improved considerably in spite of, or because of, the acute pain and discomfort which I had of my own free will undertaken. The turning of the mind from outer activity to inner contemplation was by far the most rewarding task I had ever undertaken, and unquestionably the most difficult. The outside world, when I re-entered it, appeared radiantly beautiful to my fresh gaze, and I had a serenity and equanimity which, while not yet deep, surpassed anything I had hitherto experienced. I knew I had taken my first step in the direction I wanted to travel.

JAPAN AND ZEN: The very day of my arrival in Japan my American friend conducted me to Ryutaku-ji, a Rinzai monastery perching like a giant bird amidst groves of towering pines and bamboo in the shadow of majestic Mount Fuji and looking down upon a rolling valley of breath-taking beauty. Through the generosity of its master, Soen-roshi, this was to be my home for the next five months. Under his benevolent guidance I began to learn the structure and discipline of monastery life. Summoned by the gong, I learned to rise at the unconscionable hour of 4 A.M., to leap into my monastery

---

[35] The first five of the ten Mahayana precepts. See "precepts" in section x.

robes, splash cold water on my face, and take my position with the monks in the main hall in the cold dawn for the early-morning sutra-chanting. The intoning of the sutras became one of the richest experiences of my life and inspired me profoundly.

Slowly my impatient nature began to break down and some measure of equanimity began to establish itself within me. The long hours spent shivering on agonizing knees in a drafty hall awaiting my turn to go before the roshi for *sanzen* enforced upon me a patience I had not believed myself capable of. The hours of daily zazen, and even more of sesshin, were also painfully learned lessons in patience and endurance, punctuated as they were by the smart whack of the kyosaku across my slumping shoulders. Partly it was this Rinzai method of using the stick from the front in response to a gestured request which conditioned my later acute dislike for the kyosaku when it was administered, as it is in the Soto discipline, suddenly and without warning from behind as one sits facing the wall; and partly it was my Western heritage which had taught me to regard beating as a human indignity.

My decision to marry again took me from this Rinzai monastery and I joined the Soto Zen group to which my husband belonged, at Taihei-ji, in the outskirts of Tokyo, under the direction of Yasutani-roshi. Because almost all the followers of this Zen master are laymen and laywomen, the sesshin is less rigidly scheduled than in a monastery in order to allow them to attend as much of it as their jobs permit. Consequently, there is much coming and going, which in the beginning is highly distracting. The outwardly rigorous discipline which monastery life enforces had here to be assumed by each individual for himself. I soon perceived that beneath the apparently relaxed air of the sesshin was an intense seriousness. The limited quarters of this temple brought me into closer contact with the others, and I found I could no longer retire alone to my tiny room to sleep at night, but had to content myself with just a mat spread out in a room occupied by many others. Doing zazen in these (for me) straitened circumstances was somewhat of a jolt after the strict but spacious atmosphere of the monastery. After a few sesshin at the temple, however, I came to see that sitting with individuals who, like myself, were neither nuns, monks, nor priests was mutually stimulating and inspiring.

The rohatsu sesshin at Taihei-ji was approaching and my feelings toward attending were mixed. I had heard several reports of this yearly mid-winter sesshin from people who had experienced it in monasteries. It was known to be the most arduous of the whole year, a constant battle against cold and fatigue. I had a deep fear of extreme cold. My body would become so tense from shivering that I could not keep my sitting position. And under great fatigue I would become almost lightheaded. These two I regarded as my real foes. At the same time the fact that it marked the enlightenment of the Buddha, which event fell just one day before my own birthday, moved me deeply. At length I determined to go and to put forth my every energy. This was my sixth sesshin in Japan. For the first time I had the firm conviction that it was entirely possible for me to realize my Self at this forthcoming sesshin. I also felt that I sorely needed it. For many weeks there had been a return of the old restlessness and anxiety which I had fought so hard while in the United States. This was now mixed with impatience and irritability. Added to this, I was sick to death of the inner mental and emotional surgings which had hitherto played such a dominant role in my life, and now felt that only through the experience of Self-realization could I cut my way out of this malaise.

I packed my warmest clothes, and as I turned the key in the lock a feeling of deep happiness crept over me. In my heart of hearts I knew that the person who would unlock this door after sesshin would not be the same as the one who was now locking it.

All the first day of the sesshin I found it virtually impossible to keep my mind steady. The comings and goings of the other participants, as well as the noise and confusion occasioned by the use of the kyosaku, were a source of constant interference. When I complained to the roshi how much better my zazen had been alone in my own home, he instructed me to pay no attention to the others, and pointed out how important it was to learn to meditate in distracting circumstances. At no time during the sesshin, however, was I hit with the kyosaku. I had found it so distracting at a previous sesshin that the roshi had given instructions it was not to be used on me.

By the end of the second day my concentration had grown steadier. I no longer had great pain in my legs, and the cold was bearable with all the clothing I had brought. There was, however, a problem which for me took on more and more significance. I had been told repeatedly to put my mind in the pit of my abdomen, or more exactly, in the region below the navel. The more I tried to do this, the less I understood what it was about the bottom of the abdomen which made this spot so significant. It had been called by the roshi a center, or focus, but for me this was meaningful only in a philosophical way. Now I was to put my mind in this "philosophical" spot and to keep repeating "Mu." I could find no relation between any of the organs of the abdomen and the process of Zen meditation, much less enlightenment. The roshi, it is true, had assigned me the koan Mu after satisfying himself of my earnest desire for Self-realization, and had instructed me as to its purpose and use; nevertheless, I was still perplexed about *how* to say Mu. Earlier I had tried considering it the same as the Indian mantra Om, endeavoring to be one with its vibration, and without questioning what Mu was. Now I began to conceive of Mu as the diamond at the end of a drill and of myself as a driller working through layers of the mind, which I pictured as geological strata, and through which I was eventually to emerge into something I knew not what.

On the morning of the third day I was truly concentrating, guided by the drilling analogy. I could now focus my mind somewhere in my abdomen without, however, knowing just where, and there was growing a rocklike stability to my sitting. By midmorning, just after the roshi's lecture, I settled into a fairly deep concentration, increasing the force of each breath, which had been synchronized with the repetition of Mu. I expected this increase of effort to strengthen the concentration even further. After some fifteen minutes the combination of this forceful breathing and the repetition of Mu began to produce a strange tingling in my wrists, which spread slowly downward to the hands and fingers as well as upward to the elbows. When this sensation had gotten well under way, I recognized it as identical to what I had experienced under severe emotional shock on several occasions of my life. I told myself that if I increased even further the force of my breathing and concentration, I might come to kensho. I did this and succeeded only in worsening the situation, finally reaching a fainting state. Just before this state erupted I began to feel the most profound and agonizing sorrow, with which came violent shivering spasms and a gnashing of my teeth. Nervous paroxysms shook my body again and again. I wept bitterly and writhed as though a torrent of electricity were surging through me. Then I began to perspire profusely. I felt that the sorrows of the entire universe were tearing at my abdomen and that I was being sucked into a vortex of unbearable agonies. Sometime afterward—I can't say how long—I remember my husband ordering me to stop zazen and to lie down and rest. I collapsed onto my sitting cushion and began to shiver. My hands were now quite stiff; neither my fingers, sticking out at odd angles, nor my elbows would bend. My head whirred and I lay exhausted. Slowly the nerves relaxed. In half an hour all had subsided, my energies had returned, and in all respects I was ready to resume zazen.

At the afternoon dokusan the roshi immediately asked what had happened. When I told him he said it was a makyo and to keep on doing zazen. Such things could happen from now on, he warned; they showed my meditation was deepening. He then instructed me to search for Mu in the region below the solar plexus. With the words "solar plexus" suddenly everything fell into position for the first time—I knew exactly where I was going and what I was to do.

The next morning, the fourth day, I awakened with the bell at 4 A.M. and found that I had not separated myself from Mu even while asleep, which was what the roshi had continually urged. During the first sitting period, before morning dokusan, the previous day's symptoms began to appear. This time, telling myself it was only a makyo, I kept right on, determined to "ride it out." Gradually, however, the paralysis descended into my legs as well, and I could just hear my husband say in the distance somewhere that I was in a trance. I thought my body might begin to levitate, but still I kept on with my zazen. Then I fell over helpless and lay still. By the time I felt well enough to resume, morning dokusan was over.

I began to consider that I must be doing something wrong, misdirecting my energy in some way. During the rest period after the morning lecture I suddenly realized that this center where I was being told to put my mind could only be a certain region long familiar to me. From early childhood it was the realm to which I had always retired inwardly in order to reflect. I had built up a whole set of intimate images about it. If ever I wanted to understand the "truth" of a situation, it was to this particular area that I must go to consider such problems, which had to be approached in a childlike frame of mind, free from prejudices. I would simply hold my mind there and be still, almost without breathing, until something coalesced. This I believed was the region the roshi intended. Intuitively I divined it, and with all my energy centered Mu there. In perhaps half an hour a warm spot began to grow in my abdomen, slowly spreading to my spine, and gradually creeping up the spinal column. This was what I had been striving for.

Highly elated, at the next dokusan I told the roshi that I had found the spot and described its functioning to him as I had always experienced it. "Good!" he exclaimed. "Now go on!" Returning to my place, I threw myself into zazen with such vigor that before long the paralysis began to manifest itself again—the severest attack yet. I could not move at all and my husband had to help me lie down, covering me with blankets. While lying there recuperating I thought: My body is obviously unable to stand up to the strain I am putting on it. If I am to see into Mu it must be done with my mind alone and I must somehow restrain the physical and nervous energies, which will have to be conserved for the final effort.

This time when I recovered I tried to concentrate my mind without voicing or thinking Mu, but found it difficult. In practice it meant actually divorcing concentration from breathing rhythm. However, after repeated efforts I did accomplish it and was able to hold my mind steady in my abdomen, as though staring intently at something, and just let my breathing take any rhythm it inclined to. The more I concentrated with my mind in my abdomen, the more thoughts, like clouds, arose. But they were not discursive. They were like stepping-stones directing me. I jumped from one to the next, constantly moving along a well-defined path which my own intuition bade me follow. Even so, I believed that at some point they must disappear and my mind become quite empty, as I had been led to expect, before kensho. The presence of these thoughts signaled to me that I must still be far from my goal.

In order to conserve as much energy as possible, I relaxed my posture and, to warm myself, pulled the blanket, which had been loose around my body, up over my head. I let my hands fall limply into my lap and unlocked my legs to a loose cross-legged position. Even that small amount of energy placed at the disposal of my mind increased its concentrative intensity.

The following morning at dokusan, the fifth day, the roshi told me I was at a critical stage and not to separate myself from Mu for a single instant. Fearing that the two remaining days and one night might not be sufficient time, I clung to Mu like a bulldog with its bone—so tenaciously in fact that bells and other signals became dim and unreal. I could no longer remember what we were supposed to do when signals sounded and had to keep asking my husband what they meant. In order to keep up strength I ate heartily at every meal and took all the rest the sesshin schedule allowed. I felt like a child going on a strange new journey, led step by step by the roshi.

That afternoon, going out for a bath, I walked down the road thinking about Mu. I began to get annoyed. What is this Mu, anyway? I asked. What in the name of heaven can it be? It's ridiculous! I'm sure there is no such thing as Mu. Mu isn't anything! I exclaimed in irritation. As soon as I said it was nothing, I suddenly remembered about the identity of opposites. Of course—*Mu is also everything!* While bathing I thought: If Mu is everything, so is it the bath water, so is it the soap, so is it the bathers. This insight gave fresh impetus to my sitting when I resumed it.

Each morning at about 4:30 it was the roshi's custom to inspect and address all the sitters. Using the analogy of a battle in which the forces of ignorance and enlightenment were pitted against each other, the roshi urged us to "attack" the "enemy" with greater vigor. Now he was saying: "You've reached the stage of hand-to-hand combat. You may use any means and any weapons!" Abruptly at these words I found myself in a dense jungle breaking through the darkness of the thick foliage, with a great knife swinging at my belt, in search of my "enemy." This image came again and again, and I supposed that with Mu I was somehow to overcome the "enemy" upon whom I was now closing in for the final dispatch.

On the afternoon of the sixth day, in my imagination I was again slashing a path through the jungle, babbling to myself and searching ahead for an opening in the darkness and waiting for the "flood of light" which would mean I was at the end of my trail. Suddenly, with a burst of inner laughter, I realized that the only way to over-come this "enemy" when he appeared was to embrace him. No sooner had I thought this than the "enemy" materialized before me clad in the costume of a Roman centurion, his short sword and shield raised in attack. I rushed to him and in joy flung my arms about him. He melted into nothingness. At that instant I saw the brilliant light appear through the darkness of the jungle. It expanded and expanded. I stood staring at it, and into its center leapt the words *"Mu is me!"* I stopped short—even my breathing stopped. Could that be so? Yes, that's it! *Mu is me and me is Mu!* A veritable tidal wave of joy and relief surged through me.

At the end of the next round of walking I whispered to my husband: "How much am I supposed to understand when I understand Mu?" He looked at me closely and asked: "Do you really understand?" "I want the roshi to test me at the next dokusan," I said. The next dokusan was some five hours away. I was impatient to know whether the roshi would confirm my understanding. In my heart of hearts I was certain I knew what Mu was, and I firmly told myself that if my answer was not accepted I would leave Zen forever. If I was wrong, then Zen was wrong. In spite of my own certainty, however, (since I was still unfamiliar with Zen expression) I felt I might not be able to respond to the roshi's testing in appropriate Zen fashion.

Dokusan finally came and I asked the roshi to test me. I expected him to ask only what Mu was. Instead he asked me: "What is the length of Mu? How old is Mu?" I thought these were typical Zen trick questions and I sat silent and perplexed. The roshi watched me closely, then told me that I must see Mu more clearly, and that in the time remaining I was to do zazen with the greatest possible intensity.

When I returned to my place I threw myself into zazen once more with every shred of strength. Now there were no thoughts—I had exhausted all of them. Hour after hour I sat, sat, and sat, thinking only Mu with all my mind. Gradually the heat again rose in my spine. A hot spot appeared between my eyebrows and began to vibrate intensely. From it clouds of heat rolled down my cheeks, neck, and shoulders. I believed something must surely happen, at the very least an inner explosion. Nothing did happen except that I experienced recurring visions of myself seated cross-legged on a barren mountainside meditating and trudging doggedly through thronged cities in the scorching sun. At the next dokusan I told the roshi about these visions and sensations. He told me that a good way to bring this vibrating center, now between the eyes, back to the solar plexus[36] was to trace a pathway for it by imagining something like honey, sweet and viscous, trickling downward. He also told me not to concern myself with either these visions or the clouds of heat, both of which were an outcome of the prodigious effort I was making. The important thing was only to concentrate steadily on Mu. After a few attempts I was able once more to re-establish this center in the solar plexus and to continue as he had bidden me.

The following day, the seventh, I went before the roshi at dokusan once more. From the six or seven hours of continuous zazen I was so physically exhausted I could scarcely speak. Imperceptibly my mind had slipped into a state of unearthly clarity and awareness. I *knew,* and I knew I knew. Gently he began to question me: "What is the age of God? Give me Mu! Show me Mu at the railway station!" Now my inner vision was completely in focus and I responded without hesitation to all his tests, after which the roshi, my husband, who interpreted, and I all laughed joyfully together, and I exclaimed: "It's all so simple!" Whereupon the roshi told me that henceforth my practice in connection with succeeding koans was to be different, and then explained how I was to proceed.

Too stiff and tired to continue sitting, I slipped quietly from the main hall and returned to the bathhouse for a second bath. Never before had the road been so roadlike, the shops such perfect shops, nor the winter sky so unutterably a starry sky. Joy bubbled up like a fresh spring.

The days and weeks that followed were the most deeply happy and serene of my life. There was no such thing as a "problem." Things were either done or not done, but in any case there was neither worry nor consternation. Past relationships to people which

---

[36] Ordinarily, the instruction is to direct one's attention to the *tanden,* or hara, that is, the lower belly. But since for this student the solar plexus had special significance, the roshi told her to place her attention there instead of in the usual place.

had once caused me deep disturbance I now saw with perfect under-standing. For the first time in my life I was able to move like the air, in any direction, free at last from the self which had always been such a tormenting bond to me.

SIX YEARS LATER: One spring day as I was working in the garden the air seemed to shiver in a strange way, as though the usual sequence of time had opened into a new dimension, and I became aware that something untoward was about to happen, if not that day, then soon. Hoping to prepare in some way for it, I doubled my regular sittings of zazen and studied Buddhist books late into each night.

A few evenings later, after carefully sifting through the *Tibetan Book of the Dead* and then taking my bath, I sat in front of a painting of the Buddha and listened quietly by candlelight to the slow move-ment of Beethoven's A Minor Quartet, a deep expression of man's self-renunciation, and then went to bed. The next morning, just after breakfast, I suddenly felt as though I were being struck by a bolt of lightning, and I began to tremble. All at once the whole trauma of my difficult birth flashed into my mind. Like a key, this opened dark rooms of secret resentments and hidden fears, which flowed out of me like poisons. Tears gushed out and so weakened me I had to lie down. Yet a deep happiness was there . . . Slowly my focus changed: "*I*'m dead! There's nothing to call *me!* There never was a *me!* It's an allegory, a mental image, a pattern upon which nothing was ever modeled." I grew dizzy with delight. Solid objects appeared as shadows, and everything my eyes fell upon was radiantly beautiful.

These words can only hint at what was vividly revealed to me in the days that followed:

1) The world as apprehended by the senses is the least true (in the sense of complete), the least dynamic (in the sense of the eternal movement), and the least important in a vast "geometry of existence" of unspeakable profundity, whose rate of vibration, whose intensity and subtlety are beyond verbal description.

2) Words are cumbersome and primitive—almost useless in try-ing to suggest the true multidimensional workings of an indescrib-ably vast complex of dynamic force, to contact which one must abandon one's normal level of consciousness.

3) The least act, such as eating or scratching an arm, is not at all simple. It is merely a visible moment in a network of causes and effects reaching forward into Unknowingness and back into an infinity of Silence, where individual consciousness cannot even enter. There is truly nothing to know, nothing that can be known.

4) The physical world is an infinity of movement, of Time-Existence. But simultaneously it is an infinity of Silence and Voidness. Each object is thus transparent. Everything has its own special inner character, its own karma or "life in time," but at the same time there is no place where there is emptiness, where one object does not flow into another.

5) The least expression of weather variation, a soft rain or a gentle breeze, touches me as a—what can I say?—miracle of unmatched wonder, beauty, and goodness. There is nothing to do: just to be is a supremely total act.

6) Looking into faces, I see something of the long chain of their past existence, and sometimes something of the future. The past ones recede behind the outer face like ever-finer tissues, yet are at the same time impregnated in it.

7) When I am in solitude I can hear a "song" coming forth from everything. Each and every thing has its own song; even moods, thoughts, and feelings have their finer songs. Yet beneath this variety they intermingle in one inexpressibly vast unity.

8) I feel a love which, without object, is best called lovingness. But my old emotional reactions still coarsely interfere with the expressions of this supremely gentle and effortless lovingness.

9) I feel a consciousness which is neither myself nor not myself, which is protecting or leading me into directions helpful to my proper growth and maturity, and propelling me away from that which is against that growth. It is like a stream into which I have flowed and, joyously, is carrying me beyond myself.

VI / YAEKO IWASAKI'S EN-LIGHTENMENT LETTERS TO HARADA-ROSHI AND HIS COMMENTS /

EDITOR'S INTRODUCTION / No name shines with greater luster in the history of modern Japanese Zen Buddhism than that of a twenty-five-year-old girl, Yaeko Iwasaki, who became enlightened after some five years of zazen, largely from a sickbed, and then, in the succeeding five days, deepened this realization to a degree rare in present-day Japan. A week later, fulfilling her own premonitions, she was dead. In India she would undoubtedly have been heralded as a saint and worshiped by thousands. In Japan the story of her intrepid life and its crowning achievement is scarcely known outside Zen circles.

These are the letters she wrote, in December 1935, to her preceptor, Zen Master Daiun Sogaku Harada, then sixty-five years old, relating what she perceived, felt, and thought during those five epic days, together with his cogent comments. Not many personal documents in religious literature, we believe, are as poignant or as eloquently revealing of the profoundly enlightened mind as these letters. Though few in number and relatively brief, they convey the very essence of living Buddhism. They abound in paradox and overflow with gratitude, qualities which unfailingly mark off deep spiritual experience from the shallower levels of insight. And woven through them is a thread of singular purity, an ardent yearning to achieve full enlightenment not for her own sake but that her fellow men might attain Self-fulfillment and lasting inner peace through her efforts to make known the Buddha's Way. Her "untimely" death—untimely only as men ordinarily calculate a life span—has not ended her karmic destiny to make known the Dharma. If anything, it bids fair to give it new impetus, for in Harada-roshi's words: "Her courageous life is so inspiring and its influence so far-reaching that it is certain to promote the spread of Buddhism and benefit mankind."

As a scion of the founder of the wealthy Mitsubishi industrial combine, Yaeko Iwasaki had everything money could buy except health. At the age of two she was so seriously ill she almost died, and the resultant impairment of her heart valves left her with a frail body for the rest of her brief life. Unable to withstand the demands of daily attendance at school, she was tutored at home until she was almost eleven, at which time, having become somewhat stronger, she was enrolled in the equivalent of junior high school. Despite her inability to participate in a number of school activities, she completed junior as well as senior high school with a host of friends and an excellent scholastic record. Her keen, lively mind, her joyous, sunny disposition, and her generous spirit earned for her the admiration and love of her classmates.

Upon graduation she commenced the study of flower arrangement and tea ceremony, the traditional Japanese arts through which serenity and gentleness of spirit are cultivated, and then began to learn cooking and to study the piano, all as preparation for eventual marriage and motherhood.

But her karma was to lead her abruptly in another direction. About the age of twenty she began to cough blood, and tuberculosis was diagnosed. Her doctor sent her to bed and ordered complete rest for two to three years. Very likely this prolonged inactivity, in its effect on her physical and psychic organism, developed within her a sensitivity which was crucial to her rich spiritual flowering.

More immediately, what propelled her toward Zen was a sudden development involving her father, whom she deeply loved. He was told that he had a heart condition which could prove fatal at any time, and becoming gripped by the fear of sudden death, he attended a lecture by Harada-roshi on this most fundamental human anxiety and how it could be dissolved through zazen and, ultimately, enlightenment. So convinced was Yaeko's father by what he heard that he became a disciple of Harada-roshi and in his own home began to practice zazen. Since his heart condition precluded regular attendance at sesshin, he prevailed upon Harada-roshi to come to his home once a month, on the roshi's regular trip to Tokyo, to give a lecture and private instructions (dokusan) to his family and friends.

With a zeal born of his overwhelming fear of death, Yaeko's father devoted himself to zazen and in less than a year attained kensho. This experience banished all his fears and brought him such an upsurge of vitality and self-confidence that he once more took up his duties as the head of his family's large industrial enterprise, but with an unwise vigor. The strain proved too much for him, and one day without warning he died of a heart attack.

The appalling suddenness of her father's death brought home with dramatic force to the still-bedridden Yaeko the evanescence of life and the stark reality of death, precipitating her into the most searching reflections on the meaning of human existence. Up to her father's enlightenment she had been hearing Harada-roshi's monthly lecture at her home, but as yet with no desire to receive private instructions or to attempt zazen herself. This event, however, had so fired the imaginations of herself, her mother, and her two sisters that they all began to devote themselves regularly to zazen. The roshi had assigned Yaeko the koan Mu, instructing her to absorb herself in it continuously even while lying in bed. With her father's death and the soul-searching it provoked, her zazen and overall concern with Buddhism took on a fresh and profound sense of urgency. Harada-roshi's lengthy commentary on Dogen's *Shobogenzo* she read seventeen times, devouring every word, and while yet far from strong she undertook zazen sitting in the traditional Japanese position, alternating it with the lotus posture. By now the worst stages of her tuberculosis had passed and she was no longer required to remain in bed. However, the disease had left its marks on her already delicate constitution and she was urged by her doctor to convalesce in sunny Kamakura, where her family maintained a villa.

In this new seclusion she was able to lose herself more and more in zazen, turning her back forever on the interests which had once been meaningful to her. So eager was she in her pursuit of the

Buddha's Way that she begged Harada-roshi to come to Kamakura to continue his lectures and private instructions. Seeing in her uncommon ardor and devotion a rare spirit, he made the trip regularly each month specially to guide her, as did from time to time Yasutani-roshi and Taji-roshi, two of Harada-roshi's most respected disciples.

Some five years elapsed from the time she began zazen in bed until her first enlightenment, on December 22, 1935. In the succeeding days, as these letters vividly reveal, her Mind's eye opened fully in a flood of light and understanding. Her ensuing rapture, her discovery that even perfect enlightenment adds nothing one does not already have, and that therefore this ecstasy is a kind of "madness"—this together with Harada-roshi's joyous recognition of her Bodhisattvic spirit and his gentle reproach for her "smell" of enlightenment afford an intimate insight, as rare as it is illuminating, into the complex and seemingly contradictory enlightenment process.

To die as Yaeko did, with a presentiment of death a week before, with no pain, and with utter serenity is, as Harada-roshi points out, an aim of all Buddhists, albeit one to which few attain. That Yaeko could achieve it is the measure of the extraordinarily high level of consciousness to which she had risen, and of her pureness of faith, courage, and perseverance which made it possible. Who can read Harada-roshi's poignant account of his last hours with her and not be moved by her dauntless spirit and utter selflessness?

The physician who witnessed her death, which technically he attributed to pneumonia, recalled: "Never have I seen anyone die so beautifully." But perhaps the greatest tribute to her memory was that paid at Hosshin-ji at the first sesshin which fell after her death. Toward the end of it Harada-roshi, in tears, recounted to the ninety or so participants the incidents of Yaeko's heroic struggle for Self-fulfillment and its magnificent consummation. Such was its effect that by the end of the sesshin more than twenty persons, an unprecedented number, had gained the first gate of enlightenment.

These letters first appeared in an article by Harada-roshi in a Buddhist magazine soon after the death of Yaeko Iwasaki. His remarks (here printed throughout in italics) were jotted down by him on the letters as he received them, but the general comments and the titles were added by him specifically for the article, to instruct the reader in Buddhism as much as to clarify the letters themselves. Yaeko, of course, had no opportunity to see these comments before her passing.

About a year later this same material was included in a book called *Yaezakura* (Double Cherry Blossoms), which is a brief account of Yaeko's life printed privately by the Iwasaki family as a memorial to her in December 1937. It is from this book that the present translation was made.

All bracketed matter within both the letters and Harada-roshi's comments is the translator's.

A BIOGRAPHICAL NOTE ON HARADA-ROSHI / Sogaku Harada, to whom Yaeko Iwasaki's letters are addressed and whose comments accompany them, died December 12, 1961, at the age of ninety-one. At his funeral service, next to his photograph, hung a piece of calligraphy written by him several years earlier:

> For forty years I've been selling water
> By the bank of a river.
> Ho, ho!
> My labors have been wholly without merit.

These typically Zen lines are a fitting epitaph, for no Japanese Zen master in modern times strove more arduously to teach his students that there is nothing to learn than Harada-roshi. His fourteen Dharma successors and innumerable enlightened disciples and followers throughout Japan bear witness that his efforts, if "without merit," have by no means been in vain.

Nominally of the Soto sect, he welded together the best of Soto and Rinzai and the resulting amalgam was a vibrant Buddhism which has become one of the great teaching lines in Japan today. Probably more than anyone else in his time he revitalized, through his profound spiritual insight, the teachings of Dogen-zenji, which had been steadily drained of their vigor through the shallow understanding of priests and scholars of the Soto sect in whose hands their exposition had hitherto rested. His commentary on *Shushogi*, a codification of Dogen's *Shobogenzo,* is recognized as one of the most penetrating of its kind.

Hosshin-ji, Harada-roshi's monastery on the Japan Sea, drenched by incessant rains, blanketed by frequent snowstorms, and "rocked" by unprecedentedly severe discipline from within, came to be known as the harshest Zen monastery in all Japan and Harada-roshi himself as the most exacting of Zen taskmasters. More than once he refused invitations to head monasteries in balmier districts of Japan, contending that this rigorous climate helped to drive men's minds into the pit of their bellies, where ultimately they would find the secret of the universe. Men and women by the hundreds flocked to Hosshin-ji in its heyday, drawn by the roshi's extraordinary power to inspire and lead them to Self-awakening.

Like all masters of high spiritual development, he was the keenest judge of character. He was as quick to expose pretense and sham as he was to detect it. Exceptional students he drove mercilessly, exacting from them the best of which they were capable. From all he demanded as a *sine qua non* sincerity and absolute adherence to his teaching, brooking not the slightest deviation. Casual observers often found him rigid and narrow, but disciples and students who were faithful to his teachings knew him to be wise and compassionate.

For all his sternness Harada-roshi had his gentle side, and though he never married but remained a monk in the true sense of the word, he loved to romp with children and was exceedingly fond of animals, particularly dogs.

Thoroughly grounded in both the Soto and the Rinzai doctrines and disciplines, Harada-roshi was eminently fitted to teach an integral Zen. At the age of seven he had entered Soto temple life as a novitiate monk and had continued his Soto training in several temples throughout his primary and high school years. At twenty, in the face of his Soto adviser's persistent opposition, he became a monk at Shogen-ji, in its time a great Rinzai monastery, as he had been unable to find a deeply enlightened master in the Soto sect. After two and a half years of strenuous training there, he attained kensho, but his enlightenment still fell short of total liberation.

At twenty-seven, by his father's insistence that he obtain more formal education, he quit Shogen-ji and enrolled in the Soto-sponsored Komazawa University, continuing for a further six years after his graduation to do research in Buddhism under well-known scholars. But while his knowledge of Buddhism grew, it did not bring him the emancipation he longed for. He decided therefore to go to Kyoto for the purpose of meeting Dokutan-roshi, abbot of Nanzen-ji and reputed to be the best Zen master then living.

He was accepted by Dokutan as a disciple, and for the next two years came daily for koan practice and private instructions while living with a friend in Kyoto whom he assisted with the affairs of his temple. At the end of two years Dokutan-roshi, impressed with his disciple's uncommon intelligence, ardor, and thirst for Truth, offered to make him his personal attendant. Though now almost forty, Sogaku Harada accepted this signal honor with alacrity and went to live at Nanzen-ji. There he applied himself intensively to zazen and completed all the koans, at last opening his mind's eye fully and receiving inka from Dokutan-roshi.

At this time Komazawa University recalled him to teach, in accordance with the provisions of an agreement he had made. This led to twelve years of teaching Buddhism at Komazawa, part of which time he spent as a full professor.

Harada-roshi—he now merited the title roshi—was a rare phenomenon in the Buddhist academic world: a professor during the academic year and a Zen master during his summer vacation, conducting sesshin at various temples. Within a short time he gained the reputation of a strict disciplinarian.

His dissatisfaction with the narrowness of academic life and its inevitable accent on theory, coupled with the limited opportunity it afforded him to train people through sesshin in the direct experience of the Dharma, was brought to a head by repeated requests that he assume the abbotship of Hosshin-ji. He finally accepted, and for the next forty years lived as master of this monastery, which was to be known as one of the outstanding centers of Zen training in Japan.

Until he was almost ninety Harada-roshi conducted a week of intensive sesshin at Hosshin-ji six times a year, in April, May, June, October, November, and December, and between times held sesshin in other parts of Japan. Five days before he drew his last breath he toppled over in a faint, and without pain gradually became weaker and weaker, passing from a partial coma to complete unconsciousness. The time of his death coincided exactly with low tide. Harada-roshi had literally ebbed away with the waters.

THE LETTERS AND COMMENTS / 1 / EVIDENCE OF KENSHO / DECEMBER 23:

Dear Harada-roshi:

I am so grateful that you came to see me the day before yesterday, busy though you were. Do take care of your cold.

At dokusan yesterday morning you told me: "What you have perceived is still hazy," so I felt I must search more deeply. When I awoke suddenly last midnight, it had become far clearer,

The Ox[1] has come a hundred miles nearer!

and all I could do was raise my hands palms together out of joy, sheer joy.

Truly I see that there are degrees of depth in enlightenment.

Yes, but few know this significant fact.

Even you, my roshi, no longer count for anything in my eyes. My gratitude and delight are impossible to describe. I can now affirm that so long as we are conscious of enlightenment it is not true enlightenment.

How can I express to you my gratitude for enabling me to requite, to even this small extent,[2] the incalculable debt I owe all Buddhas? My gratitude cannot be put into words—there is nothing I can write or say. I write you now only because I think you alone can understand my happiness, and will be pleased with me.

Now that my mind's eye is opened, the vow to save every living being arises within me spontaneously. I am so beholden to you and to all Buddhas. I am ashamed [of my defects], and will make every effort to discipline my character.

---

[1] "Ox" refers to the enlightened Mind. See Oxherding Pictures in Section viii.

[2] That is, through her enlightenment.

You have seen the Ox clearly, but the point of grasping it is
ten thousand miles away. Your experience is still tinged with
conceptual thinking.

I am also determined to cleanse my mind of its long-standing delusions. You are the only person I can confide in. Everyone else, I
am afraid, will misunderstand and think me boastful if I should
suddenly speak of all this.

I am pleased with your restraint.

Believe me, never in this lifetime did I expect to be thus favored
[in coming to enlightenment]. I owe you so much. I gassho in
heartfelt gratitude.

Guard yourself well against the cold. I look forward joyfully to
seeing you on the twenty-first of next month.

Yaeko

GENERAL COMMENT: *I confirm that she has truly seen the Ox, for there is*
in her experience deep self-affirmation, the desire to save all sentient beings,
and the determination to discipline herself spiritually in her daily life. Only
such an exalted state of mind can be called the mind of true children of the
Buddha. But as yet there remains a subject who is seeing. Her Mind's home
is still far distant. She must search more intensely!

2 / EVIDENCE OF GREAT ENLIGHTENMENT /

DECEMBER 25:

Dear Harada-roshi:

Today for the first time I have attained great enlightenment. I
am so overjoyed that all of me is dancing in spite of myself. No
one but you can possibly understand such ecstasy.

I have reached the point of actually grasping the Ox, and there
is absolutely no delusion.

Now for the first time you have found the Way—fully realized
your Mind. You have been delivered from delusion, which
has no abiding root. Wonderful! Wonderful!

There is neither Ox nor man. I ought to come at once to thank
you personally, but as I must watch my health I am unable to, so
I am expressing by letter my deep gratitude. From the bottom of
my heart I thank you and raise my hands in gassho to you.

Buddhas and patriarchs haven't deceived me![3] I have seen my Face before my parents were born clearer than a diamond in the palm of my hand. The absolute truth of every word of the patriarchs and the sutras has appeared before my eyes with crystal clarity. No longer have I need for dokusan, and all the koans are now like useless furniture to me. Even though I would save them, there are no sentient beings to save. Those who have only kensho do not know this state of unlimited freedom and profound peace of mind. Indeed, it cannot be known until one comes to full enlightenment. If after reading this letter you still talk nonsense[4] to me, I will not hesitate to say your own realization is lacking.

> *Good! Good! This is called the stage of standing on the summit of a lone mountain, or coming back to one's own Home. Yet I have to talk "nonsense" to you. You will understand why one day.*

I owe you so much. When I reflect that I have actually fulfilled the Great Vow made by me through numberless past lives and can now hold dokusan, I am infinitely grateful.

> *It is too early yet. Still, how many today among those called enlightened have established such inner assurance? I am delighted to see it revealed through your own words.*

My mind's eye is absolutely identical with yours—neither Buddhas nor devils can unnerve me.[5] This state defies description. I have forgotten everything and returned to my real Home empty-handed.

> *Has the Patriarch Dogen come again?[6] This is the immaculate Dharma-kaya, that is, the Buddha Birushana [Vairochana].*

---

[3] This is a traditional way of saying that the enlightenment taught by the Buddhas and patriarchs is now an actual fact of one's own experience.

[4] What is implied here is that to the truly enlightened all talk of enlightenment is meaningless.

[5] That is to say, she can stand unflinchingly before the penetrating gaze of a Buddha no less than the menacing aspect of a devil. This implies utter self-assurance and absolute fearlessness.

[6] Here Harada-roshi is likening Yaeko's statement, "I have forgotten everything and returned to my real Home empty-handed," to that made by Dogen upon his return from China, namely, "I have returned Home with empty hands. I retain no trace of Buddhism. I say only this: my eyes are horizontal, my nose is vertical."

My world has been revolutionized. How vain and needless my anxious strivings of the past! By following your wise instructions and patient counsel, I wouldn't allow myself to rest satisfied with the little peace[7] which my still-deluded mind believed adequate. I can't tell you how joyous I am and how thankful for my present state. This is all the outcome of persistent zazen, of a determination never to stop with a small success but to go on no matter how many lifetimes elapse.

Your intense devotion—and you a lay devotee!—is nothing short of astonishing.

Now I can commence the unending task of rescuing every living being. This makes me so happy I can scarcely contain myself.

All is radiance, pure radiance. I can now forever progress toward perfection in natural harmony with my daily life.

You do comprehend. That is exactly how it is. How many so-called Zen men these days have come to such profound realization?

I have been resurrected, as have you and everything else, for all eternity. When you read this letter you too, I believe, will shed tears of thanksgiving.

I am so thankful to have a disciple like you that I can now die happily.

You alone can understand my mind. Yet there is neither you nor me. My body and mind in fact have completely dropped away.

I will try to improve my health, cultivate virtue, and be alert for the opportunity to teach Buddhism. I am in the center of the Great Way where everything is natural, without strain, neither hurried nor halting; where there are no Buddhas, no you, nothing; and where I see without my eyes and hear without my ears. Not a trace remains of what I have written. There is neither pen nor paper nor words—nothing at all.

Since it is impossible to talk of all this except with one who has actually experienced it himself, I had to write you. I imagine you must be happy to have such a disciple as I who have drunk

---

[7] "Peace" here connotes the certainty and calmness arising from her initial kensho.

so deeply from the fountain of your wisdom. I prostrate myself nine times[8] to express my heartfelt gratitude.

Yaeko

GENERAL COMMENT: *This degree of realization is termed "grasping the Ox"—in other words, the true attainment of the Way. It is the return to one's own Home, or the acquisition of fundamental wisdom. To advance one more step is to realize even profounder wisdom. This "Ox" has immeasurable solemnity and radiance.*

3 / EVIDENCE OF DEEPENED ENLIGHTENMENT / DECEMBER 26:

Dear Harada-roshi:

I am filled with remorse and shame. My letter to you of the twenty-fifth must have led you to think I had gone mad.

> *You need not rebuke yourself. This delirium of joy is the initial reaction of all who have had a deep awakening.*

I had reached such a peak of ecstasy that I didn't know what I was doing and couldn't contain myself. When I recovered my senses and began to reflect, I burst into laughter at the thought of how topsy-turvy my emotions had become. I was then able to appreciate the story of Enyadatta,[9] who had gone mad believing she had lost her head, and the great to-do she made when she "discovered" it, though of course she had never been without it. But I am once more myself, so there is no need to worry about me.

I have always had feelings of anxiety arising on the one hand from the fear that my aspiration toward Buddhahood might weaken because of my insignificance and powerlessness, and on the other by the fear that if I should die without actually experiencing the truth of the Dharma I might not again be able to realize it for many lifetimes.[10]

> *Yes, it must be terribly painful for one having absolute faith in the Dharma to die without experiencing it. Only by feeling that way can one practice as devotedly as you have.*

[8] The number of times one formally makes obeisance to a Buddha.
[9] See p. 57.
[10] See footnote 7, p. 172.

But now that I have penetrated deeply and have acquired an unshakable aspiration to Buddhahood, it is clear to me that I can continue my spiritual discipline forever and in this way perfect my personality to its fullest, impelled by the Vow, which rises naturally within me, to save all sentient beings.

I am overcome by tears!

I know of no words to express my joy and gratitude.

Far from neglecting zazen, I have every intention of strengthening even further my powers of concentration.

Yes, yes, you really do understand!

I am profoundly aware of the need for diligent self-cultivation and thoroughly understand the value of dokusan. I swear never again to write anything so pretentious as I did yesterday, saying that I had become fully enlightened and therefore could instruct others in dokusan.

You have truly awakened!

Please forgive me. I was so beside myself that I simply lost all sense of proportion. After more sober reflection I see that this was rather comical, yet what a precious memory to have tasted such dazzling joy even briefly!

Buddhas and patriarchs have all experienced this great joy
at least once.

I am choked with tears of gratitude, for I can now truly understand good and evil, and can proceed steadily and without delusion to carry on my spiritual practices in and through my everyday life. From the bottom of my heart I thank you.

Do watch your health. I so look forward to your next visit.

Yaeko

GENERAL COMMENT: *At this stage one acquires what is termed "the wisdom of subtle and immaculate perception," or "subsequently attained wisdom." Her degree can be gauged according to the Five Degrees established by the Patriarch Tozan. The depth of perception revealed in her second letter corresponds to the third degree,* shochurai *[where awareness of the One is paramount and consciousness of differentiation has subsided], and that of this letter to the fourth degree,* henchushi *[wherein one lives in all things with no self-conscious trace of enlightenment]. Now it is possible to perform the benevolent and virtuous acts attributed to Fugen or Kannon. In Zen this is the fulfillment of the vow of a Bodhisattva, this is living in the Pure Land.*

Though it takes from five to ten years after kensho for most practicers to come to this stage, she has reached it in less than a week. It is doubtless due to her deep and pure faith in Buddhism, to her vast and boundless Vow [made through countless lives and embracing all sentient beings], and to her having listened with a believing heart to every word of authentic Buddhism spoken to her. Her accomplishment is rare in modern times. The remarkable story of her determination and zeal ought to be engraved in six-foot letters as an immortal inspiration for all Zen followers.

4 / EVIDENCE OF DIRECT EXPERIENCE OF THE GREAT WAY OF BUDDHISM / DECEMBER 26:

Dear Harada-roshi:

Forgive me for writing you so often. I have attained the level of realization which is the last possible while yet a disciple.

Indeed you have.

I used to think: "How grand must one become upon enlightenment!" and "How admirable is he who devotes himself so fully to Buddhist activities that he no longer thinks of himself!" But I was so mistaken! From now on I will cultivate more virtue and never cease my practice.

Before enlightenment I was so anxious for it and often thought: "How noble he who returns Home with peace and contentment." But having come to full enlightenment,

Your experience points up the difference between buji[11] *Zen and authentic Zen.*

I now say to myself: "Why were you so excited about it?" For I have a distinct aversion to being called "enlightened."[12]

---

[11] *Buji* Zen is a Zen without substance, a Zen which denies the validity of the enlightenment experience. Its adherents maintain that to speak of becoming enlightened is a contradiction in terms since we are all innately enlightened. See p. 49.

[12] Since enlightenment brought her nothing she did not already have, to accept praise for being enlightened would be like accepting praise for having, say, two feet.

I am delighted to hear you say this. Yet it is only with full
enlightenment that it is possible to put your Zen into practice
in daily life.[13]

I have utterly forgotten the moment of my enlightenment and what happened immediately after, yet I can say I have acquired the true eye of enlightenment, so to speak. It tickles me to say to myself: "So this is full enlightenment!"

I can't tell you how thankful I am to be forever one with the true Dharma, utterly and naturally. At the same time I feel so foolish for having been carried away by my delirious joy. This should make you smile: My "delusions" about everything have positively vanished. But let us not speak to anyone else of this, as the Dharma must be respected.[14]

If I am careful how I speak to others about your experience,
it may help, not harm, them, so don't be concerned.

I simply can't understand why I always made such a to-do about respecting Buddhism[15] or anyone who had attained full enlightenment. Have I been dreaming?

Yaeko

GENERAL COMMENT: *Dreaming? Certainly. Yet as dreams go in this world it is not the commonplace dream of most but a dream of tremendous and lasting significance, of intense absorption in the Buddha's Dharma.*

This stage can be equated with the fifth or most advanced degree, called kenchuto *[a condition of absolute naturalness*[16] *where the mutual inter-*

---

[13] What Harada-roshi is saying is that the fullest development of all the potentialities of personality and character can take place only after full enlightenment.

[14] This probably means that speaking of her enlightenment indiscriminately may lead to a distortion of the Dharma by those unable or unwilling to believe her experience possible.

[15] Since the essence of Buddhism is no more than living in harmony with the changing circumstances of one's life, without strain or compulsion, what is there to respect?

[16] "By naturalness I mean that all things are as they are according to their own nature, apart from all outside influences."—Kobo-daishi (quoted in *Honen the Buddhist Saint*, by Coates and Ishizuka, p. 133).

penetration of the world of discrimination and the world of equality is so thorough that one is consciously aware of neither].

I marvel that she has reached this point so quickly. That she could have done so can be attributed only to her intense faith in the Buddha's teachings and to her strong Bodhisattvic spirit. One who has attained to this degree has completed what Zen practice can be carried out under a teacher and embarked upon the path of true self-practice. Are there even a handful today who understand all this? Katsu!

5 / EVIDENCE OF ATTAINING THE NON-REGRESSING MIND OF FUGEN / DECEMBER 27:

Dear Harada-roshi:

Thanks to you, I have clearly perceived that Buddha is none other than Mind.[17] My gratitude knows no bounds. This is as much due to your benevolent guidance as to my intense longing and striving for Buddhahood that I may save all living beings.

> I had not thought of you as one with such an unusually strong aspiration toward Buddhahood. How undiscerning of me! It is evident you are the incarnation of a great Bodhisattva.

How can I ever thank you enough?

Now I see that, in terms of the Dharma, I must respect myself.[18] Please point out to me what I still need to do. How thankful I am to have been able to purge myself of every iota of delusive thinking and feeling.

> You have not yet entirely rooted out your delusive feelings,[19] but one who has perceived as profoundly as you have is nevertheless able to live a pure life.

---

[17] And Mind is total awareness, that is, *just* listening when listening, *just* seeing when seeing, etc.

[18] The sense of this may be that through her realization that she is the Dharma incarnate, she now feels a responsibility to teach Buddhism. Accordingly, by respecting and preserving herself she is respecting and preserving the Dharma.

[19] While the experience of enlightenment dispels the illusion of "myself" and "other," it does not concomitantly bring about purification of the feelings. Unremitting practice is required to accomplish this latter. See also pp. 51–52.

But in spite of this, I wish to be guided by you in all respects lest I mislead others in their practice or understanding of Buddhism.

My mind-state is quite different now from what it was at the time of kensho.

Kensho is the stage of merely seeing *the Ox.*

Indeed, the farther I advance on the Supreme Way, the more exalted it becomes. Now that I have experienced that *tada*[20] is itself perfection, I can at last repay your countless benefactions, and I am overjoyed. Having reached a deep and critical stage, I do need to see you soon.

I wish I could fly to you to advise you further. But since this is the end of the year,[21] *I am extremely busy with the affairs of the monastery and therefore unable to leave at present.*

Forgive me for making this request by letter, but my illness prevents me from coming to see you.

You must be extremely happy that I have truly graduated. Never did I dream that in my lifetime would I witness the transmission of Buddhism from a Buddha incarnate to the Bodhisattva Miroku.[22]

I promise myself over and over to act with the utmost care in every detail of my life.

I pray that you stay well.

Yaeko

GENERAL COMMENT: *The essence of living Buddhism can be summed up in the word* tada. *Who is Shakyamuni Buddha? Who is Miroku? They are no different from you. Look! Look!*

She has reached this stage of tada. *It is natural therefore that she should*

---

[20] Literally, "only," "just," "nothing but." Thus if one is eating, one must be absorbed in just eating. If the mind entertains any ideas or concepts during eating, it is not in *tada*. Every moment of life lived as tada is the eternal Now.

[21] In Zen monasteries in Japan the five-day-long New Year holidays are ushered in with elaborate rituals and ceremonies. For this reason the period preceding them is a busy one for roshi and monks alike.

[22] Living Buddhism can be said to be transmitted from Buddha to Bodhisattva whenever a disciple's enlightenment reaches the same level as his master's.

feel this deep joy as well as heavy responsibility as respects the profound Dharma. The actions flowing from such a Mind are those of Fugen or Miroku incarnate.

6 / EVIDENCE OF THE JOY AND PEACE OF BE-ING AT ONE WITH THE DHARMA / DECEMBER 27:

Dear Harada-roshi:

Rejoice with me! At last I have discerned my Face before my parents were born with a clarity that penetrates from heaven to the very bottom of the earth. And yet I have never regarded myself as a desperate seeker.

You and I have cherished a profound illusion: that it is exalting to vow to rescue all deluded creatures no matter how many aeons it takes.

> *But one so deluded is called a Bodhisattva. To realize that there is no one to save is [real] saving.*

Oh, how funny! Nonetheless, my respect for you as a roshi knows no bounds. Indeed no one but you can understand the import of my enlightenment.

I feel it would be unwise for you to tell others that I, who have no dignity or stature, have become fully enlightened, as it may cause them to think lightly of Buddhism.[23]

> *That may be true from one point of view. On the other hand, many will be inspired to a greater effort, so there is no need to be concerned.*

Only the exceptional few would not doubt my experience. What an immense relief to discover that just as I am I lack nothing! What a joy knowing you and I will be together everlastingly!

Buddhism is useless for those free of delusion. I chuckle knowing I have always been fundamentally a Buddha—I haven't the slightest doubt of this—yet I can tell it only to those whose enlightenment

---

[23] What is implied here is that there would be no cause for wonder if, for instance, a high priest were to attain full awakening, but when a frail girl of twenty-five becomes profoundly enlightened, it can very well lead to a belittling of the Dharma by those who would refuse to believe such a thing possible.

is equal to mine. To people of lesser realization I will have to preach differently.

With a heart full of gratitude I raise my hands to you palm to palm.

How supremely exalted is the true Law, how consistently reasonable from first to last—I feel this so keenly!

With a peaceful heart I look forward to the New Year.

Do take care of yourself.

Yaeko

[P.S.] I can now appreciate how dangerously one-sided a weak kensho can be.[24]

> *You are right. The enlightenment of most Zen teachers these days is of this kind, but a one-sided realization remains a one-sided realization regardless of how many koans one has passed. What these people fail to realize is that their enlightenment is capable of endless enlargement.*

GENERAL COMMENT: *To live one's life as* tada *is to walk the supremely glorious path trodden by all Buddhas. When one no longer is aware of the need for Buddhism, true Buddhism is manifesting itself. Should one, however, cherish even this conception, his life will become clouded with delusion. Devotedly wipe away [the haze of] such attachment and your life will be perpetually suffused with the warm sunshine of spring.*

7 / FURTHER EVIDENCE OF THE JOY AND PEACE OF BEING AT ONE WITH THE DHARMA /

DECEMBER 27:

Dear Harada-roshi:

Do let me write you often.

At last I have recovered my composure. With the realization that Buddha is myself,

> *I am Buddha. I am I. I am* selfless *I.*

---

[24] A weak kensho is one in which the world of Emptiness is still seen as other than the world of form. Their mutual interpenetration has as yet not been perceived.

I have come to understand clearly the single-minded love and respect I feel toward you.[25]

Already I have rid myself of the smell of enlightenment,

> *Not quite. You are even now emitting its awful smell.*

and my gratitude to you and the Dharma is all the deeper. I feel
grateful in my own mind for the realization that clinging either
to the deluded or the enlightened state gives rise, in spite of oneself,
to an increasingly ardent longing to pursue the Dharma with greater
intensity [so as to attain supreme peace of mind].[26]

> *One who never tires of performing virtuous deeds is called
> a Buddha. Attachment to the Dharma, however, is not a virtue,
> nor is this attachment easy to dissolve.*

Delusion and enlightenment are equally offensive.

You can appreciate how enormously satisfying it is for me to
discover at last, through full realization, that just as I am I lack
nothing.

> *I know how you feel. Even the honored Shakyamuni clung
> to the [delicious] taste of his enlightenment for a period of
> three weeks. Unless you rid yourself of this self-satisfaction,
> however, you cannot know true Buddhism.*

The knowledge that my karmic relation to you is profound has
made me more self-respecting and prudent.

I have now had one great enlightenment and five small ones. I
had forgotten who and where I was and what I was doing until
today.

---

[25] It is love flowing from the oneness of the awakened Buddha-mind
in Harada-roshi and herself.

[26] So long as our inner vision is out of focus and we falsely see ourselves
and the world as separate and apart instead of as one indivisible Whole,
we are deluded. This distortion (our basic ignorance) colors our view of
and reaction to everything, in consequence of which we do not see—that
is, experience—things as they are in their true nature. Enlightenment,
while revealing our solidarity with all things (thus bringing into accurate
focus our distorted inner vision), paradoxically gives rise to a fine mist
of pride in such an accomplishment, and this mars the inherent purity
of the Mind. So long as this defilement remains there is lingering disquiet.
But this very disquiet acts as a goad to continued practice until the attachment to one's enlightenment has been severed and supreme peace and
freedom attained.

Going not knowing one goes, sitting not knowing one sits—
this is true samadhi in Zen. Unless the ego is banished to this
extent there cannot be total regeneration. You have done well.
Confucius forgot about eating for three days, so absorbed did
he become in just his music.

I had swept away my "delusions" so thoroughly and penetrated
so deeply that I could not return to my usual state.

Let it be as it is.

I asked to have dokusan with Taji-roshi, and at that time he pointed
out that this was due to the effect of my profound concentration.

Yes, due to the force generated by deep mind concentration.[27]

I thought it might be necessary to ask you to come to give me
further instructions, but then a deep insight came to me and I
prayed before the Buddha, after which I lost myself in shikan-taza
for what must have been three hours.

There is no need for prayer.

At last I was able to return to my normal condition.

The Zen I practiced [after enlightenment] fancying there was
some residue that had to be swept away was actually desperate.
It is clear to me that I can never dispense with zazen. I am grateful,
so grateful for the realization that to be just as I am lifetime after
lifetime is in itself perfection.

In the whole universe I am supreme, and it is perfectly natural.

Among the innumerable phenomena in the universe One only
is immaculately manifesting itself. What is it if not you!

I am astonished

[Astonished] from the viewpoint of the delusive feelings.

that I am that One. How wonderful, how marvelous!

I am in good spirits, so please don't worry about me.

I look forward with the greatest pleasure to seeing you again.

Yaeko

P.S. Tears of gratitude and joy well up in me when I think that
I have accomplished the practice of Zen from first to last without
strain, and that I can receive your eternal guidance.[28]

---

[27] See pp. 49–50.

[28] Out of respect and humility one always looks to his teachers and
seniors for guidance. Dogen-zenji in his *hotsugammon* asks for the compassionate guidance of Buddhas and patriarchs.

GENERAL COMMENT: *An ancient Zen saying has it that to become attached to one's own enlightenment is as much a sickness as to exhibit a maddeningly active ego. Indeed, the profounder the enlightenment, the worse the illness. In her case I think it would have taken two or three months for the most obvious symptoms to disappear, two or three years for the less obvious, and seven or eight for the most insidious. Such symptoms are less pronounced in one as gentle as she, but in some they are positively nauseating. Those who practice Zen must guard against them. My own sickness lasted almost ten years. Ha!*

8 / PRESENTIMENT OF DEATH / DECEMBER 28:
Dear Harada-roshi:

I simply must see you before this year is out, come what may.

Let me tell you a disturbing thing. I feel strongly that the time of my parting from you is near, so I beg you to come to see me at any cost—for the sake of the Dharma. I ask this after serious reflection. I assure you it is not a hallucination.

Yaeko

CONCLUDING COMMENT: *In this her last letter it is clear that Yaeko has a foreboding of death. In view of the radiant tenor of the preceding seven letters, I was shocked and saddened by the ominous tone of this one. I had hoped that somehow her death would not come so soon. What a terrible pity!*

One of the sutras says that the ideal way to die is with an intimation of death a week beforehand, with little pain or affliction, and with a mind serenely unshaken, free from all attachment to the body. This is the ideal cherished by all Buddhists, but its realization is far from easy.

The patriarch Chuho once solemnly declared: "I want to die with a premonition of death the week before, with my mind serenely unshaken and free from attachment to my body, thence to be reborn into the realm of the Buddhas so as to ultimately gain supreme enlightenment through them and receive their sanction the better that I may be able to save all sentient beings throughout the innumerable worlds."

Yaeko's death was in this spirit. Prior to this letter I had received a telegram urgently asking me to come to see her. I hastened to her bedside at Kamakura on the twenty-ninth of December [1935]. Upon seeing and speaking with her, I confirmed the opening of her Mind's eye.

She was in tears. So was I. I cried from joy and sorrow. For herself she was not the least bit afraid of dying,[29] *but thinking only of the Dharma and the enlightenment of others, she was deeply apprehensive that her friends and acquaintances might mistakenly believe her practice of Zen or her experience of enlightenment had caused her death. Such an erroneous belief, she feared, might lead those not yet having true faith in Buddhism to repudiate the Dharma. If this came to pass, she would have committed a grave offense karmically not only against the Dharma but against those very persons. Moreover, she would be guilty, she felt, of unfaithfulness and irresponsibility toward Buddhas and all humanity.*

These thoughts weighed heavily upon her. Though she was willing to suffer rebirth in hell as a consequence, the thought that she might be instrumental in leading other people in the wrong direction was intolerable. During the course of the whole day and night that I remained with her she discussed these concerns with me. I assured her that she had no reason to worry, as I would set right any such misconceptions.

I had often cautioned her against overstraining herself, pointing out that it was contrary to the true Law, and further, that those who have the will to do it can carry on Zen practice without straining themselves. It is not impossible, of course, that she could have unwittingly ignored my warnings and, considering her delicate health, sapped her strength by an overexertion which hastened her death. Her greatest fear was that the cause of her death might be misunderstood by people [who, laying the blame upon the Dharma in its excessive demands upon her] would come to despise it.[30]

Be that as it may, the virtue of her life lies in its sterling example of how it is entirely feasible to practice Zen properly, and even experience perfect enlightenment, right in one's own home and partly from a sickbed. If there be strong determination, one can always practice zazen even with a frail constitution and without being able to attend sesshin. This it is which exalts

[29] Compare: "If one sees the Way in the morning, one can gladly die in the evening." (Confucius)

[30] Yaeko's deep concern over possible misunderstandings as to her death may seem unreasonable: why need she feel answerable for the way others choose to construe the cause of her passing? But her feelings are understandable when we remember that true enlightenment, by revealing the interrelation of all living beings and the repercussions on other lives of every action, generates a sense of responsibility not only for what one has done but also for what one has failed to do in any given situation.

her remarkable experience and must be recorded in the modern history of Zen.

Yaeko is dead now—a truly great loss. Her courageous life, however, is so inspiring and its influence so far-reaching that it is certain to promote the spread of Buddhism and benefit mankind.

PART THREE / SUPPLEMENTS

VII / DOGEN ON "BEING-TIME" /

EDITOR'S INTRODUCTION / In these pages we have had frequent occasion to mention the great Dogen-zenji and his foremost work, the *Shobogenzo* (A Treasury of the Eye—that is, of the opened Mind's eye—of the True Dharma). Both the man and his writings deserve a book to themselves, and here we can only give a hint of their stature.

Dogen Kigen (also known as Dogen Eihei after his temple, the Eihei-ji, or Temple of Eternal Peace) lived from 1200 to 1253 and was probably the most brilliant mind Japanese Buddhism has produced. Though Dogen is credited with bringing the teachings of the Soto sect from China to Japan, it seems clear that he never intended to establish a Soto sect as such but rather to foster an integral Zen based on the highest teachings and practices of Shakyamuni Buddha. Actually he discouraged all sectarian classifications, whether of Soto, Rinzai, or Obaku, or the broader categories of Hinayana and Mahayana.

It is misleading to describe Dogen, as some have done, as "a subtle dialectician," as though he were a philosopher rather than a Zen master. A high-minded teacher who deeply lived what he taught, Dogen sought to emancipate men from the fetters of greed, anger, and delusion by teaching them how to live a truly meaningful life based on the Way of the Buddha, and not to formulate a system of speculative thought.

The *Shobogenzo*, consisting of ninety-five sections, was written over a period of some twenty-five years and completed shortly before Dogen's death. In it Dogen deals with matters as simple and down to earth as the precise manner of performing toilet functions in monastery life, and as highly metaphysical as the relation of time and being to practice-enlightenment. Dogen's whole mode of expression is unique and can undoubtedly be ascribed to the quality of his enlightenment, believed by many to be one of the most penetrating in Japanese Buddhism, as well as to his naturally brilliant, highly creative mind. In informed Zen circles it is said that the abstruse sections of the *Shobogenzo* are the Mount Everest of Japanese Buddhism, and that he who would climb to that pinnacle must have the opened eye of full enlightenment and the climber's sureness of footing gained only with years of training.

To give the reader some idea of the style and dimension of Dogen's *Shobogenzo,* we present here a brief extract from Section II, entitled "Being-Time," perhaps the most abstruse section of the book. We believe that this translated portion, which consists of approximately one-third of the section, is peculiarly relevant for students of Zen living in the science-oriented twentieth century, revealing as it does in a unique way the meaning of time and the universe. More than this, it makes clear that Dogen's insights as to time and being, realized by him introspectively in the thirteenth century through zazen, and the views of certain contemporary micro- and macro-physicists on time and space, arrived at by them through the principles and methods of science, parallel each other to a remarkable degree. The difference, however, and a deeply significant one, is in the effect these insights had upon these men. Dogen's realization, being a Self-discovery, liberated him from the basic anxieties of human existence, bringing him inner freedom and peace and deep moral certainty. But, as far as can be seen at this time, no such inner evolution has followed in the wake of these scientific discoveries.

A word of caution. These passages ought not to be read as abstract metaphysic. Dogen is not speculating about the character of time and being, but is speaking out of his deepest experience of that reality. Always his overriding concern is with practice and enlightenment, with leading his readers to the realization of the truth of themselves and the universe. This is clearly stated in his *Fukan Zazengi* (Universal Promotion of the Principles of Zazen), where he admonishes: "You must cease concerning yourself with the dialectics of Buddhism and instead learn how to look into your own mind in seclusion."

"BEING-TIME" / An ancient Zen master[1] said: "Being-time stands on the topmost peak and in the utmost depths of the sea, being-time is three heads and eight elbows, being-time is a height of sixteen or eighteen feet, being-time is a monk's staff, being-time is a *hossu*,[2] being-time is a stone lantern, being-time is Taro, being-time is Jiro,[3] being-time is earth, being-time is sky."

"Being-time" means that time is being. Every existent thing is time. The sixteen-foot golden figure is time. As it is time it has the grandeur of time. You must learn that it is twelve hours[4] of "nowness." Three heads and eight elbows is time. Since it is time it cannot but be identical with these twelve hours this very moment. Though we do not measure twelve hours as a long or a short time, still we [arbitrarily] call them twelve hours. The traces of the ebb and flow of time are so evident that we do not doubt them; yet, though we do not doubt them, we ought not to conclude that we understand them. Human beings are changeable, at one time questioning what they do not understand and at another time no longer questioning the same thing, so their former questionings do not always coincide with their present ones. The questioning alone, for its duration, is time.

Man disposes himself and construes this disposition as the world. You must recognize that every thing, every being in this entire world is time. No object obstructs another, just as no time obstructs another. Thus the initial orientation of each different mind toward the truth exists within the same time, and for each mind there is as well a moment of commencement in its orientation toward truth. It is no different with practice-enlightenment.

[1] Yüeh-shan Wêi-yen (Yakusan Igen-zenji), a Chinese master of the T'ang period.

[2] A baton with a mane, carried by Zen masters to brush away flies or mosquitoes.

[3] These names are used in the same sense as Tom, Dick, and Harry.

[4] That is, the twelve-hour day, which could equally be the twenty-four-hour day and night.

Man disposes himself and looks upon this disposition [as the world]. That man is time is undeniably like this. One has to accept that in this world there are millions of objects and that each one is, respectively, the entire world—this is where the study of Buddhism commences. When one comes to realize this fact, [one perceives that] every object, every living thing is the whole, even though it itself does not realize it. As there is no other time than this, every being-time is the whole of time: one blade of grass, every single object is time. Each point of time includes every being and every world.

Just consider whether or not there are any conceivable beings or any conceivable worlds which are not included in this present time. If you are the ordinary person, unlearned in Buddhism, upon hearing the words *aru toki*[5] you will doubtlessly understand [that they mean "at one time," that is,] that at one time Being appeared as three heads and eight elbows, that at one time Being was a height of sixteen or eighteen feet, or that at one time I waded through the river and at one time crossed the mountain. You may think that that mountain and that river are things of the past, that I have left them behind and am now living in this palatial building—they are as separate from me as heaven is from earth.

However, the truth has another side. When I climbed the mountain and crossed the river, I was [time]. Time must needs be with me. I have always been; time cannot leave me. When time is not regarded as a phenomenon which ebbs and flows, the time I climbed the mountain is the present moment of being-time. When time is not thought of as coming and going, this moment is absolute time for me. At the time I climbed the mountain and crossed the river, did I not experience the time I am in this building? Three heads and eight elbows is yesterday's time, a height of sixteen or eighteen feet is today's; but "yesterday" or "today" means the time when one goes straight into the mountains and sees ten thousand peaks.[6] It has never passed. Three heads and eight elbows is my being-

[5] The one Chinese compound can be read either as *aru toki*, meaning "at one time" or, in a deeper sense, as *uji*, meaning "being-time."

[6] The "ten thousand peaks of the mountains" should be understood symbolically as meaning the countless and varied circumstances and activities of daily living.

time. It seems to be of the past, but it is of the present. A height of sixteen or eighteen feet is my being-time. It appears to be passing, but it is now. Thus the pine is time, as is the bamboo.

Do not regard time as merely flying away; do not think that flying away is its sole function. For time to fly away there would have to be a separation [between it and things]. Because you imagine that time only passes, you do not learn the truth of being-time. In a word, every being in the entire world is a separate time in one continuum. And since being is time, I am my being-time. Time has the quality of passing, so to speak, from today to tomorrow, from today to yesterday, from yesterday to today, from today to today, from tomorrow to tomorrow. Because this passing is a characteristic of time, present time and past time do not overlap or impinge upon one another. But the master Seigen is time, Obaku is time, Kosei is time, Sekito is time.[7] Since you and I are time, practice-enlightenment is time.

[7] What Dogen probably means here is that these ancient Chinese Zen masters, though having long passed on, still exist in the timelessness of time.

VIII / THE TEN OXHERDING PICTURES WITH COMMENTARY AND VERSES /

Among the various formulations of the levels of realization in Zen, none is more widely known than the Oxherding Pictures, a sequence of ten illustrations annotated with comments in prose and verse. It is probably because of the sacred nature of the ox in ancient India that this animal came to be used to symbolize man's primal nature or Buddha-mind.

The original drawings and the commentary that accompanies them are both attributed to Kuo-an Shih-yuan (Kakuan Shien), a Chinese Zen master of the twelfth century, but he was not the first to illustrate the developing stages of Zen realization through pictures. Earlier versions of five and eight pictures exist in which the ox becomes progressively whiter, the last painting being a circle. This implied that the realization of Oneness (that is, the effacement of every conception of self and other) was the ultimate goal of Zen. But Kuo-an, feeling this to be incomplete, added two more pictures beyond the circle to make it clear that the Zen man of the highest spiritual development lives in the mundane world of form and diversity and mingles with the utmost freedom among ordinary men, whom he inspires with his compassion and radiance to walk in the Way of the Buddha. It is this version that has gained the widest acceptance in Japan, has proved itself over the years to be a source of instruction and unfailing inspiration to Zen students, and is presented here, as explained on page xvi, with modern ink-and-brush paintings by Gyokusei Jikihara.

1 / SEEKING THE OX / The Ox has never really gone astray, so why search for it? Having turned his back on his True-nature, the man cannot see it. Because of his defilements he has lost sight of the Ox. Suddenly he finds himself confronted by a maze of crisscrossing roads. Greed for worldly gain and dread of loss spring up like searing flames, ideas of right and wrong dart out like daggers.

> Desolate through forests and fearful in jungles,
>   he is seeking an Ox which he does not find.
> Up and down dark, nameless, wide-flowing rivers,
>   in deep mountain thickets he treads many bypaths.
> Bone-tired, heart-weary, he carries on his search
>   for this something which he yet cannot find.
> At evening he hears cicadas chirping in the trees.

2 / FINDING THE TRACKS / Through the sutras and teachings he discerns the tracks of the Ox. [He has been informed that just as] different-shaped [golden] vessels are all basically of the same gold, so each and every thing is a manifestation of the Self. But he is unable to distinguish good from evil, truth from falsity. He has not actually entered the gate, but he sees in a tentative way the tracks of the Ox.

> Innumerable footprints has he seen
>   in the forest and along the water's edge.
> Over yonder does he see the trampled grass?
> Even the deepest gorges of the topmost mountains
>   can't hide this Ox's nose which reaches right to heaven.

3 / FIRST GLIMPSE OF THE OX / If he will but listen intently to everyday sounds,[1]* he will come to realization and at that instant see the very Source. The six senses are no different from this true Source. In every activity the Source is manifestly present. It is analogous to the salt in water or the binder in paint.[2] When the inner vision is properly focused, one comes to realize that that which is seen is identical with the true Source.

> A nightingale warbles on a twig,
>   the sun shines on undulating willows.
> There stands the Ox, where could he hide?
> That splendid head, those stately horns,
>   what artist could portray them?

* For all footnotes to this section see pp. 324–25.

4 / CATCHING THE OX / Today he encountered the Ox, which had long been cavorting in the wild fields, and actually grasped it. For so long a time has it reveled in these surroundings that breaking it of its old habits is not easy. It continues to yearn for sweet-scented grasses, it is still stubborn and unbridled. If he would tame it completely, the man must use his whip.

> He must tightly grasp the rope and not let it go,
>> for the Ox still has unhealthy tendencies.[3]
> Now he charges up to the highlands,
>> now he loiters in a misty ravine.

5 / TAMING THE OX / With the rising of one thought another and another are born. Enlightenment brings the realization that such thoughts are not unreal since even they arise from our True-nature. It is only because delusion still remains that they are imagined to be unreal. This state of delusion does not originate in the objective world but in our own minds.

He must hold the nose-rope tight and not allow the Ox to roam,
   lest off to muddy haunts it should stray.
Properly tended, it becomes clean and gentle.
Untethered, it willingly follows its master.

6 / RIDING THE OX HOME / The struggle is over, "gain" and "loss" no longer affect him. He hums the rustic tune of the woodsman and plays the simple songs of the village children. Astride the Ox's back, he gazes serenely at the clouds above. His head does not turn [in the direction of temptations]. Try though one may to upset him, he remains undisturbed.

> Riding free as air[4] he buoyantly comes home
>   through evening mists in wide straw-hat and cape.
> Wherever he may go he creates a fresh breeze,
>   while in his heart profound tranquility prevails.
> This Ox requires not a blade of grass.[5]

7 / OX FORGOTTEN, SELF ALONE / In the Dharma
there is no two-ness. The Ox is his Primal-nature: this he has now
recognized. A trap is no longer needed when a rabbit has been
caught, a net becomes useless when a fish has been snared. Like
gold which has been separated from dross, like the moon which
has broken through the clouds, one ray of luminous Light shines
eternally.

> Only on the Ox was he able to come Home,
> But lo, the Ox is now vanished, and alone and serene
>   sits the man.
> The red sun rides high in the sky
>   as he dreams on placidly.
> Yonder beneath the thatched roof
>   his idle whip and idle rope are lying.

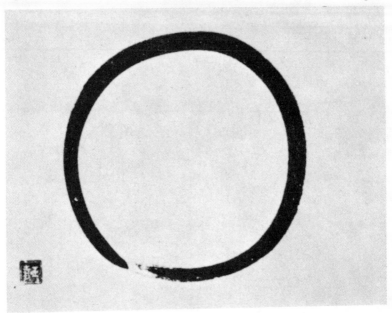

8 / BOTH OX AND SELF FORGOTTEN / All delusive feelings have perished and ideas of holiness too have vanished. He lingers not in [the state of "I am a] Buddha," and he passes quickly on through [the stage of "And now I have purged myself of the proud feeling 'I am] not Buddha.' " Even the thousand eyes [of five hundred Buddhas and patriarchs] can discern in him no specific quality.[6] If hundreds of birds were now to strew flowers about his room, he could not but feel ashamed of himself.[7]

> Whip, rope, Ox and man alike belong to Emptiness.
> So vast and infinite the azure sky[8]
>   that no concept of any sort can reach it.
> Over a blazing fire a snowflake cannot survive.[9]
> When this state of mind is realized
>   comes at last comprehension
>   of the spirit of the ancient patriarchs.

9 / RETURNING TO THE SOURCE / From the very beginning there has not been so much as a speck of.dust [to mar the intrinsic Purity]. He observes the waxing and waning of life in the world while abiding unassertively in a state of unshakable serenity. This [waxing and waning] is no phantom or illusion [but a manifestation of the Source]. Why then is there need to strive[10] for anything? The waters are blue, the mountains are green. Alone with himself, he observes things endlessly changing.

> He has returned to the Origin, come back to the Source,
>   but his steps have been taken in vain.
> It is as though he were now blind and deaf.[11]
> Seated in his hut, he hankers not for things outside.[12]
> Streams meander on of themselves,
>   red flowers naturally bloom red.

10 / ENTERING THE MARKETPLACE[13] WITH
HELPING HANDS / The gate of his cottage is closed and
even the wisest cannot find him.[14] His mental panorama[15] has finally
disappeared. He goes his own way, making no attempt to follow
the steps of earlier sages. Carrying a gourd,[16] he strolls into the
market; leaning on his staff, he returns home. He leads innkeepers
and fishmongers in the Way of the Buddha.

> Barechested, barefooted, he comes into the marketplace.
> Muddied and dust-covered, how broadly he grins!
> Without recourse to mystic powers,
>   withered trees he swiftly brings to bloom.[17]

FOOTNOTES FOR SECTION VIII

[1] See p. 171.

[2] To take the analogy of form and Emptiness, the salt corresponds to Emptiness and the water to form. Until one has known the "taste" of satori one is ignorant of this Emptiness and recognizes only the form. After enlightenment they are seen as no different from each other.

[3] Literally, "wild strength." What is implied here is that at this stage delusive feelings still persist and that their eradication requires further training.

[4] Literally, "riding upside down."

[5] That is, the Buddha-mind, symbolized by the Ox, is entirely sufficient unto itself.

[6] The implication of this passage is that Buddhas and patriarchs have a mirrorlike Wisdom which can easily discern the character of the ordinary man, tainted as it is by various defilements. But one who had cleansed himself of all impurities, including the subtlest forms of pride, would be so pure and natural that even a Buddha would be unable to look at him and say that he was this or that.

[7] This is an allusion to a parable centering around Niu-t'ou Fa-yung (Hoyu-zenji), a Zen master of the T'ang dynasty, who lived on Mount Niu-t'ou and who was widely extolled for the ardor with which he practiced zazen in his mountain retreat. Even the birds, it is said, sang his praises by offering up flowers to him as he sat in his hut. After he became fully enlightened under the Fourth Patriarch, so the story goes, the birds ceased their floral offerings, because, having attained perfect enlightenment, he no longer gave off any aura, even of devotion and virtue.

[8] "Azure sky" stands for Pure-mind.

[9] With perfect enlightenment all delusive thoughts, including those of "enlightenment" or "delusion," vanish.

[10] "If, as the sutras say, our Essential-nature is Bodhi [Perfection], why did all Buddhas have to strive for enlightenment and perfection?" asked Dogen, who was able to resolve this paradox only after years of strenuous effort, culminating in his deep enlightenment.

[11] What is implied here is that the fully enlightened man, being no longer caught up in the objects of the senses, absorbs himself so un-self-consciously in what he sees and hears that his seeing is no-seeing and his hearing no-hearing.

[12] Since with enlightenment comes the realization that one embraces the universe and all things in it, what is there to hanker for?

[13] "Marketplace" signifies the defiled world.

[14] The sense of this is that he has now become so purified, so perfected, that the wisest sage can detect about him no *marks* of perfection.

[15] That is, all concepts, opinions, assumptions, prejudices.

[16] In ancient China gourds were commonly used as wine bottles. What is implied here therefore is that the man of the deepest spirituality is not averse to drinking with those fond of liquor in order to help them overcome their delusions. Here we see a fundamental difference in emphasis between the role of the spiritually accomplished man in the Hinayana and in the Mahayana traditions. In the Hinayana the highest spiritual type, the celibate monk, is set apart from the laity. Ideally

he must be saintlike, a paragon of virtue, if he is to fulfill the role conceived for him by the community. Were it known that he indulged in alcohol, for instance, this would be regarded as the surest sign of a lingering impurity, of proof that his spirituality was not yet wholly refined. In Mahayana Buddhism, on the contrary, the man of deep enlightenment (who may be and often is the layman) gives off no "smell" of enlightenment, no aura of "saintliness"; if he did, his spiritual attainment would be regarded as still deficient. Nor does he hold himself aloof from the evils of the world. He immerses himself in them whenever necessary to emancipate men from their follies, but without being sullied by them himself. In this he is like the lotus, the symbol in Buddhism of purity and perfection, which grows in mud yet is undefiled by it.

[17] This is another way of saying that the fully enlightened man, because his whole personality is suffused with an inner radiance, brings light and hope to those in darkness and despair.

IX / POSTURES /

A / ZAZEN POSTURES ILLUSTRATED / The postures illustrated in the following pages range across history from the classic lotus pose of antiquity to a special twentieth-century zazen bench. Although Zen masters ancient and contemporary are united in proclaiming the superiority of the lotus posture over all others (for reasons which will be found in the first section of this book), the editor can testify from his own experience with each of these positions that any of them can be adequate for one sufficiently determined to pursue zazen.

The practice of sitting with the foot of each leg over the thigh of the other is one of the oldest, predating the Buddha. Not only do we know through archaeological evidence in India that millenniums before the birth of the Buddha the lotus posture was in use in that country, but wall carvings unearthed from ancient Egyptian tombs, showing figures sitting in the full-lotus, prove that civilizations other than the Indian knew the power of this unique pose.

Admittedly for Westerners, not nurtured on cross-legged sitting, the lotus posture can be difficult, but by no means is it impossible. Adult non-athletic Westerners have mastered the half-lotus in less than six months by persistent zazen coupled with simple leg-stretching calisthenics (which include pressing down of the knees with the hands after a hot bath) to gradually bring the knees down to the level of the sitting mat. The full-lotus is naturally a harder nut to crack, but it no less will yield to a systematic effort.

The posture shown in Fig. 5 is widely used in Burma and the Southeast Asian Buddhist countries. It has the advantage of being much less uncomfortable for beginners than either the half- or the full-lotus, as the legs are uncrossed, but it does not provide the strong support for the trunk that the lotus posture does; the spine, therefore, cannot be kept absolutely erect for long without strain.

The traditional Japanese sitting posture, Fig. 6, can be made comfortable for Westerners by the insertion of a cushion between the buttocks and the heels. A low bench of the type shown in Fig. 7 when placed between the buttocks and the heels renders this posture even more comfortable, since it eliminates every bit of pressure from the heels. For the novice, an absolutely straight back is easiest in this position.

An ordinary chair when sat in in the usual way, that is, with the back bent, is not satisfactory for zazen. But if used as shown in Fig. 8, with a cushion underneath the buttocks to help keep the spine erect, and with one's feet planted firmly on the floor, it can be effective.

Fig. 1 Full-lotus posture, with right foot over left thigh and left foot over right thigh, both knees touching mat. Knees should be in line with one another, the abdomen relaxed and slightly protruded. Hands rest on the heels of both feet, with thumbs touching lightly to make an oval. This posture may be reversed when the left foot gets tired.

Fig. 2 Full-lotus posture, side view, showing ears in line with shoulders, and tip of nose in line with navel. The chin should be slightly drawn in. The buttocks are thrust out, with the spine erect. A single low cushion is preferable in this posture.

Fig. 3 The half-lotus posture, with left foot over right thigh and right foot under left thigh, both knees touching mat. To facilitate the knees resting on the mat, it may be necessary to use a support cushion under the regular round one.

Fig. 4 The quarter-lotus, with the left foot resting over the calf of the right, both knees resting on the mat.

NOTE: In all postures, including that involving bench and chair, the buttocks are thrust out, the chin tucked in, and the spine held erect. The hands are kept close to the body, resting high up on the thighs or on the heels of the feet, the knees are in line with another, and the abdomen is relaxed and slightly protruded.

Fig. 5 The so-called Burmese posture, with the legs uncrossed, the left or right foot in front and both knees touching mat. Here, too, a higher sitting base may be necessary so that both knees rest squarely on the mat.

Fig. 6 Side view of the traditional Japanese sitting posture with knees in line with one another on the mat and straddling a husk cushion inserted between the heels and buttocks to relieve pressure on heels. The hands may rest on the front of the husk cushion. For extra height, the husk cushion may be placed on top of a round cushion.

Fig. 7 Side view of zazen performed on a low wooden bench with a padded seat. To prevent the hands from slipping down, a support cushion may be placed vertically on the mat under the hands.

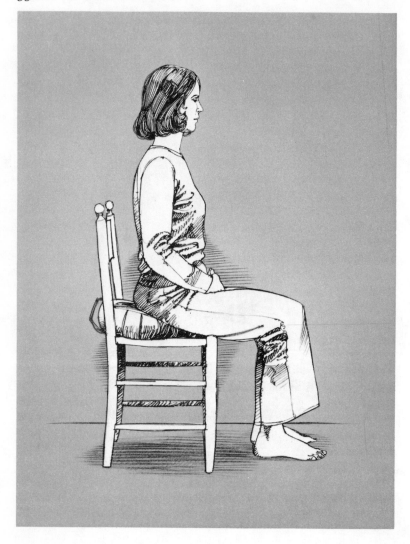

Fig. 8 Side view of zazen in a straight-back chair, with cushion under buttocks and the feet resting firmly on the floor the width of the shoulders apart.

Fig. 9 Side view of mat, round cushion, and support cushion in position for zazen. Round cushions measure anywhere from twelve to eighteen inches in diameter and from three to six in thickness. The best filler for cushions is kapok, which fluffs out when put in the sun; foam rubber tends to bounce. Cotton batting is good for mats. The best mat is not more than two inches thick, measures from thirty to thirty-six inches square, and has neither cording nor upholstery buttons. Support cushions measure about seventeen by twelve inches and two and a half inches thick. The round cushion has a handle for carrying, and pleats to provide "give."

Fig. 10 Husk cushions and low zazen bench. Husk cushions can be filled with buckwheat husks, rice husks, or any other husk which is not too hard and at the same time provides firmness. The bench measures about nineteen and a half inches by seven inches and is eight inches high in the rear, six inches in front. The seat is upholstered for greater comfort.

B / QUESTIONS AND ANSWERS

THE BACK

QUESTION: During zazen I get a weak, aching feeling in the lower part of my back. What is the reason for this?

ANSWER: This is not an uncommon problem for beginners. Usually it occurs during or after zazen because your back muscles are not strong enough to support the erect back for any length of time. The same thing may result from trying to sit with ramrod erectness. Leaning forward slightly, without rounding the back, will often eliminate the difficulty by removing the pressure from the muscles of the lower back, allowing the weight of the trunk to be supported by the hips. Sometimes pain in the lower back may be the result of sitting on a cushion that is too high or too hard. Experiment with your cushions; try using them in different ways until you find the height right for you.

You also need to strengthen your lower back through stretching exercises or sports. Here are two good stretching exercises. Standing erect, slowly bend over from the base of the spine, without rounding the back or bending your knees, as you try to touch the floor with the palms of your hands. Bend over only as far as you can comfortably; gradually you will find yourself going lower and lower until your hands touch the floor. Next sit on the floor with both legs extended. Bending from the base of the spine, try to touch your toes, keeping the knees firmly on the floor. (See sketch.)

To acquire and maintain a healthy back condition one must also learn to sit and carry oneself properly throughout the day. When you sit down, first thrust your buttocks toward the back of the chair or couch and then come up from the base of the spine. In this way it is easy to sit erect, since the weight rests squarely on the hips and thrust-out buttocks, preventing strain in the lower back. Above all, don't fall into a chair back-first, as though you were a sack of flour. And make it a point to walk erectly at all times with your center of gravity in the lower abdomen, not in the area of the shoulders. Remember, what distinguishes human beings from animals is their unique ability to keep the back erect.

The innate dignity and nobility of a human being is revealed in a straight back.

BREATHING

QUESTION 1: In zazen does one breathe from the chest or stomach? When you inhale does the stomach go in or out?

ANSWER 1: In Zen, breathing is from the lower abdomen, not the chest. When you inhale, normally the lower abdomen fills up, becoming slightly convex, and when you exhale it becomes concave. (See sketches.)

QUESTION 2: My practice is following the breath. I have read that pushing one's breath into the hara (lower abdomen) makes one's zazen more effective, but when I try to do this a pain begins to develop in the chest area. Am I doing anything wrong? What can I do to stop it?

ANSWER 2: In the beginning of one's practice there is apt to be a great deal of self-conscious effort which, when persisted in, creates pain somewhere in the body. Most people are normally shallow breathers, their exhaled breath terminating in the chest area. You need to learn how to relax the diaphragm and to breathe from the lower abdomen, not the chest. But if you try to *force* your breath down lower, it becomes dammed up and does not descend naturally into the abdomen. The result is pain either in the region of your belly, the lower back, or both.

As a way of getting beyond this self-conscious effort and of bringing your center of gravity down to the lower abdomen so that the breathing is abdominal, imagine that your nostrils are about two inches below the navel. Allow your breath to flow gently into the upper left palm of your folded hands (I assume you are holding your hands in the traditional zazen mudra and that they are resting on your heels in the region below the navel). Or imagine you have a balloon in the palm of your hands which you are inflating with each inhalation. After a while you will lose this purposeful concern with the exhalations and your respiration will become more natural. Except at the beginning of a round of zazen, when you take a deep breath and then slowly exhale, don't manipulate your breath; allow it to find its own natural passage. Sometimes the breathing will be slow, at other times fast, and still other times labored, depending on your mind state, your body condition, and other factors, but with continued zazen, you will develop poise and stability and your respiration will assume its own natural pattern. A well-known text by Zen master Dogen advises that respiration be neither gasping nor forced, neither slow nor rapid. If you concentrate your attention in the palm of your upper left hand, your center of gravity will descend effortlessly from the shoulders and chest to the hara (or *tanden*). The expansion and contraction of the respiratory muscles involved in abdominal breathing soothe and strengthen the autonomic nervous system as well as inhibit the proliferation of random thoughts.

It not infrequently happens that one becomes so preoccupied

with the mechanics of breathing, with whether the abdomen goes in or out on the inhalation or exhalation, that one's concentration on counting or following the breath, shikan-taza, or a koan becomes ineffectual. One can become like the centipede that, in trying to figure out which foot moved when, ended up in a heap, paralyzed. The reason why experienced Zen teachers do not analyze or explain the breathing process in detail is that they do not wish their students to make a technique out of breathing—or, for that matter, any other aspect of Zen practice. Techniques belong to the world of technology, not to spiritual training.

CHEST

QUESTION: Earlier you said that the chest should be held up. It seems that a conscious effort is required to do that. Won't this interfere with my zazen?

ANSWER: If you are accustomed to letting the chest sink, it does require a conscious effort to keep it up in the beginning. When it becomes natural to walk and sit with the chest open, you begin to realize the many benefits of this ideal posture. The lungs are given additional space in which to expand, thus filling and stretching the air sacs. This in turn permits a greater intake of oxygen and washes the bloodstream, which carries away fatigue accumulated in the body. Since one burns a good deal of oxygen before reaching a level of deep zazen, it is a decided advantage to have the chest open, thereby facilitating a free flow of vital energy.

EYES

QUESTION: After doing zazen for a few rounds, I find it takes a while before my eyes return to normal focus. Why is this and what can I do to correct it?

ANSWER: If the eyes are kept focused during sitting, the resultant strain from holding them this way will interfere with normal vision afterward. When sitting, keep the eyes open but unfocused; do not try to perceive anything. In the beginning this may feel strange, but with deeper involvement it will seem quite natural to keep the eyes unfocused. Even when the eyes are kept unfocused, however, they sometimes take a little time to readjust to normal focused vision due to various body-mind conditions. This should not cause concern.

If your eyes are really troubling you, there are some general eye exercises that can be done. To get the eyes quickly back into focus, blink them rapidly a few times and then bring the index finger to the tip of the nose and slowly push the finger to the left as far as you can, following it with the eyes. Then bring the finger back to the front again and do the same thing with the left index finger, to the right side. Now roll the eyes a few times clockwise, then counterclockwise. Try looking up sharply to the upper right corner, then down to the lower left corner, in a diagonal motion, then to the upper left corner and down to the lower right corner. Do this a few times and then blink the eyes rapidly again.

Another way to soothe and revitalize the eyes is to rub the palms of the hands vigorously, generating a great deal of warmth, and then place them over the eyes, blocking out all light. Now open the eyes and mentally bathe them in the warmth of the energy being emitted from the palms. This palming of the eyes can be done independently of the foregoing finger exercises.

If you wear glasses, removing them during zazen may cause eye-strain. Try sitting with them both on and off.

HANDS AND LOWER ARMS

QUESTION: Often after doing zazen for a round or two I find my hands and lower arms beginning to tense up and ache. Why is this?

ANSWER: Very likely you are creating tension by applying too much pressure against the thumbs. You must also be careful not to allow the elbows to be held out stiffly at the sides, for then the pressure on the hands becomes greater and the condition is worsened. It's almost as though you were trying to grasp your practice with your hands. This brings on stiffness, tension, and aching muscles.

The elbows should be relaxed and allowed to hang loosely, close to the body. Similarly, hold the hands with their sides resting on the thighs, free of tension, with the thumbs touching lightly to make a flattened circle. Keeping the hands flat, with the palms straight up, often creates tension in the region of the forearm and elbows.

HANDS AND SHOULDERS

QUESTION: I find that if I don't use a cushion to rest my hands on, they always seem to slip away in my lap. When this happens my shoulders are pulled down and a tiredness sets in across the top of my shoulders. How can this be avoided so that I can get rid of this hand prop? Usually I sit in the half-lotus.

ANSWER: If one can sit comfortably in the half-lotus, there should be enough lap room close to the lower abdomen to allow the hands to rest against the body, nestled in such a way that the fingers of the left hand sit within the fingers of the right in a slightly curved and relaxed manner. (See sketches of proper postures in section IX-A.)

The hands may slip out of position when the body-mind loses its tautness, that is, if you become sleepy or absentminded while sitting. The tiredness across the shoulders is due to the pull on the shoulders and shoulder blades. This unnatural drag of the weight of the shoulders saps your strength.

To correct this, bring the hands close to the lower abdomen and at the same time relax the elbows, allowing them to hang next to the body. Next take a deep breath and lift the sternum. In this way the shoulders will hang naturally, supported by the straightened shoulder blades. If the chest is permitted to drop, the shoulders will become heavy and sag.

HEAD

QUESTION: My head seems to move slowly forward as I do zazen, and it is only when corrected that I realize this has happened. How can I prevent this?

ANSWER: When one is seduced by random thoughts or fantasies, the head physically follows the thinking and projects itself forward. This can be corrected physically by feeling for the collar of your robe with the back of your neck, taking a deep breath, and then raising the sternum slightly. When the chest is raised the position of the head is corrected. The ears will automatically line up with the shoulders and the chin will tuck slightly in. No attempt should be made to *pull* the chin in as this may create tension in the back of the neck. Needless to say, an effort should be made to resist following such wandering thoughts or fantasies.

HEAD—SHARP PAINS

QUESTION: After a few minutes of sitting, I found a sharp pain coming up into the left side of my head. This happened every time a new round of sitting started.

ANSWER: In the beginning sensitive persons often have twinges of pain in different parts of their body, owing to pre-existing tensions in those areas and the strain of turning one's energies inward instead of dispersing them outwardly. It is also a strain at first for body and mind to function as a unity in zazen. If this discomfort is accompanied by feelings of apprehension, the pain and tension only increase. When you understand the reasons for the increased tension and resultant pain, and are aware that they are only temporary, the fear will evaporate. Naturally the pain will also disappear and be replaced with a sense of buoyancy and well-being.

Also remember that your discomfort can be a trick of the ego to derail your practice. Since the ego does not wish to lose its cozy dominance, it throws up all sorts of barriers to retain control, the most common of which is pain, for it knows that persistent zazen will terminate its rule. If you recognize that the pain is only a device of the ego to get you to quit, you can turn the tables on this wily phantom by refusing to give in. Pain is a challenge that sooner or later must be met, and the way to banish it is to become fully one with it.

KNEES

QUESTION: I injured my knee playing basketball and had surgery for a torn meniscus. Is it possible for me to ever attempt zazen in a half- or full-lotus?

ANSWER: If the surgery has been successful, the prognosis is generally good. The meniscus will replace itself with a thinner, more flexible tissue. There have also been cases in which the meniscus has slowly healed itself without surgery so that the knee joint was able to function as well as before the injury. As the knee begins to regain its flexibility, begin bouncing it gently a little each day until you feel able to sit comfortably in the half- or full-lotus. (See "Legs—Pain in Half-lotus.") Daily massage, herbal poultices, and herbal teas (especially those made from comfrey), as well as therapeutic doses of vitamin C, are all helpful.

LEGS—FALLING ASLEEP

QUESTION: My legs fall asleep very quickly whenever I do zazen. What can I do?

ANSWER: When the legs fall asleep during zazen it is usually because of pressure on either a nerve or a vein or both. Changing one's position on the cushion, that is, sitting farther forward or back, will relieve pressure on a nerve.

Those who are developing circulatory problems in the legs would do well to change their zazen posture frequently so as to not to cause any undue pressure for prolonged periods of time. Massaging the legs before and after zazen, thereby stimulating circulation and strengthening the nerves, is also helpful.

LEGS—PAIN IN HALF-LOTUS

QUESTION: I have a lot of pain when I try to sit in half-lotus. What can I do to help this situation?

ANSWER: Before one is ready to sit in half-lotus the ankle and knee joints must be made flexible. This may be accomplished in different ways, one of which is the following: Sit on the floor with both legs stretched out in front of you. Fold the right leg and place the right foot on top of the left thigh as far up as is comfortable for you. Hold the right foot with the left hand, and with the right hand bounce the right knee gently. If it is not possible to place the right foot on top of the left thigh, place the sole of the right foot *against* the inner left thigh and bounce the knee from this position. Continue this flipping of the knee for a few minutes and then reverse your legs and repeat on the left side. (See sketch p. 347.) Eventually, as flexibility develops and the groin area begins to open up, it will become possible to place the foot higher up on the thigh. Do this bouncing of the knees every day for a few minutes and it will soon become comfortable to sit in the half-lotus. A variant of this exercise is to place the soles of the feet together, holding onto the toes with the hands, and to flip the knees up and down. (See sketch p. 349.)

Another exercise that will open up the groin and hip areas is to clasp the lower leg and raise it high in the arms, the knee "cradled" in one elbow and the foot in the other elbow, and then to swing the leg back and forth; repeat with the other leg. (See sketch p. 348.)

Swimming is also an aid to flexibility since you can assume postures in the water that might be painful otherwise. A sauna is another advantageous place in which to first massage and manipulate the knee, ankle, and groin areas and then sit in the lotus position.

If you have mild pain during sitting because your ligaments are not yet stretched, bear with it, but if the pain is intense, unfold your legs and try another position. Don't grit your teeth, suppress the tears, and tell yourself, "I'll take the pain even if it kills me," out of a misguided belief that zazen is asceticism. Zazen should leave you with a feeling of well-being, not acute discomfort.

NECK AND HEAD

QUESTION: When I do zazen a tightness develops in my head and neck and this seems to bring on a burning sensation across the shoulder blades. What, if anything, can be done to prevent or correct this?

ANSWER: This is an example of what happens when your energy is "locked" high in the body and not allowed to flow naturally. If your attention is focused in the neck and head area, tension and pain usually develop there. The burning sensation results from an impingement that prevents a free flow of blood to the area. To remedy this, first allow the shoulders to hang effortlessly on the frame. Next take a deep breath, lift the sternum slightly, and slowly exhale. This will release the pressure in the shoulders, freeing the blocked energy. Care must be taken not to attempt to straighten the shoulders or pull them back deliberately. They will straighten of their own accord if the sternum is lifted; simultaneously the head and neck will ride freely on the spinal column. Make no conscious effort to hold on in the area of the head and neck, for this will create tension and, eventually, pain.

SALIVA

QUESTION: Sometimes my mouth fills up with saliva during zazen and I have to swallow frequently. What causes this?

ANSWER: This reaction may occur if the head is held too far forward, or with the chin lowered. To correct this, the head should be pressed back so that you feel your collar on the back of your neck. Be careful not to allow the tongue to drop from the upper palate, where it normally rests during zazen, as this, too, may cause saliva to collect in the mouth.

SLEEPY ZAZEN

QUESTION: I do about an hour of zazen in the morning before going to work, but it is not good zazen because most of the time I'm dozing off. What can I do about that?

ANSWER: Normally it takes about an hour for the body to awaken fully once you've gotten out of bed. There are ways, though, of speeding up this process. A brisk walk outdoors, filling your lungs deeply with the clear morning air, is most helpful, as are stretching exercises. Tapping the head lightly with the tips of the fingers will also clear the cobwebs from the brain. One procedure that is particularly stimulating is the following: First fill the sink with enough cold water to dip your face into; then open and shut the eyes under water while holding the breath for the count of, say, twenty, letting the cold water come in contact with your eyeballs.

Another excellent wake-up exercise is the following: As you sit with your legs crossed ready to begin zazen, clasp your hands behind you, elbows straight. Take a deep breath, then slowly bend over from the base of the back, slowly exhaling, until your forehead touches the floor. Later on you'll be able to touch the floor with your chin instead of just your forehead. Breathe normally while holding this posture for about half a minute. Then take another deep breath and slowly straighten, again from the base of the spine, while you exhale. (See sketch.) As you raise your head and trunk (your hands still clasped behind you), stretch hard, opening up the chest and thrusting out your buttocks until your trunk reaches an erect position. Now, still holding your trunk straight with your hands clasped behind you, take one final stretch, pushing your head back as far as it will go and keeping the chest open wide. Not only will this exercise awaken and invigorate you, but if you have any kind of breathing difficulties it will thoroughly clear the nasal passages.

Finally, let me point out that dozing off, at any time of day, is a common complaint of sitters. It doesn't appear to be related to whether you are tired or rested or have had your normal amount of sleep or not—the problem is one of motivation. The need for Self-realization is not yet strongly felt, and dozing off is a mild form of escape from the tedium of zazen. What you need to do is remind yourself, when dozing off, that death may come at any time, and that to have the rare opportunity of being born a human being in this lifetime and not to realize your True-nature is, as one master put it, to have lived in vain.

THOUGHTS AFFECTING POSTURE

QUESTION: I've been doing zazen for a short time and I find myself getting depressed as unpleasant memories keep coming up to consciousness. When this happens I also become aware that my posture changes for the worse, and though I try to straighten up, it doesn't stay that way for long.

ANSWER: The problem is a dual one. The invading thoughts destroy the mind's tautness and cause the body to slump. With a slumping body comes a bent spine; the sternum becomes concave, pulling the shoulders forward and down; the head juts forward, the internal organs become cramped, the hands slip away, and the whole attitude of the body is one of dejection and defeat. It is almost as if one were saying, "I can't do it. I'll never make it. I'm not strong enough." Worse, a slumping body encourages an even greater invasion of negative, unpleasant thoughts, and the cycle is enlarged.

Realize from the outset that your memories, like all thoughts, are impermanent and insubstantial, unreal in the sense that they are empty of any self-substance. Therefore you must not cling to them. Furthermore, if in your sitting you take care to keep your chest up and open, your shoulder blades will straighten and the shoulders rest easily on their frame. The head will also sit back on the cervical spine and the ears will line up with the shoulders. The internal organs will no longer be cramped. If the buttocks are thrust out in back, providing a broad base for the trunk, with the abdomen relaxed and the hands turned slightly inward, resting

close to the hara, there will be generated a totally different attitude—one of alertness, poise, and determination. Negative
thoughts will bounce off this straight alignment of body-mind as
the whole posture proclaims, "I can, and I will!"

TILTING OF TRUNK

QUESTION: The monitors are always straightening my sitting posture. Evidently I tend to lean to the right, though I'm not aware
of it, and when corrected I feel like the leaning tower of Pisa in
the other direction. Why does this happen?

ANSWER: If your body is out of alignment in general, its imbalance
will show up in your sitting. There are many causes for such an
imbalance. If one is a student and always carrying books or heavy
packages on the right side, for example, the body tends to lean
to the right because it has been pulled in that direction. Similarly,
if you are in the habit of standing at ease with one hip thrust
out, or you play a great deal of tennis, an imbalance may result.

Obviously the first step is to try to correct physically the condition
causing the imbalance, that is, to carry books or packages on both
sides, or to stand with the body weight evenly distributed on the
feet. Next, if while sitting you lean to one side or the other, you
may need to place a small, flat cushion or folded towel under one
buttock to bring the trunk back to vertical. Then when the body
has grown accustomed to sitting in an aligned position the temporary cushion or towel may be removed; it will not feel strange to
sit up straight.

There are also psychological reasons why the body will list to
one side. You will find that timid, self-deprecating persons, those
lacking a strong center, tend to walk and sit with a slump. Since
body is the physical aspect of mind, an improved posture and bearing will tend to create a healthier psychological condition—one
of poise and self-confidence. But unless the root sense of ego-I
is seen through—and in a self-deprecating person it is merely inverted, not weaker than in a domineering person—there can be
no fundamental or lasting change in personality or posture.

X / NOTES ON ZEN VOCABULARY AND BUDDHIST DOCTRINE /

Technical Zen terms and proper names, words associated with Zen (for example, *kendo*), special Buddhist terms and phrases, Buddhist doctrines, and Buddhist sects and sutras which are mentioned in the text but not explained therein are defined or explained at length here. These notes are not intended to be a dictionary of Zen terms, much less a definitive statement of Buddhist doctrine or philosophy. Yet they comprise more than a mere glossary of academic definitions. Their purpose is to help the reader understand the text and to facilitate his further study and practice.

Rather than indicate the Chinese ideographs for Japanese and Chinese names and terms, which would be meaningful only to specialists in the Japanese or the Chinese language, I have used the roman transcriptions. Where a word is better known in its original Sanskrit or Chinese than in English or Japanese, I have shown it first according to its native spelling, adding in parentheses its equivalent in English or Japanese, or both. The names of the Chinese Zen masters are listed according to the way they are pronounced in Japanese, with the Chinese reading shown in parentheses. The names of sutras are invariably given in their Sanskrit spelling as well as in Japanese and, in some cases, in English.

Japanese names and words are marked J.; Sanskrit, Skt.; and Chinese, Ch. Diacritical marks will be found only in this section.

Abhidharma (Skt.): the third of the three "baskets," or Tripitaka, of Buddhist literature, the other two being the Vinaya—that is, the precepts or moral rules given by Buddha to his followers—and the sūtras, which consist of the collection of the Buddha's sermons, discourses, and dialogues compiled after his parinirvana. The Abhidharma contains highly abstract, philosophical elucidations of Buddhist doctrine.

agura (J.): the loose cross-legged sitting position which is neither the half- nor the full-lotus.

Amitabha (Skt.; J., Amida): literally, "boundless light," or *Amitāyus*, "boundless life." Amitabha is the most widely venerated of the non-historical (that is, Dhyani) Buddhas. Indeed, in the Pure Land (J., Jōdo) sects he overshadows both Vairochana and the historic Buddha Shākyamuni.

Avatamsaka (J., Kegon) sūtra: a profound Mahāyāna sūtra embodying the sermons given by the Buddha immediately following his perfect enlightenment.

Baso (Ch., Ma-tsu): one of the great Chinese Zen masters of the T'ang dynasty (died 788); a disciple of Nangaku (Ch., Nan-yueh).

birth-and-death (J., *shōji;* Skt., *samsāra*): the world of relativity; the transformation which all phenomena, including our thoughts and feelings, are ceaselessly undergoing in accordance with the law of causation. Birth-and-death can be compared to the waves on the ocean. The rise of a wave is one "birth" and the fall one "death." The size of each is conditioned by the force of the previous one, itself being the progenitor of the succeeding wave. This process infinitely repeated is birth-and-death. See also "Six Realms of Existence," "karma," and diagram under "consciousness."

Bodhidharma (J., Daruma): the Twenty-eighth Patriarch in line from the Buddha, the First Patriarch of Zen in China. Scholars disagree as to when Bodhidharma came to China from India, how long he stayed there, and when he died, but it is generally accepted by Japanese Zen Buddhists that he came by boat from India to southern China about the year 520, and that after a short, abortive attempt to establish his teachings there he went to Lo-yang in northern China and finally settled in Shao-lin Temple, located on Mount Sū. Here for nine years he steadily did zazen, whence this period has come to be known as his "nine years of facing the wall" (J., *mempeki kunen*).

Bodhidharma and Hui-K'e (J., Eka), his disciple to whom he had transmitted the Dharma, are the subject of the forty-first kōan in the *Mumonkan* as well as of a famous painting by Sesshū, Japan's greatest painter. Hui-k'e, a scholar of some repute, complains to Bodhidharma, who is silently doing zazen, that he has no peace of mind and asks how he can acquire it. Bodhidharma turns him away, saying that the attainment of inward peace involves long and hard discipline and is not for the conceited or fainthearted. Hui-k'e, who has been standing outside in the snow for hours, implores Bodhidharma to help him. Again he is rebuffed. In desperation he cuts off his left hand and offers it to Bodhidharma. Now convinced of his sincerity and determination, Bodhidharma accepts him as a disciple.

Whether these episodes are historically true or not is less important than the fact that they symbolically reveal the importance which Zen masters attach to the hunger for Self-realization, to zazen, and to sincerity and humility, perseverance and fortitude as prerequisites to the attainment of the highest truth.

Bodhi-mind (J., *bodai-shin;* Skt., *bodhicitta*): intrinsic wisdom; the inherently enlightened heart-mind; also the aspiration toward perfect enlightenment.

Bodhisattva (Skt.; J., *bosatsu*): an enlightened being who, deferring his own full Buddhahood, dedicates himself to helping others attain liberation. In his self-mastery, wisdom, and compassion a Bodhisattva represents a high stage of Buddhahood, but he is not yet a supremely enlightened, fully perfected Buddha. "Bodhisattvas, like Buddhas, are not merely personifications of abstract principles . . . but are prototypes of those states of highest knowledge, wisdom, and harmony which have been realized in humanity and will ever have to be realized again and again . . ." (Govinda, p. 90)

Brahmajāla (Skt.; J., Bommō) sūtra: Here are to be found the ten major precepts and forty-eight lesser ones which form the ethical basis of Mahāyāna Buddhism.

Buddha (J., *butsu*): a Sanskrit word used in two senses: 1) ultimate Truth or absolute Mind, and 2) one awakened or enlightened to the true nature of existence. *The* Buddha refers to a historical person with the given name of Siddhārtha and family name of Gautama who was born around the year 563 B.C., the son of the ruler of the Shākyas, whose small kingdom lay at the foothills of present-day Nepal. In time he came to be known as Shākyamuni ("the silent sage"—that is, *muni*—"of the Shākya clan"). It is recorded that he was married at the age of sixteen and had a son, later to become his disciple. Deeply troubled by the sorrows and tribulations of human life and perplexed by the meaning of birth-and-death, the future Buddha at the age of twenty-nine could no longer bear the life of ease and luxury into which he had been born, and he fled his father's palace to become a recluse, a seeker after truth in the solitude of forests. For a time he undertook the severest ascetic practices to gain enlightenment. Close to death as a result of these austerities, he at last saw the futility of self-mortification, abandoned it, and finally won perfect enlightenment, becoming "the Buddha." Thereafter for forty-five years, until his death at the age of eighty, he not only taught his own band of monk-disciples but tirelessly trudged the roads of India preaching to all who would listen, always suiting his exposition to the capacity of his hearers' understanding. Men were moved to follow his Way to spiritual emancipation as much by his serenity and compassion as by the wisdom of his words. Eventually his sermons and dialogues were recorded and these sūtras (or scriptures) now comprise the basic doctrines of Buddhism.

The Zen sect, in common with other Buddhist sects, accepts the historic Buddha neither as a Supreme Deity nor as a savior who rescues men by taking upon himself the burden of their sins. Rather, it venerates him as a fully awakened, fully perfected human being who attained liberation of body and mind through his own human efforts and not by the grace of any supernatural being. Nor does Buddhism look upon Shākyamuni as the only true Buddha. Just as in previous world epochs other sages had trodden the same path, attained the same level of perfection, and preached the same Dharma, so would there be Buddhas in subsequent world cycles to lead men to liberation. The historic Buddha, then, is but a link in a chain of Buddhas extending from the remotest past to the immeasurable future.

The familiar statement of the Zen masters that we are all Buddhas from the very first must be understood in the sense that *potentially* everyone is a Buddha, that is, inherently endowed with the unblemished Buddha-nature, but that the candidate for Buddhahood must follow the arduous road to enlightenment if he would *realize* his innate Perfection. Anyone who has experienced his Buddha-nature, however faintly, has realized the first stage of Buddhahood, since in substance this realization is no different from the Buddha Shākyamuni's. However, in the degree of his enlightenment as well as in the perfection of his character and personality—that is, in his equanimity, compassion, and wisdom— Shākyamuni Buddha towers above the man of average enlightenment. A simple comparison would be between a Sunday painter and a Rembrandt; both are painters, but in their respective levels of attainment there is a vast difference.

Various classifications of the stages of Buddhahood are to be found in the sūtras. A Buddha in the highest stage is not only fully enlightened but "a Perfect One, one who has become *whole,* complete in himself, that is, one in whom *all* spiritual and psychic faculties have come to perfection, to maturity, to a state of perfect harmony, and whose consciousness encompasses the infinity of the universe. Such a one can no longer be identified with the limitations of his individual personality, his individual character and existence; of him it is rightly said that 'there is nothing by which he could be measured, there are no words to describe him.' " (Govinda, p. 41)

A Buddha has three "bodies" or planes of reality, though actually the three are one interrelated whole. The first is designated *dharma-kāya* (literally, "law-body"; J., *hosshin*). This is the experience of cosmic consciousness, of oneness that is beyond every conception. The unconditioned dharma-kāya is the substratum of completeness and perfection out of which arise all animate and inanimate forms and moral order. Vairochana (J., Birushana), the "All-Illuminating One," embodies this aspect of universal consciousness. The second "body" is the *sambhoga-kāya* (literally, "bliss-body"; J., *hōjin*), which is the experience of the rapture of enlightenment, of the Dharma-mind of the Buddha and the patriarchs, and of the spiritual practices which they have transmitted from generation to generation. Amitabha Buddha in his Western Paradise symbolizes this "bliss-body." The "body of transformation," *nirmāṇa-kāya* (J., *ōjin*), the third aspect, is the radiant, transformed Buddha-body, personified by Shakyāmuni, the Tathāgata, as he appears in the world with his thirty-two signs of perfection.

The interrelation of these three can be illustrated by a simple analogy. The dharma-kāya can be likened to the field of medical knowledge, the sambhoga-kāya to the doctor's training by which he acquires this knowledge, and the nirmāṇa-kāya to the application of this knowledge in the treatment of individual patients, who are thereby transformed from sickness to health.

Of the non-historical Buddhas, identified with different worlds and realms and symbolic of particular spiritual forces and powers, there is little reference made in Zen except to Vairochana (J., Birushana) and Amitabha (J., Amida).

Buddha-nature (J., *busshō*): a concrete expression for the substratum of perfection, of completeness, intrinsic to both sentient and insentient life.

Buddhism (J., *bukkyō*): Buddhism, or, more precisely, the Buddha's Dharma, has two main branches: the Southern or Theravāda (Teachings of the Elders), also known as the Hīnayāna (Lesser Vehicle; J., *shōjō*); and the Northern or Mahāyāna (Great Vehicle; J., *daijo*). The Theravāda arose in southern India, whence it spread to Ceylon, Burma, Thailand, Laos, and Cambodia; the Mahāyāna moved from northern India to Tibet, Mongolia, China, Korea, and Japan. In Vietnam both schools may be found.

Unlike Southern Buddhism, which tended to remain conservative and doctrinaire, the Mahāyāna adapted itself to the needs of peoples of diverse racial and cultural backgrounds and varying levels of understanding. Thus in China, to which country Buddhism found its way in the first century, various sects arose which elaborated certain aspects of the Buddha's Dharma in preference to others under the influence of Taoism, Confucianism, and other forms of Chinese culture. Chief among these may be mentioned the T'ien-t'ai (J., Tendai); the Ching-t'u-tsung, that is, the Pure Land (J., Jōdo); the Cha'an (J., Zen); and the Esoteric (J., Shingon) sects. In Tibet, because of unique geography, climate, and strenuous conditions of life, the Tantric elements in the Buddha's Dharma had a preponderant appeal and sects grew up which emphasized this aspect of the Buddha's teaching. In the sixth century the Buddhism that came to Japan from China via Korea was further refined and elaborated by the Japanese in terms of their hierarchical society, their highly developed esthetic sense, and their closeness to nature.

The ideal type in the Mahāyāna became the Bodhisattva, ever ready to sacrifice himself in the interest of those lost in ignorance and despair, even while striving for his own supreme enlightenment. In Theravāda the emphasis falls on the Arhat, who, having single-mindedly overcome his passions and his ego, has gained liberation for himself.

butsudan (J.): literally, "shrine of the Buddha," a Buddhist altar-shrine, a small model of which most Japanese Buddhists maintain in their own home. In addition to a figure of one of the Buddhas or Bodhisattvas, it usually contains a tablet with the names of the family dead. Offerings of food and flowers are regularly offered up to the memory of the deceased at the butsudan, and on special occasions certain sūtras are chanted before it.

cave of Satan: also called the "pit of pseudo-emancipation." This is a stage in zazen where one experiences absolute serenity and is bedeviled into believing it to be Self-realization. It requires an inspired effort to break out and go beyond this state.

Chisha (Ch., Chih-i or Chih-k'ai): founder of the T'ien-t'ai (J., Tendai) Buddhist sect in China. See also "Eight Teachings and Five Periods."

Chuang-tzu (J., Soshi): a Chinese Taoist sage of the fourth century B.C. who expounded the doctrines of Lao-tzu with wit and originality.

Chūhō Myōhon (Ch., Chung-fêng Ming-pên; 1263–1323): A Chinese Zen master. His oft-quoted statement on the significance of the kōan appears in his *"Shan-fang Yeh-hua"* (*"Evening Talks in a Mountain Hut"*).

clouds and water: Novices in Zen monasteries are called *unsui* (literally, "cloud-water") and Zen temple decorations frequently include designs of clouds and water. Clouds move freely, forming and re-forming in response to external conditions and their own nature, unhampered by obstacles. "Water is yielding but all-conquering. Water extinguishes Fire or, finding itself likely to be defeated, escapes as steam and re-forms. Water washes away soft Earth or, when confronted by rocks, seeks a way round. Water corrodes Iron till it crumbles to dust; it saturates the atmosphere so that Wind dies. Water gives way to obstacles with deceptive humility, for no power can prevent it following its destined course to the sea. Water conquers by yielding; it never attacks but always wins the last battle." (Tao Chêng of Nan Yeo, an eleventh-century Taoist scholar, quoted by Blofeld on p. 78 of his *The Wheel of Life*.) These virtues of clouds and water are the virtues of the perfected Zen man, whose life is characterized by freedom, spontaneity, humility, and inner strength, plus the resilience to adapt himself to changing circumstances without strain or anxiety.

Confucius (Ch., K'ung Fu-tzu; J., Kōshi): the celebrated Chinese sage (551–479 B.C.). The backbone of Confucius' moral and religious teachings is his *Analects*.

consciousness (J., *shiki*): Buddhism distinguishes eight classes of consciousness. The first six are the sense of sight, hearing, smell, taste, touch, and thought (intellect). While the intellect, interpreting the data of the senses, creates the illusion of a subject "I" standing apart from an object world, it is not persistently conscious of this "I." Only in the seventh class of (sub)consciousness (Skt., *manas*) is this awareness of a discrete ego-I constant. *Manas* also acts as conveyor of the seed-essence of sensory experiences to the eighth level of (sub)consciousness (Skt., *ālaya-vijñāna*), from which, in response to causes and conditions, specific "seeds" are reconveyed by *manas* to the six senses, precipitating new actions, which in turn produce other "seeds." This process is simultaneous and endless.

The diagram, based on a scheme by Harada-rōshi, shows the relation

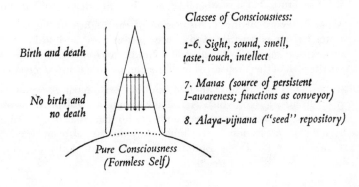

Classes of Consciousness:

Birth and death

1-6. Sight, sound, smell, taste, touch, intellect

7. Manas (source of persistent I-awareness; functions as conveyor)

No birth and no death

8. Alaya-vijnana ("seed" repository)

Pure Consciousness (Formless Self)

of the eight classes of consciousness to birth and death and to birthlessness and deathlessness. The triangular portion stands for the life of the individual, revealing his link to pure consciousness, or formless Self, sometimes called the ninth level of consciousness. This life is not unlike a wave on the vast ocean; its brief existence seems apart from the ocean—and in a sense it is not the ocean—but in *substance* it is not other than the ocean, out of which it arose, into which it will recede, and from which it will emerge again as a new wave. In just the same way, individual consciousness issues from pure consciousness and in its essential nature is indistinguishable from it. Their common element, the viable Void, is shown in the diagram by the all-pervading white background.

daishi (J.): literally, "great master," this Buddhist title is usually conferred posthumously.

Daitoku-ji (Temple of Great Virtue): a large Rinzai temple complex in Kyoto, Japan, founded in 1327 by Daito-kokushi, that is, Daito, Teacher to the Nation. Daitoku-ji is the possessor of many art treasures, among them paintings by the Zen painter Mu-ch'i (J., Mokkei).

delusion, illusion: To be deluded is to be totally deceived. Delusion implies a belief in something that is contrary to reality. Illusion, on the other hand, suggests that what is seen has objective reality but is misinterpreted or seen falsely. In Buddhism, delusion is ignorance, an unawareness of the true nature of things or of the real meaning of existence. We are deluded or led astray by our senses (which include the intellect and its discriminating thoughts) insofar as they cause us to accept the phenomenal world as the Whole of reality when in fact it is but a limited and ephemeral aspect of reality, and to act as though the world is external to us when in truth it is but a reflection of ourselves. This does not mean that the relative world has no reality whatever. When the masters say all phenomena are illusory, they mean that compared with Mind itself the world apprehended by the senses is such a partial and limited aspect of Truth that it is dreamlike. See also "Six Realms of Existence."

Denko-roku (Record of the Transmission of the Light): by Japanese Zen master Keizan, consisting of fifty-three lectures on the Buddha and the patriarchs, compiled by his disciples. Not to be confused with the *Dento-roku* (Record of the Transmission of the Lamp), by a Chinese Zen master.

Dharma (Skt.; J., *ho*): a fundamental Buddhist term having several meanings, the broadest of which is 1) "phenomenon." All phenomena are subject to the law of causation, and this fundamental truth comprises the core of the Buddha's teaching. Thus dharma also means: 2) law, 3) ultimate truth, 4) the Buddha's teaching, and 5) the doctrines of Buddhism.

"Dharma dueling" (J., *hossen*): a verbal joust or battle of "wit" as respects the Dharma, usually between two enlightened persons. In practice it is sometimes difficult to draw a clear distinction between hossen and mondo, but generally speaking, a mondo involves only a question and an answer, while a hossen can develop into an extended encounter. Dharma dueling is the typical Zen method of demonstrating Truth without recourse to logical conceptions. See also "mondo."

Dharma successor (J., *hassu*): a Zen disciple who has reached the same degree of enlightenment as his master and been given permission to carry on his line of teaching. It implies, of course, *inka*. A Dharma successor may be a layman or laywoman. Hui-neng (J., Enō), the Sixth Patriarch, was a layman when he received the seal of transmission from the Fifth Patriarch.

Diamond sūtra (Skt., Vajracchedikā Prajñā Pāramitā; J., Kongo-kyo): One of the most profound of the Mahayana sūtras, this sūtra concludes with the words: "This sacred exposition shall be known as the Vajracchedikā Prajñā Pāramitā sūtra because it is hard and sharp like a diamond, cutting off all arbitrary conceptions and leading to the other shore of Enlightenment."

dokusan: a private encounter with the rōshi in his teaching chamber. The general term for a formal appearance before the rōshi is *sanzen*. There are three types of sanzen: *sōsan*, or listening to the rōshi's general lectures on Zen practice, usually in a group—compulsory for all beginners; dokusan, or going singly before the rōshi at given periods—optional; *naisan*, or visiting the rōshi "secretly" at any time, day or night, when special circumstances warrant it. At Yasutani-rōshi's sesshin, dokusan took place three times daily: at 5 A.M., 3 P.M., and 7 P.M.

Dorin (Ch., Tao-lin): a well-known Zen master of the T'ang period. He was popularly called Niao-k'ê (Bird's Nest) from his habit of doing zazen among the branches of trees. See also "Hakurakuten."

ego: According to Buddhism, the notion of an ego, that is, awareness of oneself as a discrete individuality, is an illusion. It arises because, misled by our bifurcating intellect (the sixth sense) into postulating the dualism of "myself" and "not-myself," we are led to think and act as though we were a separated entity confronted by a world external to us. Thus in the unconscious the idea of "I," or selfhood, becomes fixed, and from this arise such thought patterns as "I hate this, I love that; this is mine, that is yours." Nourished by this fodder, the ego-I comes to dominate the personality, attacking whatever threatens its position and grasping at anything which will enlarge its power. Antagonism, greed, and alienation, culminating in suffering, are the inevitable consequences of this circular process.

Eight Teachings and Five Periods: a classification of the Buddha's teachings from the standpoint of the Tendai sect, made by its Chinese founder, Chih-i. These are divided into four doctrines plus four methods of expounding them and represent five stages of instruction given by the Buddha, from the earliest to the last and highest.

Eisai Myōan (1141–1215): The Zen sect in Japan formally begins with Eisai, a priest of high rank who had mastered the teachings of Buddhism at Mount Hiei, the foremost Buddhist center of learning, in Kyoto, in the Middle Ages. He made two trips to China, where he learned the practices of Zen at several monasteries, including the famous Zen monastery of T'ien-t'ung (J., Tendō). Upon his return to Japan in 1191 he brought the Rinzai teachings as well as tea seeds. Thus Eisai came to be known as the father of Zen and tea cultivation in Japan.

Engaku-ji (Temple of Full Enlightenment): This well-known Zen monastery was founded in Kamakura, Japan, in 1282 by the Regent Hōjō Tokimune, an ardent patron of Buddhism. Engaku-ji is the headquarters of many sub-temples scattered throughout Japan.

enlightenment: Self-realization. As used herein the term has no connection with the eighteenth-century philosophical movement characterized by rationalism. See also "kenshō" and "satori."

Enō (more fully, Daikan Enō-zenji; also Rokuso-daishi, the Sixth Zen Patriarch; Ch., Hui-nêng or Wei-lang; 638–713): One of the most distinguished of the Chinese masters of the T'ang era. Zen lore abounds with stories about him: that he was so poor he had to sell firewood to support his widowed mother; that he was illiterate; that he became enlightened in his youth upon hearing a passage from the Diamond sūtra; that he was selected to become the Sixth Patriarch through a verse he had written demonstrating his profound insight.

five deadly sins: 1) killing one's father, 2) killing one's mother, 3) killing an Arhat, 4) shedding the blood of a Buddha, 5) destroying the harmony of the Buddhist *saṅgha*.

Five Degrees of Tōzan (J., *go-i*): Like the Ten Oxherding Verses, these are different levels or degrees of Zen realization formulated by Zen master Tōzan Ryōkai (Ch., Tung-shan Liang chieh). In Japanese these five, in ascending scale, are known as 1) *shō-chū-hen*, 2) *hen-chū-shō*, 3) *shō-chū-rai*, 4) *hen-chū-shi*, and 5) *ren-chū-tō*. The key terms are *shō* and *hen*, which are two mutually related aspects of the One. Some of their complementary attributes are as follows (in each case the *shō* is followed by the *hen*): absolute, relative; emptiness, form-and-color; equality, differ-ence; oneness, manyness; absolute self, relative self. The *chū*, which can mean "within" or "among," expresses the interrelation of the *shō* and the *hen*.

1) Shō-chū-hen. At this level of realization the world of phenomena is dominant, but it is perceived as a dimension of the absolute Self. 2) Hen-chū-shō. At this second stage the undifferentiated aspect comes strongly to the fore and diversity recedes into the background. 3) Shō-chū-rai. The third grade is a level of realization wherein no awareness of body or mind remains; both "drop away" completely. 4) Hen-chū-shi. With this degree the singularity of each object is perceived at its highest degree of uniqueness. Now a cup is a Cup is a CUP. 5) Ken-chū-tō. In the fifth and highest grade, form and Emptiness mutually penetrate to such a degree that no longer is there consciousness of either. Ideas of satori or delusion entirely vanish. This is the stage of perfect inner freedom.

Four Modes of Birth (J., *shishō*): 1) birth through the womb, 2) birth through eggs hatched outside the body, 3) birth through moisture, and 4) birth through metamorphosis.

Four Vows (J., *shiku seigan*): 1) All beings, without number, I vow to liberate. 2) Endless blind passions I vow to uproot. 3) Dharma gates (that is, levels of truth), beyond measure, I vow to penetrate. 4) The Great Way of Buddha I vow to attain. These vows are as old as Mahāyāna Buddhism, being allied with the vows of a Bodhisattva. In the Zen temple they are recited three times in succession after the close of zazen. In the sūtra bearing his name the Sixth Patriarch gives these vows a profound interpretation.

gasshō (J.): the gesture of raising the hands palm to palm to indicate respect, gratitude, or humility, or all three.

Genki Taji-rōshi: a rōshi-disciple of Harada-rōshi. He died in 1953 at the age of sixty-four.

godō (J.): in the Sōtō sect the head monk in charge of the zendō, next in rank to the rōshi. The position of *jikijitsu* in the Rinzai sect approxi-mates that of the godō.

Hakuin Ekaku (1686–1769): One of the most versatile and brilliant of the Japanese Zen masters, Hakuin is often called the father of modern Rinzai by reason of the fact that he single-handedly revitalized the Rinzai teachings, which had been steadily declining, through his systematization of the kōans. Not only was Hakuin an outstanding master; he was a highly accomplished painter, calligrapher, and sculptor. *Sekishu,* or

"What is the sound of one hand?" which he devised, is the best-known kōan by a Japanese master. His popular *Zazen Wasan* (Chant in Praise of Zazen), frequently recited in Zen temples, begins: "From the beginning all beings are Buddha" and ends: "This earth where we stand is the pure lotus land, and this very body the body of Buddha."

Hakurakuten (Ch., Pai Yueh T'ien): To quote from Suzuki's third series of *Essays in Zen Buddhism* (p. 368): "Pai Yueh T'ien was a great poet of the T'ang [dynasty]. When he was officiating as governor in a certain district there was a Zen master within his jurisdiction popularly known as Niao-k'ê, the 'Bird's Nest,' for he used to practice his meditation on a seat made of the thickly growing branches of a tree. The governor-poet once visited him and said: 'What a dangerous seat you have up in the tree!' 'Yours is far worse than mine,' retorted the master. 'I am the governor of this district and I don't see what danger there is in it.' 'Then you don't know yourself! When your passions burn and your mind is unsteady, what is more dangerous than that?' The governor then asked: 'What is the teaching of Buddhism?' The master recited this famous stanza [appearing in a number of Mahāyāna and Hīnayāna sūtras]: Not to commit evils, / But to practice all good, / And to keep the heart pure— / This is the teaching of the Buddhas. Pai, however, protested: 'Any child three years old knows that.' 'Any child three years old may know it, but even an old man of eighty years finds it difficult to practice.' So concluded the Zen master up in the tree."

hanka (J.): the half-lotus posture. See also section ix.

Hekigan-roku (Ch., Pi-yen lu; Blue Rock Collection): probably the most famous Zen book, consisting of one hundred kōans compiled by Zen master Hsüeh-tou Ch'ung-hsien (J., Setchō Jūken; 980–1052), with his own commentary in verse accompanying each kōan. Every kōan is preceded by an introduction containing the gist of the kōan, by Zen master Yüan Wu (J., Bukka Engo; 1063–1135). The book derived its name from a scroll containing the Chinese characters for "blue" and "rock" which happened to be hanging in the temple where the collection was compiled, and which the compiler decided to use as a title for his wòrk.

Hō-koji (J.; Ch., P'ang Yün): literally, "the lay disciple Hō"; a T'ang-dynasty great Zen figure and man of means who, it is recorded, dumped his entire fortune of gold into the river and thereafter wandered about the country with his family, earning his living as a maker of bamboo ware and engaging in "Dharma dueling" with famous Zen masters.

Hosshin-ji (Monastery for Awakening the Bodhi-Mind): a Sōtō sect monastery located in Obama, Fukui Prefecture, Japan, of which Harada-rōshi was chief abbot for over forty years.

hotsugammon (J.): a vow or a petition. Dogen's *hotsugammon*, comprised of selections from his *Shobogenzo*, is chanted regularly in Zen monasteries.

Hyakujō Ekai (Ch., Pai-chang Huai-hai; 720–814): an outstanding Zen master, the first to establish a Zen monastic community in China with precise rules and regulations and the emphasis on manual labor.

Ikkyū Sōjun (1394–1481): A former abbot of Daitoku-ji, the large Rinzai monastery in Kyoto, Ikkyū is known in Zen history as much for his profound irreverent wit, expressed in numerous verses, as for his deep Zen insight. Both of these qualities can be seen in this poem, written by him at the age of eighty-seven as death approached: "Dimly, for thirty years; / Faintly for thirty years— / Dimly and faintly for sixty years; / At my death I pass my feces and offer them to Brahma." (Translation by R. H. Blyth)

inka shōmei (J.; seal of approval): Inka, as it is popularly called, is formal acknowledgment on the part of the master that his disciple has fully completed his training under him—in other words, "graduated." With masters who use the kōan system it implies that the disciple has passed all the kōans prescribed by that master. The bestowal of inka by masters who do not use kōans signifies their satisfaction with their disciple's level of understanding. One who receives inka may or may not be given permission by his master to begin teaching, for much depends on the depth of the student's enlightenment, the strength of his character, and the maturity of his personality. Obviously, much also depends on the personal qualities of the rōshi himself. If he is wise and accomplished, with high standards, his permission to teach will not be lightly given. But if he is mediocre, very likely his disciple, inka or no, will be "a poor stamp of a poor stamp." In Zen it is often said, "The fruit can be no better than the tree that produced it."

iron wall and silver mountain: metaphors to describe the sense of frustration of those who reach a certain point in their practice beyond which they cannot penetrate. One is unable to smash one's way through an iron wall or gain a foothold on a silver mountain.

jewel sword of the Vajra king: a metaphorical expression for indestructible Mind. See also "vajra."

Jizō (J.; Skt., Kshitigarbha): This Bodhisattva of benevolence and mercy is a beloved figure in Japanese Buddhism. On a popular level Jizō is not only the special protector of children but also the mentor and guide of any who are in danger of going astray. Stone statues of Jizō, with his monk's staff in one hand and his shaven head, can be seen at crossroads or intersections or at a spot where a child has suffered an unnatural death.

Jōshū Jūshin (Ch., Chao-chou Ts'ung-shên; 778–897): a renowned master of the T'ang period. His Mu is the best known of all kōans. Chao-chou is said to have attained kenshō at the age of eighteen and complete awakening at fifty-four. From fifty-four to eighty he made pilgrimages about China, staying with prominent masters and engaging in "Dharma dueling" with them. Not until he was eighty did he formally open a monastery and begin to teach. He then continued to instruct students until his death, at one hundred and twenty.

Like his master, Nan-ch'üan (J., Nansen), Chao-chou was mild-mannered. He eschewed the vigorous speech and violent actions of a Rinzai, yet his wisdom and acumen in dealing with students was such that he could convey more with gentle sarcasm or a tilt of the eyebrow than other masters could with a shout or a crack of the stick. This is clear from the numerous kōans which revolve around him. Chao-chou is highly admired in Japan.

kalpa: One of the sūtras defines a kalpa as the period of time it would take a heavenly being descending from heaven once a year and making one sweep of its wings across the top of a mile-high mountain to wear it down level with the ground.

Kamakura era: the troubled period in Japanese history (from about 1192 to 1336) that saw the seat of government moved to Kamakura and the rise of the Zen, Nichiren, and Pure Land sects.

Kannon (J.—also Kwannon, Kanzeon; Skt., Avalokitesvara; Ch., Kuan Yin): "The Great Compassionate One," Kannon is the Bodhisattva of all-embracing love and benevolence. He plays a central role in the devotional practices of all Buddhist sects. Although originally male, Kannon has become a feminine figure in the popular imagination in Asia.

karma (J., *gō*): One of the fundamental doctrines of Buddhism, karma is action and reaction, the continuing process of cause and effect. Thus our present life and circumstances are the product of our past thoughts and actions, and in the same way our deeds in this life will fashion our future mode of existence. The word "karma" is also used in the sense of evil bent of mind resulting from past wrongful actions. See also "birth-and-death," "consciousness," and "Six Realms of Existence."

katsu or *kwatz* (J.; Ch., *ho*): Though this exclamation has no exact meaning, it conveys a great deal. It is used by the masters to sweep from the mind of the student all dualistic, ego-centered thoughts. The expression is most often associated with Lin-chi (J., Rinzai), whose shouting and stick-wielding are legendary in Zen. Lin-chi distinguished four kinds of katsu: "Sometimes it is like the jewel sword of the Vajra king; sometimes it is like the golden-haired lion crouching on the ground; sometimes it is like a grass-tipped decoy pole; and sometimes it is no katsu at all."

Keihō Shūmitsu (Ch., Kuei-fêng Tsung-mi): a Zen master of great learning in the T'ang era.

keisu (pronounced "kay-su"): a bronze bowl-shaped gong used during chanting by all Buddhist sects in Japan. It is struck on the rim by a small padded club held with both hands.

Keizan Jōkin (1268–1325): the Fourth Patriarch of the Japanese Sōtō sect in line after Dōgen; founder of Sōji-ji, one of the two head Sōtō monasteries. The *Denkō-roku* is a compilation of his works.

kendō (literally, "the way of the sword"): Japanese-style fencing in which the sword is wielded with both hands. Traditionally, kendō adepts have disciplined themselves in Zen, the better to develop alert, wholehearted response and a fearless acceptance of death.

kenshō (literally, "seeing into one's own nature"): Semantically, kenshō and satori have virtually the same meaning and are often used interchangeably. In describing the enlightenment of the Buddha and the patriarchs, however, it is customary to use the word *satori* rather than kenshō, the term satori implying a deeper experience. (The exact Japanese expression for full enlightenment is *daigo tettei.*) When the word *godō* (literally, "the way of enlightenment") is combined with the term "kenshō," the latter word becomes more subjective and emphatic.

kōan (Ch., *kung-an;* pronounced in Japanese as two syllables, *kō-an*): Its original meaning in Chinese was a case which established a legal precedent. In Zen a kōan is a formulation, in baffling language, pointing to ultimate truth. Kōans cannot be solved by recourse to logical reasoning but only by awakening a deeper level of the mind beyond the discursive intellect. Kōans are constructed from the questions of disciples of old together with the responses of their masters, from portions of the masters' sermons or discourses, from lines of the sūtras, and from other teachings.

The word or phrase into which the kōan resolves itself when grappled with as a spiritual exercise is called in Japanese the *watō* (Ch., *hua t'ou*). Thus "Has a dog the Buddha-nature?" together with Joshu's answer, "Mu!" constitutes the kōan; "Mu!" itself is the watō.

Altogether there are said to be 1,700 kōans. Of these, Japanese Zen masters use a core of 500, more or less, since many are repetitive and others less valuable for practice. Masters have their own preferences, but invariably they employ (if they employ kōans at all) the *Mumonkan* and *Hekigan-roku* compilations of kōans. A disciple who completes his training under Yasutani-rōshi must pass the following kōans and other types of problems in this order: miscellaneous kōans, 50; *Mumonkan* (with verses), 96; *Hekigan-roku*, 100; *Shōyō-roku*, *100; Denkō-roku* (with verses), 110; *Jūjūkinkai* and others, 90; making a total of 546.

Kōbō-daishi (774–835): one of the most revered names in Japanese Buddhism. Kūkai, as he was known during his lifetime, brought Shingon Buddhism to Japan from China, where he studied it for three years. He is famous equally as an outstanding religious teacher, a talented man of letters, an artist, and an unsurpassed calligrapher. As well the inventor of the *hiragana* syllabary, he is regarded by the Japanese as one of their great benefactors.

Kōgaku-ji: literally, "Temple Facing the Mountain" (the mountain being Mount Fuji); founded by Zen master Bassui and located in the town of Enzan, Yamanashi Prefecture, Japan.

kotsu: the rōshi's baton or stick, about fifteen inches long and shaped like the human spine, used by him to emphasize a point or sometimes to rap a student.

kriyā meditation: a type of meditation used in certain branches of yoga.

Lao-tzu (J., Rōshi): Though Lao-tzu is commonly regarded as one of China's greatest sages, little is known about his actual life. He is said to have been born about 604 B.C. and to be the author of the *Tao Teh Ching* (The Way and Its Power; J., Dotokkyō), which is the bible of Taoism, as the religion which grew up around this book came to be called. The Tao has been defined as the ground of all existence, or as the power of the universe.

lotus: In Buddhism the lotus is the symbol of the purity and perfection of the Buddha-nature which is intrinsic to all. "Just as the Lotus grows up from the darkness of the mud to the surface of the water, opening its blossom only after it has raised itself beyond the surface, and remaining unsullied from both earth and water, which nourished it—in the same way the mind, born in the human body, unfolds its true qualities ('petals') after it has raised itself beyond the turbid floods of passion and ignorance, and transforms the dark powers of the depths into the radiantly pure nectar of Enlightenment-consciousness." (Govinda, p. 89)

lotus posture (Skt., *padmāsana):* the position in which the Buddha is iconographically depicted sitting on a lotus. See section IX.

Lotus sūtra (also Sūtra of the Lotus of the Wonderful Law; Skt., Saddharma Pundarīka; J., Myōhō Renge-kyō, also known as Hokke-kyō): This Mahāyāna sūtra, said to date from the first century A.D., has had a wide influence among Buddhists of China and Japan. "In vivid language overpowering the imagination it relates the final discourse on Vulture Peak of Shākyamuni before his entry into Nirvāna. Here he offers to his assembled disciples a vision of infinite Buddha-worlds, illuminated by Buddhas revealing the Truth to innumerable disciples, just as Shākyamuni does in this world. This is a foreshadowing of the later revelation that Shākyamuni is just one manifestation of the Eternal Buddha, who appears in these infinite realms whenever men threaten to be engulfed by evil . . . Shākyamuni proceeds to explain why it has been necessary for him first to preach the Hīnayāna doctrine, intended for the self-improvement of individuals, as a preparation for the final revelation of Universal Salvation . . ." (From *The Lotus of the Wonderful Law,* an abridged translation by W. E. Soothill, quoted in *Sources of Japanese Tradition,* edited by William Theodore de Bary, p. 121.)

mandala: see "Tantric Buddhism."

Manjusri: see "Samantabhadra and Manjusri."

mantra: see "Tantric Buddhism."

maya: This Sanskrit word is usually defined as illusion, but māyā is merely the medium through which we measure and appraise the phenomenal world. It is the cause of illusion when this world of form is incorrectly perceived as static and unchanging. When it is seen for what it is, namely, a living flux grounded in Emptiness, māyā is Bodhi, or inherent wisdom. See also "delusion."

Meiji Restoration: the event in Japanese history (1867) that marked the downfall of the Tokugawa shogunate, the restoration of power to the Emperor Meiji, and the beginning of the Meiji period (1867–1912).

Mencius (Ch., Meng-tzu; J., Mōshi; fourth century B.C.): a Chinese philosopher-sage. *The Book of Mencius,* his main work, is considered to be one of the classic commentaries on the Confucian writings.

mind (J., *kokoro* or *shin*): Ask the ordinary Japanese where his mind is and the chances are he will point to his heart or chest. Ask the same question of a Westerner and he will indicate his head. These two responses illustrate the difference between the conception of mind in the East and that in the West. The word *kokoro,* which is translated by the English *mind,* also means "heart," "spirit," "psyche," or "soul." Mind (with a small "m") as used in this book, therefore, means more than the seat of the intellect. Mind with a capital "M" stands for absolute reality. From the standpoint of Zen experience, Mind (or mind) is total awareness—in other words, *just* hearing when listening, *only* seeing when looking, etc.

The expression "open the mind's eye" is another way of speaking of the experience of satori or Self-realization. ". . . place the mind's eye . . ." means to direct the summation point, or focus of attention, of one's entire being.

Miroku (J.; Skt., Maitreya, the "Great Loving One"): the Bodhisattva who will become a full Buddha in the next world cycle to lead men to liberation from self-bondage.

mokugyo (literally, "wooden fish"): The mokugyo is a hollowed-out roundish wooden block, fashioned after some sort of sea creature, with a long horizontal slit for resonance, employed as an accompaniment to sūtra chanting in Buddhist temples. When struck by a padded stick it emits a distinctive sound. Originally Chinese, this wooden drum may be as large as three feet in height or small enough to hold in the lap. Frequently it is lacquered bright red. Fish, since they never sleep, are symbolic in Zen of the alertness and watchfulness required of the aspirant to Buddhahood.

mondō (literally, "question and answer"): a uniquely Zen type of dialogue between a master and a student wherein the student asks a question on Buddhism which has deeply perplexed him, and the master, skirting theory and logic, replies in such a way as to evoke an answer from the deeper levels of the student's intuitive mind. See also "Dharma dueling."

monk (priest): The Japanese language makes no distinction between the two religious types described by the English words "monk" and "priest." *Obo-san* (or less respectfully, *bōzu*) is the general term for an ordained disciple of the Buddha. There are two other related expressions: *unsui*, a novice training in a Zen monastery (see "clouds and water"), and *oshō-san*, the designation for the master, or head, of any Buddhist temple. The ancient Chinese and Japanese Zen masters and their disciples designated in English as monks were men who had taken the Mahāyāna vows to tread the Buddha's Path and who, unmarried, lived the simple life of Truth-seekers either as members of a monastic community or as itinerant followers of the Way. In present-day Japan those who most nearly approach this monkish ideal are the Zen monastery rōshi and the disciples training under them, although a few married men can be found even among them.

The English word "priest" is usually applied to obo-san resident in temples, who perform various Buddhist rites for their members, give instruction in Buddhist doctrine, and occasionally conduct zazen classes if their temple happens to belong to the Zen sect. Those among them of the stature of a rōshi hold periodic sesshin in their own temples, as well as elsewhere, chiefly for lay people. Most Japanese priests are married, living with their families in the temple inherited from their father. Nowadays neither the Zen sect nor any other Japanese Buddhist sect demands celibacy of its priests, though Zen nuns, whether resident in a nunnery (called *ni-sōdō* in Japanese) or in their own temple, are forbidden to marry. See also "temple."

mudrā: see "Tantric Buddhism."

Mumonkan (J.; Ch., Wu-mên-kuan; The Gateless Barrier): This book of forty-eight kōans, with comments in prose and verse by the compiler, Zen master Wu-mên Hui-k'ai (J., Mumon Ekai), is, next to the *Hekigan-roku*, the best-known collection of Chinese kōans. The verse accompanying each kōan is usually treated as a separate kōan.

Nakagawa-rōshi: see "Sōen Nakagawa-rōshi."

Nangaku Ejō (Ch., Nan-yuëh Huai-jang): an outstanding T'ang-dynasty Zen master; a disciple of Hui-neng, the Sixth Patriarch.

Nichiren sect: a Japanese Buddhist sect founded by Nichiren (1222–82). Nichiren believers devotedly recite "Namu Myōhō Renge-kyō" (I trust in the Sūtra of the Lotus of the Wonderful Law) to the vigorous accompaniment of their own drum-beating.

nirvāna (Skt.; J., *nehan*): extinction of ignorance and craving and awakening to inner Peace and Freedom. Nirvāna (with a small "n") stands against saṁsāra, that is, birth-and death. Nirvāna is also used in the sense of a return to the original purity of the Buddha-nature after the dissolution of the physical body, that is, to the perfect freedom of the unconditioned state.

Nirvāna sūtra (J., Nehan-kyō; Skt., Mahā-parinirvāṇa sūtra): Among other things, this sūtra contains the last words of the Buddha.

Nōh: the highly refined classical Japanese dance-drama.

Nyojō (Ch., Ju-ching; 1163–1238): the Chinese Zen master under whom Dōgen was enlightened in China at T'ien-t'ung (J., Tendō) monastery.

Ōbaku Kiun (Ch., Huang-po Hsi-yün; ?–850): another of the outstanding Zen masters of the T'ang period. One of his most celebrated disciples was Lin-chi (J., Rinzai).

Ōbaku sect (J., Ōbaku-shū): This Zen sect was introduced into Japan from China in 1654 by Zen master Yin-yuan (J. Ingen). Its head temple, built in the Chinese style, is Mampukuji, near Kyoto. Ōbaku is the least influential of the Zen sects in present-day Japan.

Oṁ: This sacred syllable is one of the principal mantra in tantric Buddhism.

"One more step!": a phrase often used by the rōshi in dokusan to imply that the student's mind has reached a point where it needs one final thrust or leap to come to its own Self-realization. It is not a definable position, but a state the rōshi senses in each individual.

oneness: With a small "o" this word means absorption to the point of self-forgetfulness. With a capital "O" it refers to the experience of the Void or Emptiness.

parinirvāna: literally, "complete extinction." This term most frequently refers to the passing away of the Buddha.

Patañjali: the putative compiler of a book of yoga aphorisms dealing with the philosophy, the disciples, and the techniques of meditation "leading to knowledge of the Godhead." So little is known of Patañjali that guesses as to the date of his work range all the way from the fourth century B.C. to the fourth century A.D.

patriarchs (J., soshigata): The patriarchs are the great masters who have received and formally transmitted the Buddha's Dharma. They number twenty-eight in India and six in China (Bodhidharma was both the twenty-eighth in India and the first in China). The Sixth Patriarch, Hui-neng, never formally passed on the patriarchy to his successor, so it lapsed. However, the outstanding masters of succeeding generations, both Chinese and Japanese, are loosely designated patriarchs by the Japanese, or elders by the Chinese, out of reverence and respect for their high attainments.

Prajñā Pāramitā Hridaya (Skt.; J., Hannya Haramita Shingyō): this heart of the Prajñā Pāramitā sūtra is recited so frequently in the temple that most Zen students chant it from memory. Its theme is: "Form is no other than Emptiness, Emptiness no other than form." Prajñā pāramitā means literally "the wisdom that leads to the other shore," that is, intuitive wisdom.

precepts (J., kairitsu): Formally to become a Zen Buddhist one must be initiated, that is, receive the precepts in a formal ceremony (called jukai in Japanese) wherein one pledges to give himself up wholly to the Three Treasures of Buddhism (q.v.); to keep the ten cardinal precepts; to avoid evil and practice goodness; and to strive toward the liberation of every sentient being. Zen master Dogen has written that the formal taking of the precepts is an essential step toward Buddhahood.

The ten cardinal Mahāyāna precepts (J., *jūjūkinkai*) exhort one to refrain from 1) the taking of life, 2) theft, 3) unchastity, 4) lying, 5) selling or buying alcoholic liquor (that is, causing others to drink or drinking oneself), 6) speaking of the shortcomings of others, 7) praising oneself and reviling others, 8) giving spiritual or material aid grudgingly, 9) anger, and 10) disparaging the Three Treasures. These are the same for laymen and monks.

The observance of the percepts is important not alone for ethical reasons. Because one cannot progress on the road to enlightenment unless his mind is free of the inner disturbance which thoughtless or wanton behavior produces, the precepts are the foundation of spiritual practice. Few novices, however, regardless of the strength of their resolve, are able to uphold every one of the commandments, so transgressions in one degree or another are inevitable. Such violations do not debar one from pursuing the Buddha's Way provided one acknowledges them, truly repents, and exerts himself to live by the precepts in the future. Transgressions become less frequent as one advances on the Way and through zazen gains in strength and purity and insight. But what is permanently damaging—in fact, fatal to one's spiritual progress—is loss of faith in the Buddha, in the Truth he revealed through his enlightenment experience, and in the confirmatory words of the patriarchs. In this event, full enlightenment—and with it the eradication of the root-source of evil, namely, ignorance and delusion—is virtually impossible.

priest: see "monk."

Pure Land (J., Jōdo): a metaphorical expression for the world of truth and purity revealed in enlightenment.

Pure Land sects (J., Jōdo-shū or Nembutsu-shū): The central doctrine of the Pure Land sects is that all who evoke the name of Amida (q.v.) with sincerity and faith in the saving grace of his vow will be reborn in his Pure Land of peace and bliss. The most important meditational practice in the Pure Land sects, therefore, is the constant voicing of the words *namu Amida butsu* (I surrender myself to Amida Buddha). In Japanese this invocation is termed *nembutsu* (*nem*, "yearning for," "surrendering to"; *butsu*, Buddha).

The Japanese Pure Land sect was established in 1175 by Hōnen, a wise and saintly monk. And his illustrious disciple, Shinran, in his turn became the central figure of the Pure Land sect called Jōdo-Shin or Shin (True Pure Land). See also "Amitabha."

Rinzai Gigen (Ch., Lin-chi I-hsüan; ?–867): the famed Chinese master of the T'ang period around whose teachings a special sect bearing his name was formed. Rinzai's *Collected Sayings* (Rinzai-roku) is a text widely used by Rinzai masters in Japan. Rinzai is famous for his vivid speech and forceful pedagogical methods.

Rinzai sect: The Rinzai teachings were firmly established in Japan by Fisai. The Rinzai sect is particularly strong in Kyoto, where many of its head temples and monasteries are located.

rohatsu sesshin: the sesshin commemorating the Buddha's own enlightenment, which is said to have taken place on December 8. It is the severest sesshin not only because it is the coldest, the last before sesshin are suspended for the winter months, but also because the rōshi and the head monks make the heaviest demands upon the participants in order that they may achieve awakening during this sesshin.

rōshi (literally, "venerable teacher"): Traditionally, training in Zen is under a rōshi, who may be a layman or a laywoman as well as a monk or priest. The function of a rōshi is to guide and inspire his disciples along the path to Self-realization; he does not attempt directly to control or influence their private lives.

In olden days rōshi was a hard-won title, conferred by the public on one who had mastered the Buddha's Dharma from the inside (which is to say through his own direct experience of Truth), who had integrated it into his own life, and who could lead others to this same experience. As a minimum it implied a pure, steadfast character and a mature personality. To become a full-fledged rōshi demanded years of practice and study, full enlightenment, and the seal of approval of one's own teacher, followed by years of ripening through "Dharma dueling" with other masters. Nowadays the standards are less rigid, but the title rōshi, if it is legitimately come by, is still a title of distinction. Unfortunately, many in Japan today are addressed as rōshi simply out of respect for their advanced age, and little more. Masters in the true sense of the word are rare.

Ryūtaku-ji (Monastery of the Pond Dragon): a Rinzai monastery founded by Hakuin, located outside Mishima City in Shizuoka Prefecture, Japan. The dragon (that is, the oriental, not the occidental), with its superhuman powers, symbolizes absolute Mind.

samādhi (Skt.; J., *zammai* or *sammai*): This term has a variety of meanings. In Zen it implies not merely equilibrium, tranquility, and one-pointedness, but a state of intense yet effortless concentration, of complete absorption of the mind in itself, of heightened and expanded awareness. Samādhi and Bodhi are identical from the view of the enlightened Bodhi-mind. Seen from the developing stages leading to satori-awakening, however, samādhi and enlightenment are different.

Samantabhadra and Mañjusri (Skt.; J., Fugen and Monju): Samantabhadra embodies calm action, compassion, and deep-seated wisdom. He is usually depicted astride a white elephant (the elephant being noted for its tranquility and wisdom), sitting in attendance on the right of the Buddha, while the Bodhisattva Mañjusri, with his delusion-cutting vajra sword in one hand, sits on the back of a lion on the Buddha's left. Mañjusri represents awakening, that is, the sudden realization of the Oneness of all existence and the power rising therefrom, of which the lion's vigor is symbolic. When the knowledge acquired through satori is employed for the benefit of mankind, Samantabhadra's compassion is manifesting itself. Accordingly, each of the Bodhisattvas is an arm of the Buddha, representing, respectively, Oneness (or Equality) and manyness.

saṁsāra: see "birth-and-death."

satori (J.): enlightenment, that is, Self-realization, opening the Mind's eye, awakening to one's True-nature and hence of the nature of all existence. See also "kenshō."

seiza: the traditional Japanese posture of sitting, with the back straight and the buttocks resting on the heels.

Sekitō Kisen (Ch., Shih-t'ou Hsi-ch'ien, 700–90): a leading Chinese Zen master of the T'ang period. He acquired the name Sekitō (literally, "rock top") from the fact that he lived in a hut he had built for himself on a large flat rock.

Self-realization: the realization of Mind; satori.

Sesshū Tōyō (1420–1506): Not only was Sesshū an accomplished Zen monk who had spent some twenty years at Shōkoku-ji, a large Zen monastery in Kyoto and one of the centers of art, culture, and learning in medieval Japan, but he is generally acknowledged to be Japan's most accomplished master of the suiboku (water and India ink) style of painting. The celebrated picture of Bodhidharma and his disciple Hui-k'e (see pp. 138 and 356–57 for descriptions) was painted by Sesshū in his seventy-seventh year.

Shingon (True Words; Skt., Mantrayana): The doctrines and practices of this sect of Buddhism were brought from China to Japan in the ninth century by Kūkai (or Kōbō-daishi, as he is more popularly known). Shingon discipline and practice revolve around three meditational devices: the maṇḍala, the mantra, and the mudrā. See also "Tantric Buddhism."

Shōbōgenzō Zuimonki: a collection of instructional talks and comments by Japanese Zen master Dōgen (1200–1253), recorded by his disciple-successor, Ejō.

Shōyō-roku (Ch., Ts'ung-jung lu; Record of Great Serenity): a book of one hundred kōans compiled by Hung-chih Chêng-chüeh (J., Wanshi Shō-kaku), a Chinese Sōtō Zen master of repute. The title is derived from the name of Wanshi's hermitage, Shōyō-an (Hermitage of Great Serenity).

Shushōgi: a classification of Dōgen's Shōbōgenzō according to the doctrines of the Sōtō sect, made by Ouchi Seiran, a Japanese priest-scholar, during the Meiji era.

sitting: immobile zazen.

Six Realms of Existence (J., *rokudō*): In ascending scale these are the realms of hell (J., *jigoku*), pretas (or hungry ghosts; J., *gaki*), beasts (J., *chikushō*), asuras (or fighting demons; J., *shura*), human beings (J., *ningen*), and devas (or heavenly beings; J., *tenjō*). All creatures in these realms are tied to the ceaseless round of birth-and-death, that is, to the law of causation, according to which existence on any one of these planes is determined by antecedent actions. In Buddhism these planes are depicted as the spokes or segments of the "wheel of life." This "wheel" is set in motion by actions stemming from our basic ignorance of the true nature of existence and by karmic propensities from an incalculable past, and kept revolving by our craving for the pleasures of the senses and by our clinging to them, which leads to an unending cycle of births, deaths, and rebirths to which we remain bound. The Six Realms are the worlds of the unenlightened.

Buddhism also speaks of four realms of enlightened existence, sometimes called the "four holy states." In ascending order these are the worlds of *sravakas, pratyekabuddhas, bodhisattvas,* and full *buddhas.* A sravaka is one who hears the teaching of the Buddha and accepts it into his heart, thereby attaining enlightenment. Pratyekabuddhas ("private buddhas") are those who carry on solitary practice and reach enlightenment without a teacher. Finally, at the highest two levels of enlightened existence are Bodhisattvas (q.v.) and full Buddhas (q.v.).

Unlike those in the lower Six Realms, the enlightened know the joy of inward peace and creative freedom because, having overcome their ignorance and delusion through Knowledge, they are freed from enslavement to karmic propensities arising from past delusive actions, and no longer sow seeds which will bear fruit in the form of new karmic bondage. Enlightenment, however, does not suspend the law of cause and effect. When the enlightened man cuts his finger it bleeds, when he eats bad food his stomach aches. He too cannot escape the consequences of his actions. The difference is that because he accepts—that is, sees into—his karma he is no longer bound by it, but moves freely within it.

Sōen Nakagawa-rōshi: the former abbot of Ryūtaku-ji.

Sōji-ji: one of the two head temples of the Japanese Sōtō sect, founded by Zen master Keizan in 1321. It is presently located near Yokohama.

Sōtō (Ch., Ts'ao-tung) sect: one of the two dominant Zen sects in Japan, the other being the Rinzai. There are several theories as to the origin of the name Sōtō. One is that it stems from the first character in the names of two masters in China, Tōzan Ryōkai (Tung-shan Liang-chieh) and Sōzan Honjaku (Ts'ao-shan Pên-chi). Another theory is that the *Sō* refers to the Sixth Patriarch, who was also known in Japan as Sōkei Enō.

The Japanese Sōtō sect venerates Dōgen as its founder. Eihei-ji, one of its two headquarters temples, in Fukui Prefecture, was founded by Dōgen in 1243. It presently consists of a mammoth complex of buildings on the site of what was once Dōgen's small mountain temple, long since destroyed by fire. In the number of its monasteries, sub-temples, and adherents the Sōtō sect greatly exceeds the Rinzai in Japan.

student: As used in this book, the term refers to one training in Zen and not one studying Zen academically.

substance: As used in this book, the word has the meaning of "real nature" or "essence." It ought not to be thought of as matter, however infinitesimal.

Śūrangama (Skt.; J., Ryōgon) sūtra: This profound writing, originally in Sanskrit, is widely venerated in all the Mahāyāna Buddhist countries. Among other things, the sūtra deals at length with the successive steps for the attainment of supreme enlightenment.

sūtras (Skt.; J., *kyō*): literally, "a thread on which jewels are strung." The sūtras are the Buddhist scriptures, that is, the purported dialogues and sermons of Shākyamuni Buddha. There are said to be over ten thousand, only a fraction of which have been translated into English. The so-called Hīnayāna were originally recorded in Pāli, the Mahāyāna in Sanskrit.

Most Buddhist sects are founded upon one particular sūtra from which they derive their authority—the Tendai and the Nichiren from the Lotus sūtra (J., Hokke-kyō), the Kegon sect from the Kegon-kyō (Avatamsaka sūtra), etc. Zen, however, is associated with no one sūtra, and this gives the masters freedom to use the scriptures as and when they see fit or to ignore them entirely. In fact, their attitude toward them is not unlike that of a skilled physician toward drugs: he may prescribe one or more for a particular illness or he may prescribe none. The familiar statement

that Zen is a special transmission outside the scriptures, with no depend-
ence upon words and letters, only means that for the Zen sect Truth
must be directly grasped and not taken on the authority of even the
sūtras, much less sought in lifeless intellectual formulas or concepts.
Still, most Japanese masters do not frown on sūtra-reading after a disciple has attained kenshō if it acts as a spur to full enlightenment.

Taihei-ji (Temple of Profound Peace): a temple formerly occupied by Yasutani-rōshi.

Taji-rōshi: see "Genki Taji-rōshi."

takuhatsu (J.): literally, "holding the bowl"; religious mendicancy. There
are many forms of takuhatsu, but Zen monks training in a monastery
usually do it in a group of ten or fifteen. As they walk through the
streets of a town in single file, they chant "Hō," that is, Dharma. Believers
and sympathizers, hearing their cry, offer them sustenance in the form
of either money, which they place in their wooden bowls, or uncooked
rice, which the monks receive in a cloth bag carried for this purpose.
Recipient and donor then bow to each other in mutual gratitude, humility, and respect. The idea behind takuhatsu is that the monks, who
are the guardians of the Dharma, offer it to the public in the example
of their own lives, and in return are sustained by believers in the truth
of the Dharma.

tan: a wooden platform covered with straw matting, about three feet high
and six and a half feet deep, built along the wall of the zendō. By day
it is used for zazen and at night for sleeping.

Tanka (Ch., T'ien-jan of Tanhsia; ?–824): a Zen master of the T'ang era
and a disciple of Ma-tsu (J., Baso). The episode of his demolishing a
wooden statue of the Buddha and using it as firewood is widely quoted
and often misunderstood.

Tantric (or sometimes Esoteric) Buddhism (J., *mikkyō*): The Buddhist
tantra consist of sūtras of a so-called mystical nature which endeavor
to teach the inner relationship of the external world and the world of
spirit, of the identity of Mind and the universe. Among the devices
employed in tantric meditational practices are the following:
  1. Maṇḍala. This word has the meaning of "circle," "assemblage,"
"picture." There are various kinds of maṇḍala, but the commonest in
Esoteric Buddhism are of two types: a composite picture graphically
portraying different classes of demons, deities, Buddhas, and Bodhisattvas (representing various powers, forces, and activities) within symbolic
squares and circles, in the center of which is a figure of the Buddha
Vairochana, the Great Illuminator; and a diagrammatic representation

wherein certain sacred Sanskrit letters (called *bīja,* or seeds) are substituted for figures.

2. Mantra. These sacred sounds—such as Oṁ, for example—are transmitted from the master to his disciple at the time of initiation. When the disciple's mind is properly attuned, the inner vibrations of this word symbol together with its associations in the consciousness of the initiate are said to open his mind to higher dimensions.

3. Mudrā. These are physical gestures, especially symbolical hand movements, which are performed to help evoke certain states of mind parallel to those of Buddhas and Bodhisattvas.

Tathāgata (Skt.; J., Nyorai): the appellation the Buddha used in referring to himself. It literally means one "thus-come," the "thus" (or "thusness") indicating the enlightened state. "Tathāgata" can therefore be rendered as "Thus enlightened I come," and would apply equally to Buddhas other than Shākyamuni.

temple (J., *tera, o-tera*): Either a temple or a monastery is indicated by the Japanese suffix *-ji* (the alternative reading of the character for *tera*). It may be a complex of buildings, consisting of the main hall, the lecture hall, the founder's room, and living quarters within a compound entered through a massive tower gateway, or it may be merely a small solitary structure. If the temple has attached to it a *sōdō* (sometimes called a *semmon dōjō*—that is, a special training place for monks under the direction of a rōshi) the English word "monastery" would be applicable.

Zen alone of all the Buddhist sects maintains a bona fide monastic system, organized on the basic principles and regulations laid down by Hyakujō in China in the eighth century. Simplicity and frugality distinguish this monastic life. The object of the training is not only awakening and its concomitant, Self-knowledge, but also the cultivation of self-control and fortitude, humility and gratitude—in other words, a strong moral character. The chief monastery disciplines are daily zazen and periodic sesshin, manual labor, and takuhatsu. In the Zen sect novices must spend an average of three years in a Zen monastery before they can become eligible to serve as a temple priest. Monastery sesshin are widely attended by lay people, who often outnumber the monks. Under special circumstances and for varying lengths of time they are permitted to live in the monastery as lay monks.

Tendai (Ch., T'ien-t'ai): The Japanese Tendai sect starts with Saichō (767–822), posthumously known as Dengyō-daishi, who brought the teachings from China in 805. The Tendai doctrines and practices are based chiefly on the Lotus sūtra and the division of the Buddha's doctrines into Eight Teachings and Five Periods as laid down by Chih-i, the Chinese founder.

ten directions (J., *jippō*): This includes the whole cosmos. Besides worlds north, south, east and west and the four intermediate points, it encompasses zenith and nadir, thus making ten points of reference in all.

ten evil deeds: 1) killing, 2) stealing, 3) committing adultery, 4) lying, 5) using immoral language, 6) gossiping, 7) slandering, 8) coveting, 9) giving vent to anger, 10) holding wrong views. See also "five deadly sins."

Three Evil Paths (J., *sanakudō*): the realms of hell, hungry ghosts, and beasts—in other words, the subhuman world.

Three Treasures or Jewels (Skt., *triratna;* J., *sambō*): The foundation of Buddhism is the Three Treasures, without trust in which and reverence for there can be no Buddhist religous life. In the Mahāyāna these are conceived broadly as: 1) the Unified Three Treasures (J., *ittai sambō;* literally "one body, three treasures"), 2) the Manifested Three Treasures (J., *genzen sambō*), and 3) the Abiding Three Treasures (J., *jūji sambō*).

For convenience of exposition these are subdivided, though in reality they are inseparable. Thus the Unified Three Treasures of the Buddha Vairochana, representing the realization of the world of Emptiness, of Buddha-nature, of unconditioned Equality; second, the Dharma, that is, the law of beginningless and endless becoming, to which all phenomena are subject according to causes and conditions; and third, the harmonious fusion of the preceding two, which constitutes total reality as experienced by the enlightened (see pp. 78 and 127).

The first of the Manifested Three Treasures is the historic Buddha Shākyamuni, who through his perfect enlightenment realized in himself the truth of the *ittai sambō.* The second is the Dharma, which comprises the spoken words and sermons of Shākyamuni Buddha wherein he elucidated the significance of the *ittai sambō* and the way to its realization. The third includes the immediate disciples of the Buddha Shākyamuni and other followers of his day who heard, believed, and made real in their own bodies the *ittai sambō* that he taught.

Of the Abiding Three Treasures the first is the iconography of Buddhas which have come down to us; the next is the written sermons and discourses of Buddhas (that is, fully enlightened beings) as found in the sūtras and other Buddhist texts still extant; while the third consists of contemporary disciples who practice and realize the saving truth of the *ittai sambō* that was first revealed by Shākyamuni Buddha.

The Three Treasures are mutually related and interdependent. One unrealized in the *ittai sambō* can neither comprehend in depth the import of Shākyamuni Buddha's enlightenment nor appreciate the infinite preciousness of his teachings nor cherish as living realities images and pictures of Buddhas. Again, the *ittai sambō* would be unknown had not it been made manifest by Shākyamuni in his own body and mind and the Way to its realization expounded by him. Lastly, without enlightened followers of the Buddhas' Way in our own time to inspire and lead others along this Path to Self-realization, the *ittai sambō* would be a remote ideal, the saga of Shākyamuni's life desiccated history, and the Buddhas' words lifeless abstractions. More, as each of us embodies the *ittai sambō,* the foundation of the Three Treasures is none other than one's own self.

Three Worlds (J., *sangai*): This is another classification of reality according to Buddhist cosmology. These three consist of, in ascending order, the domains of Desire, Form, and Non-Form. Dwellers in the first and lowest level are still strongly attached to the senses. In the second are those who have bodily form but no longer cling to the world of the senses. The inhabitants of the third are without corporeality, that is, a condition akin to pure consciousness. In Zen these are also considered as dimensions of human consciousness.

Tokusan Senkan (Ch., Tê-shan Hsüan-chien; 790—865): another of the great masters of the T'ang. He is the subject of several kōans, of which one, the twenty-eighth case of *Mumonkan,* tells how he attained enlightenment through his master's blowing out of a candle.

Tōzan Ryōkai (Ch., Tung-shan Liang-chieh; 807—69): the First Patriarch of the Sōtō sect in China and formulator of the Five Degrees (J., *Go-i*).

Ummon Bun'en (Ch., Yün-mên Wên-yen; ?—949): a noted master of the late T'ang, who, like Lin-chi, used vigorous language and jarring tactics to bring his disciples to Self-awakening. The circumstances of Yün-men's own enlightenment are known to all Zen students. Seeking dokusan with Mu-chou (J., *Bokujū*), later to become his master, Yün-men rapped on the little door on the side of the large gateway leading to Mu-chou's temple. Mu-chou called out: "Who is it?" and Yün-men answered, "Wenyen." Mu-chou, whose habit it was to refuse dokusan to all but the most ardent truth-seekers, felt satisfied from Yün-men's knock and the tone of his voice that he was earnestly striving for truth, and admitted him. Scarcely had he entered when Mu-chou, perceiving the state of his mind, seized him by the shoulders and demanded: "Quick, say it, say it!" But Yün-men not yet understanding, couldn't respond. To jolt his mind into Understanding, Mu-chou suddenly shoved him out through the partly opened door and slammed it on his leg, shouting: "You goodfor-nothing!" With a cry of "Ouch!" Yün-men, whose mind at that moment was emptied of every thought, suddenly became enlightened.

Vairochana (Skt; J. Birushana): the "All-Illuminating One." Of the non-historical Buddhas, Vairochana is supreme, symbolizing cosmic consciousness, that is, transcendental Buddha-knowledge.

vajra: (literally, "diamond" or "adamantine"): the symbol of the highest spiritual power, which is compared with the gem of supreme value, the diamond, in whose purity and radiance other hues are reflected while it remains colorless, and which can cut every other material, itself being cut by nothing.

wu wei (J., *mu-i*): This controversial Taoist term has the literal meaning of "non-doing" or "non-striving" or "not making." It does not imply inaction or mere idling. We are merely to cease striving for the unreal things which blind us to our true Self.

Yama-rāja (Skt.; J., Emma-samma): in Buddhist and Hindu mythology, the Lord or Judge of the Dead before whom all who die must come for judgment. Yama-rāja holds up his Mirror of Karma, wherein are reflected the good and evil deeds of the deceased, and the latter consigns himself either to a happy realm or, where his deeds have been preponderantly evil, to frightful tortures, of which swallowing a red-hot iron ball is one.

yaza: zazen done after 9 P.M., the usual bedtime hour in the Zen monastery.

yin and *yang* (J., *yo-in*): in Chinese cosmology, the principle of polarity, namely, earth and heaven, female and male, etc.

yoga: In its widest sense this Sanskrit term embraces the whole complex of spiritual disciplines (including doctrines and bodily postures and breathing exercises) for achieving unity (the literal meaning of yoga) with universal consciousness. In the popular mind, yoga is synonymous with hatha yoga, a branch of yoga which emphasizes breathing exercises and postures for attaining this end. Yoga is also commonly associated with physical or mental health or supranormal powers. In Mahayāna Buddhism the term has been employed chiefly to describe disciplines and doctrins of the Tantric sects.

Yōka Gengaku (Ch., Yung-chia Hsuan-chüeh; 665-713): a great Zen master of the T'ang period and a disciple of the Sixth Patriarch. His "Song of Realization" is a popular Zen writing.

zazenkai: a one-day gathering of Zen practicers for the purpose of doing zazen, listening to a Zen lecture, and receiving dokusan.

Zazen Yōjinki (Precautions to Observe in Zazen): This well-known writing on the practice of zazen is by Keizan-zenji, one of the patriarchs of the Japanese Sōtō sect. It was written in the fourteenth century.

Zen: an abbreviation of the Japanese word *zenna,* which is a transliteration of the Sanskrit *dhyāna* (*ch'an or ch'anna* in Chinese), that is, the process of concentration and absorption by which the mind is first tranquilized and brought to one-pointedness, and then awakened. As a Mahāyāna Buddhist sect, Zen is a religion free of dogmas or creeds whose teachings and disciplines are directed toward Self-consummation, that is to say, to the full awakening that Shākyamuni Buddha himself experienced under the Bo tree after strenuous self-discipline. In Japan, the Zen sect embraces the Sōtō, Rinzai, and Ōbaku sects.

zendō (sōdō): a large hall or room—in large temples or centers a separate structure—where zazen is practiced.

zenji: The last syllable of this word is the euphonic rendering of *shi,* meaning "teacher" or "master"; the entire expression thus has the meaning of great or renowned Zen master. The title is usually conferred posthumously, though some masters have achieved this distinction during their lifetime.

PRONUNCIATION GUIDE TO JAPANESE WORDS

VOWELS Vowels may be short, long or silent. Short vowels are very short.

Short Vowels

a	as in	*far (kōan)*
e	as in	*end (zendō)*
i	as in	*machine (sesshin)*
o	as in	*forest (dokusan)*
u	as in	*put (mu)*

Long Vowels

ā	as in	*park*
ō	as in	*note (rōshi)*
ū	as in	*rumor (Jōshū).*

Diphthongs

ei	as in	*labor (Eisai)*
ai	as in	*fine (daishi)*
ao	as in	*now (kao)*

Silent Vowels

The vowels *i* and *u* are silent or almost silent in many Japanese words, as in: *dokusan, takuhatsu.*

CONSONANTS The following have the same pronunciation as in English: b, d, j, k, m, n, p, t, and y.

ch	as in	*change (Chisha)*
g	as in	*grateful (gasshō)*
h	as in	*home (Heikigan-roku)*
s	as in	*silent (Sōtō)*
sh	as in	*shore (Shōyō-roku)*
z	as in	*zero (Zen)*

The letter *r* is neither the hard English sound nor the rolled sound of Spanish, but is between the English *l* and *r* sounds.

DOUBLE CONSONANTS Double consonants are stressed by holding the sound of the particular consonant longer, as in: *sesshin, gassho.*

INDEX / Numerals in italics refer to pages on which terms are defined or described in detail. Numerals in parentheses refer to footnotes.